D0146058

# OXFORD POLITICAL THEORY

*Series Editors:* Will Kymlicka, David Miller, and Alan Ryan

# INCLUSION AND DEMOCRACY

# OXFORD POLITICAL THEORY

Oxford Political Theory presents the best new work in contemporary political theory. It is intended to be broad in scope, including original contributions to political philosophy, and also work in applied political theory. The series will contain works of outstanding quality with no restriction on approach or subject-matter.

# INCLUSION
# AND DEMOCRACY

IRIS MARION YOUNG

OXFORD

UNIVERSITY PRESS

# OXFORD
UNIVERSITY PRESS

Great Clarendon Street, Oxford OX2 6DP

Oxford University Press is a department of the University of Oxford.
It furthers the University's objective of excellence in research, scholarship,
and education by publishing worldwide in

Oxford New York

Athens Auckland Bangkok Bogotá Buenos Aires Cape Town
Chennai Dar es Salaam Delhi Florence Hong Kong Istanbul Karachi
Kolkata Kuala Lumpur Madrid Melbourne Mexico City Mumbai Nairobi
Paris São Paulo Shanghai Singapore Taipei Tokyo Toronto Warsaw

with associated companies in Berlin Ibadan

Oxford is a registered trade mark of Oxford University Press
in the UK and in certain other countries

Published in the United States
by Oxford University Press Inc., New York

British Library Cataloguing in Publication Data

Data available

Library of Congress Cataloging in Publication Data
Young, Iris Marion, 1949–
Inclusion and democracy / Iris Marion Young.
(Oxford political theory)
Includes bibliographical references and index.
1. Democracy. 2. Political participation. 3. Political culture.
4. Communication in politics. I. Title. II. Series.
JC423.Y69 2000 321.8—dc21 00-025844
ISBN 0-19-829754-8

3 5 7 9 10 8 6 4 2

Typeset by Hope Services (Abingdon) Ltd.
Printed in Great Britain
on acid-free paper by
T.J. International Ltd
Padstow, Cornwall

For Dave, again

# ACKNOWLEDGEMENTS

The outline for this book was conceived for a seminar on democratic theory that I gave at the Johann Wolfgang von Goethe Universität in Frankfurt in the spring term of 1995. All of the seminar participants contributed to stimulating my thinking towards the arguments here. I would like to thank Lisa Conradi, Angelika Kreps, Amos Nasimento, Katharina Pühl, Anna Riek, Hillal Segin, and all the other regular participants in that seminar whose faces and voices remain with me but whose names have faded from my memory.

Early work on some of the ideas in these chapters was supported by a six-month grant from the American Council of Learned Societies in 1994. The University of Pittsburgh granted me a sabbatical leave during the 1996–7 academic year to work on this project at the Center for Human Values at Princeton University. I am grateful to the Center for its support, and for providing such an intellectually stimulating and humanly warm atmosphere in which to work.

Some of these chapters, or portions of chapters, have evolved from earlier essays written for conferences and later published as book chapters. I thank each of the editors for giving me the occasion and space to work out some of these ideas. A portion of Chapter 2 is based on 'Public Address as a Sign of Political Inclusion', in Claudia Card (ed.), *Feminist Ethics and Politics* (Lawrence: University of Kansas Press, 1999); a portion of Chapter 3 is based on 'Difference as a Resource in Democratic Communication', in James Bohman and William Rehg (eds.), *Deliberation and Democracy* (Cambridge, Mass.: MIT Press, 1997); Chapter 4 is a much revised version of 'Deferring Group Representation', in Ian Shapiro and Will Kymlicka (eds.), *Ethnicity and Group Rights*, NOMOS 29 (New York: New York University Press, 1997); Chapter 5 is based on 'State, Civil Society and Social Justice', in Ian Shapiro and Casiano Calderon-Hacker (eds.), *Democracy's Value* (Cambridge: Cambridge University Press, 1999); Chapter 6 is a revised and enlarged version of 'Residential Segregation and Differentiated Citizenship', in a special issue of *Citizenship Studies* entitled 'Rights to the City', edited by Engin Isen; Chapter 7 is a much revised and altered iteration of 'Self-Determination and Global Democracy: A Critique of Liberal Nationalism', in Stephen Macedo and Ian Shapiro (eds.), *Designing Democratic Institutions*, NOMOS 39 (New York: New York University Press, 2000).

I have presented ideas and arguments in these chapters at many universities and conferences in the past five years. On every occasion lively discussion has set me to further refinement, and I cannot hope to thank all those who have helped me. Several colleagues read a portion of the book and offered invaluable comments: I thank James Bohman, Lisa Brush, Robert Gooding-Williams, Pablo De Greiff, Amy Gutmann, Christian Hunold, David Ingram, Jeffrey Isaac, Alison Jaggar, Thomas McCarthy, Martin Matustik, Geraldine Pratt, Edward Soja, and James Tully. Robert Beauregard, Joan Cocks, Lisa Disch, Robert Goodin, Anne Phillips, William Scheuerman, John Trimbur, and Melissa Williams each read a draft of the entire book; without their sympathetic criticism there would be many more flaws in this book, but of course I am responsible for those that remain. Thanks also to Forrest Morgeson for research assistance.

Dave Alexander talked over many of these ideas with me on city walks or in front of evening fires. He read several drafts of every chapter, always challenging me further to sharpen my questions, concepts, and arguments. When he judged that I had worked enough, he took me out to hear some jazz. His support and companionship sustain my work and my life.

# CONTENTS

# INTRODUCTION

In January 1997 I stood on street corners in Pittsburgh soliciting signatures for a referendum petition. The temperature hovered around 15 degrees Fahrenheit in the sun. I persisted in this self-punishment because I knew that scores of other people were spread over the city also collecting signatures. The petition called for a question to be put on the May ballot asking voters to approve the creation of a Police Civilian Review Board. State law allowed us a mere six weeks to collect the required 11,000 signatures of currently registered Pittsburgh voters. Petitioners were heartened to find that many we asked were already apprised of the issue; many signed our petition, including more than a few uniformed police officers. By the closing date we had 16,000 names.

The referendum campaign came after more than four years of citizen agitation about issues of police conduct towards citizens. For African Americans in Pittsburgh these issues were always simmering, but had come to the boil with the publicized shooting in the back of a youth in a police chase. The Coalition to Counter Hate Groups joined with the newly formed Citizens for Police Accountability to develop a proposal for a Review Board. At the same time the Pittsburgh chapter of the American Civil Liberties Union began documenting cases of alleged police abuse or harassment. Gay and lesbian organizations linked with the agitation and publicized some incidents of police encounters with gay men that they claimed were abusive. The local and national press covered the story of the death of an African American in a Pittsburgh suburb while in police custody after being pulled over for an alleged traffic violation.

With the issue of police accountability so centrally in the public eye, the campaign for a Civilian Review Board had gained momentum. Citizens for Police Accountability organized several meetings attended by Pittsburghers. Soon the proposed ordinance was under discussion by the Pittsburgh City Council. The Council sponsored a series of public hearings in several neighbourhoods attended by hundreds of people representing organizations as diverse as the Fraternal Order of Police, the National Association for the Advancement of Colored People, and the Pittsburgh Mediation Center. The chief of police argued against the proposed Review Board on the grounds that the Police Department had a competent internal complaints and review system. The mayor publicly stated his opposition to the creation of a Review Board.

Citizens for Police Accountability packed the City Council chambers for every meeting during which the Council deliberated on the proposed legislation. They talked to councillors and their aides between meetings, providing them with information about civilian review processes in other cities. The Fraternal Order of Police also lobbied the councillors. In the fall of 1996 the Council voted down the proposal for a Review Board. Only then did supporters decide to take the issue to direct vote of the citizens of Pittsburgh.

We who had worked so hard to collect 16,000 signatures had little time to celebrate what we thought was our success in putting the issue on the ballot. The Fraternal Order of Police hired a consulting firm, which claimed that 9,000 of those names were invalid. Again within a short time window a small army of mostly volunteer supporters sat with petitions and voter lists, painstakingly documenting each wrongful challenge. The supporters succeeded in validating the required number of signatures.

The Fraternal Order of Police then tried to keep the issue from the ballot by means of court action. Only a few weeks before the 22 May election the court found against the objection, and supporters began a speedy campaign. On election day Pittsburgh voters approved by a margin of two to one the creation of a Police Civilian Review Board. Supporters were jubilant; the people spoke loud and clear.

The referendum vote did not itself create the Board, however; it only required the City Council to do so according to certain broad guidelines. Members of Citizens for Police Accountability wanted to go on vacation, but instead they began lobbying members of the Council about the legal language of the ordinance. Those who had opposed the creation of the Board now also turned their attention to discussion of specific language. The resulting document contained compromises, but supporters of the original idea considered the law that finally passed through the Council acceptable.

The Review Board began its work in July 1998. Citizens for Police Accountability still monitors the process, and tries to convince Pittsburghers that the Board will only work to hold police accountable if citizens hold the Board accountable. There have been complaints that the staff are not energetic enough in pursuing complaints, and that city offices have stalled in supplying information requested by investigators. Popular interest in the Board and its work has dropped off as people retreat into the pressing issues of their private lives or move on to work on other political issues. Citizens with serious complaints about police, however, now have a public forum in which to air them, whose hearings are sometimes widely publicized.

## 1. Challenges for Democracy

I begin with this story of ordinary democracy in action because it refers to most of the elements of the democratic process that this book considers. Private mumblings about a perceived problem break into a more public discussion in civil society, leading to citizens organizing to promote wider discussion of the problem and of ways for government to address it. This problem itself arises partly from structural social group differences, and the prejudices, privileges, and misunderstandings that accompany them. In this case residential racial segregation is a major component of such structural difference. The story illustrates, however, a way that public discussion and decision-making sometimes successfully crosses those differences. When the issue first emerged, many white middle-class people saw no urgency in it; having the opportunity to read about and listen to the experience of others changed the minds of many of them. Civic associations played a crucial role in promoting political discussion and government policy.

The series of events also involves a struggle among parties with different points of view and perceived interests, and this struggle takes place in several discursive terrains: in the press, in hearings and public meetings, City Council meetings, and courts. The story illustrates that more-marginalized citizens with fewer resources and official status can sometimes make up for such inequality with organization and time. Weaker parties can sometimes achieve their political goals when the democratic process is open and fair, and when there is sustained public discussion in which they have a chance to persuade fellow citizens of the justice or wisdom of their cause. This example also shows, however, that instituting a policy through democratically decided government may take a long time and require determination and continued mobilization by advocates. That process may be bureaucratic and rather boring at times. Even when principles are at stake, arriving at a decision in a democratic process requires a give and take that often leads to compromise. In this instance, even though one side in the debate may have 'won', few question the legitimacy of the outcome because the process was relatively public, inclusive, and procedurally regular.

The story also shows that active participation and political representation do not exclude one another, and sometimes even work together to produce policy outcomes. Without active citizens agitating for reform, the status quo would certainly have continued, and it was important that they had tools of direct democracy available to them. The process required mediation by representatives at many stages, however, both formally elected and as spokespeople for civic associations. The policy outcome, moreover, is the creation of a representative body. The authority of any policy-making body, however, has limited jurisdiction, and this fact may limit the real impact of a hard-won reform. In this case, the activities of the Civilian Review Board must be limited to what happens within the boundaries of the city of Pittsburgh, even though some of the most publicized and egregious cases of alleged police abuse have occurred in surrounding suburbs.

Finally, this story exhibits how democratic processes sometimes accomplish something, however small or slow to come. We have arrived at a paradoxical historical moment when nearly everyone favours democracy, but apparently few believe that democratic governance can *do* anything. Democratic process seems to paralyse policy-making. Ideals of public discussion and holding officials accountable have little institutional effect; they seem only to generate mass gossip. Today the notion that, with good institutions and goodwill, citizens can engage with one another about the problems they have in living together, and work out policies to address those problems, most often meets with a response of detached cynicism, 'Yeah, right.'

It is easy to throw sand on my story. A Civilian Review Board just adds another layer of bureaucracy that can be captured by those it is supposed to monitor, some might say, while the citizens it is supposed to serve become disconnected. It does little, moreover, to address the causes of the conflicts and abuses it is supposed to prevent or punish. These lie in structural inequalities which require attention in many disparate fields of social life—housing, employment, education, property relations.

The chapters that follow include reflections on each of these aspects of democratic practice under conditions of structural inequality: the differences and conflicts that generate problems for which authoritative decision-making seeks solutions; the meaning and role of public discussion in decision-making; the nature of political representation both through formal institutions and in civil society; as well as structural, communicative, and jurisdictional impediments to political equality and fair outcomes.

## 2. Deep Democracy

Using democratic process to promote legal, administrative, and social changes toward greater justice is hard work. I begin from a conviction, however, that democratic process is usually a necessary and proper vehicle for doing so. I shall assume a minimalist understanding of democracy as given: that democratic politics entails a rule of law, promotion of civil and political liberties, free and fair election of lawmakers. The assurance of these institutions is rare enough in the world today, and even those societies that have institutionalized them are for the most part only thinly democratic. Even the supposedly most democratic societies in the world most of the time are largely 'plebescite' democracies: candidates take vague stands on a few issues; citizens endorse one or another, and then have little relation to the policy process until the next election. A democratic spirit and practice inspires many voluntary organizations, and movements composed of such groups sometimes influence government actions and the actions of other powerful institutions. Some of the reflections in this book theorize this democratic impulse in some quarters of civil society. Where decisions are far-reaching or involve basic interests of the most powerful, however, the powerful usually try to make the decisions themselves, and often succeed, with little pretence of democracy. I write this shortly after nineteen of the world's leading liberal democracies have waged a ghastly war without any of them formally consulting with either their citizens or their elected representatives about whether to do so.

Existing democracies really are democratic in some respects, with regard to some issues and institutions. Indeed, most societies have some democratic practices. Democracy is not an all-or-nothing affair, but a matter of degree; societies can vary in both the extent and the intensity of their commitment to democratic practice. Some or many institutions may be democratically organized, and in any such nominally democratic institution the depth of its democratic practice can vary.[1] The operating conviction of this book, that democratic practice is a means promoting justice, calls for widening and deepening democracy beyond the superficial trappings that many societies endorse and take some steps to enact.

This book highlights one norm often invoked by those seeking to widen and deepen democratic practices: inclusion. The normative legitimacy of a democratic decision depends on the degree to which

---

[1] On the idea of degrees of democracy, see Frank Cunningham, *Democratic Theory and Socialism* (Cambridge: Cambridge University Press, 1987), ch. 3.

those affected by it have been included in the decision-making processes and have had the opportunity to influence the outcomes. Calls for inclusion arise from experiences of exclusion—from basic political rights, from opportunities to participate, from the hegemonic terms of debate. Some of the most powerful and successful social movements of this century have mobilized around demands for oppressed and marginalized people to be included as full and equal citizens in their polities. Demands for voting rights have focused some of these movements; especially today, however, when most adults in most societies have nominal voting rights, voting equality is only a minimal condition of political equality. *Inclusion and Democracy* explores additional and deeper conditions of political inclusion and exclusion, such as those involving modes of communication, attending to social difference, representation, civic organizing, and the borders of political jurisdictions.

The book has three parts, each guided by a question central to the democratic process: (1) What are the norms and conditions of inclusive democratic communication under circumstances of structural inequality and cultural difference? (2) How should inclusive democratic communication and decision-making be theorized for societies with millions of people? (3) What is the proper scope of the democratic polity, and how are exclusions enacted by restricting that scope?

Chapters 1, 2, and 3 address the first question by refining theories of deliberative democracy, while also criticizing certain interpretations of this model. I argue that the model of deliberative democracy implies a strong meaning of inclusion and political equality which, when implemented, increases the likelihood that democratic decision-making processes will promote justice. On a deliberative understanding of democratic practice, democracy is not only a means through which citizens can promote their interests and hold the power of rulers in check. It is also a means of collective problem-solving which depends for its legitimacy and wisdom on the expression and criticism of the diverse opinions of all the members of the society. Inclusive democratic practice is likely to promote the most just results because people aim to persuade one another of the justice and wisdom of their claims, and are open to having their own opinions and understandings of their interests change in the process.

Some formulations of ideals of deliberative democracy, however, tend to restrict their conception of political communication to argument, and to have too biased or narrow an understanding of what being reasonable means. To the extent that norms of deliberation implicitly value certain styles of expression as dispassionate, orderly, or articulate, they can have exclusionary implications. Such a focus on a narrow deliberative style, moreover, ignores the important role other forms of communication play in furthering inclusive democratic outcomes. Chapter 2 identifies three such forms or aspects of communication with unique important functions in furthering democratic deliberation. What I call *greeting* or *public address* acknowledges the presence and point of view of diverse social segments in the political public. The category I call *rhetoric* refers to the way claims and reasons are stated, and accompanies all argument. I include in this category the affective dimensions of communication, its figurative aspects, and the diverse media of communication—placards and street theatre instead of tabloids or reports. Rhetoric has the important function of *situating* those seeking to persuade others in relation to their audience. *Narrative*, finally, has many important functions in political deliberation; narratives can supply steps in arguments, but they can also serve to explain meanings and experiences when groups do not share premises sufficiently to proceed with an argument.

Another questionable assumption made by some democratic theorists is that a properly functioning democratic discussion should be oriented to a common good or common interest. They assume that politics must be either a competition among private and conflicting interests, or that political participants must put aside their particular interests and affiliations to form a deliberative public. In Chapter 3 I argue that this is a false dichotomy, and that a third possibility is more plausible. Democratic discussion and decision-making is better theorized as a process in which differentiated social groups should attend to the particular situation of others and be willing to work out just solutions to their conflicts and collective problems from across their situated positions. It is a mistake to consider the public assertion of experiences of people located in structurally or culturally differentiated social groups as nothing but the assertion of self-regarding interest. I suggest that this misconstrual derives in part from misunderstanding such group-based public expressions solely and entirely as assertions of a group 'identity'. I review arguments that question such a notion of group identity, and argue that most group-based movements and claims in contemporary democratic polities derive from relationally constituted structural differentiations. When so understood, it becomes clear that socially situated interests, proposals, claims, and expressions of experience are often an important resource for democratic discussion and decision-making. Such situated knowledges can both pluralize and relativize hegemonic discourses, and offer otherwise unspoken knowledge to contribute to wise decisions.

Chapters 4 and 5 address the second question of the book, how to understand inclusive communicative democracy in the context of mass societies. Many theorists and activists interested in deepening democratic practices have wrongly assumed that representative institutions are incompatible with deep democracy. Authentic democracy, on this view, is direct and face to face. If this is true, however, then large-scale mass societies are condemned to thin democracy. This dilemma stems partly from wrongly opposing participation and representation. On the contrary, citizens can only legitimately authorize representatives and hold them accountable if there are many avenues and institutions through which they engage with both each other and their representatives. Systems of representation are most inclusive, furthermore, when they encourage the particular perspectives of relatively marginalized or disadvantaged social groups to receive specific expression.

Mechanisms for such specific representation of marginalized social groups can involve state institutions, such as voting schemes, electoral rules, and rules about the appointment of commissions and the conduct of hearings. With a number of other contemporary democratic theorists, however, I also look to the vast range of activity often brought under the label 'civil society' for important forms of participation, of expression from a socially situated perspective, and forms of holding power accountable that a strong communicative democracy needs. Chapter 5 theorizes both private and public functions of civic associations, and expands critical theoretical ideas of the public sphere as important to deep democracy. Contrary to many today who find in civil society the primary basis for social change to promote justice, however, I argue that those who wish to undermine injustice cannot turn their backs on state institutions as tools for that end.

The last two chapters focus on a question seldom made thematic by political theorists. What should the scope of the polity be? Most democratic theory assumes the polity as given. Democratic inclusion means that all members of the given polity should have effectively equal influence over debate and decision-making within that polity. The problem with restricting the issue of inclusion in this way, however, is that by virtue of its definition or scope the polity itself may wrongfully exclude individuals or groups.

Chapter 6 explores one form of such wrongful exclusion in processes of racial and class segregation. Even when segregated groups are nominally included in a polity, processes of segregation prevent participation for some and preserve privilege for others. Segregation is often accomplished or reinforced, however, especially in the United States but also elsewhere, by the existence of separate municipal jurisdictions in metropolitan regions whose economic and social relations produce dense interdependencies among people across the region. Issues of the proper scope of the polity arise in just such situations, when the scope of social and economic interactions does not match the scope of political jurisdiction. I argue that the scope of a polity ought to correspond to the scope of relations across which obligations of justice extend. In many parts of the world with dense metropolitan regions this principle implies that the scope of polities should be regional. Regional governance is deeply democratic, however, only if combined with neighbourhood and community-based participatory institutions many of which are differentiated by group affinities on a model I call *differentiated solidarity.*

Chapter 7 extends the question of the scope of the polity to a global level. It applies the model of differentiated solidarity to world-wide interaction and interdependence among peoples. The existing nation-state system enacts and legitimizes profound exclusions, and many of these are unjust. Contemporary conditions of global interdependence imply that the actions of some people in one nation-state presume or affect the actions of distant others in other states. If the scope of democratic political institutions should correspond to the scope of obligations of justice, then this argument implies that there ought to be more global institutional capacity to govern relations and interaction among the world's peoples.

Many people rightly distrust projects of cosmopolitan governance, however, because they fear cultural homogenization or a failure to respect and recognize the specificity of peoples. Normative ideals of global justice and democracy should be articulated with commitment to cultural autonomy and the self-determination of peoples. As long as self-determination is understood as hegemony, however, wrongful exclusion and domination are likely results. I argue for a model of global democratic discussion and regulation that accommodates differentiated solidarity by giving a more relational interpretation to the meaning of self-determination. We should envision global democracy as the interaction of self-determining peoples and locales on terms of equality in which they understand obligations to listen to outsiders who claim to be affected by their decisions or actions and to resolve conflicts with them through settled procedures in a global framework of regulatory principles democratically decided on together by all the self-determining entities.

Ideally, then, inclusive democracy refuses exclusive sovereign borders, though it recognizes the importance of group affinities and structured differences in politics. Beyond membership and voting rights, inclusive democracy enables participation and voice for all those affected by problems and their proposed solutions. Democratic process cannot be centred in particular places, but rather concerns the communicative relation of broad social sectors in the public spheres of civil society and representative bodies whose diversity responds to the structural differentiations of the society.

## 3. The Approach of Critical Theory

The general theoretical approach of this book is that of critical theory, by which I mean socially and historically situated normative analysis and argument. *Inclusion and Democracy* articulates and defends principles which I argue best express ideals of a democratic politics in which citizens try to solve shared problems justly. A critical theory does not derive such principles and ideals from philosophical premisses about morality, human nature, or the good life. Instead, the method of critical theory, as I understand it, reflects on existing social relations and processes to identify what we experience as valuable in them, but as present only intermittently, partially, or potentially. Thus to identify ideals of inclusive democracy I reflect on the experience of actually existing democracy, looking for possibilities glimmering in it but which we nevertheless feel lacking—experiences such as reasonable yet passionate persuasion, accountable representation, participatory civic activity linked to authoritative state action, or transnational institutions for discussing and addressing global problems. Normative critical theory constructs accounts of these democratic ideals that render articulate and more systematic those feelings of dissatisfaction and lack which we normally experience in actual democratic politics.[2]

Ideals are neither descriptions nor blueprints; they correspond neither to a present nor to a future reality, precisely because they express ideals. They allow thinkers and actors to take a distance from reality in order to criticize it and imagine possibilities for something better. *Inclusion and Democracy* thus articulates normative ideals and moral arguments intended both to reveal moral deficiencies in contemporary democratic societies and at the same time to envision transformative

---

[2] On generating ideals from felt lack in reality, see Herbert Marcuse, *One Dimensional Man* (Boston: Beacon Press, 1964), 203–23; see also Martin Matustik, 'Back to the Future: Marcuse and New Critical Theory', foreword to William Wilkerson and Jeffrey Paris (eds.), *New Critical Theory: Essays on Liberation* (Lanham, Md.: Rowman & Littlefield, 2000); see also my own discussion of the method of critical theory in *Justice and the Politics of Difference* (Princeton: Princeton University Press, 1990), 5–7.

possibilities in those societies. These twin purposes require the collaboration of moral theory and social theory.

Thus the book analyses many normative concepts important for democracy, such as political equality, publicity, representation, and self-determination. Every chapter poses questions whose answers rely on the methods and principles of contemporary moral and political argument. Each chapter also sets such moral argument, however, in the context of a theoretical description and interpretation of the structure and processes of contemporary societies that claim to follow democratic values. Thus my social-theoretic tasks include defining and analysing several key social and communicative concepts, and setting out logical relations among them. I explicate the meaning of structural social relations and implications of the way individuals are positioned in them. I define some positive political functions of rhetoric and narrative in socially differentiated political communication. I reflect on the meaning and consequences of race and class segregation, as well as try to respond normatively to the apparently contradictory implications of claims for the self-determination of peoples and increasing global economic interdependence.

## 4. Thematizing Inclusion

Democratic theory has not sufficiently thematized a problem that people frequently identify with democratic processes that formally satisfy basic normative conditions of the rule of law, free competitive elections, and liberties of speech, association, and the like. Many criticize actually existing democracies for being dominated by groups or élites that have unequal influence over decisions, while others are excluded or marginalized from any significant influence over the policy-making process and its outcomes. Strong and normatively legitimate democracy, on this intuition, includes equally in the process that leads to decisions all those who will be affected by them. Theorists and political actors might call this theme of inclusion into question, however, from several points of view.

Some might object to a discourse of inclusion because they suspect that it presupposes an already given set of procedures, institutions, and terms of public discourse into which those excluded or marginalized are incorporated without change. In this image of inclusion, the particular interests, experiences, and ways of looking at things that the formerly excluded bring to politics make little difference to its processes or outcomes. On this image, bringing about political equality consists in extending already constituted institutions and practices to people not currently benefiting from them enough, and thereby expecting them to conform to hegemonic norms.

I agree that this is indeed an attitude implicit in the discourse and behaviour of some well-meaning people who both consider themselves included and advocate greater inclusion of particular groups or individuals in a political process. The arguments of this book continue some of those of earlier work, however, to the effect that inclusive political processes should not be thought of as enfolding its participants in a single public with a single discourse of the common good.[3] Thus Chapter 2 argues that political inclusion specifically requires openness to a plurality of modes of communication, and Chapter 3 argues that inclusive political discussion should recognize and attend to social differences in order to achieve the wisest and most just political judgements for action. On this view, one of the purposes of advocating inclusion is to allow transformation of the style and terms of public debate and thereby open the possibility for significant change in outcomes. Chapter 6 perhaps most directly addresses the sorts of worries behind this objection, by arguing that some interpretations of the ideal of racial integration are overly assimilationist and obscure the most important harms of residential segregation. The image of inclusive politics this book aims to conjure, then, is that of a heterogeneous public engaged in transforming institutions to make them more effective in solving shared problems justly.

Others might object that an ideal of inclusion is itself both under- and over-inclusive. On the one hand, a concept of inclusion presupposes some bordered unit into which those excluded can be included. As a concept it thus depends on some continued exclusion. On the other hand, accusations of exclusion and calls for inclusion are often vague, and seem to cover every form of injustice and remedy.

In his critique of the discourse of inclusion Robert Goodin makes both these points, though he concentrates on the first.[4] The ideal of inclusion presupposes bounded states whose function is as much to exclude some people as to include others. Calls for inclusion rarely question this nation-state form, and merely aim to rectify political and social inequalities among people already dwelling under the jurisdiction of a nation-state. Goodin argues that those concerned with relations of privilege and disadvantage should question this nation-state system and conceive instead a system of multiple, overlapping

---

[3] Young, *Justice and the Politics of Difference*.
[4] Robert E. Goodin, 'Inclusion and Exclusion', *Archives of European Sociology*, 37/2 (1966), 343–71.

sovereignties each of which is open to others and which does not subject individuals to the vulnerabilities of having only one jurisdiction within which to appeal to redress injustice.

As I indicated earlier, the third major question this book takes up concerns the scope of the polity. I agree that societies and political institutions enact some of their most grievous exclusions by the way they define political jurisdictions themselves—who has a right to influence their operations and who does not. Chapter 6 examines how local politics often perpetuates segregation and other harms by allowing discrete autonomous municipalities within regions of significant interdependence. Chapter 7 argues along with Goodin and others that the nation-state is an inappropriately exclusive political form, and that inclusive politics in our world normatively requires a more open system of global regulation and local and regional interaction.

There is also some point to the objection that much of the way contemporary social critics call for inclusion seems to cover too much. Especially in Europe a myriad of problems seem to come under the general umbrella of 'social exclusion', and this language of exclusion sometimes seems to be a euphemism for the presence of misfits, particularly immigrants experienced as racially or culturally different and unemployed youth. The promotion of inclusion in some of this discourse, or 'social cohesion', as it is sometimes called, refers to a diverse set of policies, social services, and civic education aimed to support such populations and ease their interaction with better-off citizens. Policies and policy proposals in this context, however, sometimes appear to aim at making social and economic deviants fit into dominant norms and institutions, as well as to give them opportunities for political participation, educational development, and welfare benefits. Suspicion of such attitudes that require adjustment returns us to the first objection.

The concepts of exclusion and inclusion lose meaning if they are used to label all problems of social conflict and injustice. Where the problems are racism, cultural intolerance, economic exploitation, or a refusal to help needy people, they should be so named. My subject in this book is *political* exclusion and marginalization in particular, and I aim to theorize principles and ideals of political inclusion based on common critical reactions to such political exclusion. I focus on political processes that claim to be democratic but which some people reasonably claim are dominated by only some of those whose interests are affected by them. If inclusion in decision-making is a core of the democratic ideal, then, to the extent that such political exclusions exist, democratic societies do not live up to their promise. Cultural intolerance, racism, sexism, economic exploitation and deprivation, and other social and economic inequalities help to account for these political exclusions. For the most part this book assumes such causal relations between social and economic inequality, on the one hand, and political equality, on the other, without theorizing those other inequalities in any detail.

## 5. Situated Conversation

I do not present the chapters of this book as constituting a single, self-enclosed, logically integrated theory. While there are many arguments in the book, moreover, and more than one extends over several chapters, I do not think of the book as putting forward one major argument where each chapter contains one step towards the conclusion. Instead I think of these chapters as contributing to a set of overlapping conversations with people of diverse interests and backgrounds whose writing has stimulated me to think or with whom I have spoken over time. In these discussions I aim to advance both my own thinking, and the thinking of those with whom I have engaged and other readers, about issues crucial to democratic practice. In some places my intention is to bring certain interlocutors into conversation with one another. In others I wish to turn the attention of interlocutors and listeners towards some issues I think they have not attended to sufficiently.

Critical theory, as I understand it, abjures the stance of theoretical universality that academic writing sometimes adopts. Normative theorists sometimes speak from a position abstracted from social context, and assert general principles that they claim have the same meaning in all contexts. Such abstraction is sometimes useful, and I rely on some of this work in my discussion. Nor would I deny that some general principles can meaningfully be asserted across social contexts. The approach of critical theory, however, suggests that there are dangers in abstract and generalized normative theorizing, involving, for example, importing into supposedly general theories assumptions derived from the particular socio-historical context in which one thinks, or from the structured social positions conditioning one's own life in that context. Once having adopted a stance of abstraction and generality, furthermore, normative theorizing often has some difficulty in showing its relevance to engaged political action.

For the most part the book stays closer to particular contemporary social contexts and the problems for democratic theory and practice they generate. Since I am writing from the context of the United States, this situatedness means that the scholarly interlocutors, social conditions, and political debates that most influence these pages are from the United States. I very much hope, however, that the questions I raise, and the reflections, analyses, and arguments I offer to address these questions, may fruitfully contribute to the thinking of those concerned to further democratic practice anywhere in the world. Thus I have tried in many places in these pages to refer to issues, writers, and social conditions in other places with which I have some familiarity, where I have had conversations with colleagues and have had some opportunity to follow current affairs—particularly Canada, New Zealand, Australia, Germany, South Africa, and Northern Ireland. No doubt my work falls short of a complete engagement with issues of inclusion and democracy in any context, but I hope that it provides enough stimulus to begin a conversation in many.

# CHAPTER 1

## Democracy and Justice

Democracy is hard to love. Perhaps some people enjoy making speeches, or confronting those with whom they disagree, or standing up to privileged and powerful people with claims and demands. Activities like these, however, make many people anxious. Perhaps some people like to go to meetings after a hard day's work and try to focus discussion on the issue, to haggle over the language of a resolution, or gather signatures for a petition, or call long lists of strangers on the telephone. But most people would rather watch television, read poetry, or make love. To be sure, democratic politics has some joys: the thrill of being part of a crowd of thousands marching down the street chanting and singing for a cause we believe in; the sense of solidarity with others as we work in a campaign; the excitement of victory. Defeat, co-optation, or ambiguous results are more common experiences than political victory, however. Citizens must often put in a great deal of time to gain a small reform. Because in a democracy nearly everything is revisable, and because unpredictable public opinion often counts for something, uncertainty shadows democracy.[1]

If democracy is such a lot of trouble for uncertain results, then why do so many people value it? Some political theorists praise democracy for its intrinsic values—the way it enlarges the lives of active citizens, develops capacities for thought, judgement, and co-operation, and gives people opportunities for glory. There are real intrinsic values of democracy. It is not clear, however, that these rewards outweigh the pleasures of rewards forgone in order to engage in democratic practice. Nor is it obvious that the intrinsic values of democracy compensate for the angers, frustrations, fears, uncertainties, drudgery, disappointments, and defeats that are democratic daily fare. Most honest folk

---

[1] See Mark Warren, 'What should we Expect from More Democracy? Radically Democratic Responses to Politics', *Political Theory*, 24/2 (May 1996), 241–70.

must admit, then, that if democracy is valuable at all, it is for instrumental reasons primarily. We believe that democracy is the best political form for restraining rulers from the abuses of power that are their
inevitable temptations. Only in a democratic political system, furthermore, do all members of a society in principle have the opportunity to
try to influence public policy to serve or protect their interests.
Judging from the claims often made in public debates, finally, we also
believe that democratic process is the best means for changing conditions of injustice and promoting justice. Individuals and social movements frequently appeal to governments and their fellow citizens that
they suffer injustice, or that some proposals would produce injustice
or fail to challenge injustice, and they expect democratic publics and
governments to redress injustices.[2]

This chapter explicates a normative theoretical connection between
democracy and justice. To do so I rely on the approach to democratic theory and practice usually called deliberative democracy. After
reviewing criticisms of the aggregative model of democracy, I formulate an account of the model of deliberative democracy that emphasizes the ideals of inclusion, political equality, reasonableness, and
publicity. I show that this model supports a tight theoretical connection between democracy and justice; under ideal conditions of inclusive political equality and public reasonableness, democratic
processes serve as the means of discovering and validating the most
just policies.

Ours is not the ideal society, however, in the sense prescribed by the
theory. In the real world some people and groups have significantly
greater ability to use democratic processes for their own ends while
others are excluded or marginalized. Our democratic policy discussions do not occur under conditions free of coercion and threat, and
free of the distorting influence of unequal power and control over
resources. In actually existing democracies there tends to be a reinforcing circle between social and economic inequality and political
inequality that enables the powerful to use formally democratic
processes to perpetuate injustice or preserve privilege. One means of
breaking this circle, I argue, is to widen democratic inclusion.
Democratic political movements and designers of democratic
processes can promote greater inclusion in decision-making processes
as a means of promoting more just outcomes. The model of democracy

---

[2] Ian Shapiro conceives of democracy as what he calls a 'subordinate good', where its
role in promoting justice is primary. See *Democratic Justice* (New Haven: Yale University
Press, 1999). See also Philippe Van Parijs, 'Justice and Democracy: Are they
Incompatible?', *Journal of Political Philosophy*, 4/2 (June 1996), 101–17.

many theorists call deliberative democracy provides important ideals for such inclusive practices.

While my theoretical starting-point is this model of deliberative democracy, I nevertheless find several shortcomings with some formulations of the model. Some proponents of the model tend to assume that proper settings of deliberation are face to face; others focus on argument as the primary form of political communication. Some advocates of deliberative processes, moreover, claim that democratic commitment requires attending only to a common good, and some assume norms of orderliness which can, in my view, be exclusionary. I argue that a theory of inclusive democratic interaction and decision-making should attend to important functions that forms of communication additional to argument sometimes serve. The model should be applicable to mass society, moreover, which means theorizing the meaning of inclusive representation. Finally, in my conception, a communicative model of democratic inclusion theorizes differentiated social segments struggling and engaging with one another across their differences rather than putting those differences aside to invoke a common good.

## 1. Two Models of Democracy

In contemporary political theory two models of democracy stand centre-stage, often called aggregative and deliberative. Both models share certain assumptions about the basic framework of democratic institutions: that democracy requires a rule of law, that voting is the means of making decisions when consensus is not possible or too costly to achieve, that democratic process requires freedoms of speech, assembly, association, and so on.[3] The models focus less on institutional frameworks of democracy than on the *process* of decision-making to which the idea of democracy refers. I call these 'models' to suggest that each functions as an ideal type; each picks out features of existing democratic practices and systematizes them into a general account of an ideal of democratic process.

---

[3] James Bohman suggests that formulations of the model of deliberative democracy have not always accepted the institutional assumptions of liberal and representative institutions, and that more recent theorizing is close to the assumptions of liberal pluralism in these respects. See, 'The Coming of Age of Deliberative Democracy', *The Journal of Political Philosophy*, Vol. 6, No. 4, December 1998, pp. 400–425.

## The Aggregative Model

The first model interprets democracy as a process of aggregating the preferences of citizens in choosing public officials and policies. The goal of democratic decision-making is to decide what leaders, rules, and policies will best correspond to the most widely and strongly held preferences. A well-functioning democracy allows for the expression of and competition among preferences, and has reliable and fair methods for adding them to bring a result. Jane Mansbridge describes this model of democracy as follows:

Voters pursue their individual interest by making demands on the political system in proportion to the intensity of their feelings. Politicians, also pursuing their own interests, adopt policies that buy them votes, thus ensuring accountability. In order to stay in office, politicians act like entrepreneurs and brokers, looking for formulas that satisfy as many, and alienate as few, interests as possible. From the interchange between self-interested voters and self-interested brokers emerge decisions that come as close as possible to a balanced aggregation of individual interests.[4]

The aggregative model describes democratic processes of policy formation something like this. Individuals in the polity have varying preferences about what they want government institutions to do. They know that other individuals also have preferences, which may or may not match their own. Democracy is a competitive process in which political parties and candidates offer their platforms and attempt to satisfy the largest number of people's preferences. Citizens with similar preferences often organize interest groups in order to try to influence the actions of parties and policy-makers once they are elected. Individuals, interest groups, and public officials each may behave strategically, adjusting the orientation of their pressure tactics or coalition-building according to their perceptions of the activities of competing preferences. Assuming the process of competition, strategizing, coalition-building, and responding to pressure is open and fair, the outcome of both elections and legislative decisions reflects the aggregation of the strongest or most widely held preferences in the population.[5]

---

[4] Jane Mansbridge, *Beyond Adversary Democracy* (New York: Basic Books, 1980), 17.

[5] The model I am calling aggregative is similar to the way of thinking about democracy that some have called pluralist or interest group pluralist. I choose to use the term 'aggregative' instead of 'interest group pluralist' because I find neither pluralism nor the promotion of legitimate interests objectionable or incompatible with a deliberative interpretation of the democratic process. The features of this model that are most objected to by deliberative theorists are those that tend to interpret democratic political processes as like market

This preference aggregation model of democracy has several problems, especially for a theoretical stance that aims to flesh out the intuition that democratic process ought sometimes to be connected to an interest in justice.[6]

First, in this description of democratic process, we take individuals' preferences, whatever they happen to be, as given. There is no account of their origins; they may have been arrived at by whim, reasoning, faith, or fear that others will carry out a threat. While some preferences may be motivated by self-interest, others by altruistic care for others, and still others by a sense of fair play, the aggregative model offers no means of distinguishing among such motives. There are no criteria for distinguishing the quality of preferences by either content, origin, or motive. Where common sense might be inclined to rank some preferences as more intrinsically valuable than others because of their reflective origins or comprehensive content, this model values some more than others only extrinsically according to how many or few hold them or how strongly. Because preferences are conceived as exogenous to the political process, furthermore, there can be no account of how people's political preferences may change as a result of interacting with others or participating in the political process.[7]

On this understanding, furthermore, democracy is a mechanism for identifying and aggregating the preferences of citizens, in order to learn which are held in the greatest number or with the greatest intensity. Citizens never need to leave the private realm of their own interests and preferences to interact with others whose preferences differ. This model lacks any distinct idea of a *public* formed from the interaction of democratic citizens and their motivation to reach some decision. Thus there is no account of the possibility of political co-ordination and co-operation.

A third problem with the aggregative model of democracy is that it carries a thin and individualistic form of rationality. Each political actor may engage in instrumental or strategic reasoning about the best

---

economic processes, and the reasoning of political actors as analogous to strategic reasoning in a competitive market context. For some summaries and critiques of this model, see C. B. Macpherson, *The Life and Times of Liberal Democracy* (Oxford: Oxford University Press, 1977), ch. 4; Thomas Christiano, *The Rule of the Many* (Boulder, Colo.: Westview Press, 1996), 133–50; David Ingram, *Reason, History and Politics* (Albany: State University of New York Press, 1995), ch. 1.

[6] For criticisms of the aggregative model in addition to the above, see Benjamin Barber, *Strong Democracy* (Berkeley: University of California Press, 1984), esp. 132–43; John Dryzek, *Discursive Democracy* (Cambridge: Cambridge University Press, 1990), esp. ch. 1.

[7] See Cass R. Sunstein, 'Preferences and Politics', *Philosophy and Public Affairs* 20 (Winter 1991), 3–34.

means of realizing their preferences, but the aggregate outcome has no necessary rationality and itself has not been arrived at by a process of reasoning.[8] Indeed, the aggregate outcome can just as easily be irrational as rational, even measured in terms of the preferences themselves; preference orderings when aggregated may yield a different ordering than those the individuals hold singly.[9]

The aggregative model of democracy, finally, is sceptical about the possibility of normative and evaluative objectivity. It denies that people who make claims on others about what is good or just can defend such claims with reasons that are objective in the sense that they appeal to general principles beyond the subjective preferences or interests of themselves or others.[10] On this subjecitivist interpretation, if people use moral language, they are simply conveying a particular kind of preference or interest which is no more rational or objective than any other.[11] Although in everyday political life sometimes people do claim that certain policies ought to be put in place because they are right, the aggregative model of democracy offers no way to evaluate the moral legitimacy of the substance of decisions. Without any notion of normative reasons in the process, there is also no basis for normatively evaluating the substance of the result.

The model therefore offers only a weak motivational basis for accepting the outcomes of a democratic process as legitimate. If even at its best democracy is simply a mechanism for aggregating preferences which are subjective and non-rational, and if the fair outcome reflects which preferences are more widely or strongly held, then there is no reason why those who do not share those preferences ought to abide by the results. They may simply feel that they have no choice but to submit, given that they are in the minority.

## The Deliberative Model

The model of democracy as a process of aggregating preferences does loosely describe some aspects of democratic process in the world today, and also expresses the way many political actors think about democracy. Not only political scientists and economists, but many journalists, politicians, and citizens, implicitly share the assumptions

---

[8] Thomas Spragens, *Reason and Democracy* (Durham, NC: Duke University Press, 1990).

[9] See David Miller, 'Deliberative Democracy and Social Choice', in David Held (ed.), *Prospects for Democracy* (Oxford: Polity Press, 1993).

[10] See Dryzek, *Discursive Democracy*, 125.

[11] Mansbridge, *Beyond Adversary Democracy*, 18.

of this model that ends and values are subjective, non-rational, and exogenous to the political process. Consequently, they believe that democratic politics is nothing other than a competition between private interests and preferences. The operation of liberal democratic politics corresponds to these assumptions. Voting—the expressing of preferences among a list of candidates or referendum choices—is the primary political act. The democratic process consists in various groups putting out their interests and competing for those votes. Such a mass plebiscite process treats citizens as atomized, privately responding to itemized opinion poll questions.[12]

Even in our imperfect democracies, however, another model of democracy lies in the shadows. Wherever the democratic impulse emerges, many people associate democracy with open discussion and the exchange of views leading to agreed-upon policies. In parliamentary discussions participants often claim that theirs is the most just and reasonable proposal. Most democracies contain other institutions and practices of political discussion and criticism in which participants aim to persuade one another of the rightness of their positions.

Contemporary political theorists usually call this alternative model deliberative democracy. A number of important theories of deliberative democracy have appeared in recent years, sparking a renewed interest in the place of reasoning, persuasion, and normative appeals in democratic politics.[13] In the deliberative model democracy is a form of practical reason. Participants in the democratic process offer proposals for how best to solve problems or meet legitimate needs, and so on, and they present arguments through which they aim to persuade others to accept their proposals. Democratic process is primarily a discussion of problems, conflicts, and claims of need or interest. Through dialogue others test and challenge these proposals and arguments.

---

[12] On the idea of and for a critique of plebiscite democracy, see James Fishkin, *the Voice of the People* (New Haven: Yale University Press, 1991).

[13] Among the writers whom I include as theorists of deliberative democracy are Joshua Cohen, 'Deliberation and Democratic Legitimacy', in Alan Hamlin and Philip Pettit (eds.), *The Good Polity* (London: Blackwell, 1989); Spragens, *Reason and Democracy*; Barber, *Strong Democracy*; Cass R. Sunstein, *The Partial Constitution* (Cambridge, Mass.: Harvard University Press, 1993), esp. ch. 8; Frank Michelman, 'Traces of Self-Government', *Harvard Law Review*, 100 (1986), 4–77; Jane Mansbridge, 'A Deliberative Theory of Interest Representation', in Mark P. Patracca (ed.), *The Politics of Interest: Interest Groups Transformed* (Boulder, Colo., Westview Press, 1992); Dryzek, *Discursive Democracy*; James Bohman, *Public Deliberation* (Cambridge, Mass.: MA: MIT Press, 1996); Fishkin, *The Voice of the People*; Jurgen Habermas, *Between Facts and Norms* (Cambridge, Mass.: MIT Press, 1996); Amy Gutmann and Dennis Thompson, *Democracy and Disagreement* (Cambridge, Mass.: Harvard University Press, 1996); Christiano, *The Rule of the Many*, esp. ch. 3; Ingram, *Reason, History and Politics*.

Because they have not stood up to dialogic examination, the deliberating public rejects or refines some proposals. Participants arrive at a decision not by determining what preferences have greatest numerical support, but by determining which proposals the collective agrees are supported by the best reasons. This model of democratic processes entails several normative ideals for the relationships and dispositions of deliberating parties, among them inclusion, equality, reasonableness, and publicity. These ideals are all logically related in the deliberative model.

*Inclusion.* On this model a democratic decision is normatively legitimate only if all those affected by it are included in the process of discussion and decision-making. This simple formulation opens many questions about the way in which they are affected, and how strongly; it might be absurd to say that everyone affected by decisions in any trivial way ought to be party to them. To limit this question somewhat, we can say that 'affected' here means at least that decisions and policies significantly condition a person's options for action. As an ideal, inclusion embodies a norm of moral respect. Persons (and perhaps other creatures) are being treated as means if they are expected to abide by rules or adjust their actions according to decisions from where determination their voice and interests have been excluded. When coupled with norms of political equality, inclusion allows for maximum expression of interests, opinions, and perspectives relevant to the problems or issues for which a public seeks solutions.

*Political equality.* As a normative ideal, democracy means political equality. Not only should all those affected be nominally included in decision-making, but they should be included on equal terms. All ought to have an equal right and effective opportunity to express their interests and concerns.[14] All also ought to have equal effective opportunity to question one another, and to respond to and criticize one another's proposals and arguments. The ideal model of deliberative democracy, that is, promotes free and equal opportunity to speak. This condition cannot be met, however, without a third condition of equality, namely freedom from domination. Participants in an ideal process of deliberative democracy must be equal in the sense that none of them is in a position to coerce or threaten others into accepting certain proposals or outcomes.

While I have distinguished the terms 'inclusion' and 'political equality' in order to specify their normative import, for the rest of this book

[14] For a comprehensive theory of political equality in the deliberative mode, see Charles Beitz, *Political Equality* (Princeton: Princeton University Press, 1990).

when I refer to a norm of inclusion I shall understand it to entail the norm of political equality. In real political conflict, when political actors and movements protest exclusion and demand greater inclusion, they invariably appeal to ideals of political equality and do not accept token measures of counting people in. When discussion is inclusive, in this strong sense, it allows the expression of all interests, opinions, and criticism, and when it is free from domination, discussion participants can be confident that the results arise from good reasons rather than from fear or force or false consensus. This confidence can be maintained, however, only when participants have a disposition to be reasonable.

*Reasonableness*. In the context of the model of deliberative democracy, I take reasonableness to refer more to a set of dispositions that discussion participants have than to the substance of people's contributions to debate. Reasonable people often have crazy ideas; what makes them reasonable is their willingness to listen to others who want to explain to them why their ideas are incorrect or inappropriate. People who think they know more or are better than others are sometimes too quick to label the assertions of others as irrational, and thereby try to avoid having to engage with them. Since reasonable people often disagree about what proposals, actions, groundings, and narratives are rational or irrational, judging too quickly is itself often a symptom of unreasonableness.

Reasonable people enter discussion to solve collective problems with the aim of reaching agreement. Often they will not reach agreement, of course, and they need to have procedures for reaching decisions and registering dissent in the absence of agreement. Reasonable people understand that dissent often produces insight, and that decisions and agreements should in principle be open to new challenge. While actually reaching consensus is thus not a requirement of deliberative reason, participants in discussion must be *aiming* to reach agreement to enter the discussion at all. Only if the participants believe that some kind of agreement among them is possible in principle can they in good faith trust one another to listen and aim to persuade one another.

Thus reasonable participants in democratic discussion must have an open mind. They cannot come to the discussion of a collective problem with commitments that bind them to the authority of prior norms or unquestionable beliefs.[15] Nor can they assert their own interests above all others' or insist that their initial opinion about what is right

---

[15] Cohen, 'Deliberation and Democratic Legitimacy', 22–3.

or just cannot be subject to revision. To be reasonable is to be willing to change our opinions or preferences because others persuade us that our initial opinions or preferences, as they are relevant to the collective problems under discussion, are incorrect or inappropriate. Being open thus also refers to a disposition to listen to others, treat them with respect, make an effort to understand them by asking questions, and not judge them too quickly. A reasonable respectful process of discussion exhibits deliberative uptake; when some speak, others acknowledge the expression in ways that continue the engagement.[16]

*Publicity.* The conditions of inclusion, equality, and reasonableness, finally, entail that the interaction among participants in a democratic decision-making process forms a public in which people hold one another accountable.[17] A public consists of a plurality of different individual and collective experiences, histories, commitments, ideals, interests, and goals that face one another to discuss collective problems under a common set of procedures. When members of such a public speak to one another, they know they are answerable to that plurality of others; this access that others have to their point of view makes them careful about expressing themselves. This plural public-speaking context requires participants to express themselves in ways accountable to all those plural others. They must try to explain their particular background experiences, interests, or proposals in ways that others can understand, and they must express reasons for their claims in ways that others recognize could be accepted, even if in fact they disagree with the claims and reasons. Even when they address a particular group with a particular history, as is usually the case, they speak with the reflective idea that third parties might be listening.[18] For the content of an expression to be public does not entail that it *is* immediately understood by all, or that the principles to which argument appeals *are* accepted by all, but only that the expression aims in its form and content to be understandable and acceptable. Deliberative exchange thus entails expressions of puzzlement or disagreement, the posing of questions, and answering them.

[16] Of deliberative theorists, Bohman has made the most of this idea of uptake; *Public Deliberation*, 58–9, 116–18.

[17] Publicity and accountability are the core of Amy Gutmann and Dennis Thompson's conception of deliberation. See *Democracy and Disagreement*.

[18] See Jodi Dean, *Solidarity of Strangers* (Berkeley: University of California Press, 1994). Dean develops an idea of a universalist open relation of solidarity among particular group members, where they are united by their relation to a 'hypothetical third'. Some writers put this publicity condition in terms of Kantian universalizability, but I think that this is a mistake, because it removes the discourse from its situatedness. See Bohman, *Public Deliberation*, 35–47.

## The Adequacy of the Deliberative Model

Though both models rely on the actual experience of democracy, the deliberative model is more adequate to the set of commitments that bring us to value democratic practice than is the aggregative. The latter model responds primarily to democracy's purpose as a protection against tyranny and the ability of individuals and groups to promote and protect their interests in politics and policy. The deliberative model responds to these purposes, but also corresponds to other purposes people express for valuing democracy, such as promoting cooperation, solving collective problems, and furthering justice.

The interactive aspect of this model accounts for its greater comprehensiveness. In the deliberative model political actors not only express preferences and interests, but they engage with one another about how to balance these under circumstances of inclusive equality. Because this interaction requires participants to be open and attentive to one another, to justify their claims and proposals in terms acceptable to all, the orientation of participants moves from self-regard to an orientation towards what is publicly assertable. Interests and preferences continue to have a place in the processes of deliberative democracy, but not as given and exogenous to the process. Most proponents of deliberative democracy emphasize that this model conceptualizes the process of democratic discussion as not merely expressing and registering, but as *transforming* the preferences, interests, beliefs, and judgements of participants. Through the process of public discussion with a plurality of differently opinioned and situated others, people often gain new information, learn of different experiences of their collective problems, or find that their own initial opinions are founded on prejudice or ignorance, or that they have misunderstood the relation of their own interests to others'.[19]

I endorse the basic outlines of the model of deliberative democracy as I have formulated them here. It is the best way to think about democracy from the point of view of an interest in a politics of inclusion and promoting greater justice. Some formulations of the model should be criticized, however, and the model also needs refinement in several respects in order to a serve a theory of inclusive democratic process.

---

[19] Most deliberative theorists thematize this transformative aspect of discursive interaction. See e.g. Barber, *Strong Democracy*, 136–58; Jane Mansbridge, 'Self-Interest and Political Transformation', in George E. Marcus and Russell L. Hanson (eds.), *Reconsidering the Democratic Public* (University Park: Pennsylvania State University Press, 1993).

## 2. An Ideal Relation between Democracy and Justice

People value democracy, I have suggested, at least partly because we believe it is the best political means for confronting injustice and promoting justice. Are there grounds for this belief? Experience offers many counter-examples. Certainly many democracies have enacted unjust laws or sanctioned the performance of unjust actions. Even when democracies do not directly enact injustices, their processes and policies often reinforce or fail to change social and economic injustices they have not created. Democrats nevertheless persist in the faith that there is a connection between democracy and justice. I will return to consider the problem that the democratic processes we know too often produce or reinforce injustice in the societies. Now I will elaborate how the ideals of deliberative democracy give theoretical support for the persistent faith that democratic procedures are likely to promote the most just policies.

I assume a polity within which there are differences and conflicts, problems that the collective must face in order to get on with their individual business and collective project of living with one another. A polity is a collective whose members recognize themselves as governed by common rule-making and negotiating procedures. The ideal model of deliberative democracy says that all those whose basic interests are affected by a decision ought to be included in the deliberatively democracy process. Democratic theory does not often raise the question of whether the scope and membership of the *actual* polity dealing with specific problems corresponds to the scope of what the polity *ought* to be if the discussions are to include all those affected by decisions. A theory of democratic inclusion, however, must consider the question of the correspondence of the polity with the proper moral scope of the issues of justice that arise. Chapters 6 and 7 of this book deal explicitly with this question. For now I leave it aside, and simply assume polities whose decision-making procedures consider questions that the collective faces. On this general account a polity need not be a legally defined state, but may refer also to non-state governing bodies in private businesses, universities, churches, and other such institutions.

In addition to the question of who is included in deliberation, we need to know what is the object of their discussion. The object of their discussion is contested problems. People who live and work together face some problems, whether external or internal, which can best be addressed by some co-operative action. The problems may be as limited as where to locate a school and how it should be designed, or how to divert traffic around the city centre without harming the businesses there. Or the problems may be as protracted as how to resolve long-standing disputes over land distribution among persons and groups of differing historical origins with complex histories of conflict, or how to design a tax system that is fair, generates sufficient revenue, is difficult to cheat, and is easy to administer. A useful way to conceive of democracy is as a process in which a large collective discusses problems such as these that they face together, and try to arrive peaceably at solutions in whose implementation everyone will co-operate.[20]

The problems that collectives face for which they seek solutions through a political process usually have both a technical and a normative aspect. They concern not only accomplishing some ends in the most efficient manner, but also, in the process, not wrongfully burdening some members of the polity or undervaluing their rights and interests. Seeking a solution to problems a large collective faces, that is, always entails considerations of justice, even though it usually entails other considerations as well. Often the problems are posed as issues of justice directly; they arise because some individual or group claim they suffer injustice and call upon the polity to enact measures to redress or eliminate such injustices.

Importantly, however, the problems a collective faces and seeks to solve through a democratic process rarely, if ever, receive the formulation that philosophers often give to issues of justice: what are the two or three principles of justice that right-thinking polities ought to accept to guide their decision-making? Constructing the problem in this way invites us to imagine a more abstract and comprehensive decision situation than politics usually exhibits. Even during those rare moments when polities engage in constitutional discussions, the object of their discussion is not to reach agreement on principles of justice, but rather to agree on the design of institutions. Most political decisions, however, are more specific and contextualized than such constitutional decisions. The outcome of political discussion and decision-making is almost never some conception of justice, but rather a

---

[20] Defining democracy as a method of collective problem-solving recalls John Dewey's approach to democratic theory and practice; see Dewey, *The Public and its Problems* (Chicago: Swallow Press, 1927). For two rather different recent interpretations of a deliberative understanding of democracy along Dewey's lines, see Hilary Putnam, 'A Reconsideration of Deweyan Democracy', *Southern California Law Review*, 63/6 (Sept. 1990), 1671–97; and Axel Honneth, 'Democracy as Reflexive Cooperation: John Dewey and the Theory of Democracy Today', *Political Theory*, 26/6 (Dec. 1998), 763–83. Honneth gives an account of Dewey's conception of democracy as an alternative both to an aggregative conception and to Habermas's overly procedural conception.

*particular judgement* about what actions and policies *this* collective should adopt to address *these* circumstances.[21]

This does not mean that there is no role for principles and theories about justice in political discussion. On the contrary, to the extent that people require justification from one another for their claims and proposals, they must often appeal to principles and values of justice. To the extent that some people doubt or disagree with the principles that others appeal to, reasonable political discussion also calls for justifying principles, theorizing their coherence with one another, or arguing that some take precedence over others. Appeals to principles of justice have a more pragmatic function in political interaction than many theories of justice attribute to them. Where practical judgements are the result at which discussants aim, appeals to principles of justice are steps in arguments about what should be done.

Members of a polity, then, need not seek and arrive at agreement on a general conception of justice in order to argue productively about their problems and come to morally legitimate resolutions. Recognizing this can make political agreement seem less intractable than is sometimes supposed; it is often easier for people facing shared problems or conflicts to agree on a particular judgement about ways to address those problems than to commit themselves to a set of general principles to apply to all their collective dealings. While considerations of justice are nearly always morally at stake in political decision-making, justice 'in itself' is a limit concept at which we always aim as the moral horizon of our political dealings.[22]

We can now return to the major point at hand: What are the theoretical reasons for thinking that a democratic political process is likely to promote the most just outcomes? The argument assumes the ideal conditions I specified above for the model of deliberative democracy. If all significantly affected by problems and their solutions are included in the discussion and decision-making on the basis of equality and non-domination, and if they interact reasonably and constitute

---

[21] Contemporary moral and political theorists pay too little attention to judgement as the conclusion of moral reasoning, as distinct from a general theory or set of principles, and particular statements or actions that follow from these. Charles Larmore is one moral theorist who recommends judgement; see *Patterns of Moral Complexity* (Cambridge: Cambridge University Press, 1987), esp. ch. 1; Jennifer Nedelsky reflects on the role of judgement in Kant and Arendt to develop an account useful for democratic theory; see Jennifer Nedelsky, 'The Problem of Judgment', unpublished manuscript, University of Toronto.

[22] See Jacques Derrida, 'Force of Law: The "Mystical Foundation of Authority"', in Drucilla Cornell, Michel Rosenfeld, and David Gray Carlson (eds.), *Deconstruction and the Possibility of Justice* (New York: Routledge, 1992).

a public where people are accountable to one another, then the results of their discussion is likely to be the most wise and just.

A process of public deliberation under these ideal conditions provides both the motivation to take all needs and interests into account and knowledge of what they are. The conditions of equal opportunity to speak and freedom from domination encourage all to express their needs and interests. The equality condition also requires a reciprocity such that each acknowledges that the interests of the others must be taken into account in order to reach a judgement. Knowing that they are answerable to others, and that they are mutually committed to reaching agreement, means that each understands that his or her best interests will be served by aiming for a just result. Each is thus motivated to express her interests or preferences in terms that aim to persuade others that they are compatible with justice in this case, which is to say that they do not seek to ignore or cancel the legitimate interests of others. Since individuals and groups often initially construct their interests and preferences in ways that cancel out or ignore the legitimate interests of others, this accountability to others means that they must often transform their interests and preferences, so that they can be publicly expressed as compatible with justice.[23]

The structure and norms of ideal deliberative democracy, furthermore, provide the epistemic conditions for the collective knowledge of which proposals are most likely in fact to promote results that are wise and just. If discussion reflects all social experience, and everyone can speak and criticize freely, then discussion participants will be able to develop a collective account of the sources of the problems they are trying to solve, and will develop the social knowledge necessary to predict likely consequences of alternative courses of action meant to address them. Their collective critical wisdom thus enables them to reach a judgement that is not only normatively right in principle,

---

[23] I mean this paragraph to echo the pragmatic theory of rightness expressed in discourse ethics. On this theory a norm is valid if it is the result of free discussion and agreement under circumstances of inclusive equality. See Jurgen Habermas, *Moral Consciousness and Communicative Ethics* (Cambridge, Mass.: MIT Press, 1990), esp. chs. 3 and 4. In earlier formulations Habermas says that the dialogic process sifts out interests that are *generalizable* from those that are not. I interpret 'generalizable' here to mean not that they are interests that everyone shares (which is one interpretation Habermas has given to the idea), but rather interests that can be promoted in public in the sense that others can recognize those interests as legitimate without denying their own legitimate claims to self-determination and self-development. In later formulations Habermas attends more to the way that preferences and experiences of concrete particular subjects in a discursive situation become transformed towards a more objective constitution of a social perspective. See Habermas, 'A Genealogical Analysis of the Cognitive Content of Morality', in *The Inclusion of the Other: Studies in Political Theory* (Cambridge, Mass.: MIT Press, 1998).

but also empirically and theoretically sound. I will elaborate this function of democracy to produce social knowledge more in Chapter 3.[24]


## 3. Ideals of Self-Determination and Self-Development

This book reflects on the conditions of inclusive decision-making that might help bring about more just and wise political judgements. What counts as a just result is what participants would arrive at under ideal conditions of inclusion, equality, reasonableness, and publicity. A comprehensive theory of justice is neither necessary nor appropriate for thinking about deepening democracy. In the same manner that ideas of justice must arise in the middle of discussing particular political problems in practice, however, so appeals to some notions of justice are unavoidable in political theorizing. At several points in the chapters that follow I appeal to two ideals of social justice that I believe in this general form are fairly uncontroversial, but which I should state explicitly as assumptions. I call these values self-development and self-determination. As I understand them, these two general values correspond to two general conditions of injustice: oppression, institutional constraint on self-development, and domination, institutional constraint on self-determination.[25] I shall briefly elaborate on each of these general notions of social justice, as they have been theorized by others.

I interpret the value of self-development along lines similar to the values Amartya Sen calls equality as capabilities. Just social institutions provide conditions for all persons to learn and use satisfying and expansive skills in socially recognized settings, and enable them

[24] I am relying here on what many writers call an epistemic interpretation of deliberative democracy. If the model of deliberative democracy interprets democracy as a form of collective practical reason, then the outcome of deliberation has a 'truth' value. Deliberators make claims and arguments in order to find the best judgement. In *On Liberty* J. S. Mill expresses the classic argument that freedom of deliberation is more likely to lead to wise conclusions. For discussions of epistemic virtues of deliberative democracy, see Joshua Cohen, 'An Epistemic Conception of Democracy', *Ethics*, 97 (Oct. 1986), 26–38; David Estland, 'Making Truth Safe for Democracy', in D. Copp, J. Hampton, and J. Roemer (eds.), *The Ideal of Democracy* (Cambridge: Cambridge University Press, 1993); Estland, 'Beyond Fairness and Deliberation: The Epistemic Dimension of Democratic Authority', in Bohman and Rehg (eds.), *Deliberative and Democracy* (Cambridge, Mass.: MIT Press, 1996); Bohman, *Public Deliberation*, 27; Christiano, *The Rule of the Many*, 31–7.

[25] See Iris Marion Young, *Justice and the Politics of Difference* (Princeton: Princeton University Press, 1990), 33–8. Carol Gould develops a thorough account of freedom as self-development; see Gould, *Rethinking Democracy: Freedom and Social Cooperation in Politics, Economy and Society* (Cambridge: Cambridge University Press, 1988), esp. 40–1.

to play and communicate with others or express their feelings and perspectives on social life in contexts where others can listen.[26] Self-development in this sense certainly entails meeting people's needs for food, shelter, health care, and so on. With Sen, however, I find focus on distribution of goods or income *per se* too limited a way of evaluating justice or well-being.[27] Because of their differing attributes or situation, some people need more or different kinds of goods to enable equal levels of capability with others. Perhaps more importantly, there are aspects of this value of self-development which are only accidentally related to goods or income. Using satisfying skills and having one's particular cultural modes of expression and ways of life recognized depend on the organization of the division of labour and the structures of communication and co-operation. While the distribution of resources and positions is a central issue for the value of self-development, this value also raises questions about the institutional organization of power, status, and communication in ways not reducible to distributions.

Self-determination, the second aspect of justice as I understand it, consists in being able to participate in determining one's action and the condition of one's action; its contrary is domination. Persons live within structures of domination if other persons or groups can determine without reciprocation the conditions of their action, either directly or by virtue of the structural consequences of their actions.[28] Philip Pettit offers a useful political theory of freedom as non-domination. A person is free if she is able to pursue her life in her own way. Pettit disagrees, however, with an interpretation of autonomy in this sense as reducible non-interference. The ability to follow one's own pursuits in one's own way is often restricted not only by direct interference by other agents, but more importantly by institutional relations, including those that award differential power to some agents to constrain the choices and actions of others. These are institutional relations of domination. Real freedom means the absence of such relations of domination. Pettit argues that institutions should promote

---

[26] Young, *Justice and the Politics of Difference*, 38.

[27] Amartya Sen, *Inequality Reexamined* (Cambridge, Mass.: Harvard University Press, 1992), esp. ch. 2; see also Sen, 'Justice: Means versus Freedoms', *Philosophy and Public Affairs*, 19 (Spring 1990), 111–21; for a comprehensive reconstruction of Sen's theory of justice as the conditions for capability, see David Crocker, 'Functioning and Capability: The Foundations of Sen's and Nussbaum's Development Ethic', in Martha Nussbaum and Jonathan Glover (eds.), *Women, Culture and Development: A Study in Human Capabilities* (Oxford: Oxford University Press, 1995); see also Young, *Justice and the Politics of Difference*, ch. 1.

[28] Young, *Justice and the Politics of Difference*, 37.

and preserve non-domination for everyone. To do so they must sometimes regulate and interfere with actions in order to restrict dominative power and promote co-operation. To arrive at a concept of
self-determination, I add an element that Pettit does not emphasize,
namely participation in making the collective regulations designed to
prevent domination. Democracy in that respect is entailed by self-
determination, though the value of self-determination does not reduce
to democratic participation.

I define social justice, then, as the institutional conditions for promoting self-development and self-determination of a society's members. This expresses an ideal of justice which is even more abstract than
a set of principles. The ideal may be controversial, but at this level of
abstraction I will assume in this book that it is not enormously controversial. Interpretation and application of these ideals in a particular
political situation, however, is always controversial. We may agree on
goals and values in this most abstract sense, but disagree strongly on
what are the best means of promoting these values in that context,
what are the acceptable priorities and trade-offs, and so on. We may
disagree about what actions and institutions will in fact further these
ideals, or just how the interests of different social segments are served
or how they conflict. Political judgements concern resolving those
particular and contextual disagreements. At several points in the coming chapters I invoke these general ideas of justice to discuss issues of
inclusion and democracy in particular contexts.

## 4. Democratic Theory for Unjust Conditions

I have explained how the theory of deliberative democracy supports
the intuition that democratic processes are most likely to undermine
injustice and promote justice. Before continuing, the problem of the
logical circle in this theory should be addressed. As ideal, the theory
expresses conditions that often operate as implicit regulative norms
guiding social co-operation, but which are never perfectly realized.
The model of deliberative democracy assumes that participants in a
decision-making process are not pressed for time, and that they can
concentrate significant energies to their discussion. It rules out the
influence of prior commitments, unconscious prejudices, and authority which often colour even the most well-intentioned deliberations in
actual democracies. The theory says that justice is nothing other than
what the members of an inclusive public of equal and reasonable citizens would agree to under these ideal circumstances.

Put this way, the connection between democracy and justice appears circular. Ideal processes of deliberative democracy lead to substantively just outcomes because the deliberation begins from a starting-point of justice. All potentially affected persons are included in the discussions, and all are able to speak freely and criticize, under circumstances where no one is in a position to threaten or coerce others into accepting their proposals. Such conditions would seem to exist only within just institutions that enable the self-development of everyone and where no one is subject to domination by others.

No existing democracy is as just as that. Our democracies contain structural inequalities—for example, inequalities of wealth, social and economic power, access to knowledge, status, work expectations. These structural inequalities are unjust to the extent that they help produce or perpetuate institutional conditions which support domination or inhibit self-development. We are all dismally familiar, moreover, with many of the ways that social and economic inequality produces political inequality. Money often has greater influence than open debate in determining the outcomes of elections, referendum campaigns, or legislative battles. Economic power and the interests of financiers often operate to confine alternative policy proposals to a narrow set.[29] The harms of poverty, or exploitative overwork, or domestic violence, or racial prejudice often inhibit the political participation of some citizens with formally equal rights at the same time that they relatively empower others. Structural social and economic inequalities thus often operate to exclude or marginalize the voice and influence of some groups while magnifying the influence of others.

So we have a different circle: Where there are structural inequalities of wealth and power, formally democratic procedures are likely to reinforce them, because privileged people are able to marginalize the voices and issues of those less privileged. Because these are some of the realities of democracy under conditions of structural inequalities, some theorists of deliberative democracy claim that a political process can only be properly democratic if the society in which it takes place is free of domination, especially that produced by economic power.[30]

[29] See Adam Pzeworski and Immanuel Wallterstein, 'Structural Dependence of the State on Capital', *American Political Science Review* 82 (1989), 11–29.

[30] See Joshua Cohen, 'The Economic Basis of Deliberative Democracy', *Social Philosophy and Policy*, 6/2 (Spring 1989), 25–50. Gutmann and Thompson build the meeting of an economic minimum into their conception of deliberative democracy; *Democracy and Disagreement*. See my essay 'Justice, Inclusion and Deliberative Democracy', in Stephen Macedo (ed.), *Deliberative Politics: Essays on Democracy and Disagreement* (Oxford: Oxford University Press, 1999), 151–8.

For democracy to promote justice it must already be just. Formally democratic processes in societies with structural inequalities seem as likely to reinforce injustice as to promote greater justice. Must we accept these circles? They seem to imply that real-world political actors cannot use democratic means to seek greater justice. But what alternatives are there for those who seek social change to bring about more just institutions and relations?

Political actors can try to impose their idea of more just conditions through authoritarian or revolutionary force. I would not say that trying to do so is always wrong, but only rarely is it a live option. The use of undemocratic means to try to create conditions of greater freedom from social and economic domination and possibilities for self-development for more people, moreover, itself carries risks of producing or reinforcing injustice. Organizing and political mobilization within formally democratic institutions and norms is usually the only realistic option for oppressed and disadvantaged people and their allies to improve social relations and institutions.[31]

Democrats believe that the circles can be broken. In formally democratic societies with serious injustices it must be possible to promote social changes towards greater justice through democratic means. The history of many societies offers inspiring examples of social movements and government reform efforts that have indeed undermined injustices by democratic means. Such efforts rely on what Frank Cunningham calls a 'democratic fix' for social harms and problems; impediments to the ability of democracies to enact more just policies are best addressed by deepening democracy.[32]

Political practice guided by norms of deliberative democracy that I have articulated above can deepen democracy to make it more inclusive of plural claims and perspectives and empowering for less privileged participants. Proponents of the application of a model of deliberative democracy to actual political processes in imperfect democracies with injustices suggest that the more that public life and political decision-making motivate political actors to justify their claims and actions and be accountable to their fellow citizens, the more the arbitrariness of greed, naked power, or the cynical pursuit of self-interest can be exposed and limited. When public debate gets beyond soundbites and manipulated opinion polls, issues often are seen as more complex and less polarized, and thus more open to minority voices. Relatively small or weak social segments have more

[31] Compare Van Parijs, 'Justice and Democracy: Are they Incompatible?'.
[32] Frank Cunningham, *The Real World of Democracy Revisited* (Atlantic Highlands, NJ: Humanities Press, 1994), esp. chs. 2 and 3.

chance of influencing political outcomes in a process where people are expected to justify their opinions and actions and listen to others than in a competition that aggregates pre-existing preference. Increasing opportunities for serious and plural public debate that both holds powerful actors accountable and is connected to institutional or policy outcomes, then, may be a means by which democratic processes in a society with structural social and economic inequalities can address some of their injustices.

In existing democracies there is more agreement on the norms of inclusive democracy than there is agreement on whether social and economic arrangements are just. Even many who do not agree that the economic inequalities of these societies are unjust, for example, nevertheless criticize moves by the economically and socially powerful to avoid public scrutiny, buy influence, or exclude individuals and groups from participation. Many democracies have some provisions for confronting the ways in which the socially privileged sometimes exclude others from influencing policy outcomes. Campaign finance regulation, lobbying regulation, corruption investigation, rules for hearings, procedures for public comment, and so on, all attempt to regulate decision-making processes to make them more inclusive. Accusations of exclusion or marginalization often send political leaders and movements scrambling to become more inclusive, or at least to appear to be. In taking up the task of deepening democracy, then, citizens must struggle to ensure such measures are enacted and enforced.

## 5. Limitations of Some Interpretations of the Deliberative Model

Because inclusion is a basic and widely accepted condition of legitimacy in democratic politics, it can be a tool to break the circle by which the political inequality produced by social and economic inequality reinforces those inequalities. While full political equality requires conditions of social justice, political inequalities can nevertheless be attacked directly, and institutions and actors can be effectively criticized for excluding or marginalizing some members of the polity. The model of deliberative democracy offers a useful beginning for criticizing exclusion and offering a vision of the meaning of inclusion. Certain interpretations of the model of deliberative democracy, however, make it too narrow or itself exclusionary to aid the task of deepening democracy in mass societies with structural injustices. While these assumptions are not shared by all promoters of the deliberative model, they are held commonly enough by both advocates and detractors to warrant their examination.

## Privileging Argument

In some formulations of the model of deliberative democracy argument constitutes the primary form of political communication. By argument I mean the constuction of an orderly chain of reasoning from premises to conclusion. While argument is an important contributor to political discussion, there are reasons to be suspicious of privileging argument, and especially certain interpretations of what good argument means, over other forms of communication. On these accounts, deliberation cannot proceed unless there are some premises that all the discussants accept, and a generally accepted conceptual and normative framework for framing the issues. Discussion should proceed, this interpretation assumes, by identifying such mutually accepted premises and frameworks, and should aim to base arguments on them. Given the heterogeneity of human life and the complexity of social structures and interaction, however, the effort to shape arguments according to shared premises within shared discursive frameworks sometimes excludes the expression of some needs, interests, and suffering of injustice, because these cannot be voiced with the operative premises and frameworks. Jean-François Lyotard calls this the problem of the 'differend', or

the case where the plaintiff is divested of the means to argue and becomes for that reason a victim. If the addressor, the addressee, and the sense of the testimony are neutralized, everything takes place as if there were no damages. A case of differend between two parties takes place where the 'regulation' of the conflict that opposes them is done in the idiom of one of the parties while the wrong suffered by the other is not signified in that idiom.[33]

Silencing some problem or experience is an ever-present danger in communication, and no general rules or practices of discussion can ensure against it. Inclusive democratic communication, however, should be alert to the possibility that a public that appears to have shared understandings might exclude some needs which do not find expression within those shared understandings. A lack of shared premises or discursive framework for making an argument about a need or injustice, however, does not imply that there are no ways to communicate the need or injustice to others. Such communication,

---

[33] Jean-François Lyotard, *The Differend: Phrases in Dispute* (Minneapolis: University of Minnesota Press, 1988), 9.

however, must be more particularistic than argument from shared premises can be.

Even where participants in political discussion do share premises and idiom of discussion, the norms that practices and theories of deliberation often assume can privilege some and disadvantage others. In particular, expectations about norms of articulateness and dispassionateness sometimes serve to devalue or dismiss the efforts of some participants to make their claims and arguments to a political public.

Being reasonable in a discussion means being open to listening to others and having them influence one's views, and expressing one's own claims upon them in ways that aim to reach their assent or understanding. The desire and ability to be reasonable in this sense lies in the practices of communicative action themselves, in so far, as when people talk, they aim to understand one another.[34] Being reasonable in this sense requires no special education or training beyond the significant demands of co-operative social interaction.

Often, however, norms of speaking that I bring under the label 'articulateness' privilege the modes of expression more typical of highly educated people. Spoken expression that follows the structure of well-formed written speech is privileged over other modes. Speech or writing framed as straightforward assertion is privileged over more circuitous, hesitant, or questioning expression. The norms of deliberation also often privilege speech that is formal and general. They value expression that proceeds from premise to conclusion in an orderly fashion, formulating general principles and applying them to particular cases.[35]

Unlike a norm of reasonableness, which is a general norm of communicative action that aims to reach understanding, these norms of 'articulateness' are culturally specific. Those who exhibit such

[34] Here I appeal to Habermas's notion of communicative action. Habermas theorizes communicative interaction, that is, language as practice, as itself a process implicitly guided by regulative norms of respect and reasonableness. To be sure, humans are horribly selfish, irrationally hateful, and violent. Everyday communication, however, also frequently exhibits a desire on people's part to understand one another and affirm that we understand one another's meanings and intentions, and this effort of co-ordination is no small achievement. See Habermas, *The Theory of Communicative Action*, i (Boston: Beacon Press, 1984).

[35] See Susan Bickford, *The Dissonance of Democracy* (Ithaca, NY: Cornell University Press, 1996), 97–8. Compare Nancy Fraser, 'Rethinking the Public Sphere: A Contribution to the Critique of Actually Existing Democracy', in Bruce Robbins (ed.), *The Phantom Public Sphere* (Minneapolis: University of Minnesota Press, 1993). Fraser argues that social inequality often surfaces within contexts of deliberation that claim to have bracketed such inequalities in the modes of speaking of different groups. She claims that theorists of the public sphere often assume that public discussion is culturally neutral when in fact some cultural styles are more valued than others.

articulate qualities of expression are usually socially privileged. Actual situations of discussion often do not open themselves equally to all ways of making claims and giving reasons.[36] Many people feel intimidated by the implicit requirements of public speaking; in some situations of discussion and debate, such as classrooms, courtrooms, and city council chambers, many people feel they must apologize for their halting and circuitous speech. While all of us should admire clarity, subtlety, and other excellences of expression, none of us should be excluded or marginalized in situations of political discussion because we fail to express ourselves according to culturally specific norms of tone, grammar, and diction.[37]

Thirdly, some interpretations of norms of deliberation privilege speech which is dispassionate and disembodied. Defences of these norms tend to presuppose an opposition between reason and emotion. They tend falsely to identify objectivity with calm and the absence of emotional expression. For those suspicious of emotion, expressions of anger, hurt, or passionate concern taint whatever claims and reasons they accompany. Wide gestures, movements of nervousness, or bodily expression of emotion, furthermore, are taken as signs of weakness that cancel out one's assertions or reveal a person's lack of objectivity and control. Some advocates of deliberative norms privilege 'literal' language over figurative language that uses metaphor, hyperbole, and so on. An appropriate conception of democratic communication should reject this opposition between reason and emotion, literal and figurative. As I will discuss more in the next chapter, emotional and figurative expression are important tools of reasonable persuasion and judgement.[38]

The privileging of allegedly dispassionate speech styles, moreover, often correlates with other differences of social privilege. The speech culture of white, middle-class men tends to be more controlled, without significant gesture and expression or emotion. The speech culture of women, racialized or ethnicized minorities, and working-class

---

[36] Compare Lynn Sanders, 'Against Deliberation', *Political Theory*, 25/3 (June 1997), 349.

[37] Compare Stanley Aronowitz, 'Is a Democracy Possible? The Decline of the Public in the American Debate', in Robbins (ed.), *The Phantom Public Sphere*. Aronowitz argues that a disdain for 'mass' culture has underlain some democratic theory. While endorsing inclusion and political equality in principle, writers such as Walter Lipmann tend to reserve political participation for those educated in high culture. Aronowitz claims that a truly egalitarian approach to democracy must cease to privilege literacy and education in this way.

[38] See Jane Mansbridge, 'Activism Writ Small, Deliberation Writ Large', Paper presented to the American Political Science Association, Washington, Sept. 1997.

people, on the other hand, often is, or is perceived to be, more excited and embodied, values more the expression of emotion, uses figurative language, modulates tones of voice, and gestures widely.[39]

A conception of discussion-based democracy that emphasizes inclusion as a means for enlarging the ability of opinions and experiences to be voiced in public should be careful not to assume too restrictive a notion of legitimate political communication. Because for many the term 'deliberation' carries connotations of the primacy of argument, dispassionateness, and order in communication, for the rest of the book I will often use the term 'communicative' democracy instead, to denote a more open context of political communication.

## Privileging Unity

For many theorists of deliberative democracy, the subject of public discussion is the common good. According to Thomas Spragens, the idea of the common good functions for the public reason of democracy as the ideal of truth functions in theoretical disciplines.[40] The idea of the common good *can* be interpreted simply as the addressing of problems that people face together, without any assumption that these people have common interests or common way of life, or that they must subordinate or transcend the particular interests and values that differentiate them. Some theorists adopt the stronger traditional interpretation of the idea of the common good, however, to imply that the members of the polity have common interests and agreement on principles and policies. I see two distinct approaches in deliberative theory to the assumption of commonness for a deliberative public. Either theorists assume such commonness as a prior condition of deliberation, or they see it as a goal. Both approaches are problematic.

A number of writers with a generally deliberative approach to democracy appear to think that a successful democratic process

[39] Jane Mansbridge cites studies that show that female state legislators speak less than their male counterparts, and that in public meetings women tend more to give information and ask questions, while men state opinions and engage in confrontation. Mansbridge, 'Feminism and Democratic Community', in John W. Chapman and Ian Shapiro (eds.), *Democratic Community*, NOMOS 35 (New York: New York University Press, 1991). Anthony Cortese argues that the model of moral reasoning presupposed by Kohlberg and Habermas is ethnocentric and culturally biased, and tends to locate Chicano speaking and reasoning styles lower in his scale; see *Ethnic Ethics* (Albany: State University of New York Press, 1990). Charles Henry discusses the tendency of African Americans more than whites to couple emotion and anger with argument, influencing African American styles of public debate; see *Culture and African American Politics* (Bloomington: Indiana University Press, 1990).

[40] Spragens, *Reason and Democracy*, 120.

depends on a prior unity among its participants. Michael Walzer, for example, argues that the effective social critic locates and appeals to a community's prior 'shared understanding' in levelling her or his criticism.[41] A people has a core of shared values and traditions, he says, which can be renewed and reinvoked to motivate reflective social critique and action. Even more strongly, David Miller argues that only the sense of commonality provided by nationality can support the trust and mutual respect necessary for deliberation to begin.[42] Though not appealing to commonality of culture or nation, in *Beyond Adversary Democracy* Jane Mansbridge suggests that a participatory democratic forum that relies on discussion applies only in contexts where people already share many goals, interests, and premises, and much life experience. Where these are not shared, she suggests, an adversary democracy is more appropriate.[43]

There are at least two problems with the assumption that deliberative democracy must proceed on the basis of common understanding. First, in pluralist societies we cannot assume that we sufficiently share understanding to which we can appeal in many situations of conflict and solving collective problems. Most political units, even at a local level, are multicultural. Every political unit has gender differences, moreover, that are sources of different social experience and often different interests. Differences of class and/or occupation importantly separate experience and culture in most societies. Under circumstances of pluralism, appeals to supposedly shared understandings may be completely fair; on the other hand, they may exclude or marginalize some people or groups. This assumption of commonality constructs the political public as enclosed, implicitly saying that we can co-operate with each other only if we distinguish ourselves together from outsiders whom we define as different.[44] A political theory more useful to the realities of plural and structurally differentiated societies, and which furthers a norm of respect and co-operation, should give an account of the practice and function of openness to difference. This will be my task in Chapter 3.

---

[41] Michael Walzer, *The Company of Critics: Social Criticism and Political Commitment in the Twentieth Century* (New York: Basic Books, 1990).

[42] David Miller, *On Nationality* (Oxford: Oxford University Press, 1995), 96–8.

[43] Mansbridge, *Beyond Adversary Democracy*.

[44] See Chantal Mouffe, 'Democracy, Power and the "Political"', in Seyla Benhabib (ed.), *Democracy and Difference* (Princeton: Princeton University Press, 1996), 255; William Connolly, *Identity/Difference* (Ithaca, NY: Cornell University Press, 1993), 93; Iris Marion Young, 'The Ideal of Community and the Politics of Difference', in Linda Nicholson (ed.), *Feminism/Postmodernism* (New York: Routledge, 1990).

Another problem with the assumption of a common good or shared understanding prior to or as a condition of political communication is that it obviates the need for the transformations from self-regarding to enlarged thought which I earlier argued is an important aspect of a discussion-based model of democracy. If dialogue succeeds primarily when it appeals to what the participants all already share, then none need revise their opinions or viewpoints in any serious way in order to take account of other interests, opinions, or perspectives. Beyond this, even if we understand that we need others to see what we all share, it can easily happen that we each find in the other only a mirror for ourselves.[45]

Recognizing these problems, some theorists of deliberative democracy conceptualize unity not as the starting-point but as a goal of political dialogue. On this view, participants transcend their subjective, self-regarding perspective on political issues by putting aside their particular interests and seeking the good of the whole. While participants in a democratic dialogue often begin with differences of culture, perspective, and interest, the goal of discussion is to locate or create common interests that all can share. To arrive at the common good it may be necessary to work through differences, but difference itself is something to be transcended, because it is partial and divisive.

Benjamin Barber is particularly strong on how processes of public discussion move people from private interests to common interests.

It is as a citizen that the individual confronts the Other and adjusts his own life plans to the dictates of a shared world. *I* am a creature of need and want; *we* are a moral body whose existence depends on the common ordering of individual needs and wants into a single vision of the future in which all can share.[46]

This understanding of the deliberative process as seeking a common interest or common good regards differences of identity, culture, interests, social position, or privilege as something to be bracketed and transcended in public discourse and decision-making. Differences of experience, interest, group solidarity, and social perspective are merely private. Asserting them and seeking their recognition in public political debate, on this view, only serves to divide people, produce unworkable conflict, and remove the possibility for a genuinely public discourse in which people look beyond their private interest and

---

[45] See Iris Marion Young, 'Asymmetrical Reciprocity: On Moral Respect, Wonder and Enlarged thought', in *Intersecting Voices: Dilemmas of Gender, Political Philosophy and Policy* (Princeton: Princeton University Press, 1997).

[46] Barber, *Strong Democracy*, 224.

experience. This view sees the only alternatives as either a process of aggregation of preferences in which each interest competes with the others to get the most for themselves, without concern for others, or a public-spirited dialogue which puts aside private interests and affiliation.[47] In Chapter 3 I argue that this is a false dichotomy.

I find three problems with the view that the goal of public discussion ought to be the identification and implementation of a common good or interest that transcends the particularities of interest, experience, and affiliation in the society.

First, under circumstances of social inequality, the idea of a common good or general interest can often serve as a means of exclusion. Assuming a discussion situation in which participants are differentiated by social position or culture, and where some groups have greater symbolic or material privilege than others, or where there are socially or economically weak minorities, definitions of the common good are likely to express the interests and perspectives of the dominant groups in generalized terms. The less privileged are asked to put aside the expression of their experience, which may require a different way of speaking, or their grievances and demands must be suspended for the sake of a common good whose definition is biased against them.[48] The idea of a generalized and impartial public interest that transcends all difference and division makes it more difficult to expose how the perspective of the privileged dominates the public agenda than it is when people believe that politics is nothing but the naked competition of interest.

Putting such a premium on a common good in the sense of values and interests we all agree we share, furthermore, is liable to narrow the possible agenda for deliberation and thereby effectively silence some points of view. A deliberative process will be a sham if participants are not committed to trying to come to an agreement about how to address collective problems. People can aim at agreement in the sense of being open to changing their positions as a result of discussion, however, without acceding to the claim that there is a single set of interests and order of goods to which they can all agree. Agreement is best reached when it is treated as a means of co-operation and of addressing collective problems which is situation-specific, thus not binding for further problems, and thus provisional and renewable. Agreement on ways of addressing specific problems, moreover, can

---

[47] Jean Elshtain, *Democracy on Trial* (New York: Basic Books, 1995), esp. ch. 3.
[48] See Young, *Justice and the Politics of Difference*, ch. 4.

leave intact differences of affiliation and perspective, and even give them prominence in discussion.[49]

Although the ideal of aiming to reach agreement normatively regulates meaningful dialogue, conflict and disagreement are the usual state of affairs even in a well-structured deliberative democratic setting. Dialogue participants open to and aiming for agreement must nevertheless acknowledge that conflict and disagreement are frequent, and not be frightened away from democratic practice by their emergence. Too strong a commitment to consensus as a common good can incline some or all to advocate removing difficult issues from discussion for the sake of agreement and preservation of the common good. Sometimes those difficult issues matter deeply to one group because they perceive themselves as suffering a basic injustice, but they are the sources of deep disagreement because others in the society perceive rectifying this alleged injustice as coming at too great a cost to them. Deep disagreement can also arise when various groups have very different values, perspectives, and assumptions they bring to the issue. In both of these sorts of situations—of basic conflict of interest or value—the sources and terms of disagreement are exactly what everyone should come to understand if they are to do justice. Serious and open public dialogue is more likely under these circumstances to reveal differences than a common good.[50] A discussion is liable to break down if participants with deep conflicts of interest and value pretend they have common interests, because they are unable to air their differences. If, on the other hand, they mutually acknowledge their differences, and thereby mutually acknowledge that co-operation between them requires aiming to make each understand the others across those differences, then they are more likely to maintain co-operation and occasionally arrive at rough-and-ready provisional agreement. Where there are structural conflicts of interest generating deep conflicts of interest, processes of political communication are more about struggle than agreement.

## Assuming Face-to-Face Discussion

Many contemporary theorists of deliberative democracy at least implicitly assume that deliberations occur in a single forum where

[49] I take this to be the spirit behind Rawls's notion of an 'overlapping consensus'. See *Political Liberalism* (New York: Columbia University Press, 1993).

[50] See Jack Knight and James Johnson, 'Aggregation and Deliberation: On the Possibility of Democratic Legitimacy', *Political Theory*, 22/2 (May 1994), 277–98. Mansbridge makes a similar point in her essay 'Activism Writ Small, Deliberation Writ Large'.

deliberators face each other directly, whether in small civic settings or in legislatures. Jane Mansbridge looks to the New England town meeting and small co-operative service-providers for her theorizing an alternative to interest-based adversary democracy. Benjamin Barber recommends neighbourhood meeting groups as the basis of strong discussion-based participatory institutions. While he thinks that discursive designs should extend to global as well as local issues, John Dryzek rejects representative institutions from the ideal of discursive democracy.[51] James Fishkin proposes a 'deliberative opinion poll' as a means of adapting the requirement of small-group face-to-face discussion and decision-making to the context of mass democracy.

Without question, democracy cannot function well unless there is freedom of association and civic culture that encourages people to meet in small groups to discuss the issues that press on their collective life. A discussion-based democratic theory will be irrelevant to contemporary society, however, unless it can apply its values, norms, and insights to large-scale politics of millions of people linked by dense social and economic processes and legal framework. The major problems and conflicts that face most democracies now appear within the context of large-scale mass society, indeed global society: how to get relief to victims of disaster thousands of miles away; how to structure the relations of millions of people from diverse ethnic and religious groups densely packed in the neighbourhoods of a city so that there will be less violence and more co-operation among them; how to organize and finance a national retirement system most prudently and justly. Transportation, communication, and economic interdependence have made it unlikely that we could reverse the process of the globalization of societies. Democratic politics must respond to this scale, and thus must involve millions of people related to one another through democratic institutions. The challenge for a theory of discussion-based democracy is to explain how its norms and values can apply to mass polities where the relations among members are complexly mediated rather than direct and face to face. This requires, among other things, a political theory of representation consistent with those norms. Chapter 4 proposes some elements of such a theory of representation.

Bewitched by the image of small-group face-to-face interaction, a model of deliberative democracy often implicitly assumes what Jurgen Habermas calls a 'centred' image of the democratic process.[52] In this image a single deliberative body, say a legislature or a constitutional

---

[51] Dryzek, *Discursive Democracy*, 41.
[52] Habermas, *Between Facts and Norms*, 296–307.

convention, can take the society as a whole as the object of its deliberations, and discuss the best and most just way to order its institutions
and make its rules. While the decision-making process takes place over
time, it is a single process with a beginning and an end. The centred
image of deliberative democracy implicitly thinks of the democratic
process as one big meeting at the conclusion of which decisions are
made, we hope justly. In contrast to this image, with Habermas I
advocate a 'decentred' conception of politics and society. According to
this concept, we cannot conceive of the subject-matter of democracy
as the organization of society as a whole. Society is bigger than politics and outruns political institutions, and thus democratic politics
must be thought of as taking place within the context of large and
complex social processes the whole of which cannot come into view,
let alone under decision-making control.

In a decentred model of deliberative democracy, moreover, the
democratic process cannot be identified with one institution or set of
institutions—the state, or legislative bodies, or courts, etc. Rather, the
processes of communication that give normative and rational meaning
to democracy occur as flows and exchanges among various social sectors not brought together under a unifying principle.[53] While there are
meetings and discussion in this process, there is no final moment of
decision, such that the democratic forum can itself come under review.
The norm-guided communicative process of open and public democracy occurs across wide distances and over long times, with diverse
social sectors speaking to one another across differences of perspective
as well as space and time. As I will elaborate in Chapter 5, such a
decentred view of the democratic process gives more prominence to
processes of discussion and citizen involvement in the associations of
civil society than do most theories of deliberation. On this conception,
democratic communication and influence flows between non-state
institutions of civil society and state institutions.[54]

The notion that democracy is *decentred* differs from saying that its
jurisdictions and authority are *decentralized*. Democracy is decentralized, as I understand that term, when its policy-making and enforcement authority is dispersed among small, relatively unco-ordinated
jurisdictions. These two concepts are independent. A decentralized
democracy is likely to be centred in the sense that Habermas and I

---

[53] See Claude Lefort, *The Political Forms of Modern Society* (Cambridge, Mass.: MIT
Press, 1986), chs. 9 and 10; see also Chantal Mouffe, 'Democratic Citizenship and the
Political Community', in *The Return of the Political* (London: Verso, 1993).

[54] See Jean Cohen and Andrew Arato, *Civil Society and Political Theory* (Cambridge,
Mass.: MIT Press, 1992); Bohman, *Public Deliberation*, ch. 4.

reject; people often advocate decentralization, that is, because they desire or have an image of authentic democratic process as occurring in a single face-to-face forum. As I will discuss in Chapter 6, the virtues of localism should be rethought precisely in light of the facts of interdependent mass societies.

## Assuming a Norm of Order

None of the theoretical advocates of a model of deliberative democracy explicitly specify that deliberation carries particular norms of order. Nevertheless, in everyday political contexts the invocation of deliberative norms frequently appeals to the good of deliberation as a means of discrediting or excluding modes of political communication deemed disorderly or disruptive. Not infrequently those who assume a stance of rational deliberators in public discourse invoke a narrow image of 'civility' that rules 'out of order' forms of political communication other than prepared statements calmly delivered. On this view, rowdy street demonstrations where thousands of people carry funny or sarcastic banners and chant slogans directed critically at powerful actors, which disrupt normal traffic and force bystanders to listen and look at their signs, go beyond the bounds of deliberative civility. Such an attitude that equates deliberation with orderliness similarly condemns and excludes actions like unfurling banners or displaying symbolic objects with the intent of disrupting bureaucratic or parliamentary routines in order to call attention to issues or positions that those performing the acts believe have been wrongly excluded from a deliberative agenda.[55]

These examples refer to the way that critics sometimes bring their issues before a public. Ideas of deliberation, reasonableness, or civility are often used to locate some people as temperate and to label as 'extreme' others who use more demonstrative and disruptive means. An opposition between 'moderate' and 'extreme' often appears as a description of views expressed, moreover, and not merely their manner of expression. In this construction, orderly deliberation stays within a certain 'moderate' range of assumptions, alternatives, or forms of expression. Those who question those assumptions or the range of alternatives dominant discourse offers for addressing an issue are labelled 'extreme'. The label suggests that the people who hold those views are unreasonable, and excludes their views from consideration without giving them any hearing.

---

[55] Compare Sanders, 'Against Deliberation', 361.

To the extent that norms of deliberative democracy oppose disorderly, demonstrative, and disruptive political behaviour or label a certain range of positions extreme in order to dismiss them, such norms wrongfully exclude some opinions and modes of their expression. A discussion-based model of democracy must not devalue public political demonstration in particular, which is usually disorderly and disruptive to some degree, and whose planners sometimes aim to maximize its disruptiveness. Public demonstration is a most important and often effective mode of expressing opposition and criticism, and of calling powerful actors to account. Without creative protest action and mass mobilization, a democracy is insipid and weak. Yet many whose voices and opinions would receive more attention by means of public demonstration decline to engage in or support such actions, for fear of being thought uncivil and unreasonable.

In criticizing an implicit norm of orderliness I do not mean to suggest that in politics anything goes. As I articulated it earlier in this chapter, the norm of reasonableness is central to political communication that aims to solve collective problems and promote justice. There I specified that being a reasonable citizen means pressing one's claims on others with the conviction that they are just claims. The reasonable person is therefore obliged to try to persuade others of the justice of his or her claims and to exhibit a willingness to be persuaded by them. Being reasonable thus entails non-violence: one does not attempt or threaten to harm or eliminate those with whom one disagrees, or those who challenge one's privilege, or those one believes are dominative or oppressive, or just plain wrong. Some images of civility, however, tend to categorize as a weaker form of violence certain forms of protest or demonstration that aim to make a point to others, call attention to issues, or otherwise address others in a rowdy and insistent way. What are the appropriate limits to demonstration and protest is surely contestable, but in a deep democratic society the presumption should be in favour of the protesters that their purpose is to persuade.

Being reasonable, furthermore, entails expressing persuasive disagreement in terms of basic respect: one cannot express disagreement with, or criticism and judgement of, the actions and opinions of others in terms that imply that one's opponents are less than human or that their views do not deserve an equal hearing because of who they are—as long as they are willing to listen in turn. Thus 'hate speech' aimed at denigrating the persons or affiliations of some members of the polity, or which threatens them with violence or aims to incite violence against or harassment of some members of the polity, is rightly condemned as 'uncivil'. Especially under circumstances where there are serious conflicts that arise from structural positions of privilege and disadvantage, and/or where a subordinated, less powerful or minority group finds its interests ignored in public debate, members of such groups do not violate norms of reasonableness if they engage in seriously disruptive actions, or express their claims with angry accusations. Disorderliness is an important tool of critical communication aimed at calling attention to the unreasonableness of others—their domination over the terms of debate, their acts of exclusion of some people or issues from consideration, their use of their power to cut off debate, their reliance on stereotypes and mere derision.[56]

Both here and in some of my earlier criticisms of some accounts and images of deliberative democracy[57] I aim to challenge an identification of reasonable open public debate with polite, orderly, dispassionate, gentlemanly argument. As against this image of a normative ideal of democratic politics I join with several other contemporary political theorists in endorsing a more 'agonistic' model of democratic process.

According to Chantal Mouffe, for example, some theories of liberal democracy attempt to resolve social pluralism into a political unity in a manner that subordinates political expression to an overly rationalistic set of normative requirements and thereby theorizes away antagonism and contestation as endemic to the process of democratic politics. Mouffe proposes an 'agonistic pluralism' as constitutive of modern democracy. Modern societies are rife with conflict deriving from injustice, greed, bias, and value difference. Democracy is a set of institutions that transforms mere exclusion and opposition to the other into engaged antagonism within accepted rules. A pluralistic democratic order

is based on a distinction between 'enemy' and 'adversary.' It requires that, within the context of the political community, the opponent should be considered not as an enemy to be destroyed, but as an adversary whose existence is legitimate and must be tolerated. We will fight against his ideas but we will not question his right to defend them.[58]

---

[56] Holloway Sparks proposes an idea of 'dissident' citizenship in which disorderly expression sometimes has a role but which nevertheless preserves the possibility of ongoing debate and disagreement; 'Dissident Citizenship: Democratic Theory, Political Change, and Activist Women', *Hypatia: Journal of Feminist Philosophy*, 12/4 (Fall 1997), 74–109.

[57] Iris Marion Young, 'Communication and the Other: Beyond Deliberative Democracy', in Seyla Benhabib (ed.), *Democracy and Difference* (Princeton: Princeton University Press, 1996).

[58] Mouffe, *The Return of the Political*, 4. For such an 'agonistic' view of democratic politics, see also Connolly, *Identity/Difference*; Wendy Brown, *States of Injury* (Princeton: Princeton University Press, 1995); and Bonnie Honig, *Political Theory and the*

I prefer to call to the normal condition of democratic debate a process of *struggle*. In a society where there are social group differences and significant injustice, democratic politics ought to be a process of struggle. Far from a face-off in enemy opposition, struggle is a process of communicative *engagement* of citizens with one another. People of differing social positions or interests must struggle to raise issues because others may be threatened by those issues or they may simply think that different issues are more important. Once the issues that concern them are on the agenda, citizens must struggle with others over the terms in which they will engage the issue, they must struggle to get their views heard, and must struggle to persuade others. The field of struggle is not level; some groups and sectors are often at a disadvantage. Fair, open, and inclusive democratic processes should attend to such disadvantages and institutionalize compensatory measures for exclusion. Because disadvantaged and excluded sectors cannot wait for the process to become fair, because there are often so many contending interests and issues, oppressed and disadvantaged groups have no alternative but to struggle for greater justice under conditions of inequality. The process of democratic struggle is an attempt to engage others in debate about social problems and proposed solutions, engage them in a project of explaining and justifying their positions. Disorderly, disruptive, annoying, or distracting means of communication are often necessary or effective elements in such efforts to engage others in debate over issues and outcomes.

In response to this depiction of democratic process as agonistic, a process of engaged struggle, one might raise the following question. How is this endorsement of institutionalized conflict and struggle different from the aggregative model of democracy I rejected at the beginning of this chapter? The aggregative model, you recall, understands democracy as a process of competition among divergent policy preferences, where the preferences held by the majority wins the policy battle. I criticized this model of democracy because it has no way of distinguishing normatively legitimate outcomes from the will of the powerful, and makes no distinction between subjective preferences and more objective judgements of justice or rightness.

*Displacement of Politics* (Ithaca, NY: Cornell University Press, 1993). Both some of those who promote this agonistic interpretation of democratic politics and those suspicious of it suggest that such an interpretation is incompatible with an attitude of reasonableness where participants aim at agreement even as they are willing to uncover disagreement. Maria Pia Lara argues, however, that a robust communicative democracy contains both agonistic and consensual moments; see Lara, *Moral Textures: Feminist Narratives in the Public Sphere* (Cambridge: Polity Press, 1998), introd.

Some of those political theorists who express an agonistic model of democratic politics do not express a view very different from a model of interest group competition in which aggregated might makes right. They decline to endorse norms of either justice or legitimacy, and indeed some argue that appeals to justice or rightness function as mere ideology.

The model of democratic process I advocate here, however, retains deliberative democracy's account both of communicative orientation towards normative reason and of the transformation of private, self-regarding desire into public appeals to justice. In democratic struggle citizens engage with others in the attempt to win their hearts and minds, that is, their assent. To do so they should be open and reasonable, and be prepared to challenge others through criticism and not merely the assertion of opposition. One should therefore be wary of political moves to restrict discourses or their mode of expression to formal argument, appeals to a common good, or to those that some label as moderate and civil.

# CHAPTER 2

# Inclusive Political Communication

The previous chapter endorsed a normative ideal of democracy as a process of communication among citizens and public officials, where they make proposals and criticize one another, and aim to persuade one another of the best solution to collective problems. Participants in the processes of communication must be reasonable in the sense of willing to be accountable to others. The process must be open in the sense of public and accessible for it to count as normatively legitimate.

Most importantly, democratic norms mandate inclusion as a criterion of the political legitimacy of outcomes. Democracy entails political equality, that all members of the polity are included equally in the decision-making process and have an equal opportunity to influence the outcome. Inclusion increases the chances that those who make proposals will transform their positions from an initial self-regarding stance to a more objective appeal to justice, because they must listen to others with differing positions to whom they are also answerable. Even if they disagree with an outcome, political actors must accept the legitimacy of a decision if it was arrived at through an inclusive process of public discussion. The norm of inclusion is therefore also a powerful means for criticizing the legitimacy of nominally democratic processes and decisions.

Democracies frequently violate this norm of inclusion. In this chapter I distinguish two forms of exclusion from political discussion and decision-making. The most obvious forms of exclusion are those that keep some individuals or groups out of the fora of debate or processes of decision-making, or which allow some individuals or groups dominative control over what happens in them. I call this *external* exclusion. While no democracy does enough to criticize external exclusions, much democratic theory and practice notices them and discusses what ought to be done to mitigate such exclusions.

Less noticed are those forms of exclusion that sometimes occur even when individuals and groups are nominally included in the discussion and decision-making process. In the previous chapter I referred to several of these forms of *internal* exclusion: the terms of discourse make assumptions some do not share, the interaction privileges specific styles of expression, the participation of some people is dismissed as out of order.

This chapter theorizes three modes of communication attention to which can mitigate such internal exclusions: greeting, rhetoric, and narrative. With these three categories I reflect on modes of communication that already appear in everyday interaction. I interpret their communicative and normative functions in processes of political discussion among differently situated or disagreeing individuals or groups. In doing so I adopt a method like that of Habermas's discourse ethics, a method of normative theorizing that makes explicit the implicit norms guiding everyday communicative interaction.[1] Greeting, or in political contexts public acknowledgement, is a form of communication where a subject directly recognizes the subjectivity of others, thereby fostering trust. Rhetoric, the ways that political assertions and arguments are expressed, has several functions that contribute to inclusive and persuasive political communication, including calling attention to points and situating speakers and audience in relation to one another. Narrative also has several functions that counter exclusive tendencies and further argument. Among other functions, narrative empowers relatively disfranchised groups to assert themselves publicly; it also offers means by which people whose experiences and beliefs differ so much that they do not share enough premisses to engage in fruitful debate can nevertheless reach dialogical understanding.

## 1. External and Internal Exclusion

Norms of democracy call for inclusion and political equality, because political outcomes can only be considered morally legitimate if those who must abide by or adjust to them have had a part in their formation. Even in democratic societies, however, struggles over resources and power motivate efforts to exclude many affected people from decision-making processes. *External* exclusion names the many ways

[1] Jurgen Habermas, 'Discourse Ethics: Notes on a Program of Philosophical Justification', in *Moral Consciousness and Communicative Action* (Cambridge, Mass.: MIT Press, 1990).

that individuals and groups that ought to be included are purposely or inadvertently left out of fora for discussion and decision-making.

Back-door brokering, for example, is a typical form of political exclusion. The easiest way for powerful people to get what they want out of the political process is to set up exclusive self-appointed committees that deliberate privately to set the agenda and arrive at policies which they then introduce to public debate as accomplished facts. Such activities violate the most basic democratic norms of publicity. They are difficult to combat precisely because others affected are likely not to be aware of them until too late. Both public regulation and civic activity in most democracies have some methods of effecting the 'transparency' in political decisions, however, because the temptation to private control is otherwise so pervasive.

Also common in the best democracies are various ways that formally public discussion and decision-making processes are nevertheless difficult to access. The American Civil Rights movement exposed cumbersome and discriminatory voter registration rules in the United States, and struggles continue over the ease or difficulty of access to voting. The location and timing of meetings and public hearings present a formidable obstacle for many people who might wish to participate. The relative inaccessibility of otherwise public discussions and decision-making processes often results from unconscious bias and thoughtlessness on the part of the designers of such processes, but is no less exclusive on that account.

Perhaps the most pervasive and insidious form of external exclusion in modern democracies is what I referred to in the previous chapters as the ability for economically or socially powerful actors also to exercise political domination. If some citizens are able to buy sufficient media time to dominate public discussion of an issue, others are effectively excluded. When industrialists or financiers threaten to disinvest in a region unless political decisions go the way they wish, they exercise exclusive tyranny. When political candidates must depend on huge contributions from particular individuals or organizations to win elections, then political influence is wrongly unequal.

Inequalities of power and resources frequently lead to outcomes such as these, where some citizens with formally equal rights to participate nevertheless have little or no real access to the fora and procedures through which they might influence decisions. External exclusions of this sort occur in all existing democracies. When political outcomes demonstrably result from an exclusive process, where those with greater power or wealth are able to dominate the process, then from the point of view of democratic norms that outcome is illegitimate.

Many of the struggles within formal democracies concern efforts to expose such exclusion and press for institutional changes that will better ensure the real inclusion of more affected people in decision-making processes. One task of democratic civil society is to expose and criticize exclusions such as these, and doing so sometimes effectively challenges the legitimacy of institutional rules and their decisions. Most democracies have some provisions for confronting the ability of more powerful or wealthy actors effectively to exclude others from influencing policy outcomes. Campaign finance regulation, lobbying regulation, corruption investigation, mandates for hearings, procedures for public comment, commission membership, voting procedures, and so on, all attempt to regulate decision-making processes to promote the presence of potentially marginalized constituencies.

I call these issues of *external* exclusion because they concern how people are kept outside the process of discussion and decision-making. Most theorists of strong democracy pay attention to such issues of external exclusion. They call for limiting the influence of wealth or position on the ability to participate in a democratic process, and they make transparency, accountability, and access to deliberative publics central to their normative accounts. Less noticed are situations that concern what I call *internal* exclusion and inclusion.

Excluded groups protest a political process and shame its designers to such a degree that procedures are put into place that bring them into the public. New rules give free television or radio time to consumer groups with little funds; the doors of the city council chamber open to poor people and their advocates wishing to testify at budget hearings; new rules ensure that there are greater numbers of women on important committees and commissions. Having obtained a presence in the public, citizens sometimes find that those still more powerful in the process exercise, often unconsciously, a new form of exclusion: others ignore or dismiss or patronize their statements and expressions. Though formally included in a forum or process, people may find that their claims are not taken seriously and may believe that they are not treated with equal respect. The dominant mood may find their ideas or modes of expression silly or simple, and not worthy of consideration. They may find that their experiences as relevant to the issues under discussion are so different from others' in the public that their views are discounted. I call these familiar experiences *internal* exclusion, because they concern ways that people lack effective opportunity to influence the thinking of others even when they have access to fora and procedures of decision-making.

The sections that follow focus on three modes of political communication, attention to which, I suggest, responds to such issues of internal exclusion. This focus does not imply that issues of internal exclusion are more important than issues of external exclusion. On the contrary, mechanisms by which people are excluded from access to democratic processes more fundamentally impede political equality than interactive and communicative exclusions. I concentrate on internal exclusion and inclusion here because these have received less theoretical attention, and because responding to these internal exclusions completes the refinement of the model of deliberative democracy that I began in the previous chapter.

Chapter 1 argued that some interpretations of a model of deliberative democracy tend to restrict their conception of proper political communication to arguments, the making of assertions and proposals, and providing reasons for them that they claim ought to be acceptable to others. There is no question that argument in this sense is a necessary element of public discussion that aims to make just and wise decisions. The epistemic function of political discussion cannot be served unless participants question one another, test one another's claims and opinions through discussion, and have an account of why they assent. Arguments require shared premises, however, which are not always present in a situation of political conflict. Unless there are other forms of political communication that further understanding, possibilities for deliberation may be restricted to a narrow range of situations.

Focus on argument, furthermore, tends to enact internal exclusions of style and idiom. A norm of 'articulateness' devalues the speech of those who make claims and give reasons, but not in a linear fashion that makes logical connections explicit. A norm of dispassionateness dismisses and devalues embodied forms of expression, emotion, and figurative expressions. People's contributions to a discussion tend to be excluded from serious consideration not because of what is said, but how it is said. Norms of orderliness sometimes exclude disruptive or emotional forms of expression that can be very effective in getting people's attention and making important points.

A theory of democratic inclusion requires an expanded conception of political communication, both in order to identify modes of internal inclusion and to provide an account of more inclusive possibilities of attending to one another in order to reach understanding. In the pages that follow I explicate the political functions of three modes of communication in addition to making arguments: greeting, rhetoric, and narrative.[2] A more complete account of modes of political communication not only remedies exclusionary tendencies in deliberative practices, but more positively describes some specific ways that communicatively democratic processes can produce respect and trust, make possible understanding across structural and cultural difference, and motivate acceptance and action.

The purpose of theorizing these modes of political communication is to add to rather than replace theorizing that emphasizes the role of argument. With the three categories of greeting, rhetoric, and narrative I reflect on everyday modes of communication that also already appear in political discussion. I aim to make explicit their communicative and normative functions in processes of political discussion among differently situated or disagreeing groups. Rather than substituting for the role of political argument, I offer practices of greeting, rhetoric, and narrative as enriching both a descriptive and normative account of public discussion and deliberation. All three modes of communication aid the making of arguments and enable understanding and interaction in ways that argument alone cannot. While each is subject to abuse or manipulation, so is argument.

## 2. Greeting, or Public Acknowledgement

It is not uncommon to hear a complaint from individuals or groups who have tried to make claims and arguments in a political discussion that they have been ignored, or worse, spoken about by others as though they were not there, deprecated, stereotyped, or otherwise insulted. No rules or formalities can ensure that people will treat others in the political public with respect, and really listen to their claims. I suggest, however, that situations of political communication, in which participants explicitly acknowledge the other participants, are more substantively inclusive than those that do not. What I call greeting, or public acknowledgement, is thus a specific communicative gesture with important and not sufficiently noticed functions for democratic practice.

My method begins by reflecting on and making explicit the normative implications of the most everyday non-political communication gestures. At that most basic level, 'greeting' refers to those moments in everyday communication where people acknowledge one another in

---

[2] I expand considerably the discussion of these categories in an earlier paper, 'Communication and the Other: Beyond Deliberative Democracy', in Seyla Benhabib (ed.), *Democracy and Difference* (Princeton: Princeton University Press, 1996).

their particularity. Thus it includes literal greetings, such as 'Hello', 'How are you?', and addressing people by name. In the category of greeting I also include moments of leave-taking, 'Good-bye', 'See you later', as well as the forms of speech that often lubricate discussion with mild forms of flattery, stroking of egos, deference, and politeness. Greeting includes handshakes, hugs, the offering of food and drink, making small talk before getting down to real business.

I begin my understanding of the role of greeting in a communicative ethics from a reading of Emmanuel Levinas. In *Otherwise than Being, or Beyond Essence* Levinas distinguishes one aspect of communication, a process of subject-to-subject recognition, on the one hand, from an aspect of expressing content between the subjects, on the other. The former he calls Saying and the latter the Said. Prior to and a condition for making assertions and giving reasons for them is a moment of opening to and directly acknowledging the others, without the mediation of content that refers to the world. Prior to a thought to be conveyed, a world to refer to, act in, and share is the gesture of opening up to the other person where the speaker announces 'Here I am' for the other, and 'I see you'.

For Levinas, this act of signification is one of exposure, vulnerability, risk. In such announcement the speaker responds to the other person's sensible presence, by taking responsibility for the other's vulnerability, but without promise of reciprocation. Communication would never happen if someone did not make the 'first move', out of responsibility for the other to expose herself without promise of answer or acceptance. Greeting (which is my term, not Levinas's) is this communicative moment of taking the risk of trusting in order to establish and maintain the bond of trust necessary to sustain a discussion about issues that face us together.

Levinas describes the most primordial moment of an ethical relation between one person and another as a condition of being *hostage*. To recognize another person is to find oneself already claimed upon by the other person's potential neediness. The sensual, material proximity of the other person in his or her bodily need and possibility for suffering makes an unavoidable claim on me, to which I am hostage. Often a person turns her back on this claim of the other upon her, or is indifferent. Sometimes she may react with selfish greed or cruelty to the claim. But when she acknowledges the other, she responds to the other and acknowledges an ethical relation of responsibility for the other person. 'It is through the condition of being hostage that there can be in the world pity, compassion, parody, and proximity—even the little that there is, even the simple, "After you, sir." The unconditionality of being hostage is not the limit case of solidarity, but the condition for all solidarity.'[3]

In the moment of communication I call greeting, a speaker announces her presence as ready to listen and take responsibility for her relationship to her interlocutors, at the same time that it announces her distance from the others, their irreducible particularity. Greetings in this broad sense are a constant aspect of everyday communicative interaction. Without these gestures of respect and politeness, that are only Saying without anything said, people would probably stop listening to one another. If we were to imagine a communicative interaction in which such mode of greeting were absent, it would feel like the science fiction speech of an alien, some sort of heartless being for whom speech is only for getting things said, interrogating their truth or rightness, and getting things done. Greeting has a very important place, moreover, in situations of communication among parties who have a problem or conflict, and try to reach some solution through discussion.

I refer to Levinas's theory of speech and the ethical relation because I agree with Jurgen Habermas that a theory of communicative democracy should be grounded in everyday communicative ethics. Levinas's account of the moment of Saying, I think, can supplement Habermas's account of the Said. Levinas expresses his theory at the level of ethics and ontology, however, not at the level of politics. How do greetings, or what can also be called public acknowledgement, appear in political interaction, and what functions do they serve there?

Rituals of greeting are a formal part of the political practices of many non-Western and traditional societies. Meetings of different villages or clans among the Maori people, for example, begin with several stages and forms of greeting; Maori engage in these rituals today in their political life, which has also influenced the political practices of New Zealand society more generally.[4] The gestures of greeting function to acknowledge relations of discursive equality and mutual respect among the parties to discussion, as well as to establish trust and forge connection based on the previous relationships among the parties. In modern Western political processes the role of greeting is not so self-conscious, but I suggest that it is often quite ritualized. Most fora of political discussion, dispute, and negotiation are peppered with gestures of greeting, as are most non-political interactive situations.

[3] Emmanuel Levinas, *Otherwise than Being, or Beyond Essence*, trans. Alphonso Lingis (The Hague: Nijhoff, 1981), 117.

[4] For one account of Maori greeting protocol, see Joan Metge, *The Maoris of New Zealand: Tauhai* (London: Routledge & Kegan Paul, 1976), 249–53.

The political functions of such moments of greeting are to assert dis-cursive equality and establish or re-establish the trust necessary for discussion to proceed in good faith.

Before the guest speaker begins her speech on an issue of the day to a public forum, she must be introduced by an official of the hosting organization. The official recites the speaker's background and achievements, often incorporating a narrative about the hosting organ-ization and its connection with the speaker and her activities. When the speaker finally takes the podium, she does not usually get right to the point, but instead thanks her introducers, says some words of praise about her hosts, tells a narrative of her own about their connec-tion, perhaps makes a joke.

Delegates come to the annual convention of a large citizens' organ-ization or to a legislative session knowing in each case that the agenda is fraught with some hotly contested issues. Especially when groups or factions confront one another over issues about which they will decide, rituals of greeting and politeness are important for getting and keeping the discussion going through difficult times. Contentious meetings often begin or end with receptions during which individuals greet each other personally. People disagreeing with each other often acknowledge the importance of the group on the other side, its integrity and goodwill, before they give their reasons for disagree-ment. Such gestures do not offer information or further arguments directly by giving reasons or criticisms. But without such spoken moments of politeness, deference, acknowledgement of the particular perspective of others, their goodwill and contribution to the collect-ive, discussion itself would often break down. To be sure, such ges-tures of flattery and deference are often absent from political contest, often making discussion impossible because some or all contestants do not believe the others respect them as political equals. Then there is only power politics.

Gestures of greeting are most elaborate and ritualized in inter-national relations. Indeed, much of diplomacy consists in state leaders, ambassadors, and other high officials visiting high officials of other states to do little else than greet one another: give speeches that affirm that country's friendship and mutual respect but say nothing of sub-stance about policy, attend balls and dinners. A cynic can say such activity is simply playing to media and crowds while the real inter-national politics goes on as a power struggle behind closed doors. If gestures of greeting are divorced from ongoing processes of political discussion, debate, and decision-making, they do indeed become diverting political window-dressing.

Greeting, which I shall also call public acknowledgement, names communicative political gestures through which those who have conflicts aim to solve problems, *recognize* others as included in the discussion, especially those with whom they differ in opinion, interest, or social location. By such Sayings discussion participants acknowledge that the others they address are part of the process, and that we who address them must be accountable to them, as they to us. The intuition underlying Levinas's account of Saying is that this acknowledgement cannot come in the form of a general appeal to 'all reasonable persons'. It must be more particular: I or we must try to persuade you who are in this social situation. We must be responsive to you who have this claim on us, listen seriously to you, even though we may perceive that our interests conflict fundamentally or we may come from different ways of life with little mutual understanding. In practice in mass politics this means public acknowledgement by some groups of the inclusion of other social groups or social segments.

Charles Taylor has proposed that a politics of recognition is a basic element of justice. He expresses it as a political end, an ultimate goal that cultural groups seek in their interaction with others.[5] In a diverse society with complex problems and conflicts, I suggest, at least one level of recognition is best thought of as a condition rather than a goal of political communication that aims to solve problems justly. A communicative model of democracy says that democratic legitimacy requires that all those affected by decisions should be included in discussions that reach them. Greeting names those communicative political gestures through which participants in democratic discussion recognize other specific groups as included in the discussion that will issue in decisions. By such gestures of greeting, discussion participants acknowledge that they are together with those they name, and that they are obliged to listen to their opinions and take them seriously. As a political issue of inclusion, recognition is primarily a starting-point for political interaction and contest, rather than its end.

To be sure, gestures of acknowledgement are often pro forma and superficial, and political discussants often fail to respect those whom they have acknowledged. Thus less powerful groups often must struggle for recognition over and over, and call to the political public to make good on the promise of inclusion contained in its greeting gestures. Without the moment of greeting, however, no discussion can take place at all, because the parties refuse to face one another as

---

[5] Charter Taylor, 'Multiculturalism and the Politics of Recognition', in Amy Gutmann (ed.), *Multiculturalism* (Princeton: Princeton University Press, 1992). Compare Axel Honneth, *The Struggle for Recognition* (Cambridge, Mass.: MIT Press, 1995), esp. ch. 8.

dialogue partners. When Yasir Arafat and Yitzak Rabin shook hands in 1993 some wrongly celebrated this moment as the arrival of peace. The moment was and remains a historical turning-point, however, as the moment when Israel for the first time gave greeting to the Palestinians as a group with whom they are obliged to discuss their mutual problems and conflicts. In this case as in many others, when discussion breaks down, greetings may have to be renewed.

The uses of a theory of communicative democracy are primarily critical. With the norms and ideals expressed in the theory one can evaluate how most political processes fall short of what is necessary to do justice. Understanding the political function of greeting gives an important criterion for assessing actual political processes. Actual political discussion should be examined not only for what it says, whether the issues are well formulated, the arguments coherent, and so on. We should also ask whether the major contributions to a political debate show discursive signs that they are addressing all those who should be included in the debate. One sign of the absence of such greeting is that a public debate across mass society refers to persons or social segments only in the third person, never addressing them in the second person. If a social segment rarely if ever appears as a group to whom deliberators appeal, and if there are few signs that participants in public debate believe themselves accountable to that social segment among others, then that social segment has almost certainly been excluded from discussion.

For example, the American welfare reform debate of 1992–6 fails this test of inclusion. Lower-income people, and in particular lower-income single mothers—the social segment arguably the most directly affected by the reforms—on the whole have not been included as participants in the deliberations. In this debate lower-income single mothers have not been treated as equal citizens with opinions and perspectives that deserve to be taken into account to make just and wise decisions about public assistance. Instead, they have been treated almost entirely as the *objects* of the debate: there has been a great deal of talk about lower-income single mothers, especially those on welfare, as a *problem*, and many experts have analysed the sources of this problem and made predictions about how policy will produce behavioural change in this problem group. The actual voices, evaluations, and reasons of lower-income people have rarely been heard in the public debate. The category of greeting thus adds something important to ideals of inclusive public reason. It is not simply that participants in public discussion should have reasons that others can accept, but they must also explicitly *acknowledge* the others whom they aim to persuade.

## 3. Affirmative Uses of Rhetoric

Some theorists of deliberative democracy maintain a Platonic distinction between rational speech and mere rhetoric, and in doing so they often denigrate emotion, figurative language, or unusual or playful forms of expression. Rational speech, on this view, the speech to which deliberative democracy should be confined, consists of universalistic, dispassionate, culturally and stylistically neutral arguments that focus the mind on their evidence and logical connections, rather than move the heart or engage the imagination. Thus Thomas Spragens, for example, invokes Hitler's disdain for the rationality of the masses as a warning against rhetorical speech that aims to move the masses with hot passion. A rational democracy, he claims, will engage the mind rather than ignite the passions.[6] As James Bohman points out, in his theory of discourse ethics Habermas also aims to distinguish rational speech from rhetoric, the first of which has a communicative and the second a strategic function. Communicative action involves speech that makes assertions about the natural or human world and signals in its illocutionary acts its commitment to those claims and a willingness to defend them with reasons. Rhetorical speech, on the other hand, aims not to reach understanding with others, but only to manipulate their thought and feeling in directions that serve the speaker's own ends.[7]

As I discussed in the previous chapter, to the extent that democratic theory and practice privilege such a standard of allegedly dispassionate, unsituated, neutral reason, it has exclusionary implications. The ideal of disembodied and disembedded reason that it presupposes is a fiction. What such privileging takes to be neutral, universal, and dispassionate expression actually carries the rhetorical nuances of particular situated social positions and relations, which social conventions do not mark as rhetorical and particular in the same way that they notice others. Many politicians, not to mention many academics and policy advisers, are very good at adopting a stance of controlled and measured expression of the neutral facts that commands authority just because it claims to be impartial and dispassionate, transcending the dirty world of interest and passion. Against this stance, whose

[6] Thomas Spragens, *Reason and Democracy* (Durham, NC: Duke University Press, 1990); Gary Remer cites Simone Chambers as saying that emotional manipulation is a kind of force; see Chambers, *Reasonable Democracy* (Ithaca, NY: Cornell University Press, 1996), 151.

[7] James Bohman, 'Emancipation and Rhetoric: The Perlocutions and Illocutions of the Social Critic', *Philosophy and Rhetoric*, 21/3 (1988), 185–203; cf. Bill Rehg, 'Reason and Rhetoric in Habermas's Theory of Argumentation', in Walter Jost and Michael Hyde (eds.), *Rhetoric and Hermeneutics in our Time* (New Haven: Yale University Press, 1997).

rhetorical effect is to deflect attention from its particularity, more explicitly situated, imaginative, inflected forms of political communication are often dismissed as less worthy of attention. When Jesse Jackson ran for the Democratic presidential nomination in the United States in the 1980s, for example, commentators remarked on his flamboyant preacher style more than on the critical issues he wished to bring to public discussion. The only remedy for the dismissiveness with which some political expressions are treated on grounds that they are too dramatic, emotional, or figurative is to notice that any discursive content and argument is embodied in situated style and rhetoric. Rhetoric, then, becomes a feature of political expression to which we ought to attend in our engagement with one another, rather than an aspect of expression we try to bracket in order to be truly rational.

Some theorists of communicative democracy do explicitly attend to the role of figurative language, emotional expression, or specific forms of addressing particular audiences as means of furthering deliberation.[8] Nevertheless, theories of deliberative democracy tend to bracket rhetoric, even when they do not explicitly denigrate rhetorical modes of discourse. Here I will argue that rhetoric has a place in any thorough theory of communicative democracy. Because rhetoric is an aspect of all discourse, the temptation should be resisted to base a theory of deliberative democracy on a notion of non-rhetorical speech that is coolly and purely argumentative. Explicit reflection on the function of rhetoric in political communication, moreover, reveals several uniquely positive contributions rhetoric can and sometimes does make to democracy.

The concept of rhetoric assumes a distinction between *what* a discourse says, its substantive content or message, and *how* it says it. The general category of 'rhetoric', as I understand it, refers to the various

---

[8]  Benjamin Barber explicitly appeals to a broad conception of democratic communication, or 'political talk'. Talk, says Barber, is not only speech, but every human interaction that involves language or linguistic symbols. It entails listening no less than speaking, and it is affective as well as cognitive. 'Talk appears as a mediator of affection and affiliation as well as of interest and identity. . . . It offers, along with meanings and significations, silences, rituals, symbols, myths, expression and solicitations, and a hundred other quiet and noisy manifestations of our common humanity' (*Strong Democracy (Berkeley: University of California Press, 1984)*, 177). Amy Gutmann and Dennis Thompson allow that 'impassioned and immoderate speech' can be consistent with the aims of deliberative democracy, and are sometimes important for calling attention to issues and claims. Their acknowledgement of a role for rhetoric and passion in democratic discussion nevertheless maintains a distinction between a kind of expression that *is* rational and dispassionate and a kind of speech that is not. See *Democracy and Disagreement* (Cambridge, Mass.: Harvard University Press, 1996), 134–7; see n. 11 below. See also Susan Bickford, 'Beyond Reason: Political Perception and the Political Economy of Emotion Talk', Paper presented to the American Political Science Association, Boston, Sept. 1998.

ways something can be said, which colour and condition its substantive content. Thus rhetoric includes at least the following aspects of
communication, which overlap and can occur together: (*a*) the emotional tone of the discourse, whether its content is uttered with fear,
hope, anger, joy, and other expressions of passion that move through
discourse. No discourse lacks emotional tone; 'dispassionate' discourses carry an emotional tone of calm and distance. (*b*) The use in
discourse of figures of speech, such as simile, metaphor, puns, synec-
doche, etc., along with the styles or attitudes such figures produce—
that is, to be playful, humorous, ironic, deadpan, mocking, grave, or
majestic. (*c*) Forms of making a point that do not only involve speech,
such as visual media, signs and banners, street demonstration, guerrilla
theatre, and the use of symbols in all these contexts. (*d*) All these
affective, embodied, and stylistic aspects of communication, finally,
involve attention to the particular audience of one's communication,
and orienting one's claims and arguments to the particular assumptions, history, and idioms of that audience.

In all of these ways, rhetoric constitutes the flesh and blood of any
political communication, whether in a neighbourhood meeting or on
the floor of Parliament. Rhetoric concerns the way content is conveyed as distinct from the assertive value of the content, but this does
not imply that the content has the same 'meaning' in varying rhetoric
contexts. Understanding the role of rhetoric in political communication is important precisely because the *meaning* of a discourse, its
pragmatic operation in a situation of communicative interaction,
depends as much on its rhetorical as its assertoric aspects.

At least since Plato a strain of Western philosophy has tried to theorize modes of rational discourse purified of rhetoric. Such allegedly
purely rational discourse abstracts from or transcends the situatedness
of desire, interest, or historical specificity, and can be uttered and criticized solely in terms of its claims to truth. A recent version of a theory
of language that aims to purify rational argument from rhetoric
appears in Habermas's theory of communicative action, a theory most
relevant to a theory of deliberative democracy. Habermas takes up
terms from the tradition of speech-act theory, and distinguishes locution, illocution, and perlocution. Locution refers to the content of a
speech act, that about which there can be truth-value. The illocutionary component of a speech act, on the other hand, is the performative
force with which the locution is uttered ('I am telling you, I saw
him!'). The perlocution aspect of a proposition is its effect on the
hearer (e.g. to produce alertness or fear). This latter we can associate
with rhetoric. In this theory of communicative action Habermas tends

to associate the illocutionary force of speech acts with a performative intention to communicate to reach understanding. Perlocutionary acts, on the other hand, he associates with the strategic action by which people manipulate others into serving their own ends. Aiming to produce specific effects on listeners, that is, according to this account, distorts the communicative interaction by introducing this instrumental element.[9]

It is arbitrary, however, to separate speech acts whose function is solely to communicate meaning and reach understanding from speech acts that serve a strategic goal of the speaker by producing specific effects on listeners. As Thomas Farrell points out, it deviates from the speech act theory of Austin and Searle, who theorized both illocution *and* perlocution as aspects of *all* speech acts. Every communicative effort both intends a contextualized force for its assertion and aims to produce specific effects on those to whom it communicates. Such perlocutionary effects, moreover, are often crucial to successful understanding and response to an expression. While it is appropriate to distinguish between communicative acts that aim to further understanding and co-operation and those that operate strategically as means of using others for one's own ends, this distinction cannot be made by means of a distinction between purely rational and merely rhetorical speech.[10]

The claim that political argument is inevitably suffused with rhetoric can sound like a submission to the constraints and necessities of real life that ideally ought to be otherwise. There is, however, another more positive claim to make, namely that rhetoric serves several uniquely positive functions in furthering political communication in which participants aim to solve collective problems or resolve conflict. I find three such uniquely positive functions of rhetoric that accompany argument in political communication.

*Rhetorical moves often help to get an issue on the agenda for deliberation.* Gutmann and Thompson make this point through the example of Carol Mosley Braun's impassioned rhetoric when the US Senate was about to renew the patent on the Confederate flag insignia, without any debate. They suggest that without her emotional rhetoric

---

[9] See Jurgen Habermas, *The Theory of Communicative Action*, i (Boston: Beacon Press, 1984), ch. 3. For a very helpful exposition of this aspect of Habermas's theory, see Kenneth Baynes, *The Normative Grounds of Social Criticism* (Albany: State University of New York Press, 1992), 86–104.

[10] See Thomas B. Farrell, *Norms of Rhetorical Culture* (New Haven: Yale University Press, 1993), ch. 5; cf. Jonathan Culler, 'Communicative Competence and Normative Force', *New German Critique*, 35 (Spring–Summer 1985), 133–44; cf. Bohman, 'Emancipation and Rhetoric', 185–203.

the Senate would not have taken the issue seriously, and that therefore her extreme and even disruptive speech contributed positively to a deliberative process by motivating officials to discuss an important issue.[11]

Questions of what gets on the agenda of political discussion and how seriously participants take positions put forward in a discussion are crucial for an inclusive democratic process. It is easy enough to have a harmonious and expeditious decision-making process if the dominant voices do not take seriously those opinions, analyses, perspectives, and arguments that they regard as extreme, dangerous to their interests, or overly contentious. Demonstration and protest, the use of emotionally charged language and symbols, publicly ridiculing or mocking exclusive or dismissive behaviour of others, are sometimes appropriate and effective ways of getting attention for issues of legitimate public concern, but which would otherwise not be likely to get a hearing, either because they threaten powerful interests or because they particularly concern a marginalized or minority group. Every liberal and many illiberal polities offer countless examples of the use of rhetoric as the best means to get publics to discuss important issues and have all the opinions and perspectives on them taken seriously. To be sure, not every issue, position, or discourse that individuals or groups insist on having heard by speaking emotionally or engaging in rowdy demonstration is legitimate. Some formulations of positions can be ruled out of order by a deliberative public on the grounds that they fail to show respect for some members of the polity. Since whether an issue or position does assume respect is itself often a matter for dispute, however, rhetorical vehicles are appropriate for getting the issue to the point where the public decides whether it should be discussed.

*Rhetoric fashions claims and arguments in ways appropriate to a particular public in a particular situation.* Theorists of deliberative

---

[11] Gutmann and Thompson, *Democracy and Disagreement*, 135–6. Though Gutmann and Thompson give a positive role for rhetoric in deliberation in this way, they nevertheless seem to distinguish reason from rhetoric in their discussion. Non-deliberative means such as expressing emotion, they say, may be necessary to achieve deliberative ends. They also oppose reason to passion in a misrepresentation of the position of some critics of deliberative democracy. They claim that some people say that for disadvantaged groups to gain an effective voice in the public forum, their representatives must make passionate *rather than* rational appeals (p. 134). As I have said above, the claim that deliberative democracy wrongly privileges argument does not wish to replace reason with passion, but rather claims that passion accompanies reason. Carol Mosley Braun, in the example that Gutmann and Thompson cite, was not making an emotional appeal instead of an argument; she was arguing in a rhetorical and emotional way that the Senate should not routinely approve the Confederate seal.

democracy usually specify publicity as a norm of political communication. This requirement entails, of course, that deliberations leading
to legitimate binding decisions cannot take place in closed fora from
which potentially affected parties are excluded.[12] This openness
requirement in turn conditions publicity as a constraint on the content
of utterances. Claims and reasons should be uttered in a way that can
be accepted by anyone. Public utterance must be open to the possibility that anyone could be listening, and that anyone can question or
challenge them. This public reason condition by no means implies that
anyone and everyone *does* accept the claims. It only means that the
claims or reasons are not uttered in a way that others could not accept
as consistent with their own worth and dignity. In this respect the
norms of deliberative democracy are universalistic.

At the same time, however, any actual situation of political discussion is particular with respect to forum, participants, audience, issue,
and the history that has called forth the discussion. Rhetoric helps
situate claims and arguments that meet the universalistic criterion of
publicity within the particular context of discussion. As dialogic, an
effective contribution to public discussion engages with its audience,
and reflectively includes in its mode of expression attention to the
interests, assumptions, values, meanings, and situation of this particular audience.[13] With rhetorical figures a speech constructs a relation of
speaker to listeners.[14] The speaker appeals to assumed history or set of
values salient for this audience. He uses jokes, figures of speech,
idioms, that resonate with this particular audience and may not with
others. Rhetoric also constructs the occasion of the utterance—today
we commemorate, or we've just had an urgent phone call, or we are
engaged in an ongoing discussion. Rhetoric constructs the speaker,
audience, and occasion by invoking or creating specific connotations,
symbols, and commitments. Through rhetoric we construct our posi-

---

[12]   Gutmann and Thompson, *Democracy and Disagreement*, ch. 3.

[13]   See Gary Remer, 'Political Oratory and Conversation: Cicero versus Deliberative
Democracy,' *Political Theory*, 27/1 (Feb. 1999), 39–64; Remer criticizes contemporary theories of deliberative democracy for ignoring or bracketing rhetoric. He appeals to the writings of Cicero for insight into the importance of rhetoric for situating political claims in
terms of the particular circumstance in which they are made. Compare Farrell, *Norms of
Rhetorical Culture*, 238.

[14]   Benjamin Barber is one of the few theorists of discussion-based democracy who
emphasizes listening as much as speaking in the situation of discursive democracy. See
*Strong Democracy*, 175–7. It is no coincidence, I think, that Barber also reflects on the
*affective* power of talk (see p. 190). Susan Bickford has developed a sustained account of
the process and norms of listening in situations of political conflict. See *The Dissonance of
Democracy* (Ithaca, NY: Cornell University Press, 1996), esp. chs. 1 and 5.

tions and messages in a way appropriate to the particular context and audience to which we are speaking.[15]

Thus we rely on rhetoric to construct and respond to the many particular and diverse publics appearing in modern mass democracies. Some who describe deliberative democracy give a misleading picture of a process in which the whole polity is present to itself as a single public discussing its problems and coming to decisions. Modern mass democracies are necessarily decentred, however, composed of multiple overlapping and interacting publics distanced in space and time. Some publics are organized around marginalized social positions; others are interest groups or publics sharing particular values or culture. Ways of speaking that resonate and appeals that resonate in one may be poorly comprehended in another. In so far as the many sub-publics in a large and free society themselves sometimes must communicate with one another to solve problems or resolve conflict, however, rhetoric aims to help translate across them.

*Rhetoric motivates the move from reason to judgement.* As I emphasized in the previous chapter, political debate does not conclude simply with a well-founded proposition, account, or set of principles. Political argument usually aims ultimately at making *judgements* about institutions, situations, people, and solutions to problems. The situated, figured, and affective appeal of rhetoric helps make possible the move from thinking to committed action that such political judgement involves.[16] The good rhetorician is one who attempts to persuade listeners by orienting proposals and arguments towards their collective and plural interests and desires, inviting them to transform these in the service of making a judgement together, but also acceding to them as the judges, rather than claiming himself or herself to 'know'.[17] To make judgements with pragmatic consequences, political publics must not only believe and accept claims and arguments, but

[15] Farrell, *Norms of Rhetorical Culture*, ch. 5.

[16] See Douglas Walton, *The Place of Emotion in Argument* (University Park: Pennsylvania State University Press, 1992). Walton sees a role for appeals to emotion as 'steering' mechanisms that lead listeners towards consideration of proper courses of action or lead people to positions for which they develop reasoned opinion.

[17] Danielle Allen reflects on Aristotle's theory of rhetoric as the vehicle through which speakers enlist the trust of audiences and claim to befriend them. This means that the speakers do not claim superiority to the audience, but rather that they and their listeners are equal and reciprocal; a test of such reciprocity is speaking as though it is the audience that judges the quality of one's claims and that the political public makes political judgements. See Allen, 'Good Will and Equitable Persuasion: Reading Aristotle's *Rhetoric* for a Theory of Democratic Judgment', Paper presented to the American Political Science Association, Boston, Sept. 1998.

also care about and commit their will to the outcomes.[18] It sometimes happens, moreover, that several proposals are roughly equivalent in their rational acceptability. When it is possible to accept several claims on rational grounds, rhetoric provides contextual and motivational grounds for choosing between rationally acceptable positions.[19]

In sum, a normative theory of discussion-based democracy should attend to the rhetorical aspects of communication both in order to criticize exclusion and to foster inclusion. As I pointed out earlier, in real situations of political communication, people sometimes reject claims and arguments not on their rational merits, but because they do not like their modes of expression. They dismiss those who do not express themselves in the 'proper' accent or grammatical structure, or who display wild and funny signs instead of write letters to the editor. One reason to bring the category of rhetoric explicitly into focus is to notice in a situation of political conflict how some people can be excluded from the public by dismissal of their style. An inclusive communicative democracy presumes an obligation on everyone's part to listen to claims being made on the public, however expressed, unless and until they can be demonstrated as completely lacking in respect for others, or as incoherent.

To this obligation for discussion participants to listen, on the other hand, corresponds an obligation for speakers to attend to the conditions of listening. Political communication entails a reflexivity according to which anyone who wishes to persuade others of the justice or wisdom of his or her claims must aim to attend to the specifics of this audience, their interests, experience and idiom. This does not mean that one must share those interests, experiences, and idiom, but that appropriate political communication aims to be inclusive by acknowledging the specificity of context and audience, and exhibiting a desire to accommodate to it.

## 4. Narrative and Situated Knowledge

Some internal exclusions occur because participants in a political public do not have sufficiently shared understandings to fashion a set of

---

[18] See Thomas McCarthy, 'Practical Discourse: On the Relation of Morality to Politics', in Craig Calhoun (ed.), *Habermas and the Public Sphere* (Cambridge, Mass.: MIT Press, 1992). Compare Bickford, *The Dissonance of Democracy*, 48–9; there is more to figuring out how to act, she says, than producing or promoting agreement.

[19] Bill Rehg, 'Reason and Rhetoric in Habermas's Theory of Argumentation'. Rehg accepts the critiques of Habermas's efforts to separate reason from rhetoric and attempts to reconstruct a Habermasian account which includes a role for rhetoric.

arguments with shared premisses, or appeals to shared experiences and values. Too often in such situations the assumptions, experiences, and values of some members of the polity dominate the discourse and that of others is misunderstood, devalued, or reconstructed to fit the dominant paradigms. In such situations arguments alone will do little to allow public voice for those excluded from the discourse. Another mode of expression, narrative, serves important functions in democratic communication, to foster understanding among members of a polity with very different experience or assumptions about what is important.

In recent years a number of legal theorists have turned to narrative as a means of giving voice to kinds of experience which often go unheard in legal discussions and courtroom settings, and as a means of challenging the idea that law expresses an impartial and neutral standpoint above all particular perspectives. Some legal theorists discuss the way that storytelling in the legal context functions to challenge a hegemonic view and express the particularity of experience to which the law ought to respond but often does not.[20]

Several scholars of Latin American literature offer another variant of a theory of the political function of storytelling, in their reflections on *testimonio*. Some resistance movement leaders in Central and South America narrate their life stories as a means of exposing to the wider literate world the oppression of their people and the repression they suffer from their governments. Often such *testimonios* involve one person's story standing or speaking for that of a whole group to a wider, sometimes global, public, and making claims upon that public for the group. This raises important questions about how a particular person's story can speak for others,[21] and whether speaking to the literate First World public changes the construction of the story.[22] While these are important questions, here I wish only to indicate a debt to both of these literatures, and analyse these insights with an account of some of the political functions of storytelling.

Suppose we in a public want to make arguments to justify proposals for how to solve our collective problems or resolve our conflicts

[20] Kathryn Abrams, 'Hearing the Call of Stories', *California Law Review*, 79/4 (July 1991), 971–1052; Thomas Ross, 'Despair and Redemption in the Feminist Nomos', *Indiana Law Review*, 69/1 (Winter 1993), 101–36.

[21] Doris Sommer, 'Not Just a Personal Story: Women's *Testimonios* and the Plural Self', in Bella Brodzski and Celeste Schenk (eds.), *Lifelines: Theorizing Women's Autobiography* (Ithaca, NY: Cornell University Press, 1988).

[22] John Beverley, 'The Margin at the Center: On *Testimonio* (Testimonial Narrative)', *Modern Fiction Studies*, 35/1 (1989), 11–28; '"Through All Things Modern": Second Thoughts on *Testimonio*', *boundary* 2, 18/2 (1989), 1–21.

justly. In order to proceed, those of us engaged in meaningful political discussion and debate must share many things. We must share a description of the problem, share an idiom in which to express altern- ative proposals, share rules of evidence and prediction, and share some normative principles which can serve as premises in our arguments about what ought to be done. When all these conditions exist, then we can engage in reasonable disagreement. Fortunately, in most political disputes these conditions are met in some respect and to some degree, but for many political disputes they are not met in other respects and degrees. When these conditions for meaningful argument do not obtain, does this mean that we must or should resort to a mere power contest or to some other arbitrary decision procedure? I say not. Where we lack shared understandings in crucial respects, sometimes forms of communication other than argument can speak across our differences to promote understanding. I take the use of narrative in political communication to be one important such mode.

Political narrative differs from other forms of narrative by its intent and its audience context. I tell the story not primarily to entertain or reveal myself, but to make a point—to demonstrate, describe, explain, or justify something to others in an ongoing political discussion. Political narrative furthers discussion across difference in several ways.

*Response to the 'differend'.* Chapter 1 discussed how a radical injustice can occur when those who suffer a wrongful harm or oppres- sion lack the terms to express a claim of injustice within the prevailing normative discourse. Those who suffer this wrong are excluded from the polity, at least with respect to that wrong. Lyotard calls this situ- ation the *differend.* How can a group that suffers a particular harm or oppression move from a situation of total silencing and exclusion with respect to this suffering to its public expression? Storytelling is often an important bridge in such cases between the mute experience of being wronged and political arguments about justice. Those who experience the wrong, and perhaps some others who sense it, may have no language for expressing the suffering as an injustice, but neverthe- less they can tell stories that relate a sense of wrong. As people tell such stories publicly within and between groups, discursive reflection on them then develops a normative language that names their injustice and can give a general account of why this kind of suffering constitutes an injustice.

A process something like this occurred in the United States and else- where in the 1970s and 1980s, as injustice we now call sexual harass- ment gradually came into public discussion. Women had long experienced the stress, fear, pain, and humiliation in their workplace that courts today name as a specific harm. Before the language and theory of sexual harassment was invented, however, women usually suffered in silence, without a language or forum in which to make a reasonable complaint. As a result of women telling stories to each other and to wider publics about their treatment by men on the job and the consequences of this treatment, however, a problem that had no name was gradually identified and named, and a social moral and legal theory about the problem developed.

*Facilitation of local publics and articulation of collective affinities.* Political communication in mass democratic societies hardly ever consists in all the people affected by an issue assembling together in a single forum to discuss it. Instead, political debate is widely dispersed in space and time, and takes place within and between many smaller publics. By a 'local public' I mean a collective of persons allied within the wider polity with respect to particular interests, opinions, and/or social positions.[23] Storytelling is often an important means by which members of such collectives identify one another, and identify the basis of their affinity. The narrative exchanges give reflective voice to situated experiences and help affinity groupings give an account of their own individual identities in relation to their social positioning and their affinities with others.[24] Once in formation, people in local publics often use narrative as means of politicizing their situation, by reflecting on the extent to which they experience similar problems and what political remedy for them they might propose. Examples of such local publics emerging from reflective stories include the processes of 'consciousness-raising' in which some people in the women's movement engaged, and which brought out problems of battering or sexual harassment where these were not yet recognized as problems.

*Understanding the experience of others and countering pre-understandings.* Storytelling is often the only vehicle for understanding the particular experiences of those in particular social situations,

[23] Compare Nancy Fraser, 'Rethinking the Public Sphere: A Contribution to the Critique of Actually Existing Democracy', in Bruce Robbins (ed.), *The Phantom Public Sphere* (Minneapolis: University of Minnesota Press, 1993); she discusses the need for a theory of deliberative democracy to recognize that there are many publics, and that it is important for marginalized and disadvantaged groups to form 'subaltern counter-publics' in which they develop their own idiom and position. See also Hilde Nelson, 'Resistance and Insubordination', *Hypatia: A Journal of Feminist Philosophy*, 10/2 (Spring 1995) 23–40. Communities of choice can come together and tell counter-stories that redefine their lives.

[24] See Maria Pia Lara, *Moral Textures: Feminist Narratives in the Public Sphere* (Cambridge: Polity Press, 1998), chs. 1–5; see also Seyla Benhabib, 'Sexual Difference and Collective Identities: The New Global Constellation', *Signs: A Journal of Women in Culture and Society*, 24/2 (Winter 1999), 335–62.

experiences not shared by those situated differently, but which they must understand in order to do justice.[25] Imagine that people who move in wheelchairs make claims upon city resources to remove wrongful impediments to their social, political, and economic participation, and positively to aid them in ways they claim will equalize their ability to participate. A primary way they make their case will be through telling stories of their physical, temporal, social, and emotional obstacles. Such testimony often provides an answer to people who doubt the legitimacy of a claim of need or right. Relating stories alone will not legitimize such claims; political communication also requires general normative arguments. Stories often serve as the only means, however, for people in one social segment to gain some understanding of experiences, needs, projects, problems, and pleasures of people in the society differently situated from themselves, to the description of which general normative principles must be applied to do justice.[26]

While it sometimes happens that people know they are ignorant about the lives of others in the polity, perhaps more often people come to a situation of political discussion with a stock of empty generalities, false assumptions, or incomplete and biased pictures of the needs, aspirations, and histories of others with whom or about whom they communicate. Such pre-understandings often depend on stereotypes or overly narrow focus on a particular aspect of the lives of the people represented in them. People with disabilities, to continue the example, too often must respond to assumptions of others that their lives are joyless, that they have truncated capabilities to achieve excellence, or have little social and no sex lives.[27] Narratives often help target and correct such pre-understandings.[28]

[25] Seymour Mandelbaum appeals to the knowledge-producing power of stories in contexts of public hearings in city planning processes; Seymour Mandelbaum, 'Telling Stories', *Journal of Planning Research*, 10/3 (1991), 109–214.

[26] Gutmann and Thompson argue that testimony has uses in deliberative democracy, enlarging thought, but that they are futile gestures when not coupled with appeals that reach out to others to make arguments that claim to start from shared premises and appeal to reasons others ought to be able to accept; see *Democracy and Disagreement*, 136–7. Kimberly K. Smith argues that storytelling made contributions to the anti-slavery movement in the United States that no amount of general argument could have made, in expressing the experience of slaves in ways that pulled on the imagination and identification of others, and in offering exemplars of courage and integrity; Smith, 'Storytelling, Sympathy and Moral Judgment in American Abolitionism', *Journal of Political Philosophy*, 6/4 (1998), 356–77.

[27] For a thorough and philosophically sophisticated account conceptualizing the situation of people with disabilities as a function of social prejudice and institutional structure, primarily see Anita Silvers, 'Formal Justice', in Anita Silvers, David Wasserman, and Mary B. Mahowald (eds.), *Disability, Difference, Discrimination: Perspectives on Justice in Bioethics and Public Policy* (Lanham, Md.: Rowman & Littlefield, 1998).

[28] Marc A. Fajer, 'Can Two Real Men Eat Quiche Together? Storytelling, Gender-Role Stereotypes, and Legal Protection for Lesbians and Gay Men', *University of Miami Law*

*Revealing the source of values, priorities, or cultural meanings.* For an argument to get off the ground, its auditors must accept its premisses. Pluralist polities, however, often face serious divergences in value premisses, cultural practices, and meanings, and these disparities bring conflict, insensitivity, insult, and misunderstanding. Lacking shared premisses, communicatively democratic discussion cannot proceed through reasoned argument under these circumstances.

Under such circumstances, narrative can serve to explain to outsiders what practices, places, or symbols mean to the people who hold them and why they are valuable. Values, unlike norms, often cannot be justified through argument. But neither are they arbitrary. Their basis often emerges from the situated narrative of persons or groups. Through narrative the outsiders may come to understand why the insiders value what they value and why they have the priorities they have.

Members of a polity with very different histories and traditions than others in it, for example, often find things important to them that have no meaning or which seem trivial to others. Indigenous people in Anglo settler societies, for example, too often encounter incredulity, mockery, or hostility from whites, when they try to make major political issues out of holding or regaining control over a particular place, or insist on their right to fishing or gaming particular species in particular ways, or face police batons in protest of development projects that they believe desecrate burial sites. The meanings and values at stake here cannot be explained in universalizable arguments. Those facing such lack of understanding often rely on myths and historical narratives to convey what is meaningful to them and why, to explain 'where they are coming from'.

Stephen White articulates this function of narrative as explicating normative starting-points which different groups may have in a deliberative context.

If one is persistently pressed to say why the criteria of normative justification ought to be understood in a certain way, one is forced to contextualize that judgment progressively up to the most general and comprehensive level of narrative about one's culture. And at this level, what we have is not simply another, slightly bigger, narrative than all the others floating round in our culture. Rather, we have a narrative that is recounted to those with whom we

*Review*, 46 (Jan. 1992), esp. 524–8. Compare Diana Tietzejs Meyers's notion of 'dissident speech'; this is a kind of speaking where excluded or stereotyped groups aim to reconfigure how they are represented in public. See Meyers, *Subjection and Subjectivity* (New York: Routledge, 1994), esp. 113–35.

radically disagree, with the intention of showing them that they could freely recognize themselves as having a place within it.[29]

Understanding normative starting-points of a group, then, often means that we have travelled through their overlapping narratives rather than worked through a coherent exposition.

*Aid in constituting the social knowledge that enlarges thought.* Narrative, finally, not only exhibits experience and values from the point of view of the subjects that have and hold them. It also reveals a total social knowledge from particular points of view. Stories not only relate the experiences of the protagonists, but also present a particular interpretation of their relationships with others. Each person and collective has an account not only of their own life and history, but of every other position that affects their experience. Thus listeners can learn about how their own position, actions, and values appear to others from the stories they tell. Narrative thus exhibits the situated knowledge available from various social locations, and the combination of narratives from different perspectives produces a collective social wisdom not available from any one position. By means of narratives expressed in public with others differently situated who also tell their stories, speakers and listeners can develop the 'enlarged thought' that transforms their thinking about issues from being narrowly self-interested or self-regarding about an issue, to thinking about an issue in a way that takes account of the perspectives of others.[30] Narrative contributes to political argument by the social knowledge it offers of what are the likely effects of policies and actions on people in different social locations. Stories of police harassment or abusive treatment coming from people in some neighbourhoods of Pittsburgh related to others with a different experience of police, for example, were crucial to the process that brought about citizen demand for a Civilian Review Board in the case I discussed in this book's Introduction. The next chapter will theorize more thoroughly this function of political communication in producing social knowledge.

[29] Stephen White, *Political Theory and Postmodernism* (Cambridge: Cambridge University Press, 1991).

[30] Lisa Disch, 'More Truth than Fact: Storytelling as Critical Understanding in the Writings of Hannah Arendt', *Political Theory*, 21/4 (Nov. 1993), 665–94; Seyla Benhabib, 'Sexual Difference and Collective Identities: The New Global Constellation', *Signs: A Journal of Women in Culture and Society*, 24/2 (Winter 1999), 335–62. Margaret Walker, *Moral Understandings: Feminist Studies in Ethics* (New York: Routledge, 1997), esp. ch. 5; James Tully, *Strange Multiplicity* (Cambridge: Cambridge University Press, 1995): 'By listening to the different stories others tell, and giving their own in exchange, the participants come to see their common and interwoven histories together form a multiplicity of paths' (p. 26).

The general normative functions of narrative in political communication, then, refer to teaching and learning. Inclusive democratic communication assumes that all participants have something to teach the public about the society in which they dwell together and its problems. It assumes as well that all participants are ignorant of some aspects of the social or natural world, and that everyone comes to a political conflict with some biases, prejudices, blind spots, or stereotypes. Frequently in situations of political disagreement, one faction assumes that they know what it is like for others, or that they can put themselves in the place of the others, or that they are really just like the others. Especially in mass society, where knowledge of others may be largely mediated by statistical generalities, there may be little understanding of lived need or interest across groups. A norm of political communication under these conditions is that everyone should aim to enlarge their social understanding by learning about the specific experience and meanings attending other social locations. Narrative makes this easier and sometimes an adventure.

## 5. Dangers of Manipulation and Deceit

I have argued that an inclusive conception of democracy requires an account of how modes of communication additional to making assertions and giving reasons can contribute to political discussion that aims to solve collective problems justly. I regard greeting, rhetoric, and narrative as three important additional modes of communication, but there might be others. These three modes of communication can and sometimes do operate to enlarge the scope of discussion and its participants, and transform their ways of seeing problems and possible solutions in more subtle ways that take more needs and perspectives into account.

I hear the voice of the sceptic, though, still staying that this account minimizes the dangers that attend validations of such modes of communication. The purpose of privileging argument, this voice says, is to distinguish truth from falsity, honesty from deceit, rational consent from manipulation. Calling on inclusive democratic theory and practice to be open and attentive to the political functions of greeting, rhetoric, and narrative devalues or dismisses these central normative concerns. Each of these forms of communication can be and often is superficial, insincere, strategically manipulated to win the assent of others simply by flattery or fantasy and not by reason.[31]

---

[31] Seyla Benhabib has objected to my earlier and more sketchy exposition of these categories on two grounds. While greeting, rhetoric, and narrative are indeed aspects of

Examples of manipulative uses of each of these modes of communication certainly are not hard to find. Both in everyday life and in public discourses interlocutors sometimes make a great show of greeting
particular individuals or groups, only to ignore them once serious
matters are under discussion. Indeed, sometimes the fact of having
greeted serves as a way of deflecting complaints that the views of some
people are being excluded from consideration. Well, now, we have
taken a lot of trouble already to recognize the important contribution
of those people to our collective history, so you have no grounds for
complaint.

There is no question, furthermore, that public discussion often
involves irrational appeals or manipulation of unconscious desires and
fear. Audiences are often dazzled by the excitement and sparkle of a pre-
sentation and distracted from its substance, or lack thereof. Appealing
to people's basest desires for amusement and self-aggrandizement, the
clever rhetorician tricks his audience into accepting harmful decisions
and policies. Narratives, too, sometimes manipulate irrational assent.
Stories may be false, misleading, or self-deceiving. Too often in politics,
moreover, people wrongly generalize from stories. A congressperson
tells the story of one welfare mother who spends her days watching
television and drinking beer, thereby suggesting that such behaviour is
common. Narratives can create stereotypes as well as challenge them.

Such dangers of irrational and manipulative discourses dominating
and determining policies appear in multicultural societies with deep
structural injustices whose public discussion is most influenced by
private corporate-dominated mass media, and not only in political
contexts where public discourse is more tightly controlled. In such
societies it is very difficult to create and maintain a meaningful public
where discussion is open, critical, and takes place with good will.
These ends are not served, however, by trying to purify discussion of

informal communication in everyday life, she says, they do not belong in the public language of institutions and legislatures of a democracy. These should contain only shared
public reasons. Benhabib seems here to limit the concept of political communication to the
language of statute, which excludes most engaged activities of debate and discussion in
mass-mediated public spheres. Her second objection claims that the effort to theorize
greeting rhetoric and narrative as modes of political communication builds an opposition
between these and critical argument. These modes of communication are irrational, arbitrary, capricious, she says, and only rational argument contributes to deliberation. Thus
Benhabib joins those who construct an opposition between the rational purity of argument
and the irrationality of other forms of communication. I have aimed to describe the political functions of these modes of communication, however, as accompanying rather than
alternatives to argument. They give generalized reason orientation and body. See Seyla
Benhabib, 'Toward a Deliberative Model of Democratic Legitimacy', in Benhabib (ed.),
*Democracy and Difference* (Princeton: Princeton University Press, 1996).

embodied, situated, affective elements, leaving a kernel of supposedly universal unassailable rational argument. How, then, does this conception of inclusive communication respond to these dangers?

First, I do not offer practices of greeting, rhetoric, and narrative as substitutes for argument. Normative ideals of democratic communication crucially entail that participants require reasons of one another and critically evaluate them. These modes of communication, rather, are important additions to argument in an enlarged conception of democratic engagement. Greeting, I claim, *precedes* the giving and evaluating of reasons in discussion that aim to reach understanding. If parties do not recognize and acknowledge one another, they will not listen to arguments. Rhetoric always *accompanies* argument, by situating the argument for a particular audience and giving it embodied style and tone. Narratives sometimes are important parts of larger arguments, and sometimes enable understanding across difference in the absence of shared premisses that arguments need in order to begin.

We should not need much reminding, moreover, that people can also be deceived or manipulated by argumentative discourse. The truth of an argument is only as good as the truth of its premisses, and the assertions people make are often knowingly or unknowingly false. Purported experts and politicians frequently rely on the apparent unassailability of statistics or other technical discourse to produce the appearance of good reasons for flimsy conclusions. Every speechmaker knows how easy it is to confuse naïve or inattentive people into thinking that a set of assertions leads to the conclusion. We would not need the discipline of logic if fallacies were not common and often went undetected.

The only remedy for false or invalid arguments is criticism. Similarly, listeners to greetings, rhetoric, and narrative should be critically vigilant, and should apply standards of evaluation to them as well as to argument. Is this discourse respectful, publicly assertable, and does it stand up to public challenge? The only cure for false, manipulative, or inappropriate talk is more talk that exposes or corrects it, whether as a string of reasons, a mode of recognition, a way of making points, or a narrative.

Enlarging a conception of political communication for a theory of inclusive democracy in this way may make political communication more disorderly and confusing than it appears if restricted to argument. If democratic communication is not simply deliberation among gentlemen who already share basic understandings, however, but is often a struggle among society's members to have their interests, experiences, and opinions recognized by others, and a struggle to persuade others of the justice of their claims, then a theory of communicative democracy should reflect on the normative meaning of all the communicative inter-action brought to such struggles.

I have argued that an inclusive theory and practice of communicative democracy should not privilege specific ways of making claims and arguments. Participants in communicative democracy should listen to all modes of expression that aim to co-operate and reach a solution to collective problems. One might object that such a norm of inclusion would seem to imply that no particular political communication is *better* than any other. How can a theory of communicative democracy both be inclusive in this broad sense, and also distinguish good arguments from bad arguments, expressions that further discussion from those that get us nowhere, ways of making points that are more and less persuasive? Surely it is better to be clear than confused, to get to the point rather than waste people's time, to attend to subtlety and complexity rather than be simple-minded. Without such means of evaluating better and worse expression, all the critical capacity of deliberative democracy evaporates.

It would appear that the injunction to include not only diverse speakers but diverse modes of speaking in legitimate democratic communication implies a communicative levelling, that speakers or particular contributions to a discussion cannot be singled out for their excellence. If such levelling were a consequence of this expanded conception of political communication, that would be a troubling result. I do not think that it follows from the obligation and responsibility to listen to everyone in their particular mode of communication that we cannot distinguish better and worse expressions. Standards of political communication should be thought of as *virtues*, however, rather than as conditions of entry into public deliberation. Arguments, greetings, stories, and rhetoric all have their virtues. While most people most of the time do not achieve excellence in any of them, most of us recognize and admire excellence in others when we see it performed. Capacities for communicating in situations of social difference and conflict can be developed and deepened, and a public is always better if more of its members have more developed capacities than fewer. The expanded conception of political communication I have proposed here provides theorists and those who wish to design inclusive deliberative practices with more attentive ways of allowing for and evaluating the contributions people and groups make to political discussion than have most deliberative theories so far.

# CHAPTER 3

## Social Difference as a Political Resource

Many advocates of a deliberative model of democracy appeal to the republican ideal of a common good as what distinguishes it from an aggregative model of democracy. To form a deliberative public, in this interpretation, citizens must leave aside their parochial concerns of local loyalty and particular affiliation. Deliberating citizens co-operate by looking for what they have in common, seeking similarities among themselves. On this construction of politics and deliberation, there are only two alternatives, which correlate with a distinction between aggregative and deliberative models of democracy. Either people mobilize in self-regarding interest groups that compete for goods without any concern for justice, or citizens engage in rational discussion to identify the policies that unite them in a shared vision of their common interests.

Social movements mobilizing around experiences and analyses of the oppressive and unequal consequences of social differentiations of gender, race, sexuality, national origin, or religion, along with class, have expressed scepticism about appeals to a common good. The claims of workers or poor people to higher wages or more social supports too often appear as 'special interests' in such constructions of the common interest. Such claims of unity, these movements assert, often bias the interpretation of a common good in ways that favour dominant social groups and position women, or indigenous people, or Blacks, or homosexuals, or Muslims as deviant Other. Many in these social movements thus claim that it is important to notice differences of social position, structured power, and cultural affiliation in political discussion and decision-making that aims to promote justice. Issues of justice vary for structurally different groups, this politics of difference argues; oppressions and wrongful inequalities take many forms, and appeals to a common good do not adequately respond to and notice such differences.

Social movements arguing that politics aiming to promote justice should attend to social differences of gender, race, cultural age, ability, and so on have had considerable influence in many parts of the world since the 1970s. Recently some political theorists articulating a discussion-based view of democratic process, however, have criticized such a politics of difference as just another form of selfish interest group politics. This chapter considers the claims of some of those who assert that public-spirited democratic politics requires commitment to a common good, and thus criticize the politics of feminism, gay and lesbian rights, anti-racism, and multiculturalism. I examine three variations of the claim that justice-oriented politics requires transcending social difference towards a common good: neo-republican, liberal nationalist, and socialist. All claim that group-specific political movements endanger democracy and make meaningful communication impossible. Focusing on issues of gender, sexuality, race, ethnic disadvantage, these critics assert, only divides and destroys public discussion, creating bickering and self-interested enclaves with no orientation towards transformative deliberation or co-operation. Each critic would agree that democracy requires all persons affected by decision to be included in the process that leads to them. Each implicitly constructs this ideal, however, as the inclusion of individual citizens in a single discursive public with other undifferentiated citizens who leave behind their particular social situations to seek their common interests.

I argue that political claims asserted from the specificity of social group position, and which argue that the polity should attend to these social differences, often serve as a resource for rather than an obstruction of democratic communication that aims at justice. Critics of such claims wrongly reduce this politics of difference to 'identity politics'. While this label is appropriate to describe certain aspects of group-based social movements, or certain issues important to them, on the whole the label 'identity politics' is misleading. Political theory would do well to disengage social group difference from a logic of identity, in two ways. First, we should conceptualize social groups according to a relational rather than a substanstialist logic. Secondly, we should affirm that groups do not have identities as such, but rather that individuals construct their own identities on the basis of social group positioning.

I distinguish cultural and structural social groups, and argue that the latter are more important for most appeals to justice. The chapter briefly theorizes structural social groups and structural inequality. Differentiations of gender, race, or ability are more like class than ethnicity, I argue, inasmuch as they concern structural relations of power, resource allocation, and discursive hegemony. Even where the basis of group differentiation more concerns culture than structure, furthermore, claims to cultural recognition usually are means to the end of undermining domination or wrongful deprivation.

A strong communicative democracy, I conclude, needs to draw on social group differentiation, especially the experience derived from structural differentiation, as a resource. A democratic process is inclusive not simply by formally including all potentially affected individuals in the same way, but by attending to the social relations that differently position people and condition their experiences, opportunities, and knowledge of the society. A democratic public arrives at objective political judgement from discussion not by bracketing these differences, but by communicating the experiences and perspectives conditioned by them to one another. Communication of the experience and knowledge derived from different social positions helps correct biases derived from the dominance of partial perspective over the definition of problems or their possible solutions. Such differentiated communication also enables a public collectively to construct a more comprehensive account of how social processes work and therefore of the likely consequences of proposed policies. Not only does the explicit inclusion of different social groups in democratic discussion and decision-making increase the likelihood of promoting justice because the interests of all are taken into account. It also increases that likelihood by increasing the store of social knowledge available to participants.

## 1. Critique of a Politics of Difference

Writers with varying political sympathies have criticized claims of justice and political inclusion made on the basis of specific social group experiences of women, gay men and lesbians, racial minorities, or people with disabilities. Nevertheless, these criticisms take a similar form. They each construct group-specific justice claims as an assertion of group identity, and argue that the claims endanger democratic communication because they only divide the polity into selfish interest groups. I shall review the accounts of communitarian Jean Elshtain, liberal nationalist David Miller, and socialists Todd Gitlin and David Harvey.

### Destroys the common good

For Jean Elshtain, workable democracy involves active citizens in a vibrant civil society who work together in a public spirit that seeks their common good. Democratically committed citizens should adopt a public orientation of commitment and responsibility in which they leave behind what differentiates them. Workable democratic communication and decision-making, according to Elshtain, requires that citizens be able to transcend the parochialism of their private associations, affections, and affiliations.

Recent movements asserting the importance of attending to social group difference, such as feminists, gay rights activists, or post-civil-rights African American activism, do not, in Elshtain's view, display such public-spiritedness. On the contrary, a politics of difference destroys public commitment to a common good. These movements have turned politics into a cacophony of self-interested demands for recognition and redress, where groups within their private identities are unwilling or unable to communicate and co-operate.

To the extent that citizens begin to retribalize into ethnic or other 'fixed identity' groups, democracy falters. Any possibility for dialogue, for democratic communication and commonality, vanishes as so much froth on the polluted sea of phony equality. Difference becomes more and more exclusive. If you are black and I am white, by definition I do not and cannot in principle 'get it'. There is no way that we can negotiate the space between our given differences. We are just stuck with them in what political theorists used to call 'ascriptive characteristics'—things we cannot change about ourselves. Mired in the cement of our own identities, we need never deal with one another. Not really. One of us will win and one of us will lose the cultural war or the political struggle. That's what it's all about: power of the most reductive, impositional sort.[1]

Feminists and gay rights activists, in Elshtain's view, drag private issues of reproduction and sexuality into the public, where they inappropriately demand inclusion and equal opportunity without shedding or hiding their bodily specificity. Blacks or Latinos or Native Americans claim that American history has left a legacy of discrimination and disadvantage reproduced in schools, workplaces, and public policy, but in their claims for redress they ignore their responsibilities for promoting the common good of everyone. These politics of difference are only a crass interest group politics that makes dialogue impossible.

### Weakens national identity

David Miller largely reduces group-based social movements to claims of minority ethnicities for recognition in the context of a nation-state.

[1] Jean Bethke Elshtain, *Democracy on Trial* (New York: Basic Books, 1995), 74.

Feminist or gay rights movements, in his construction, appear to be just another identity, gender identity or sexuality, seeking recognition in public life.

Group identity, whether sexual, cultural, or ethnic, should not merely be expressed in private settings, but should be carried into the arenas of politics—that is, one should participate politically *as* a gay, a religious fundamentalist, or a black—and political institutions should operate in such a way as to respect these group differences. On the one hand, they must validate group identities by ensuring that the various groups are represented in politics *as* groups; on the other hand, they must ensure that the policies that emerge show equal respect for the values and cultural demands of each group—there should, if necessary, be subsidies for the activities that each group regards as central to its identity; educational materials must avoid discriminatory judgments which imply that one cultural norm might be superior to another; and so forth.[2]

Miller does not entirely reject the idea that minority cultures should receive public recognition and expression. To the extent that some groups tend to be excluded from full participation in public deliberation, moreover, he agrees that special representation for groups may sometimes be necessary. A politics of difference taken too far, however, on his account, endangers the national identity, which ought to be the primary focus of political debate. In a deliberative democratic setting, if groups make claims on one another for justice, they can do so effectively on the basis of sharing a common national identity. That national identity is the basis of the trust among groups necessary to an orderly and human democratic government. Individuals can develop and express their ethnic and other group identities, such as their gender identity or their Jewish identity, but the national identity must be universal and neutral, as the commitment to a common political culture that transcends these specificities.

## Undermines class solidarity

Surprisingly, perhaps, the radical socialist critique of new social movements has a form similar to the communitarian or the liberal nationalist critique. Feminist, indigenous, or anti-racist movements and claims for justice, according to leftists such as Todd Gitlin or David Harvey, have splintered progressive politics into separatist enclaves. Attention to issues like sexual harassment or police abuse diverts egalitarian socialists from the power of capitalism that oppresses all of the groups.

---

[2] David Miller, *On Nationality* (Oxford: Oxford University Press, 1995), 132.

Concern with culture and identity freezes different groups in opposition to one another, rather than uniting everyone who has reason to oppose the power that corporate imperatives have over the lives of most people. As the gap between rich and poor grows, and increasing numbers of people world-wide are hurled into poverty or economic insecurity, emancipatory politics requires that all who are interested in justice put aside their particular claims of gender, sexual, race, or ethnic oppression and unite behind the common dream of a society that meets everyone's basic needs. The politics of difference only deflects from such concerns. Those group-based claims are particularist and self-regarding, unlike the claims of working-class struggle, which transcend those group particularities towards a vision of universal human emancipation.[3]

All these criticisms reduce group-based social movements to the label 'identity politics'. They all construe this identity politics as either the assertion of a group interest without regard for the interests of others, and/or the demand that others in a polity recognize their group identity as such. There is some basis for these interpretations: Essentialist modes of asserting group identity can be found in the behaviour and discourse of some people speaking out of movements of women, Blacks, indigenous people, people with disabilities, migrants, and similar social movements. The primary claims of these movements, however, and those that deserve to be taken the most seriously, have been claims for political equality, inclusion, and appeals to justice directed at a wider public which they claim that public ought to accept. These movements have made claims upon dominant political, social, and economic institutions that their interests, needs, and particular points of view should be better taken into account in decision-making processes and policies.

In what follows I will argue that labelling these movements and their claims 'identity politics' is largely misleading. The specificity of group difference out of which these movements arise is best conceptualized through a relational logic, rather than the substantive logic assumed in most notions of group identity. The primary form of social difference to which the movements respond, moreover, is structural difference, which may build on but is not reducible to cultural differences of gender, ethnicity, or religion. Social structures often position people unequally in processes of power, resource allocation, or dis-

---

[3] Todd Gitlin, *Twilight of Common Dreams* (New York: Metropolitan Books, 1995); David Harvey, *Justice, Nature and the Geography of Difference* (Oxford: Blackwell, 1996), esp. ch. 12.

cursive hegemony. Claims of justice made from specific social group positions expose the consequences of such relations of power or opportunity. Where there are such social group differences, moreover, they often produce social problems or conflicts. Democratic communication best responds to these problems and conflicts not by invoking a common good, but by taking account of the specificities of differentiated relations.

## 2. Social Difference is not Identity

Those who reduce group difference to identity implicitly use a logic of substance to conceptualize groups. Under this logic a group is defined by a set of essential attributes that constitute its identity as a group. Individuals are said to belong to the group in so far as they have the requisite attributes. On this sort of account, the project of organizing in relation to group-based affiliation and experience requires identifying one or more personal or social attributes which make the group what it is, shared by members of the group, and which clearly exclude others. Identifying the group of Latinos, for example, means finding the essential attributes of being Latino, such as biological connection, language, national origin, or celebration of specific holidays. Saying that gay people are a group, to take another example, means identifying the essential attributes that members of the group share that make the group a group. In their efforts to discover the specificities of their group-based social positions and forge relations of solidarity among those similarly located, group-based social movements themselves have sometimes exhibited these essentializing tendencies. We did not need to wait for neo-republican or socialist critics of 'identity politics' to point out the problems with such identity claims. Group-differentiated political movements themselves, along with their theoreticians, have developed sophisticated critiques of such tendencies.[4]

Whether imposed by outsiders or constructed by insiders to the group, attempts to define the essential attributes of persons belonging

[4] For some examples of critiques of essentialism and a politics of identity from within theories and movements that support a politics of difference, see Elizabeth V. Spelman, *Inessential Woman* (Boston: Beacon Press, 1988); Anna Yeatman, 'Minorities and the Politics of Difference', in *Postmodern Revisions of the Political* (New York: Routledge, 1994); Michael Dyson, 'Essentialism and the Complexities of Racial Identity', in David Theo Goldberg (ed.), *Multiculturalism* (Cambridge, Mass.: Blackwell, 1994); Steven Seidman, 'Identity and Politics in a "Postmodern" Gay Culture', in *Difference Troubles: Queering Social Theory and Sexual Politics* (Cambridge: Cambridge University Press, 1997).

to social groups fall prey to the problem that there always seem to be persons without the required attributes whom experience tends to include in the group or who identify with the group. The essentialist approach to defining social groups freezes the experienced fluidity of social relations by setting up rigid inside-outside distinctions among groups. If a politics of difference requires such internal unity coupled with clear borders to the social group, then its critics are right to claim that such politics divides and fragments people, encouraging conflict and parochialism.

A politics that seeks to organize people on the basis of a group identity all members share, moreover, must confront the fact that many people deny that group positioning is significant for their identity. Some women, for example, deny reflective awareness of womanly identity as constitutive of their identity, and they deny any particular identification with other women. Many French people deny the existence of a French identity and claim that being French is nothing particularly important to their personal identities; indeed, many of these would be likely to say that the search for French identity that constitutes the personal identities of individual French men and women is a dangerous form of nationalism. Even when people affirm group affinity as important to their identities, they often chafe at the tendency to enforce norms of behaviour or identity that essentialist definitions of the groups entail.

Thirdly, the tendency to conceive group difference as the basis of a common identity which can assert itself in politics implies for many that group members all have the same interests and agree on the values, strategies, and policies that will promote those interests. In fact, however, there is usually wide disagreement among people in a given social group on political ideology. Though members of a group oppressed by gender or racial stereotypes may share interests in the elimination of discrimination and dehumanizing imagery, such a concern is too abstract to constitute a strategic goal. At a more concrete level members of such groups usually express divergent and even contradictory interests.[5]

The most important criticism of the idea of an essential group identity that members share, however, concerns its apparent denial of differentiation within and across groups. Everyone relates to a plurality of social groups; every social group has other social groups cutting across it. The group 'men' is differentiated by class, race, religion, age, and so on; the group 'Muslim' differentiated by gender, nationality, and so on. If group identity constitutes individual identity and if indi-

[5] Compare Anne Phillips, *The Politics of Presence* (Oxford: Oxford University Press, 1995), ch. 6.

viduals can identify with one another by means of group identity, then how do we deal theoretically and practically with the fact of multiple group positioning? Is my individual identity somehow an aggregate of my gender identity, race identity, class identity, like a string of beads, to use Elizabeth Spelman's metaphor. In addition, this ontological problem has a political dimension: as Spelman, Lugones, and others argue, the attempt to define a common group identity tends to normalize the experience and perspective of some of the group members while marginalizing or silencing that of others.[6]

Those who reduce a politics of difference to 'identity politics', and then criticize that politics, implicitly use a logic of substance, or a logic of identity, to conceptualize groups. In this logic an entity is what it is by virtue of the attributes that inhere in it, some of which are essential attributes. We saw above that attempts to conceptualize any social group—whether a cultural group like Jews, or structural groups like workers or women—become confused when they treat groups as substantially distinct entities whose members all share some specific attributes or interests that do not overlap with any outsiders. Such a rigid conceptualization of group differentiation both denies the similarities that many group members have with those not considered in the group, and denies the many shadings and differentiations within the group.

By conceiving social group differentiation in relational rather than substantial terms, we can retain a description of social group differentiation, but without fixing or reifying groups. Any group consists in a collective of individuals who stand in determinate relations with one another because of the actions and interactions of both those associated with the group and those outside or at the margins of the group.[7] There is no collective entity, the group, apart from the individuals who compose it. A group is much more than an aggregate, however. An aggregate is a more or less arbitrary collection of individuals according to one or more attributes; aggregation, when it occurs, is from the point of view of outsiders, and does not express a subjective social experience. Insurance companies may aggregate smokers for the purposes of actuarial tables, and the Cancer Society may aggregate persons known to have contributed to health insurance advocacy groups. When constituted as aggregates, individuals stand in no determinate relations to one another. The members of groups, however, stand in

[6] Spelman, *Inessential Woman*; Maria Lugones, 'Purity, Impurity and Separation', *Signs: A Journal of Women in Cultural and Society*, 19/2 (Winter 1994), 458–79.

[7] For an account of groups as constituted relations, see Larry May, *The Morality of Groups* (Chicago: University of Chicago Press, 1988); and *Sharing Responsibility* (Chicago: University of Chicago Press, 1993).

determinate relations both to one another and to non-members. The group, therefore, consists in both the individuals and their relationships.

Associations are one kind of group. An association is a group that individuals purposefully constitute to accomplish specific objectives. These may be as minor and transient as forming a neighbourhood welcoming committee or as grand and long-lasting as a constitutional state. Certainly associations are constituted relationally. Their members or affiliates stand in certain relations with one another around particular objectives, and those relations are often defined by explicit rules and roles, although many of the relationships in associations will also be informal and tacit. The argument of this chapter requires conceptualizing *social* groups, however, as distinct from associations.[8]

Considered relationally, a social group is a collective of persons differentiated from others by cultural forms, practices, special needs or capacities, structures of power or privilege. Unlike associations, social groups are not explicitly constituted. They emerge from the way people interact. The attributes by which some individuals are classed together in the 'same' group appear as similar enough to do so only by the emergent comparison with others who appear more different in that respect. Relational encounter produces perception of both similarity and difference. Before the British began to conquer the islands now called New Zealand, for example, there was no group anyone thought of as Maori. The people who lived on those islands saw themselves as belonging to dozens or hundreds of groups with different lineage and relation to natural resources. Encounter with the English, however, gradually changed their perceptions of their differences; the English saw them as similar to each other in comparison to the English, and they found the English more different from them than they felt from one another.

In a relational conceptualization, what makes a group a group is less some set of attributes its members share than the relations in which they stand to others. On this view, social difference may be stronger or weaker, it may be more or less salient, depending on the point of view of comparison. A relational conception of group difference does not need to force all persons associated with the group under the same attributes. Group members may differ in many ways, including how strongly they bear affinity with others of the group. A relational approach, moreover, does not designate clear conceptual and practical

---

[8] In earlier work I have distinguished these three terms, aggregates, associations, and social groups, and I rely on these conceptualizations here. See *Justice and the Politics of Difference* (Princeton: Princeton University Press, 1990), ch. 2.

borders that distinguish all members of one group decisively from members of others. Conceiving group differentiation as a function of relation, comparison, and interaction, then, allows for overlap, interspersal, and interdependence among groups and their members.[9]

Groups differentiated by historic connection to territories and by culture have received the most attention both in recent political theory and practical politics, for example in nationalist politics, on the one hand, and in efforts to institute multicultural policies, on the other. Cultural groups are differentiated by perceived similarity and dissimilarity in language, everyday practices, conventions of spirituality, sociability, production, and the aesthetics and objects associated with food, music, buildings, the organization of residential and public space, visual images, and so on. For those within it or who practice it, culture is an environment and means of expression and communication largely unnoticed in itself. As such, culture provides people with important background for their personal expression and contexts for their actions and options. Culture enables interaction and communication among those who share it. For those unfamiliar with its meanings and practices, culture is strange and opaque. Cultural difference emerges from internal and external relations. People discover themselves with cultural affinities that solidify them into groups by virtue of their encounter with those who are culturally different in some or many respects. In discovering themselves as distinct, cultural groups usually solidify a mutual affinity and self-consciousness of themselves as groups.

Political conflict between cultural groups is common, of course. Outsiders condemn or denigrate a group's practices or meanings, and/or assert the superiority of their own, sometimes attempting to suppress the denigrated group's practices and meanings, and impose its own on them. It is important to remember, however, that much of the ground for conflict between culturally differentiated groups is not cultural, but a competition over territory, resources, or jobs. The last chapter of this book focuses on some issues of cultural difference by examining contemporary arguments about liberal nationalism and

---

[9] Martha Minow proposes a relational understanding of group difference; see *Making All the Difference* (Ithaca, NY: Cornell University Press, 1990), pt. II. I have referred to a relational analysis of group difference in *Justice and the Politics of Difference*, ch. 2; in that earlier formulation, however, I have not distinguished group affiliation from personal identity as strongly as I will later in this chapter. For relational understandings of group difference, see also William Connolly, *Identity/Difference* (Ithaca, NY: Cornell University Press, 1993); and Chantal Mouffe, 'Democracy, Power and the "Political"', in Seyla Benhabib (ed.), *Democracy and Difference* (Princeton: Princeton University Press, 1996).

self-determination. Later in this chapter I will discuss the politics of multiculturalism as a kind of 'identity politics'.

More important for the central argument of this chapter, however, is the concept of *structural*, as distinct from cultural, group. While they are often built upon and intersect with cultural differences, the social relations constituting gender, race, class, sexuality, and ability are best understood as structural.[10] The social movements motivated by such group-based experiences are largely attempts to politicize and protest structural inequalities that they perceive unfairly privilege some social segments and oppress others. Analysing structural difference and structural inequality, then, helps to show why these movements are not properly interpreted as 'identity politics'. I turn, then, to an account of structural differentiation.

## 3. Structural Difference and Inequality

Appeal to a structural level of social life, as distinct from a level of individual experience and action, is common among social critics.[11] Appeal to structure invokes the institutionalized background which conditions much individual action and expression, but over which individuals by themselves have little control. Yet the concept of structure is notoriously difficult to pin down. I will define social structure, and more specifically structural inequality, by rebuilding elements from different accounts.

Marilyn Frye likens oppression to a birdcage. The cage makes the bird entirely unfree to fly. If one studies the causes of this imprisonment by looking at one wire at a time, however, it appears puzzling. How does a wire only a couple of centimetres wide prevent a bird's flight? One wire at a time, we can neither describe nor explain the inhibition of the bird's flight. Only a large number of wires arranged in

[10]   The following effort to articulate the naming of structural social groups and use that concept to argue against an 'identity politics' interpretation of the claims of difference-based social movements is partly motivated by a desire to think through further some of the issues raised in an exchange I have had with Nancy Fraser. See Fraser, 'From Redistribution to Recognition? Dilemmas of Justice in a "Post-Socialist" Age', *New Left Review*, 212 (July–Aug. 1995), 68–99; and Iris Marion Young, 'Unruly Categories: A Critique of Nancy Fraser's Dual Systems Theory', *New Left Review*, 222 (Mar.–Apr. 1997), 147–60. Fraser's initial paper importantly reminded theorists of justice and multiculturalism of issues of structural oppression and possible transformation. Fraser herself oversimplifies the meaning of a politics of difference as identity politics, however, and I believe inappropriately dichotomizes issues of culture and structure.

[11]   See e.g., William Julius Wilson, *When Work Disappears* (New York: Knopf, 1997); see also Jean Hampton, *Political Philosophy* (Boulder, Colo.: Westview Press, 1997), 189–90.

a specific way and connected to one another to enclose the bird and reinforce one another's rigidity can explain why the bird is unable to fly freely.[12]

At a first level of intuition, this is what I mean by social structures that inhibit the capacities of some people. An account of someone's life circumstances contains many strands of difficulty or difference from others that, taken one by one, can appear to be the result of decision, preferences, or accidents. When considered together, however, and when compared with the life story of others, they reveal a net of restricting and reinforcing relationships. Let me illustrate.

Susan Okin gives an account of women's oppression as grounded in a gender division of labour in the family. She argues that gender roles and expectations structure men's and women's lives in thoroughgoing ways that result in disadvantage and vulnerability for many women and their children. Institutionally, the entire society continues to be organized around the expectation that children and other dependent people ought to be cared for primarily by family members without formal compensation. Good jobs, on the other hand, assume that workers are available at least forty hours per week year round. Women are usually the primary caretakers of children and other dependent persons, due to a combination of factors: their socialization disposes them to choose to do it, and/or their job options pay worse than those available to their male partners, or her male partner's work allows him little time for care work. As a consequence the attachment of many women to the world of employment outside the home is more episodic, less prestigious, and less well paid than men's. This fact in turn often makes women dependent on male earnings for primary support of themselves and their children. Women's economic dependence gives many men unequal power in the family. If the couple separates, moreover, prior dependence on male earnings coupled with the assumptions of the judicial system makes women and their children vulnerable to poverty. Schools', media, and employers' assumptions all mirror the expectation that domestic work is done primarily by women, which assumptions in turn help reproduce those unequal structures.[13]

This is an account of gender difference as structural difference. The account shows gender difference as structured by a set of relationships and interactions that act together to produce specific possibilities and preclude others, and which operate in a reinforcing circle. One can

[12] Marilyn Frye, 'Oppression', in *The Politics of Reality* (Trumansburg, NY: Crossing Press, 1983).

[13] Susan Okin, *Justice, Gender and the Family* (New York: Basic Books, 1989).

quarrel with the content or completeness of the account. To it I would add, for example, the structures that organize the social dominance of norms of heterosexual desire, and the consequences of this heterosexual matrix for people of both sexes and multiple desires. The example can show at an intuitive level the meaning of structural social group difference. Social groups defined by race or class are also positioned in structures; shortly I will elaborate these examples. Now I will systematize the notion of structure by building up definitions from several social theorists.

Peter Blau offers the following definition. 'A social structure can be defined as a multidimensional space of differentiated social positions among which a population is distributed. The social associations of people provide both the criterion for distinguishing social positions and the connections among them that make them elements of a single social structure.'[14] Blau exploits the spatial metaphor implied by the concept of structure. Individual people occupy varying *positions* in the social space, and their positions stand in determinate relation to other positions. The structure consists in the connections among the positions and their relationships, and the way the attributes of positions internally constitute one another through those relationships.

Basic social structures consist in determinate social positions that people occupy which condition their opportunities and life chances. These life chances are constituted by the ways the positions are related to one another to create systematic constraints or opportunities that reinforce one another, like wires in a cage. Structural social groups are constituted through the social organization of labour and production, the organization of desire and sexuality, the institutionalized rules of authority and subordination, and the constitution of prestige. Structural social groups are relationally constituted in the sense that one position in structural relations does not exist apart from a differentiated relation to other positions. Priests, for example, have a particular social function and status in a particular society by virtue of their structured and interdependent relations with others who believe they need specialists in spiritual service and are willing to support that specialization materially. The prestige associated with a caste, to take another example, is bought only through reproduced relations of denigration with lower castes. The castes exist by virtue of their interactive relations with one another, enacted and re-enacted through rituals of deference and superiority enforced through distributions, material dependencies, and threats of force.

[14] Peter Blau, *Inequality and Heterogeneity* (New York: Free Press, 1977), 4.

More generally, a person's social location in structures differentiated by class, gender, age, ability, race, or caste often implies predictable status in law, educational possibility, occupation, access to resources, political power, and prestige. Not only do each of these factors enable or constrain self-determination and self-development, they also tend to reinforce the others. One reason to call these structural is that they are relatively permanent. Though the specific content and detail of the positions and relationships are frequently reinterpreted, evolving, and even contested, the basic social locations and their relations to one another tend to be reproduced.

It is certainly misleading, however, to reify the metaphor of structure, that is, to think of social structures as entities independent of social actors, lying passively around them, easing or inhibiting their movement. On the contrary, social structures exist only in the action and interaction of persons; they exist not as states, but as processes. Thus Anthony Giddens defines social structures in terms of 'rules and resources, recursively implicated in the reproduction of social systems'.[15] In the idea of the duality of structure, Giddens theorizes how people act on the basis of their knowledge of pre-existing structures and in so acting reproduce those structures. We do so because we act according to rules and expectations and because our relationally constituted positions make or do not make certain resources available to us.

Economic class is the paradigm of structural relations in this sense. Understood as a form of structural differentiation, class analysis begins with an account of positions in the functioning of systems of ownership, finance, investment, production, and service provision. Even when they have shares of stock or participate in pension funds, those who are not in a position to live independently and control the movement of capital must depend on employment by others in order to gain a livelihood. These positions of capitalist and worker are themselves highly differentiated by income and occupation, but their basic structural relation is an interdependency; most people depend on employment by private enterprises for their livelihoods, and the owners and managers depend on the competence and co-operation of their employees for revenues. Important recent scholarship has argued that a bipolar understanding of economic class in contemporary societies is too simple, and we must also analysis the structural differences of professional and non-professional employees, as well

[15] Anthony Giddens, *The Constitution of Society* (Berkeley: University of California Press, 1984).

as self-employed, and those more or less permanently excluded from employment.[16]

People are born into a particular class position, and this accident of birth has enormous consequences for the opportunities and privileges they have for the rest of their lives. Without a doubt, some born to wealth-owner families die paupers, and others born poor die rich. Nevertheless, a massive empirical literature shows that the most consistent predictor of adult income level, educational attainment, occupation, and ownership of assets is the class situation of one's parents. While class position is defined first in terms of relations of production, class privilege also produces and is supported by an array of assets such as residence, social networks, access to high-quality education and cultural supplements, and so on. All of these operate to reinforce the structural differentiations of class.

Defining structures in terms of the rules and resources brought to actions and interactions, however, makes the reproduction of structures sound too much like the product of individual and intentional action. The concept of social structure must also include conditions under which actors act, which are often a *collective* outcome of action impressed onto the physical environment. Jean-Paul Sartre calls this aspect of social structural the *practico-inert*.[17] Most of the conditions under which people act are socio-historical: they are the products of previous actions, usually products of many co-ordinated and unco-ordinated but mutually influenced actions over them. Those collective actions have produced determinate effects on the physical and cultural environment which condition future action in specific ways. As I understand the term, social structures include this practico-inert physical organization of buildings, but also modes of transport and communication, trees, rivers, and rocks, and their relation to human action.

Processes that produce and reproduce residential racial segregation illustrate how structural relations become inscribed in the physicality of the environment, often without anyone intending this outcome, thereby conditioning future action and interaction. A plurality of expectations and actions and their effects operate to limit the options of many inner-city dwellers in the United States. Racially discriminatory behaviour and policies limit the housing options of people of colour, confining many of them to neighbourhoods from which many

---

[16] For a clear and thorough account of class in a contemporary Marxist mode, see Eric Olin Wright, *Class Counts* (Cambridge: Cambridge University Press, 1997).

[17] Jean-Paul Sartre, *Critique of Dialectical Reason*, *trans.* Alan Sheridan-Smith (London: New Left Books, 1976), bk. 1, ch. 3.

of those whites who are able to leave do. Property-owners fail to keep up their buildings, and new investment is hard to attract because the value of property appears to decline. Because of more concentrated poverty and lay-off policies that disadvantage Blacks or Latinos, the effects of an economic downturn in minority neighbourhoods are often felt more severely, and more businesses fail or leave. Politicians often are more responsive to the neighbourhoods where more affluent and white people live; thus schools, fire protection, policing, snow removal, garbage pick-up, are poor in the ghetto neighbourhoods. The spatial concentration of poorly maintained buildings and infrastructure that results reinforces the isolation and disadvantage of those there because people are reluctant to invest in them. Economic restructuring independent of these racialized processes contributes to the closing of major employers near the segregated neighbourhoods and the opening of employers in faraway suburbs. As a result of the confluence of all these actions and processes, many Black and Latino children are poorly educated, live around a higher concentration of demoralized people in dilapidated and dangerous circumstances, and have few prospects for employment.[18]

Reference to the physical aspects of social structures helps to lead us to a final aspect of the concept. The actions and interactions which take place among persons differently situated in social structures using rules and resources do not only take place on the basis of past actions whose collective effects mark the physical conditions of action. They also often have future effects beyond the immediate purposes and intentions of the actors. Structured social action and interaction often have collective results that no one intends, and which may even be counter to the best intentions of the actors.[19] Even though no one intends them, they become given circumstances that help structure future actions. Presumably no one intends the vulnerability of many children to poverty that Okin argues the normal gender division of labour produces.

In summary, a structural social group is a collection of persons who are similarly positioned in interactive and institutional relations that condition their opportunities and life prospects. This conditioning occurs because of the way that actions and interactions conditioning that position in one situation reinforce the rules and resources available for other actions and interactions involving people in the structural positions. The unintended consequences of the confluence of

[18] See Douglas Massey and Nancy Denton, *American Apartheid* (Cambridge, Mass.: Harvard University Press, 1993).
[19] Sartre calls such effects counter-finalities; see *Critique of Dialectical Reason*, 277–92.

many actions often produce and reinforce such opportunities and constraints, and these often make their mark on the physical conditions of future actions, as well as on the habits and expectations of actors. This mutually reinforcing process means that the positional relations and the way they condition individual lives are difficult to change.

Structural groups sometimes build on or overlap with cultural groups, as in most structures of racialized differentiation or ethnic-based privilege. Thus cultural groups and structural groups cannot be considered mutually exclusive or opposing concepts. Later I will elaborate on the interaction of cultural groups with structures, in the context of evaluating what should and should not be called identity politics. Not all ethnic or cultural group difference, however, generates structural group difference. Some structural difference, moreover, is built not on differences of cultural practice and perception, but instead on bodily differences like sex or physical ability. Some structures position bodies with particular attributes in relations that have consequences for how people are treated, the assumptions made about them, and their opportunities to realize their plans. In so far as it makes sense to say that people with disabilities are a social group, for example, despite their vast bodily differences, this is in virtue of social structures that normalize certain functions in the tools, built environment, and expectations of many people.[20]

People differently positioned in social structures have differing experiences and understandings of social relationships and the operations of the society because of their structural situation. Often such differences derive from the structural inequalities that privilege some people in certain respects and relatively disadvantage others. Structural *inequality* consists in the relative constraints some people encounter in their freedom and material well-being as the cumulative effect of the possibilities of their social positions, as compared with others who in their social positions have more options or easier access to benefits. These constraints or possibilities by no means determine outcomes for individuals in their ability to enact their plans or gain access to benefits. Some of those in more constrained situations are particularly lucky or unusually hard-working and clever, while some of those with an open road have bad luck or squander their opportun-

---

[20] Anita Silvers develops a thorough and persuasive account of why issues of justice regarding people with disabilities should focus on the relation of bodies to physical and social environments, rather than on the needs and capacities of individuals called disabled. See Silvers, 'Formal Justice', in Anita Silvers, David Wasserman, and Mary B. Mahowald (eds.), *Disability, Difference, Discrimination: Perspectives on Justice in Bioethics and Public Policy* (Lanham, Md.: Rowman & Littlefield, 1998).

ities by being lazy or stupid. Those who successfully overcome obstacles, however, cannot be judged as equal to those who have faced fewer structural obstacles, even if at a given time they have roughly equivalent incomes, authority, or prestige.

## 4. Social Groups and Personal Identity

So far I have aimed to disengage group difference from identity by suggesting that social groups do not themselves have substantive unified identities, but rather are constituted through differentiated relations. The other task of this disengagement concerns the relation of individuals to groups. Some ethnic-, national-, gender-, or race-conscious social movement activists talk as though affinity with these groups constitutes their identity as individual people, which they share with all others of the group. Such discourse, however, quickly runs up against the problem I discussed earlier, namely that every individual necessarily has affinities with many social groups, and that the lives of different individuals are structured by differing constellations of groups. If each group defines a person's identity, then how are a person's multiple group affiliations conjoined? Many people rightly resist the suggestion, moreover, that who they are as individuals is determined in specific ways by social group membership. Such a notion of personal identity as constituted by an alleged group identity fails to give sufficient force to personal freedom and individuality.

From these failings it does not follow that groups are fictions or have no significant relation to individual possibilities. The relation of individuals to groups, however, is not one of identity. Social groups do indeed position individuals, but a person's identity is her own, formed in active relation to social positions, among other things, rather than constituted by them. Individual subjects make their own identities, but not under conditions they choose.

An important strand of social theory describes individual subjectivity and identity as constituted or conditioned by the social relations into which a person is born and grows up, and through which he or she moves in his or her life. Social relationships, institutions, and structures are prior to individual subjects, both temporally and ontologically. A person encounters an already structured configuration of power, resource allocation, status norms, and culturally differentiated practices.[21] Particular individuals occupy particular positions in these

---

[21] There are different theoretical approaches to such an idea that subjects are positioned by prior social relations. Lacanian-inspired theories describe the positioning of persons in

fields. The positioning of individuals occurs through processes of communicative interaction in which persons identify one another as belonging to certain social categories, as standing in specific relations to themselves or others, and enforce norms and expectations in relation to one another. While no individual is in exactly the same position as any other, agents are 'closer' or 'farther' from one another in their location with respect to the relations that structure that field. Agents who are similarly positioned experience similar constraints or enablements, particular modes of expression and affinity, in social relations. Persons are thrown into a world with a given history of sedimented meanings and material landscape, and interaction with others in the social field locates us in terms of the given meanings, expected activities, institutional rules, and their consequences. We find ourselves positioned in relations of class, gender, race, nationality, religion, and so on, which are sources of both possibilities of action and constraint.

In another place I have suggested that Sartre's concept of 'seriality' can be useful for theorizing structural positioning that conditions the possibility of social agents without constituting their identities. In Sartre's theory to be working-class (or capitalist class) is to be part of a series that is constituted by the material organization of labour ownership, and the power of capital in relation to labour. I have suggested that the gender position of being a woman does not itself imply sharing social attributes and identity with all those others called women. Instead, 'women' is the name of a series in which some individuals find themselves positioned by virtue of norms of enforced heterosexuality and the sexual division of labour.[22] Both the norms and expectations of heterosexual interaction and the habits developed in certain social

terms of dominant discourses constituting social positions and their relative power and status; see Rosalind Coward and John Ellis, *Language and Materialism* (London: Routlege & Kegan Paul, 1977), 49–60; Diana Fuss, *Essentially Speaking: Feminism, Nature and Difference* (New York: Routledge, 1989); Bill Martin, *Matrix and Line* (Albany: State University of New York Press, 1993); Liz Bondi discusses the meaning of a shift from identity to position in the terms for thinking about the relation of individuals to social groups. She argues that the shift does not entirely avoid problems of essentialism, but that it better enables thinking of groups as constituted through relations among persons. Bondi, 'Locating Identity Politics', in Michael Keith and Steve Pile (eds.), *Place and the Politics of Identity* (London: Routledge, 1993). Other theories rely on the tradition of interactionism begun by George Herbert Mead, which describes the formation of the self through the internalization of naming and norming relations of others; see Jurgen Habermas, *The Theory of Communicative Action*, i (Boston: Beacon Press, 1984); Axel Honneth, *Struggle for Recognition* (Cambridge, Mass.: MIT Press, 1995).

[22] Iris Marion Young, 'Gender as Seriality: Thinking about Women as a Social Collective', in *Intersecting Voices: Dilemmas of Gender, Political Philosophy and Policy* (Princeton: Princeton University Press, 1997).

activities such as caring for children will condition the dispositions and affinities of people, without constituting their identities.

Social processes and interactions position individual subjects in prior relations and structures, and this positioning conditions who they are. But position neither determines nor defines individual identity. Individuals are agents: we constitute our own identities, and each person's identity is unique. We do not choose the conditions under which we form our identities, and we have no choice but to become ourselves under the conditions that position us in determinate relation to others. We act in situation, in relation to the meanings, practices, and structural conditions and their interaction into which we are thrown. Some of the recent literature on the moral value of cultural membership discusses one such mode of the conditioning of selves. The language and historical narratives of a group, its literature, symbols, modes of celebration, and so on give individuals both context and media for expressing their individuality and interpreting the world.[23] Positioning in social structures such as class, gender, race, and age condition individual lives by enabling and constraining possibilities of action, including enabling relations of superiority and deference between people.

None of this, however, determines individual identities. Subjects are not only conditioned by their positions in structured social relation; subjects are also *agents*. To be an agent means that you can take the constraints and possibilities that condition your life and make something of them in your own way. Some women, for example, affirm norms of femininity and internalize them; others resist evaluations of their actions and dispositions in such terms. Some people whose class status makes their childhood relatively difficult develop an attitude of working-class militancy against bosses, while others become determined to enter the upper class. Our experiences of cultural meaning and structural positioning occur in unique events and interactions with other individuals, and the unique events are often more important to our sense of ourselves than are these social facts. How we fashion ourselves is also a function of our attitudes towards our multiple cultural and structural group memberships.[24] In the words of Kwame

[23] Charles Taylor, 'Multiculturalism and the Politics of Recognition', in Amy Cutmann (ed.), *Multiculturalism* (Princeton: Princeton University Press, 1992). Taylor theorizes culture as a source of the self in just this way, not as determinative, but as providing meanings through which individuals exercise their freedom. See also Yael Tamir, *Liberal Nationalism* (Princeton: Princeton University Press, 1993).

[24] Gloria Anzaldua expresses this active appropriation of one's own multiple group positionalities as a process of 'making faces': 'Haciendo Caras, una entrada/an Introduction', in Gloria Anzaldua (ed.), *Making Face, Making Soul/ Haciendo Caras* (San Francisco: Aunt Lute Foundation, 1990).

Anthony Appiah, 'We make up selves from a tool kit of options made available by our culture and society. We do make choices, but we do not determine the options among which we choose.'[25]

Understanding individuals as conditioned by their positioning in relation to social groups without their constituting individual identities helps to solve the problem of 'pop-bead' identity: A person's identity is not some sum of her gender, racial, class, and national affinities. She is only her identity, which she herself has made by the way that she deals with and acts in relation to others social group positions, among other things.

This way of conceptualizing the relation of individual identities to social position, moreover, has several implications for the argument I make below to the effect that social group difference is a resource in democratic communication that aims to promote justice. First, it allows us to notice structural relations of dominance and subordination among groups that raise important issues of justice for individuals. The metaphor of positioning, furthermore, helps to point to ways that individual people have similar kinds of knowledge about the workings of society or have similar kinds of routine experiences because of the social relations and possibilities in which they act. Understanding social positioning as conditioning rather than determining individual identity, however, gives voice to the intuition that social group members do not have some 'fixed' or 'authentic' group identity that they share. We know from experience that people often have very different attitudes towards being Jewish, say, or being a woman, and act in very different ways regarding these facts. That individual persons freely act in relation to social group positioning makes the possibility of collective action to transform those social relations possible. The multiple positioning of individuals also enables individuals as political actors themselves to draw on knowledge of difference kinds of social and cultural relations for different purposes.

## 5. What is and is not Identity Politics

Some critics of a politics of difference wrongly reduce them to 'identity politics'. They reduce political movements that arise from specificities of social group difference to assertions of group identity or

[25] Kwami Anthony Appiah, 'Identity, Authenticity, Survival: Multicultural Societies and Social Reproduction', in Amy Gutmann (ed.), *Multiculturalism* (Princeton: Princeton University Press, 1994), 155.

mere self-regarding interest. Often group-conscious social movements claim that social difference should be taken into account rather than bracketed as a condition of political inclusion for furthering social justice. Yet the label 'identity politics' is not entirely misplaced as a characterization of some claims and self-conceptions of these movements. Now I want to sort out those concerns and public activities plausibly called identity politics from those that are not.

Historically excluded or dominated groups all have organized discourses and cultural expressions aimed at reversing the stereotypes and deprecations with which they claim dominant society has described them. Politically conscious social movements of indigenous people, for example, promote a positive understanding of indigenous governance forms, technology, and art, as a response to colonialist definitions of 'civilized' institutions and practices. Many African Americans in the United States historically and today cultivate pride in the ingenuity of African American resistance institutions and cultural expression as a response to the invisibility and distortion of their lives and experience they have seen in dominant discourses. Where dominant understandings of femininity equate it with relative weakness and selfless nurturing, some feminists have reinterpreted typically womanly activities and relationships as expressions of intelligence and strength. Interpretations and reinterpretations of typical experiences and activities of group members in response to deprecating stereotpyes can rightly be called 'identity politics'. They are often expressed in cultural products such as novels, songs, plays, or paintings. Often they are explicit projects that individual persons take up as an affirmation of their own personal identities in relation to group meaning and affinity with others identified with the group. Their function is partly to encourage solidarity among those with a group affinity, and a sense of political agency in making justice claims to the wider society.

Any movements or organizations mobilizing politically in response to deprecating judgements, marginalization, or inequality in the wider society, I suggest, need to engage in 'identity politics' in this sense. Working-class and poor people's movements have asserted positive group definition in this sense as much as gender, racialized, or colonized groups. Such solidarity-producing cultural politics does consist in the assertion of specificity and difference towards a wider public, from whom the movement expects respect and recognition of its agency and virtues. The public political claims of such groups, however, rarely consist simply in the assertion of one identity as against others, or a simple claim that a group be recognized in its distinctiveness. Instead, claims for recognition usually function as part of or means to claims against discrimination, unequal opportunity, political marginalization, or unfair burdens.

Another kind of movement activity often brought under the label 'identity politics', however, I find more ambiguous. The project of revaluation and reclaiming identity often involves individual and collective exploration of the meaning of a cultural group's histories, practices, and meanings. Many people devote significant energy to documenting these meanings and adding to their creative expression in music, visual images, and written and visual narratives. The exploration of positioned experience and cultural meaning is an important source of the self for most people. For this reason exploring the expressive and documentary possibilities especially of cultural meaning is an intrinsically valuable human enterprise, and one that contributes to the reproduction of social groups. In themselves and apart from conflict and problems of political and economic privilege or civil freedom, however, these are not *political* enterprises. To the extent that social movements have mistaken these activities for politics, or to the extent that they have displaced political struggles in relation to structural inequalities, critics of identity politics may have some grounds for their complaints.

Projects of the exploration of cultural meaning easily become political, however, under at least the following circumstances. (1) Sometimes people find their liberty to engage in specific cultural practices curtailed, or they face impediments in forming associations to express and preserve their cultural identity. (2) Even where there is social and cultural tolerance, sometimes political conflict erupts over educational practices and curricular context because different groups believe they are entitled to have their children learn their cultural practices and meanings in public schools. (3) Even when they have a formal liberty to explore their affinity group meanings, engage in minority practices, and form associations, sometimes groups find that they cannot get access to media, institutions, and resources they need to further their projects of exploring and creating cultural meaning. These are all familiar and much discussed conflicts often brought under the rubric of 'multicultural' politics. I do not wish to minimize the difficulty and importance of working through such issues. The point here is that most group-based political claims cannot be reduced to such conflicts concerning the expression and preservation of cultural meaning.

Charles Taylor's theory of the politics of recognition is a very influential interpretation of a politics of difference. Taylor argues that cultural group affinity, as well as respect for and preservation of their culture, is deeply important to many people because they provide sources of their selves. A person lacks equal dignity if a group with which he or she is associated does not receive public recognition as having equal status with others. Some political movements thus seek recognition in that sense, as a claim of justice.[26] While I agree that claims for recognition and respect for cultural groups judged different are often made and are claims of justice, I disagree with Taylor and those who have taken up his account that misrecognition is usually a political problem independent of other forms of inequality or oppression. On his account, groups seek recognition for its own sake, to have a sense of pride in their cultural group and preserve its meanings, and not for the sake of or in the process of seeking other goods. But I do not believe this describes most situations in which groups demand recognition. Where there are problems of lack of recognition of national, cultural, religious, or linguistic groups, these are usually tied to questions of control over resources, exclusion from benefits of political influence or economic participation, strategic power, or segregation from opportunities. A politics of recognition, that is, usually is part of or a means to claims for political and social inclusion or an end to structural inequalities that disadvantage them.

Political movements of African Americans today have been interpreted by many as 'identity politics'. An examination of some of the central claims made by African American activists, however, puts such a label into question. Many African Americans call for stronger measures to prevent race-motivated hate crimes and to pursue and punish those who commit them. Agitation continues in many cities to make police more accountable to citizens, in an effort to prevent and punish abuse and arbitrary treatment which African Americans experience more than others. African American politicians and activists continue to argue that institutional racism persists in the American educational, labour market, and housing allocation system, and that more active measures should be taken to enforce anti-discrimination and redistribute resources and positions for the sake of the development of disadvantaged African American individuals and neighbourhoods. Making many of these claims involves asserting that African Americans as a group are positioned differently from other people in American society, and sometimes activists also assert a pride in African American cultural forms and solidarity. The primary claims of justice, however, refer to experiences of structural inequality more than cultural difference.

[26] Taylor, 'Multiculturalism and the Politics of Recognition'.

What of movements of indigenous people? Indigenous politics certainly does entail a claim to recognition of the cultural distinctness of these groups. Indigenous peoples everywhere have suffered colonialist attempts to wipe out their distinct identities as peoples. They have been removed, dispersed, killed; their languages, religious practices, and artistic expression suppressed. They demand of the societies that continue to dominate them recognition and support for their distinct cultures and the freedom to express and rejuvenate those cultures. Colonialist oppression of indigenous people has involved not only cultural imperialism, however, but at the same time and often in the same actions deprivation of the land and resources from which they derived a living, and suppression of their governing institutions. As a result of conquest and subsequent domination and economic marginalization, indigenous people today are often the poorest people in the societies to which they are connected. Primary indigenous demands everywhere, then, are for self-determination over governance institutions and administration of services, and restoration of control over land and resources for the sake of the economic development of the people. Self-determination also involves cultural autonomy.

The 'identity' assertions of cultural groups, I suggest, usually appear in the context of structural relations of privilege and disadvantage. Many Muslims in Europe or North America, for example, assert their right to wear traditional dress in public places, and make claims of religious freedom.[27] Many Middle Eastern, North African, and South Asian migrants claim that Germany, the Netherlands, or France ought to accept them with their difference as full members of the society in which they have lived for decades, where their children were born and now live marginal youthful lives. Many of them experience housing, education, and employment discrimination, are targets of xenophobic acts of violence or harassment, and are excluded from or marginalized in political participation. In this sort of context claims for cultural recognition are rarely asserted for their own sake. They are part of demands for political inclusion and equal economic opportunity, where the claimants deny that such equality should entail shedding or privatizing their cultural difference.

Let me review one final example of political claims of justice critics often deride as divisive identity politics: political claims of gay men and lesbians. Especially after internal movement criticisms of efforts

---

[27] See Joseph Carens and Melissa Williams, 'Muslim Minorities in Liberal Democracies: Justice and the Limits of Toleration', in Carens (ed.), *Culture, Citizenship, and Community: A Contextual Exploration of Justice as Evenhandedness* (Oxford: Oxford University Press, 2000).

to 'identify' what it means to 'be' gay, more people whose desires and actions transgress heterosexual norms, and who find affinities with gay and lesbian institutions, would deny that they have or express a 'gay identity' they share with others. They do claim that they ought to be free to express their desires and to cultivate institutions without hiding, and without fear of harassment, violence, loss of employment, or housing. Many claim, further, that same-sex partners should have access to the same material benefits in tax law, property relations, and access to partner's employment benefits as heterosexual couples can have through marriage. For the most part, these claims of justice are not 'identity' claims. Nor are they simple claims to 'recognition'. They are claims that they should be free to be openly different from the majority without suffering social and economic disadvantage on account of that difference.

To summarize, I have argued in this section that some group-based political discourses and demands can properly be labelled 'identity politics'. Sometimes groups seek to cultivate mutual identification among those similarly situated, and in doing so they may indeed express conflict and confrontation with others who are differently situated, against whom they make claims that they wrongfully suffer domination or oppression. Such solidarity-forming 'identity politics' is as typical of obviously structurally differentiated groups such as economic classes, however, as of marginalized cultural groups. Multicultural politics concerning freedom of expression, the content of curricula, official languages, access to media, and the like, moreover, can properly be called 'identity politics'. Most group-conscious political claims, however, are not claims to the recognition of identity as such, but rather claims for fairness, equal opportunity, and political inclusion.

Critics of the politics of difference worry about the divisiveness of such claims. There is no question that such claims often provoke disagreement and conflict. When diverse groups makes claims of justice, however, we cannot reject them simply on the grounds that others' disagreement with or hostility to them produces conflict. Norms of inclusive communicative democracy require that claims directed at a public with the aim of persuading members of that public that injustices occur must be given a hearing, and require criticism of those who refuse to listen. Appeals to a common good that exhort people to put aside their experienced differences will not promote justice when structural inequality or deep disagreement exist. I shall now argue that such group-based conflict or disagreement is more likely to be avoided or overcome when a public includes differently situated voices that speak across their difference and are accountable to one another.

## 6. Communication across Difference in Public Judgement

We can now return to arguments such as Elshtain's that a politics of difference endangers democracy because it encourages self-regarding parochialism and destroys a genuine public life. Elshtain conceptualizes genuine democratic process as one in which participants assume a public mantle of citizenship which cloaks the private and partial and differentiated, on the one hand, and enters an impartial and unitary realm, on the other. Either politics is nothing but competition among private interests, in which case there is no public spirit; or politics is a commitment to equal respect for other citizens in a civil public discussion that puts aside private affiliation and interest to seek a common good. I believe that this is a false dichotomy.

### Difference, Civility, and Political Co-operation

When confronted so starkly with an opposition between difference and civility, most must opt for civility. But a conception of deliberative politics which insists on putting aside or transcending partial and particularist differences forgets or denies the lesson that the politics of difference claims to teach. If group-based positional differences give to some people greater power, material and cultural resources, and authoritative voice, then social norms and discourses which appear impartial are often biased. Under circumstances of structural social and economic inequality, the relative power of some groups often allows them to dominate the definition of the common good in ways compatible with their experience, perspective, and priorities. A common consequence of social privilege is the ability of a group to convert its perspective on some issues into authoritative knowledge without being challenged by those who have reason to see things differently. Such a dynamic is a major way that political inequality helps reproduce social and economic inequality even in formally democratic processes.

It is especially ironic that some critics on the left, such as Gitlin and Harvey, reject a politics of difference, and argue that class offers a vision of commonality as opposed to the partiality of gender or race. For those aiming to speak from the perspective of the working class have long argued that the economic and social power of the capitalist class allows that class perspective to dominate political and cultural institutions as well, and to pass for a universal perspective. The capitalist class is able to control deliberative modes and policy decisions for the sake of its interests and at the same time to represent those interests as common or universal interests. On this account, the only way to expose that such claims to the common good serve certain particular interests or reflect the experience and perspective of particular social segments primarily is publicly to assert the interests not served by the allegedly common policies, and publicly to articulate the specificity of the experiences and perspectives they exclude. Claims by feminists that the formulation and priorities of issues often assume masculine experience as normative, or by racialized or ethnic minorities that the political agenda presumes the privilege and experience of majorities, are extensions of this sort of analysis. To the degree that a society is in fact differentiated by structural relations of privilege and disadvantage, claims that everyone in the society has some common interests or a common good must be subject to deep scrutiny, and can only be validated by critical discussion that specifically attends to the differentiated social positions.

At least while circumstances of structural privilege and disadvantage persist, a politics that aims to promote justice through public discussion and decision-making must theorize and aim to practise a third way, alternative to either private interest competition or difference-bracketing public discussion of the common good. This third way consists in a process of public discussion and decision-making which includes and affirms the particular social group positions relevant to issues. It does so in order to draw on the situated knowledge of the people located in different group positions as resources for enlarging the understanding of everyone and moving them beyond their own parochial interests.[28]

It is simply not true that, when political actors articulate particularist interests and experiences and claim that public policy ought to attend to social difference, they are necessarily asserting self-regarding interests against those of others. Undoubtedly groups sometimes merely assert their own interests or preferences, but sometimes they make claims of injustice and justice. Sometimes those speaking to a

---

[28] I find the conception of deliberative democracy elaborated by James Bohman a version of this third way. Bohman criticizes communitarian or neo-republican interpretations of publicity and deliberation as requiring too much consensus. He constructs a weaker version of publicity and legitimacy that are explicitly open to social difference and inequality which recognizes that ideals of impartiality and common good are problematic in complex democracies with cultural differences and structural inequalities. See *Public Deliberation* (Cambridge, Mass.: MIT Press, 1996). In some of his most recent work Jurgen Habermas has shifted from a more unifying view to one which emphasizes more the need to attend to social differences. See 'Does Europe Need a Constitution? Reponse to Dieter Grimm', and 'Struggles for Recognition in the Democratic Constitutional State', both in *The Inclusion of the Other: Studies in Political Theory* (Cambridge, Mass.: MIT Press, 1998).

wider public on behalf of labour, or women, or Muslims, or indigenous peoples make critical and normative appeals, and they are prepared to justify their criticisms and demands. When they make such appeals with such an attitude, they are not behaving in a separatist and inward-looking way, even though their focus is on their own particular situation. By criticizing the existing institutions and policies, or criticizing other groups' claims and proposals, they appeal to a wider public for inclusion, recognition, and equity. Such public expression implies that they acknowledge and affirm a political engagement with those they criticize, with whom they struggle.

Critics who emphasize appeals to a common good are surely right to claim that workable democratic politics requires of citizens some sense of being together with one another in order to sustain the commitment that seeking solutions to conflict under circumstances of difference and inequality requires. It is far too strong, however, to claim that this sense of being together requires mutual identification. Nor should such togetherness be conceived as a search for shared interests or common good beyond the goal of solving conflicts and problems in democratically acceptable ways. Trying to solve problems justly may sometimes mean that some people's perceived interests are not served, especially when issues involve structural relations of privilege. Even when the most just solutions to political problems do not entail promoting some interests more than others, fairness usually involves co-ordinating diverse goods and interests rather than achieving a common good.

Political co-operation requires a less substantial unity than shared understandings or a common good, which I reviewed in Chapter 1. It requires first that people whose lives and actions affect one another in a web of institutions, interactions, and unintended consequences acknowledge that they are together in such space of mutual effect. Their conflicts and problems are produced by such togetherness. The unity required by political co-operation also entails that the people who are together in this way are committed to trying to work out their conflicts and to solve the problems generated by their collective action through means of peaceful and rule-bound decision-making. Political co-operation requires, finally, that those who are together in this way understand themselves as members of a single polity. That means only that they conduct their problem-solving discussions and decision-making under agreed-upon and publicly acknowledged procedures.

These unity conditions for democratic decision-making are certainly rare enough in the world, difficult both to produce and maintain. Common good theorists no doubt fear that attending to group differences in public discussion endangers commitment to co-operative decision-making. Perhaps sometimes it does. More often, however, I suggest, groups or factions refuse co-operation because, at least from their point of view, their experience, needs, and interests have been excluded or marginalized from the political agenda, or are suppressed in discussions and decision-making. Only explicit and differentiated forms of inclusion can diminish the occurrence of such refusals, especially when members of some groups are more privileged in some or many respects.

## Difference and the Public

Understanding how social difference is a potential resource for democratic communication means interpreting the meaning of a *public* differently from the way Elshtain and others do. As I showed earlier, Elshtain opposes the public to particular, partial, and differentiated social segments. As citizen, a person leaves behind or brackets the particularities of her life to enter a common space where she shares with others the universal and impartial perspective of the citizen. In my view, however, such an interpretation of the universality of citizenship actually obliterates the possibility of publicity. I follow Hannah Arendt and recent interpretations of her political thought in understanding *plurality* rather than unity as a defining characteristic of a public.

For Arendt the public is not a comfortable place of conversation among those who share language, assumptions, and ways of looking at issues. Arendt conceives the public as a place of appearance where actors stand before others and are subject to mutual scrutiny and judgement from a plurality of perspectives. The public consists of multiple histories and perspectives relatively unfamiliar to one another, connected yet distant and irreducible to one another. A conception of publicity that requires its members to put aside their differences in order to uncover their common good destroys the very meaning of publicity because it aims to turn the many into one. In the words of Lisa Disch,

The definitive quality of the public space is particularity: that the plurality of perspectives that constitute it is irreducible to a single common denominator. A claim to decisive authority reduces those perspectives to a single one, effectively discrediting the claims of other political actors and closing off public discussion. Meaning is not inherent in action, but public, which is to say, constituted by the interpretative contest among the plurality of perspectives in the public realm that confer plurality on action and thereby make it real.²⁹

Differently situated actors create democratic publicity by acknowledging that they are together and that they must work together to try to solve collective problems. Creation and sustenance of publicity in this sense, as I discussed in Chapter 1, involves the willingness on the part of participants to make claims and proposals in ways that aim to achieve understanding by others with different interests, experience, and situation, and to try to persuade them of the justice of their claims. It requires openness to the claims of others, and, as discussed in Chapter 2, a willingness to listen to their particular mode of expression. At the same time it involves holding others accountable through questioning and criticizing their communication and action.

A democratic public ought to be fully inclusive of all social groups because the plurality of perspectives they offer to the public helps to disclose the reality and objectivity of the world in which they dwell together. Thus Arendt says that the public 'signifies the world itself, insofar as it is common to all of us and distinguished from our privately owned place in it. . . . To live together in the world means essentially that a world of things is between those who have it in common, as a table is located between, relates and separates men at the same time.'³⁰ The appearance of a shared world to all who dwell within it precisely requires that they are plural, differentiated, and separate, with different locations in and perspectives on that world that are the product of their social action. By communicating to one another their differing perspectives on the social world in which they dwell together, they collectively constitute an enlarged understanding of that world.

## Difference, Knowledge, and Objectivity

A key feature of the normative ideal of communicative democracy is that it facilitates the transformation of the desires and opinions of citizens from an initial partial, narrow, or self-regarding understanding

---

²⁹ Lisa Disch, *Hannah Arendt and the Limits of Philosophy* (Ithaca, NY: Cornell University Press, 1994), 80; compare Anna Yeatman, 'Justice and the Sovereign Self', in Anna Yeatman and Margaret Wilson (eds.), *Justice and Identity: Antipodean Practices* (Wellington: Bridget Williams Books, 1995). On an interpretation of the Arendtian public in terms of plurality, see Susan Bickford, *The Dissonance of Democracy* (Ithaca, NY: Cornell University Press, 1996), ch. 3.
³⁰ Hannah Arendt, *The Human Condition* (Chicago: University of Chicago Press, 1998) 52.

of issues and problems, to a more comprehensive understanding that takes the needs and interests of others more thoroughly into account. Processes of political communication ought and sometimes do move people from a merely subjective to a more objective way of looking at problems and solutions. The thinking of the participants in a public inclusive communicative process is enlarged: instead of understanding issues only from the point of view of my partial and parochial experience and interests, I move to a point of view that aims to make a judgement of justice that places my interests among others.

Modern thought has often conceptualized objectivity as achieved by transcending particularities of social position and experience, abstracting from them to construct a standpoint outside and above them that is general rather than particular. All the critics of a politics of difference whom I have cited appear to assume that a normatively objective concern for justice requires such bracketing or transcending of particular social location and adopting a 'view from nowhere'. There are at least two problems with such an interpretation of objectivity, especially when the inquiry involves assessment of social problems and rival proposals for solving them justly.

First, a monological method of bracketing or abstracting from the particularities of social position is notoriously unreliable. How can I and others be confident that I have not carried over assumptions and conclusions derived from my particular standpoint into the supposedly objective general standpoint? In making judgements about public or political action, how can I be sure that I have not given more weight to my own desires and interests than to the legitimate interests of others? Only the critical and differentiated perspectives of a plurality of others who discuss my claims and judgements can validate the objectivity of the latter.

Secondly, even if the previous problem were solved, in political communication our goal is not to arrive at some generalities, certainly not generalizations about social interaction or principles of justice. Instead, we are looking for just solutions to particular problems in a particular social context. The conclusions to political discussion and argument, that is, are particular judgements about what ought to be done. Appeals to principle have a place in such discussion, but they must be applied to particular situations in the context of particular social relationships. Thus participants in political discussion cannot transcend their particularity. If participants are to make objective judgements appropriate for their context, they must express their own particularity to others and learn of the particularity of those differently situated in the social world where they dwell together.

We thus need a different account of the distinction between a merely subjective or self-regarding point of view and an objective point of view. On this account, objectivity is an achievement of democratic communication that includes all differentiated social positions. Objectivity in political judgement, as I understand that term, does not consist in discovering some truth about politics or institutions independent of the awareness and action of social members. But it is also not simply some kind of sum of their differentiated viewpoints. An objective account of social relations and social problems, and an objective judgement of what policies and actions would address those problems, instead are accounts and judgements people construct for themselves from a critical, reflective, and persuasive interaction among their diverse experiences and opinion.

Hilary Putnam offers one such theory of objectivity. Interpreting Dewey's understanding of intelligence and democracy as a method of solving social problems, Putnam argues that objectivity is a product of inclusive democratic communication. Without such inclusive discussion, privileged social positions are able to make judgements and take actions that suit themselves and rationalizations for them that go unchallenged.[31]

Feminist epistemologists offer an account of objectivity as a product of what Donna Haraway calls 'situated knowledges'.[32] In socially differentiated societies, individuals have particular knowledge that arises from experience in their social positions, and those social positionings also influence the interests and assumptions they bring to inquiry.[33] All positionings are partial with respect to the inquiry. Where there are structural differences of privilege and disadvantage,

---

[31] See Hilary Putnam, 'A Reconsideration of Deweyan Democracy', *Southern California Law Review*, 63/6 (Sept. 1990), 1671–97; and 'Pragmatism and Moral Objectivity', in Martha Nussbaum and Jonathan Glover (eds.), *Women, Culture and Development* (Oxford: Oxford University Press, 1995); see also Linda Alcoff's comment on Putnam in the same volume; see also Cheryl Misak, 'Pragmatism, Truth, and the Worthwhile', University of Toronto; Mishak also connects objectivity, esp. about moral matters, to the enactment of democratic principles of openness and understanding perspectives and experiences of others.

[32] Donna Haraway, 'Situated Knowledges: The Science Question in Feminism and the Privilege of Partial Perspective', in *Simians, Cyborgs, and Women* (New York: Routledge, 1991).

[33] See Jennifer Hochschild, 'Where you Stand Depends on What you See: Connections among Values, Perceptions of Fact, and Prescriptions', in James Kuklinski (ed.), *Citizens and Politics: Perspectives from Political Psychology* (Cambridge: Cambridge University Press, 2000). Hochschild reviews survey results that show that people often misperceive social facts in similar ways according to social positions of class, race, gender, and the like, and also that people's opinions about priority issues and their correct perception of certain facts often correlate with their social group position.

and where these have conditioned the discourses of received knowledge, the explicit voicing of the plurality of positions and their confirming or criticizing one another is necessary for objectivity.[34]

## From Obstacle to Resource

Especially where there are structural relations of privilege and disadvantage, then, explicit inclusion and recognition of differentiated social positions provides experiential and critical resources for democratic communication that aims to promote justice. Inclusion of differentiated groups is important not only as a means of demonstrating equal respect and to ensure that all legitimate interests in the polity receive expression, though these are fundamental reasons for democratic inclusion. Inclusion has two additional functions. First, it motivates participants in political debate to transform their claims from mere expressions of self-regarding interest to appeals to justice. Secondly, it maximizes the social knowledge available to a democratic public, such that citizens are more likely to make just and wise decisions. I will elaborate each of these points.

Having to be accountable to people from diverse social positions with different needs, interests, and experience helps transform discourse from self-regard to appeals to justice. Because others are not likely to accept 'I want this' or 'This policy is in my interest' as reasons to accept a proposal, the requirement that discussion participants try to make their claims understandable and persuasive to others means they must frame the proposals in terms of justice. Appealing to justice here does not necessarily mean that the others agree with a person's or group's principle or judgements of what justice requires. It means only that they frame their assertions to the others in terms of fairness of

---

[34] See Sandra Harding, *Whose Science? Which Knowledge? Thinking from Women's Lives* (Ithaca, NY: Cornell University Press, 1991); Ismay Barwell, 'Towards a Defense of Objectivity', in Kathleen Lennon and Margaret Whitford (eds.), *Knowing the Difference: Feminist Perspectives in Epistemology* (London: Routledge, 1994). Patricia Hill Collins develops the idea that there are specific social knowledges arising from social structural location in her account of an Afrocentric feminist epistemology; see *Black Feminist Thought* (New York: Routledge, 1991), esp. chs. 10 and 11; Linda Martin Alcoff, *Real Knowing; New Versions of Coherence Theory* (Ithaca, NY: Cornell University Press, 1996), esp. ch. 3; Satya Mohanty has developed an account of social objectivity as a product of the interaction of ideas based in social locations. See Mohanty, 'The Epistemic Status of Cutlural Identity', *Cultural Critique*, 24 (Spring 1993), 41–80; Paula Moya has applied Mohanty's approach to the specific context of Latina feminism; see Moya, 'Postmodernism, "Realism" and the Politics of Identity: Cherrie Moraga and Chicana Feminism', in Chandra Talpade Mohant and M. Jacquie Alexander (eds.), *Feminist Genealogies, Colonial Legacies, Democratic Futures* (New York: Routledge, 1997).

rights that they claim take others' interests into account and which others *ought* therefore to accept. Contrary to what some theorists of deliberative democracy suggest, policy proposals need not be expressed in terms of a common interest, an interest all can share. Indeed, some claims of justice are not likely to express an interest all can share, because they are claims that actions should be taken to reduce the privilege some people are perceived to have. Many other claims or proposals will not directly confront privilege, but will be multiple expressions of need and preference among which a polity must sort out relative moral legitimacy and relative priority. To make such claims, social difference must be generally recognized.

Inclusion of and attention to socially differentiated positions in democratic discussion tends to correct biases and situate the partial perspective of participants in debate. Confrontation with different perspectives, interests, and cultural meanings teaches each the partiality of their own and reveals to them their own experience as perspectival. Listening to those differently situated from myself and my close associates teaches me how my situation looks to them, in what relation they think I stand to them. Such a contextualizing of perspective is especially important for groups that have power, authority, or privilege. Those in structurally superior positions not only take their experience, preferences, and opinions to be general, uncontroversial, ordinary, and even an expression of suffering or disadvantage, as we all do, but also have the power to represent these as general norms. Having to answer to others who speak from different, less privileged, perspectives on their social relations exposes their partiality and relative blindness.[35] By including multiple perspectives, and not simply two that might be in direct contention over an issue, we take a giant step towards enlarging thought. Where there are differences in interests, values, or judgements between members of two interdependent but differently positioned groups, the fact that both must be accountable to differently situated others further removed from those relations can motivate each to reflect on fairness to all.[36] Where such

[35] In the context of legal judgment and the responsibilities of judges, Martha Minow discusses the importance of multiple perspectives as a means of dislodging unstated assumptions about social relations and their consequences or assumptions about what is normal that are influenced by particular social positions; see *Making All the Difference* (Ithaca, NY: Cornell University Press, 1990), esp. ch. 11; compare Bohman *Public Deliberation* 102.

[36] Jodi Dean argues for a model of dialogic solidarity in which participants do not merely address one another but speak in the presence of a 'situated hypothetic third'. This appeal to the 'third' invokes the function of more distant third parties in motivating parties who either think they are allied or think they are in conflict to remember the interests and perspectives of those outside this relationship; in the above point I wish to emphasize the

exposure to the public judgement and criticism of multiply situated others does not lead them to shut down dialogue and instead leads some to try to force their preferences on policy, this process can lead to a better understanding of the requirements of justice.

By pointing out how the standpoint of those in less privileged positions can reveal otherwise unnoticed bias and partiality I do not mean to suggest, as have some standpoint theorists, that people in less advantaged social positions are 'epistemically privileged'. They too are liable to bias and self-regard in overstating the nature of situations, misunderstanding their causes, or laying blame in the wrong place. Some partialities and misunderstandings can best be exposed by discussion with differently situated others. Susan Wendell offers one example of how the experience and perspective of a structural social group can contribute to the social knowledge of everyone in order to promote more justice. When people with disabilities have the opportunity to express their perceptions of biases in the socially constructed environment or expectations of functions needed to perform tasks, then everyone learns how to see the social environment differently.[37]

Aiming to promote social justice through public action requires more than framing debate in terms that appeal to justice. It requires an objective understanding of the society, a comprehensive account of its relations and structured processes, its material locations and environmental conditions, a detailed knowledge of events and conditions in different places and positions, and the ability to predict the likely consequences of actions and policies. Only pooling the situated knowledge of all social positions can produce such social knowledge.

Among the sorts of situated knowledge that people in differentiated social positions have are: (1) an understanding of their position, and how it stands in relation to other positions; (2) a social map of other salient positions, how they are defined, and the relation in which they stand to this position; (3) a point of view on the history of the society; (4) an interpretation of how the relations and processes of the whole society operate, especially as they affect one's own position; (5) a position-specific experience and point of view on the natural and physical environment.

Norms of communicative democracy assume that differently situated individuals understand that they are nevertheless related in a

importance of the actual presence of thirds. Nevertheless, I see the point of Dean invoking a 'hypothetical' third as the position of the differend that may always be there but silenced and not included. See Jodi Dean, *Solidarity of Strangers* (Berkeley: University of California Press, 1994).

[37] Susan Wendell, *The Rejected Body* (New York: Routledge, 1996), 66–9.

world of interaction and internal effects that affects them all, but differently. If they aim to solve their collective problems, they must listen across their differences to understand how proposals and policies affect others differently situated. They learn what takes place in different social locations and how social processes appear to connect and conflict from different points of view. By internalizing such a mediated understanding, participants in democratic discussion and decision-making gain a wider picture of social processes structuring their own partial experience. Such an enlarged view better enables them to arrive at wise and just solutions to collective problems to the extent that they are committed to doing so.

Paying specific attention to differentiated social groups in democratic discussion and encouraging public expression of their situated knowledge thus often makes it more possible than it would otherwise be for people to transform conflict and disagreement into agreement. Speaking across differences in a context of public accountability often reduces mutual ignorance about one another's situations, or misunderstanding of one another's values, intentions, and perceptions, and gives everyone the enlarged thought necessary to come to more reasonable and fairer solutions to problems. Complete agreement is rare, of course, even when people act with a co-operative spirit, for contingent reasons: there isn't enough time, organizing discussion is too difficult, people lose concentration and become frustrated, and so on. Procedures of majority rule and compromise are thus often necessary, and do not violate commitments to democratic legitimacy as long as persons and groups have reason to believe that they have had opportunity to influence the outcome.

As I discussed in Chapter 1, however, some disagreement may be endemic on certain issues in the context of social structures differentiated by interdependent relations of privilege and disadvantage. Many contemporary political theorists conceptualize the sources of such deep disagreement in cultural differences or differences in basic world-view and value framework; fundamental disagreements of that sort certainly do surface in most societies over some issues. Such attention to cultural pluralism, however, has diverted attention from a more common source of deep disagreement: structural conflict of interest. A basis of many disagreements about wage, trade, or welfare policy within capitalist structural relations, for example, is neither ill will nor ignorance nor difference in cultural meaning, but the structural fact that, at least sometimes, wages or public services provided for workers implies profit forgone for firms. One can argue that some disagreements over reproductive policy, the care of children, and the proper relationship of workplace to family responsibility reflect the structural inequalities of gender. By including diverse social positions in political discussion, we may not bring about agreed-on solutions so much as reveal the structural conflicts of interest that would be obscured by discussion which successfully claimed that at bottom we have common interests. If in fact a society is structurally divided in this way, then deliberative processes ought to aim to reveal and confront such division, rather than exhort those who may have morally legitimate grievances to suppress them for the sake of some people's definition of a common good.

The claim that social difference provides a resource for democratic communication, then, does not necessarily imply that inclusion will make political communication easier, more efficient, or better able to arrive at agreement. On the contrary, in some situations greater inclusion may lead to greater complexity and difficulty in reaching decisions. This is an argument against attending to situated knowledge only if the political goal is to arrive at public decisions as quickly and with as little contest as possible. Public and private policy-makers often do have this goal, of course, but to reach it they often need to keep a process under tight and exclusive control. For many routine, trivial, or administrative decisions such a goal may not be inappropriate, though it can be called democratic only if the decisions are embedded in a wider and more contestable public policy discussion. A primary goal of democratic discussion and decision-making ought to be to promote justice in solving problems, however, and I have argued that this goal requires inclusion even if it creates complexity and reveals conflicts of interest that can only be resolved by changing structural relations.

The argument of this chapter fills out the meaning of inclusive democracy. Inclusion ought not to mean simply the formal and abstract equality of all members of the polity as citizens. It means explicitly acknowledging social differentiations and divisions and encouraging differently situated groups to give voice to their needs, interests, and perspectives on the society in ways that meet conditions of reasonableness and publicity. This thicker meaning of inclusion highlights the importance of valuing diverse models of communication in democratic discussion. Greeting, or public address, is a mode of communication in which members of a public recognize the plurality of groups and perspectives that constitute it. Narrative is an important means of conveying the situated knowledge of differently positioned people; without the thick description of needs and problems and consequences that concrete stories can provide, political judgements may rest on social understandings that are too abstract. Narrative is also a necessary means of relating both the history of socially differentiated groups and their perceptions of the history of the whole society in its relationships. Finally, open listening involves attending to diverse ways that people express themselves by idiom, tone, and image. Thus, as I argued in the previous chapter, rhetoric is an important means by which people situated in particular social positions can adjust their claims to be heard by those in differing social situations.

# CHAPTER 4

## Representation and Social Perspective

Few advocates of a deliberative or communicative model of democracy would assert that this model applies primarily to situations where people are present to one another on one occasion in the same place to face one another and speak directly. Both in theory and in practice, however, there is nevertheless a tendency to associate communicative democratic processes with face-to-face interaction. Whether they take the site of democratic discussion to be a legislative session or the meeting of a citizens' action group, advocates usually present the process of democratic communication as centred in some place where participants are present to one another.

Strong democracy certainly requires many occasions when public officials and citizens meet to discuss experiences and issues with each other. Theorizing democracy as a process of communication to arrive at decisions, however, has not sufficiently grappled with the need to conceptualize democracy as decentred in large-scale mass societies. In a complex polity of many millions democratic communication consists in fluid, overlapping, and diverging discussions and decisions, dispersed in both space and time. What are inclusive communicative relations in such flowing, decentred, mass politics?

In the context of complex mass politics, a frequently heard complaint of exclusion invokes norms of representation. People often claim that the social groups they find themselves in or with which they claim affinity are not properly represented in influential discussions and decision-making bodies, including legislatures, commissions, boards, task forces, media coverage of issues, and so on. Such claims recognize that in a large polity with many complex issues formal and informal representatives mediate the influence people have.

For these reasons many recent calls for greater political inclusion in democratic processes argue for measures that encourage more representation of under-represented groups, especially when those groups are minorities or subject to structural inequalities. Women's movement activists in many parts of the world, for example, claim that legislatures peopled mostly by men cannot be said properly to represent women. In response to such claims, some governments have enacted legislation designed to encourage more women legislators, usually requiring that party lists include a certain portion of women.[1] Women's agitation for similar provisions in their countries is increasing in many places without such provisions. Even where the law does not require it, many parties around the world have decided that their lists are not properly representative without certain numbers of women.

In the United States similar discussions take place about the specific representation of racial or ethnic minorities. Some districts have been drawn or voting processes adjusted to make the election of African Americans or Latinos more likely. Both the idea and practice of promoting specific representation of minorities are controversial, but the issue will not fade from the American public agenda. Many other countries of the world have or discuss schemes for specific social group representation, whether in the form of corporatist councils, reserved seats, party list rules, commissions, and so on.

Policies, proposals, and arguments for the special representation of groups, however, face many objections. One of these is particularly relevant to the issues treated in earlier chapters, because this objection presumes a commitment to attend to rather than submerge social difference. The idea of group representation, this objection claims, assumes that a group of women, or African Americans, or Maori, or Muslims, or Deaf people has some set of common attributes of interests which can be represented. But this is usually false. Differences of race and class cut across gender, differences of gender and ethnicity cut across religion, and so on. Members of a gender or racial group have life histories that make them very different people, with different interests and different ideological commitments. The unifying process required by group representation tries to freeze fluid relations into a unified identity, which can re-create oppressive exclusions.[2]

---

[1] For a good discussion of the politics of gender quotas in India, see Meena Dhanda, 'Justifications for Gender Quotas in Legislative Bodies: A Consideration of Identity and Representation', *Women's Philosophy Review*, 20 (Winter 1998–9), 44–62.

[2] For examples of works that make this sort of objection, see Anne Phillips, 'Democracy and Difference', in *Democracy and Difference* (University Park: Pennsylvania State University Press, 1993); Chantal Mouffe, 'Feminism, Citizenship and Politics', in *The Return of the Political* (London: Verso, 1993); Cathy J. Cohen, 'Straight Gay Politics: The Limits of an Ethnic Model of Inclusion', in Ian Shapiro and Will Kymlicka (eds.), *Ethnicity and Group Rights*, Nomos 29 (New York: New York University Press, 1997).

This objection to policies and arguments for special representation of groups which tend otherwise to be excluded from discussion and decision-making coheres with the critique of a logic of identity referred to in Chapter 3. On one interpretation of this critique, no single representative could speak for any group, because there are too many intersecting relationships among individuals. Yet calls for special representation of marginalized groups do not seem to be muted by these critiques, because in the context of practical affairs many people believe that such measures are the best way to gain voice for many wrongly excluded issues, analyses, and positions.

The chapter aims to clarify the meaning of such group representation, and to provide further arguments for such differentiated representative practices as an important enactment of political inclusion. Doubts about such practices derive in part from misunderstandings about the nature of representation more generally. Implicitly much discourse about representation assumes that the person who represents stands in some relation of substitution or identity with the many represented, that he or she is present for them in their absence. Against such an image of representation as substitution or identification I conceptualize representation as a *differentiated relationship* among political actors engaged in a process extending over space and time. Considering the temporality and mediated spatiality of the process of representation decentres the concept, revealing both political opportunities and dangers.

After theorizing representation in general terms, I return to the question of group representation. Many objections to practices of the specific representation of structurally disadvantaged groups derive from the assumption that groups do not have one set of common interests or opinions. Building on the discussion of structural positioning and situated knowledge in Chapter 3, I argue that being similarly positioned in the social field generates a social *perspective* the inclusion of which in public discussion processes of group representation can facilitate. I conceptualize a distinction between *interests*, *opinions*, and *perspectives* and the role of each in political participation. After making arguments for the special representation of otherwise excluded or marginalized social perspectives, I briefly evaluate several institutional means for enacting such group representation.

Before we turn to this chapter's general account of the meaning of representation and arguments for group representation, however, I review reasons that some democratic theorists have for saying that representation is incompatible with authentic democracy. The first task of the chapter is to rebut those reasons, and to explain why representation need not undermine inclusive participation. Indeed, in large-scale mass society, representation and participation mutually require each other for politics to be deeply democratic.

## 1. Participation and Representation

Radical democrats frequently distrust institutions of political representation. They often present representation as violating the values of democracy themselves. Representation, they suggest, 'alienates political will at the cost of genuine self-government', 'impairs the community's ability to function as a regulating instrument of justice', and 'precludes the evolution of a participating public in which the idea of justice might take root.'[3]

Without question a strong democracy should have institutions of direct democracy such as referendum as part of its procedural repertoire. As society is more deeply democratic, moreover, the more it has state-sponsored and civic fora for policy discussion at least some of which ought procedurally to influence authoritative decisions. The anti-representation position, however, refuses to face complex realities of democratic process, and wrongly opposes representation to participation.

Representation is necessary because the web of modern social life often ties the action of some people and institutions in one place to consequences in many other places and institutions. No person can be present at all the decisions or in all the decision-making bodies whose actions affect her life, because they are so many and so dispersed. Though her aspirations are often disappointed, she hopes that others will think about situations like hers and represent them to the issue forum.[4]

One might object that this argument presupposes a large-scale society and polity which a preference for direct democracy rejects. A democracy without representation must consist of small, decentralized, self-sufficient units. Robert Dahl gives a compelling set of arguments, however, that even this vision of decentralized direct

---

[3] Benjamin Barber, *Strong Democracy* (Berkeley: University of California Press, 1984), 145–6. Compare Paul Hirst, *Representative Democracy and its Limits* (Oxford: Polity Press, 1990); John Dryzek, *Discursive Democracy* (Cambridge: Cambridge University Press, 1990), 42–3.

[4] Linda Alcoff argues that the position that a person can and should speak only for herself is an abrogation of responsibility. It ignores the fact that people's lives are affected by the congruence of many distant actions, and that the participation of people in institutions here in turn affects others. See 'The Problem of Speaking for Others', *Cultural Critique*, 20 (Winter 1991), 5–32.

democracy cannot avoid representation. The equal participation of everyone in political deliberation, he argues, can occur only in small committees. Even in assemblies of a few hundred people most people will be more passive participants who listen to a few people speak for a few positions, then think and vote. Beyond the small committee, that is, features of time and interaction produce *de facto* representation. But such *de facto* representation is arbitrary; in fact direct democracies often cede political power to arrogant loudmouths whom no one chose to represent them. Thus even in relatively small units of political de-cision-making like neighbourhoods or workplaces, political equality may best be served by institutions of formal representation, because the rules concerning who is authorized to speak for whom are public and there are some norms of accountability. Dahl also argues, I think plausibly, that in the normal course of social life small decentralized political units are likely to grow larger by means of either conquest or coalition. As soon as scale returns, then, representation also returns.[5]

Critics of representative democracy might object that this enhanced participation, to the degree that it exists, comes at the expense of cit-izen participation in the deliberative process. Citizens vote for their representatives, and then there is no further need for them. The insti-tutions and culture of some representative democracies do indeed dis-courage citizens from participating in political discussion and decision-making. One can argue, however, that if they do, so they are not properly representative, because under such circumstances repre-sentatives have only a very weak relation to their constituents. Under normative ideals of communicative democracy, representative institu-tions do not stand opposed to citizen participation, but require such participation to function well.[6] Below I develop an account of repre-sentation as a process of anticipation and recollection flowing between representative and constituents' participation in activities of author-ization and accountability.

## 2. Representation as Relationship

The claim that authentic democracy is not compatible with represen-tation implicitly relies on the logic of identity I referred to in Chapter

---

[5] Robert Dahl, *Democracy and its Critics* (New Haven: Yale University Press, 1989), ch. 16.

[6] See David Plotke, 'Representation is Democracy', *Constellations*, 4/1 (Apr. 1997), 19–34. See also Philip Green, *Retrieving Democracy* (Totowa, NJ: Rowman & Allenheld, 1985), ch. 9.

3, or what Jacques Derrida calls a metaphysics of presence.[7] It imagines an ideal democratic decision-making situation as one in which the citizens are *co-present*. Like at a town meeting, in this image of authentic democracy citizens meet in one place and make their decisions on one occasion.

This image of authentic democracy also assumes an *identity* of the rulers and the ruled. The critic rejects representation because its institutions separate power from the people; those who make the rules are not identical with all those who are obliged to follow them. Once again, Benjamin Barber's words are particularly strong: 'Men and women who are not directly responsible through common deliberation, common decision, and common action for the policies that determine their common lives are not really free at all.'[8]

On this image of democracy, representatives could only properly express the 'will of the people' if they are *present for* their constituents, and act as they would act. On this image, the representative *substitutes* for the constituents, stands for them in a relation of identity. Critics of representation rightly note that it is not possible for one person to be present in place of many, to speak and act as they would if they were present. It is impossible to find the essential attributes of constituents, the single common good that transcends the diversity of their interests, experiences, and opinions. The objection that some people make to the notion of specific representation for marginalized gender or ethnic groups in fact can be extended to all representation. Political representatives usually have a large constituency that is diverse in its interests, backgrounds, experiences, and beliefs. It is perhaps even more difficult to imagine a shared will for the residents of a metropolitan legislative district than for members of an ethnic group.

If we accept the argument that representation is necessary, but we also accept an image of democratic decision-making as requiring a co-presence of citizens, and that representation is legitimate only if in some way the representative is identical with the constituency, then we have a paradox: representation is necessary but impossible. There is a way out of this paradox, which involves conceptualizing representation outside a logic of identity. Taking seriously the decentred nature of large-scale mass democracy entails discarding images of the co-presence of citizens or that representatives must be present for citizens, and instead conceiving democratic discussion and decision-making as mediated through and dispersed over space and time.

[7] Jacques Derrida, *On Grammatology* (Baltimore: Johns Hopkins University Press, 1973).
[8] Barber, *Strong Democracy*, 146.

Rather than a relation of identity or substitution, political representation should be thought of as a process involving a mediated relation of constituents to one another and to a representative.

I rely on the Derridian concept of *différance* to formulate another account of representation. Where the metaphysics of presence generates polarities because it aims to reduce the many to one identity, thinking of entities in terms of *différance* leaves them in their plurality without requiring their collection into a common identity. Things take their being and signs take their meaning from their place in a process of differentiated relationships. Things are similar without being identical, and different without being contrary, depending on the point of reference and the moment in a process. As emphasizing process and relationship more than substance, *différance* foregrounds intervals of space and time. Oppositions such as substance–accident, cause–effect, presence–absence, reality–sign locate authentic being in an origin, an always earlier time for which the present process is a derivative copy. Derrida proposes to rethink such oppositions in terms of the idea of the *trace*, a movement of temporalization that carries past and future with it. The moment in the conversation, this moment in the being of the mountain, and, as we shall see, this moment in the representative relationship each carry traces of the history of relationships that produced it, and its current tendencies anticipate future relationships.[9]

Conceptualizing representation in terms of *différance* means acknowledging and affirming that there is a difference, a separation, between the representative and the constituents. Of course, no person can stand for and speak as a plurality of other persons. The representative function of *speaking for* should not be confused with an identifying requirement that the representative *speak as* the constituents would, to try to be present for them in their absence. It is no criticism of the representative that he or she is separate and distinct from the constituents. At the same time, however, conceiving representation under the idea of *différance* means describing a relationship between constituents and the representative, and among constituents, where the temporality of past and anticipated future leave their traces in the actions of each.

Conceiving representation as a differentiated relationship among plural actors dissolves the paradox of how one person can stand for the experience and opinions of many. There is no single will of the people that can be represented. Because the constituency is internally

---

[9] I derive my account of *différance* primarily from Derrida's essay of that title in *Speech and Phenomena and Other Essays: Husserl's Theory of Signs* (Evanston, Ill.: Northwestern University Press, 1973).

differentiated, the representative does not stand for or refer to an essential opinion or interest shared by all the constituents which she should describe and advocate.[10]

Rather than construe the normative meaning of representation as properly standing for the constituents, we should evaluate the process of representation according to the character of the relationship between the representative and the constituents. The representative will inevitably be separate from the constituents, but should also be *connected* to them in determinate ways. Constituents should also be connected to one another. Representation systems sometimes fail to be sufficiently democratic not because the representatives fail to stand for the will of the constituents, but because they have lost connection with them. In modern mass democracies it is indeed easy to sever relations between representatives and constituents, and difficult to maintain them.

## 3. Anticipating Authorization and Accountability

In her classic work on representation Hanna Pitkin analyses several meanings that attach to the term. Some writers understand what constitutes a representative as the fact that he or she is *authorized* to act by a set of official institutions that also bind together the represented group. Others focus on demands that a legitimate representative must be *accountable* to those whom he or she represents; otherwise the agent who claims to represent is simply acting on his or her own.

Pitkin discusses the debate about whether a representative is properly a *delegate* who carries the mandate of a constituency which he or she advocates, or rather ought to act as a *trustee* who exercises independent judgement about the right thing to do under these political circumstances. Pitkin argues that the debate is misconstrued. Both sides are correct in their way; the specific function of legitimate representation consists in exercising independent judgement but in knowledge and anticipation of what constituents want.

Conceptualizing political representation also raises the question of whether representative bodies ought to mirror the population represented, and whether the interests represented in such bodies should be construed as objective, or simply as a product of the subjective perceptions and preferences of constituencies. Pitkin concludes that all

[10] Derrida himself points towards a theorizing of political representation under the idea of *différance*. See 'Sending: On Representation', trans. Peter Dews and Mary Dews, *Social Research*, 49 (Summer 1982), 294–326.

these concepts and issues are aspects of the complex relationship called representation, and that both theory and practice require understanding that the agency of the representative ought to stay within the several limits bounded by these diverse issues.[11]

The account of political representation I give below owes much to Pitkin's. I follow her in theorizing representation as involving both authorization and accountability, and agree with her that the dichotomy of delegate–trustee is a false polarization. Pitkin asserts that all of these apparently divergent conceptualizations of representation are in fact diverse aspects of a complex set of institutions and practices. She does not fully theorize how to bring them together, however. I suggest that emphasizing representation as a process differentiated and mediated in space and time provides a way to think these different aspects together.

Thinking of representation in terms of *différance* rather than identity means taking its temporality seriously. Representation is a process that takes place over time, and has distinct moments or aspects, related to but different from one another. Representation consists in a mediated relationship, both among members of a constituency, between the constituency and the representative, and between representatives in a decision-making body. As a deferring relationship between constituents and their agents, representation moves between moments of authorization and accountability. Representation is a cycle of anticipation and recollection between constituents and representative, in which discourse and action at each moment ought to bear *traces* of the others.

Thus the account proposed here is primarily normative. I aim to identify ideals of well-functioning representation, which promotes democratic legitimacy and political inclusion. In accord with a concept of democracy as a matter of degree, good representation itself is a matter of degree. In the next section I suggest one measure of good representation as the number of aspects or modes through which people are represented. Here I consider the extent of connection between constituents and representative as a measure of the degree of representation. Conceptualized as difference, representation necessarily involves distinction and separation between representatives and constituents. Representation is a differentiated relationship between constituents and representative where disconnection is always a possibility, and connection maintained over time through anticipation and recollection in moments of authorization and accountability. A representative

[11] Hanna Pitkin, *The Concept of Representation* (Berkeley: University of California Press, 1971).

process is worse, then, to the extent that the separation tends towards severance, and better to the extent that it establishes and renews connection between constituents and representative, and among members of the constituency.

Pitkin agrees that authorization is an important sign of representation. One who represents others in an official institutionalized sense must be authorized to speak for and perhaps bind them. Elections are the most common and obvious means of authorizing representations, but other forms of delegate selection to discussion and decision-making bodies sometimes obtain. The delegate model of the representative's responsibility is one interpretation of authorization. On this interpretation, a constituency is an already formed cohesive group with a single will that can be conveyed to the representative as a mandate. Such an image relies on an identity interpretation, where the many people represented are identical with one another in at least the respect that they agree on this mandate, which the delegate can carry to a representative body untransformed.[12]

In fact, however, in most situations the specific constituency exists at best potentially; the representative institutions and the process of authorization themselves call its members into action.[13] Anticipating the moment when representatives will claim to act at their behest and on their behalf, individuals in the defined constituency go looking for each other. They organize and discuss the issues that are important to them, and call on candidates to respond to their interests. While there is usually a moment when they authorize representatives, in doing so the constituency rarely brings itself to affirm a common will. The constituency is usually too large, or the varying activities of its members are too dispersed, or its definition and borders too vague, to expect a time when the constituency at one moment arrives at a collective will. Instead, in a well-functioning process a public sphere of discussion sets an issue agenda and the main terms of dispute or struggle. For parliamentary processes to be effective as representative, and not merely as a stage on which élites perform according to their own script, the

---

[12] Nancy Schwartz criticizes what she calls a 'transmission belt' theory of representation which has this form. On this image, the individuals represented need do nothing but express their wills, and the representative functions as a mediator. Neither constituents nor representative are active, and the political judgements of neither are transformed in the representative process. See Schwartz, *The Blue Guitar: Political Representation and Community* (Chicago: University of Chicago Press, 1988).

[13] Melissa Williams discusses this fact of the mutual constitution of constituency and representative. See *Voice, Trust and Memory: Marginalized Groups and the Failure of Liberal Representation* (Princeton: Princeton University Press, 1998), 203–5.

democratic process of the authorization of representatives should be both participatory and inclusively deliberative.

As Pitkin maintains, conceptualizing the representative either purely as a delegate with a clear mandate, or entirely as a trustee who acts only according to his or her own lights, dissolves the specific meaning of representative activity. Well-functioning representation stands between and incorporates both. The representative's responsibility is not simply to express a mandate, but to participate in discussion and debate with other representatives, listen to their questions, appeals, stories, and arguments, and with them to try to arrive at wise and just decisions. Different groups and segments of the polity best talk across their difference through representatives who meet together and listen to one another, open to the possibility of changing their positions.

During these sustained moments of independent action and judgement, however, the representative ought to recollect the discussion process that led to his authorization and anticipate a moment of being accountable to those he claims to represent. The representative is authorized to act, but his judgement is always in question. Whether he acted on authority is a question deferred to a later time, when he will be held accountable. The representative acts on his or her own, but in anticipation of having to give an account to those he or she represents. While there is no authorized mandate for many decisions, representation is stronger when it bears the traces of the discussion that led to authorization or in other ways persuasively justifies itself in a public accounting.

In the process of calling representatives to account for what they have decided, citizens continue to form themselves into a constituency, and they engage anew in debate and struggle over the wisdom and implications of policy decisions. Such renewed opinion formation may bear the traces of the process of authorization, but it also has new elements, because previously the constituents did not know just how issues would be formulated in the representative body, and what expression, appeals, and arguments would be offered there. The responsibility of the representative is not simply to tell citizens how she has enacted a mandate they authorized or served their interests, but as much to persuade them of the rightness of her judgement.[14]

---

[14] See Amy Gutmann and Dennis Thompson, *Democracy and Disagreement* (Cambridge, Mass.: Harvard University Press, 1996), ch. 4. Accountability, including the accountability of representatives to constituents, is one of the three procedural principles of deliberative democracy for Gutmann and Thompson. They somewhat emphasize the representative's giving his or her reasons for doing as he or she did, it seems to me, at the expense of articulation of the reasons they have for disagreeing.

In most actually existing democracies, the moment of accountability is weaker than the moment of authorization. For many systems of representation, the only form of being held to account is re-authorization by means of re-election. The cycle that returns to authorization is indeed important for motivating accountability. Strong communicative democracy, however, also requires some processes and procedures where constituents call representatives to account over and above re-authorizing them. As with authorization, accountability should occur both through official institutions and in the public life of independent civic association. All existing representative democracies could be improved by additional procedures and fora through which citizens discuss with one another and with representatives their evaluation of policies representatives have supported. Official means of accountability distinct from election campaigns can include civic review boards, implementation studies, and periodic official participatory hearings following the policy-making process. Public spheres of civil society can further accountability by means of independent questioning, praise, criticism, and judgement.

The major normative problem of representation is the threat of disconnection between the one representative and the many he or she represents. When representatives become too separated, constituents lose the sense that they have influence over policy-making, become disaffected, and withdraw their participation. Establishing and maintaining legitimate and inclusive processes of representation calls up responsibilities for both officials and citizens. Citizens must be willing and able to mobilize one another actively to participate in processes of both authorizing and holding to account. Representatives should listen to these public discussions and diverse claims, stay connected to constituents, and be able to convey reasons for their actions and judgements in terms that recollect their discussions. Such mobilization, listening, and connectedness can be either facilitated or impeded by the design of representative institutions.

Thus I can here cash in on the claim made earlier that representation and participation are not alternatives in an inclusive communicative democracy, but require each. Institutions of representation help organize political discussion and decision-making, introducing procedures and a reasonable division of labour. Thereby citizens have objectives around which they can organize with one another and participate in anticipatory and retrospective discussion, criticism, and evaluation. Without such citizen participation, the connection between the representative and constituents is most liable to be broken, turning the representative into an élite ruler. For their part, representatives should respond to such participatory process. Public spheres of civil society, which I will discuss in Chapter 5, serve as important arenas for citizen participation that help maintain these connections.

## 4. Modes of Representation

The representative should not be thought of as a substitute for those he or she represents, I have suggested, nor should we assume that the representative can or should express and enact some united will of the constituency. The representative can stand for neither the identity of any other person nor the collective identity of a constituency. There is an inevitable difference and separation between the representative and constituents, which always puts in question the manner and degree to which constituents participate in the process that produces policy outcomes. Yet representation is both necessary and desirable in modern politics. Rather than devaluing representation as such, participatory and radical democrats should evaluate the degree to which processes of authorization and accountability exist, are independent, and activate the constituency-inclusive participatory public opinion.

Another measure of the degrees of democracy, I suggest, is whether people are connected through relationships of authorization and accountability to a plurality of representatives who relate to different aspects of their lives. The assumption that representatives should in some fashion be identical to constituents implicitly carries the impossible requirement that a person is represented only if everything about her potentially has a voice in the political process. Since the representative is necessarily different from the constituents, a democracy is better or worse according to how well those differentiated positions are connected. Democracy can also be strengthened by pluralizing the modes and sites of representation. Systems of political representation cannot make individuals present in their individuality, but rather should represent *aspects* of a person's life experience, identity, beliefs, or activity where she or he has affinity with others. Potentially there are many such aspects or affinity groups. I propose to distinguish here three general modes through which a person can be represented: according to interest, opinion, and perspective. Within a particular political context, a person may be represented in several ways within each of these modes. Explication of what it means to represent perspective in particular provides arguments for the special representation of oppressed or disadvantaged social groups while avoiding the problem of attributing to all members of those groups common opinions or interests.

What do I mean when I say that I feel represented in the political process? There are many possible answers to this question, but three stand out for me as important. First, I feel represented when someone is looking after the interests I take as mine and share with some others. Secondly, it is important to me that the principles, values, and priorities that I think should guide political decisions are voiced in discussion. Finally, I feel represented when at least some of those discussing and voting on policies understand and express the kind of social experience I have because of my social group position and the history of social group relations. I will discuss interest and opinion only briefly, because these have been much discussed in political theory. I will focus more attention on representing perspectives because this idea is less familiar.

*Interest.* I define interest as what affects or is important to the life prospects of individuals, or the goals of organizations. An agent, whether individual or collective, has an interest in whatever is necessary or desirable in order to realize the ends the agent has set. These include both material resources and the ability to exercise capacities—e.g. for cultural expression, political influence, economic decision-making power, and so on. I define interest here as self-referring, and as different from ideas, principles, and values. The latter may help define the ends a person sets for herself, where the interest defines the means for achieving those ends.

Interests frequently conflict, not only between agents, but also in the action of a single agent. Where agents need resources to accomplish a variety of ends, they are likely to find some of the resources they need to be relatively scarce. Sometimes the means one agent needs to pursue a certain end implies directly impeding another agent's ability to get what he needs to pursue his ends. It is important to note, however, that interests do not necessarily conflict. The pursuit of ends in society and the setting of political frameworks to facilitate that pursuit need not necessarily be structured as a zero-sum relationship among agents.

The representation of interest is familiar in political practice, and there exists more theory of interest representation perhaps than any other kind. I do not here wish to review the huge literature on interest groups and the means by which they can achieve political influence. I only note that it is a part of the free associative process of communicative democracy that people have the freedom to press politically for policies that will serve their interest and to organize together with others with similar interests in order to gain political influence.

*Opinions.* I define opinions as the principles, values, and priorities held by a person as these bear on and condition his or her judgement about what policies should be pursued and ends sought. This is the primary sphere of what Anne Phillips refers to as the 'politics of ideas',[15] on which much contemporary discussion of pluralism focuses. Rawls's recent discussion of the principles and problems of political liberalism, for example, concentrates on the fact of plural ideas and belief systems in modern societies, how these legitimately influence political life, and how people with differing beliefs and opinions can maintain a working polity.[16] By opinion, I mean any judgement or belief about how things are or ought to be, and the political judgements that follow from these judgements or beliefs. Opinions may be religious, or derive from religious reasons, or they may be culturally based in a world-view or history of social practices. They may be based in disciplinary or knowledge systems, as might be political opinions derived from certain premisses of neo-classical economics, or based in a set of normative principles such as libertarianism or radical ecology. While I doubt that most people's opinions on public matters all derive from a single 'comprehensive doctrine', I do assume that most people make judgements about particular social and political issues with the guidance of some values, priorities, or principles that they apply more broadly than that case, if not to all cases. Opinions are certainly contestable, and often some can be shown to be more well founded than others. A communicative democracy, however, requires the free expression and challenging of opinions, and a wide representation of opinions in discussions leading to policy decisions.

Political parties are the most common vehicle for the representation of opinions. Parties often put forward programmes that less express the interests of a particular constituency, and more organize the political issues of the day according to principles, values, and priorities the party claims generally to stand for. Smaller or more specialized associations, however, can and often do form to represent opinions in public life and influence public policy. Traditionally interest group theory has treated such associations as another kind of interest group, and for most purposes this is a harmless conflation. I think it important to distinguish, however, in general between kinds of political association

[15] Anne Phillips, *The Politics of Presence* (Oxford: Oxford University Press, 1995).

[16] John Rawls, *Political Liberalism* (New York: Columbia University Press, 1993). With the term 'opinion', however, I do not necessarily intend something so all-encompassing and fundamental as what Rawls calls 'comprehensive doctrine', partly because I doubt that most people in modern societies hold or have most or all of their moral and political judgements guided by a single comprehensive doctrine. See Iris Marion Young, 'Rawls's *Political Liberalism*', *Journal of Political Philosophy*, 3/2 (June 1995), 181–90.

motivated by an instrumentalist interest, on the one hand, and kinds of association motivated by commitment to beliefs and values, on the other. Whereas the former sort of motivation is selfish, even if selfish for a group, the latter often takes itself to be impartial or even altruistic.

*Perspective.* In Chapter 3 I argued against the claim that structural social groups should be thought of in a substantial logic that would define them according to a set of common attributes all their members share and that constitute the identities of those members. Social group differentiation should be understood with a more relational logic, I argued, and individuals should be understood as positioned in social group structures rather than having their identity determined by them. Contrary to those who find that group-differentiated politics only create division and conflict, I argued that group differentiation offers resources to a communicative democratic public that aims to do justice, because differently positioned people have different experience, history, and social knowledge derived from that positioning. I call this social *perspective*.

Because of their social locations, people are attuned to particular kinds of social meanings and relationships to which others are less attuned. Sometimes others are not positioned to be aware of them at all. From their social locations people have differentiated knowledge of social events and their consequences. Because their social locations arise partly from the constructions that others have of them, as well as constructions which they have of others in different locations, people in different locations may interpret the meaning of actions, events, rules, and structures differently. Structural social positions thus produce particular location-relative experience and a specific knowledge of social processes and consequences. Each differentiated group position has a particular experience or point of view on social processes precisely because each is part of and has helped produce the patterned processes. Especially in so far as people are situated on different sides of relations of structural inequality, they understand those relations and their consequences differently.

Following the logic of the metaphor of group differentiation as arising from differing positions in social fields, the idea of social perspective suggests that agents who are 'close' in the social field have a similar point of view on the field and the occurrences within it, while those who are socially distant are more likely to see things differently. While different, these social perspectives may not be incompatible. Each social perspective is particular and partial with respect to the whole social field, and from each perspective some aspects of the reality of social processes are more visible than others.

Thus a social perspective does not contain a determinate specific content. In this respect perspective is different from interest or opinion. Social perspective consists in a set of questions, kinds of experience, and assumptions with which reasoning begins, rather than the conclusions drawn. Critiques of essentialism rightly show that those said to belong to the same social group often have different and even conflicting interests and opinions. People who have a similar perspective on social processes and issues—on the norms of heterosexual interaction, for example—nevertheless often have different interests or opinions, because they reason differently from what they experience, or have different goals and projects.

Perspective is a way of looking at social processes without determining what one sees. Thus two people may share a social perspective and still experience their positionality differently because they are attending to different elements of the society. Sharing a perspective, however, gives each an affinity with the other's way of describing what he experiences, an affinity that those differently situated do not experience. This lesser affinity does not imply that those differently positioned cannot understand a description of an element of social reality from another social perspective, only that it takes more work to understand the expression of different social perspectives than those one shares.[17]

Social perspective is the point of view group members have on social processes because of their position in them. Perspectives may be lived in a more or less self-conscious way. The cultural experiences of distinct peoples or religious groups, as well as groups responding to a history of grievance or structural oppression, often offer refined interpretations of their own situation and their relations to others. Perspective may appear in story and song, human and word play, as well as in more assertive and analytical forms of expression. Let me give an example.

[17] A number of political theorists have used a similar idea of social perspective to describe socially situated ways of looking at issues and others. See Martha Minow, *Making All the Difference* (Ithaca, NY: Cornell University Press, 1990), 60–70. Melissa Williams appeals to an idea of social perspective in her arguments for group representation. Her notion of the 'voice' model of representation most resonates with the idea of social perspective; see *Voice, Trust and Memory*, esp. ch. 4. Thomas Christiano also argues that differing social groups often have differing points of view on social and political issues that all benefit from being voiced; see Christiano, *The Rule of the Many* (Boulder, Colo.: Westview Press, 1996), 189–90; Kristin Renwick Monroe and Lina Hadda Kreidi develop a somewhat different but similarly functioning idea of social perspective to theorize the social psychology of the distinctive group of Islamic fundamentalists in Western predominantly secular societies; see Monroe and Kreidi, 'The Perspective of Islamic Fundamentalists and the Limits of Rational Choice Theory', *Political Psychology*, 18/1 (1997), 19–43.

For more than fifty years the *Pittsburgh Courier* has been an important newspaper for African Americans in the city of Pittsburgh and for many of those years in other parts of the United States as well. I think that this newspaper illustrates well the difference between perspective, on the one hand, and interest and opinion, on the other. In the pages of this newspaper each week appear reports of many events and controversies that exhibit the plurality of interests, not all of them compatible, that African Americans in Pittsburgh and elsewhere have. On the opinion pages, moreover, appear editorials that cover the range from right-wing libertarianism to left-wing socialism, from economic separatism to liberal integrationism. Despite this variety of interests and opinions, it is not difficult to identify how the *Pittsburgh Courier* nevertheless speaks an African American perspective. Most of the events discussed involve African Americans as the major actors, and take place at sites and within institutions which are majority African American or otherwise specifically associated with African Americans. When the paper discusses local or national events not specifically identified with African Americans, the stories usually ask questions or give emphases that are particularly informed by issues and experiences more specific to African Americans.[18]

One might object that the idea of an African American perspective, or a female gendered perspective, is just as open to criticism as the idea of a single group interest or opinion. Isn't it just as inappropriately reductive to talk about *one* American Indian perspective as one American Indian interest? To be sure, each person has his or her own irreducible history which gives him or her unique social knowledge and perspective. We must avoid, however, the sort of individualism that would conclude from this fact that any talk of structured social positions and group-defined social location is wrong, incoherent, or useless. It makes sense to say that non-professional working-class people have predictable vulnerabilities and opportunities because of their position in the occupational structure. The idea of perspective is meant to capture

[18] Lynn Sanders appeals to the idea of social perspective in the context of democratic communication, particularly the differing perspectives expressed by Blacks and whites in the United States; 'Against Deliberation', *Political Theory*, 25/3 (June 1997), 347–76. With Donald Kinder, Sanders has documented such differing perspectives of these structurally differentiated groups in their understandings of American politics; see Sanders and Kinder, *Divided by Color: Racial Politics and Democratic Ideals* (Chicago: University of Chicago Press, 1996). Jennifer Hochschild also documents through synthesis of many empirical studies that African Americans and whites have rather different understandings of many aspects of American society, one another, and the opportunities it offers; see Hochschild, *Facing up to the American Dream: Race, Class, and the Soul of the Nation* (Princeton: Princeton University Press, 1995). Hochschild also documents difference of *class* perspective within each racial group on opportunity and social problems.

that sensibility of group-positioned experience without specifying unified content to what the perceptive sees. The social positioning produced by relation to other structural positions and by the social
processes that issue in unintended consequences only provide a background and perspective in terms of which particular social events and
issues are interpreted; they do not make the interpretation. So we can
well find different persons with a similar social perspective giving different interpretations of an issue. Perspective is an approach to looking
at social events, which conditions but does not determine what one sees.

Suppose we accept this claim that individuals positioned in similar
ways in the social field have a similar group perspective on that society. What does this imply for individuals, who are positioned in terms
of many group-differentiated relations? Since individuals are multiply
positioned in complexly structured societies, individuals interpret the
society from a multiplicity of social group perspectives. Some of these
may intersect to constitute a distinctive hybrid perspective, a Black
woman's perspective, perhaps, or a working-class youth perspective.
But individuals may also move around the social perspectives available
to them depending on the people with whom they interact or the
aspect of social reality to which they attend. The multiple perspectives
from which persons may see society may reinforce and enhance one
another, or it may be impossible to take one without obscuring
another, as in a duck-rabbit figure. The perspectives available to a person may be incommensurable, producing ambiguity or confusion in
the person's experience and understanding of social life; or their multiplicity may help the person form a composite picture of social
processes. However they are experienced, the availability of multiple
perspectives provides everyone with the resources to take a distance
on any one of them, and to communicate in certain ways with people
with whom one does not share perspectives in others.

Melissa Williams objects to an earlier statement of the distinction
between interests, opinions, and perspectives that perspectives and
interests cannot be neatly separated. 'My understanding of the relationships between perspectives and interests is rather that a group's
shared perspective helps to define the boundaries within which different interpretations of interest are possible.'[19] It is useful to regard
social perspective as helping to set a framework of interpretation.
Doing so may indeed help individuals reason through what they find
to be in their interests. Nevertheless, theorizing in this regard ought to

[19] Williams, *Voice, Trust and Memory*, 171. She is commenting on an earlier essay of
mine, 'Deferring Group Representation', in Ian Shapiro and Will Kymlicka (eds.),
*Ethnicity and Group Rights*, Nomos 29 (New York: New York University Press, 1997).

recognize that sometimes individuals similarly positioned in social structures find that there are many interests they do not share. Representing an interest or an opinion usually entails promoting certain specific outcomes in the decision-making process. Representing a perspective, on the other hand, usually means promoting certain starting-points for discussion. From a particular social perspective a representative asks certain kinds of questions, reports certain kinds of experience, recalls a particular line of narrative history, or expresses a certain way of regarding the positions of others. These importantly contribute to the inclusion of different people in the decision-making process and nurture attention to possible effects of proposed policies on different groups. Expressing perspective, however, does not usually mean drawing a conclusion about outcomes.

Let me give another example to illustrate the expression of perspective. Several years ago US Senator Robert Packwood was accused of sexual harassment of several of his aides. After the story broke, many in the Senate seemed disinclined to bring the matter to hearing for potential ethics sanction. Packwood had a distinguished record serving in the Senate, and many of his colleagues took the attitude that this tawdry accusation was not worth taking a Senate committee's time. In response nearly all the women legislators in both the House of Representatives and the Senate held a joint press conference to demand that the Senate hold hearings seriously to consider the charges against Packwood. These women did not agree on political values and they had many divergent interests; they did not agree in their opinions of whether Packwood was guilty of harassment. Their purpose was to influence the Senate's agenda, and in doing so they expressed a similar perspective on the meaning and gravity of accusations of sexual harassment, a perspective that many of the men seemed not to understand, at least at first.

Interests, opinions, and perspectives, then, are three important aspects of persons that can be represented. I do not claim that these three aspects exhaust the ways people can be represented. There may well be other possible modes of representation, but I find these three particularly salient in the way we talk about representation in contemporary politics, and in answering the conceptual and practical problems posed for group representation. None of these aspects reduce to the identity of either a person or a group, but each is an aspect of the person. None of these aspects of persons, moreover, is reducible to the others. They are logically independent in the sense that from a general social perspective one can immediately infer a set of neither interests nor opinions.

Unlike interests or opinions, moreover, social perspectives cannot easily be thought of as conflicting. Put together they usually do not cancel each other out, but rather offer additional questions and fuller social knowledge. Perspectives may often seem incommensurate, however. An account of post-war America from the perspective of those now in their eighties cannot be made in the same language and with the same assumptions as an account made from the perspective of those now in their twenties.

## 5. Special Representation of Marginalized Groups

Few would deny that members of less privileged structural social groups are under-represented in most contemporary democracies. As I discussed in Chapter 1, structural social and economic inequality often produces political inequality and relative exclusion from influential political discussion. Thus poor and working-class people often do not have their interests and perspectives as well represented as the rich or middle-class. In most political systems women occupy a small proportion of elected offices, and relatively few positions of power and influence in public and private life more generally. Minority cultural groups and those positioned in devalued racial positions usually also lack effective political voice. Many people regard this political exclusion or marginalization of subordinate groups and persons as wrong because it undermines promises of equal opportunity and political equality implied by democratic commitments. As I suggested in Chapter 1, such judgements about the injustice of political inequality can be used to break the circle by which formal political democracy tends to reproduce social inequality. More inclusion of and influence for currently under-represented social groups can help a society confront and find some remedies for structural social inequality.[20]

One important way to promote greater inclusion of members of under-represented social groups is through political and associational institutions designed specifically to increase the representation of women, working-class people, racial or ethnic minorities, disadvantaged castes, and so on. Techniques of quotas in electoral lists, proportional representation, reserved seats, the drawing of boundaries for electoral jurisdictions, have all been proposed and many implemented to promote group representation. Social movements increasingly call for forms of group representation not only in legislatures, but also in

[20] Melissa Williams gives a similar account of the potential connection between norms of representation and structural inequality; *Voice, Trust and Memory*, 194.

various kinds of commissions and boards, private corporate governing bodies, and in civic associations, as well as state institutions. Although proposals for group representation are nearly always controversial, structural exclusions that lead to such proposals do not seem to fade away. As Anne Phillips points out, however, specific representation of otherwise marginalized groups does not follow immediately from commitment to political equality.[21] Additional normative arguments are required.

Many doubt the justice or wisdom of efforts at the specific representation of social groups. Some claim that individuals should relate directly to political institutions without the mediation of groups, and that districts aggregating individual votes to obtain one representative is the only way to implement such political individualism.[22] As I discussed earlier, others object to group representation because they suspect it of invidious and false essentializing. Several theorists raise objections to what is called 'descriptive' or 'mirror' representation.

A conception of 'descriptive' or 'mirror' representation says that a representative body ought to appear as a copy of the whole polity. Thus it should contain members of obvious social groups in the proportions they are found in the general public. Pitkin argues that such an image of mirror representation considers representation only as a function of substitution or 'standing for', rather than asking about representation as an activity.[23] If to be properly representative all that matters is that legislators have specific attributes, furthermore, then random sampling might be a more effective means of choosing representatives than election.[24]

Many who advocate the specific representation of women, or African Americans, or classes, or Aboriginals, however, would find absurd the suggestion that the physical or membership attributes of people *as such* are grounds for their representing those with similar attributes. Instead, they argue that women, or Aboriginals, have similar experiences that only others of the group can understand with the

---

[21] Phillips, *The Politics of Presence*, 33–6.      [22] See Schwartz, *The Blue Guitar.*

[23] Pitkin, *The Concept of Representation*, 90.

[24] Ibid. 73; Will Kymlicka, *Multicultural Citizenship* (New York: Oxford University Press, 1996), 139. This sounds like a *reductio ad absurdum* argument directed against using sampling techniques for purposes of forming diverse groups. Such methods are not obviously ridiculous, however. James Fishkin uses random sampling for his deliberative opinion polls, for example; see Fishkin, *The Voice of the People* (New Haven: Yale University Press, 1995). He argues that this is an efficient and fairly reliable way to produce the multiplicity of social perspectives that I argue is necessary for informed deliberation, and he may be right about that. Still, the groups that he assembles are not properly political representatives precisely because they have no institutional or active connection to a constituency.

same immediacy. Others worry, however, that justifying group representation in terms of experiences, interests, or opinions allegedly
shared by all members of the group obscures differences within the
group, wrongly reduces all members of the group to a common
essence, and thereby also divides groups so much from each other that
understanding and co-operation across the differences may become
impossible.[25]

The theory of representation I have offered above can respond to
some of these worries about group representation. Whatever it is,
group representation is not properly conceived as an attention only to
attributes people share, nor is it a making present of some set of opinions, interests, or experiences that all members of the group share. As
I discussed earlier, such an interpretation follows a logic of identity
rather than conceptualizing representation as a differentiated process
relating the representative and constituents.

This theory of representation, on the other hand, rejects the
assumption implicit in many objections to group representation: that
a person's participation in large-scale politics can somehow be individualized. All systems and institutions of representation group individuals according to some kind of principles, and none are innocent or
neutral.[26] Any form or system of representation poses the problem of
the one and the many, and, in my view, this problem is best addressed
by active relationships of authorization and accountability between
constituents and representatives. Whether the principle of constituency is geography, residence, belief, financial interest, organizational or occupational interest, or social group position, members of
the constituency are better represented when they organize together
to discuss their agreements and differences with each other and with
officials. In the first place, any constituency is internally differentiated
and has to be organized in relation to a representative. Individuals are
better represented, furthermore, when representative bodies are
plural, and when individuals have plural relationships to representatives, in both political and civic organizations. The distinction drawn
above among modes of representation by opinion, interest, and
perspective describes such pluralization. The notion of representing
a perspective in particular aims to respond to objections to group
representation which claim that social groups cannot be defined by
common interests or opinions. To the extent that what distinguishes
social groups is structural relations, particularly structural relations of

[25] Compare Kymlicka, *Multicultural Citizenship*, 139; Phillips, *The Politics of Presence*,
ch. 2.
[26] Williams, *Voice, Trust and Memory*, 26.

privilege and disadvantage, and to the extent that persons are positioned similarly in those structures, then they have similar perspectives both on their own situation and on other positions in the society.

Arguments for the special representation of structural social groups that would otherwise be under-represented, therefore, appeal to the contribution such practices can and should make to inclusive political discussion and engagement with those who are different and with whom there may be conflicts.[27] First, when there has been a history of the exclusion or marginalization of some groups from political influence, members of those groups are likely to be disaffected with that political process; they may be apathetic or positively refuse to try to engage with others to solve shared problems. Under such circumstances, the specific representation of disadvantaged groups encourages participation and engagement.[28] Secondly, where some structural social groups have dominated political discussion and decision-making, these social perspectives have usually defined political priorities, the terms in which they are discussed, and the account of social relations that frames the discussion. At the same time these perspectives are not experienced as only one way to look at the issues, but rather often taken as neutral and universal. Special representation of otherwise excluded social perspectives reveals the partiality and specificity of the perspectives already politically present.[29] Special representation of marginalized social groups, finally, bring to political discussion and decision-making the situated knowledges I discussed in Chapter 3. Because of their social positioning, members of structurally

---

[27] What follows extends and revises arguments I have made in previous work; *Justice and the Politics of Difference* (Princeton: Princeton University Press, 1990), ch. 6. Although the earlier work did not intend to restrict the site of group representation to legislatures, nor to specify that the form such representation ought to take is through reserved seats, many interpreted the arguments as implying this. Thus in the discussion here I take up more explicitly issues of the sites and means of group representation. In this account I have also bracketed what seemed a particularly controversial aspect of the earlier account, namely the specification that disadvantaged groups should have veto power over decisions about issues that most specifically affect them. For some sympathetic yet critical interpretations of these earlier arguments, see Kymlicka, *Multicultral Citizenship*, 141; Phillips, *The Politics of Presence*, 54; David Ryden, *Representation in Crisis: The Constitution, Interest Groups, and Political Parties* (Albany: State University of New York Press, 1996), 88–91.

[28] Melissa Williams refers to this as a 'trust' argument for the special representation of marginalized groups; *Voice, Trust and Memory*, ch. 5. Jane Mansbridge also appeals to the development of trust as one argument for what she calls descriptive representation; see 'Should Blacks Represent Blacks and Women Represent Women? A Contingent "Yes"', *The Journal of Politics*, 61/3 (Aug. 1997), 628–57.

[29] Compare Pablo De Greiff, 'Deliberative Democracy and Group Representation', in Jorge Gracia and Pablo De Greiff (ed.), *Hispanics/Latinos in the US* (New York: Routledge, 2000).

differentiated groups often have different understandings of the causes of the problems and conflicts and the possible effects of proposed solutions. They have differing perceptions of one another and different understandings of the society's history and current relationships. If only a few of those understandings influence discussion and decision-making, political actors are more likely to perpetuate injustice or take imprudent action.[30]

Will Kymlicka endorses two arguments for the special representation of social groups which are likely to be marginalized without such measures. He claims, first, that such group representation is justified to combat systematic discrimination, both in the political system and in the society more widely. This set of reasons coheres with the arguments I have just made. Kymlicka's second reason, however, is rather different. Group representation is also justified, he argues, on grounds of self-government. Some groups, which Kymlicka calls nations, have rights to self-government; indigenous peoples are his paradigm of such groups. In multicultural societies many groups that deserve self-government are and should be parts of larger polities with whom they ought to stand in complex federated relationships. Groups that have a right to self-government but are also part of larger polities ought to be represented as groups in the decision-making bodies of these larger politics, as well as in intergovernment commissions, boards, and negotiations.[31]

Kymlicka is right to distinguish these two justifications for group representation, and I agree with him that self-government in the context of larger political relations offers a justification additional to those I have made above. As I suggested in Chapter 3, however, distinct peoples with claims to self-government also often stand in relations of structural inequality or potential domination with other groups. I will take up the question of distinct people, self-government, and group representation in federated polities most directly in Chapter 7, though some of the arguments of Chapter 6 begin to address these issues.

[30] The last argument and this both might be aspects of the argument Melissa Williams makes that group representation promotes political 'voice'. See also Susan Bickford, 'Reconfiguring Pluralism: Identity and Institutions in the Inequalitarian Polity', *American Journal of Political Science*, 43/1 (Jan. 1999), 86–108. Bickford develops a particularly nuanced argument for the specific representation of marginalized groups in circumstances of structural inequality. By emphasizing the plurality of the contexts and forms of representation, and understanding that processes of representation themselves influence the way groups understand themselves and relate to one another, Bickford suggests that theories and practices of group representation need not assume an essential group identity. The purpose of the specific representation of structural groups, she suggests, is not to express an identity, but rather to voice the experiences and perspectives of those socially positioned in what I referred to in ch. 3 as a social series.

[31] Kymlicka, *Multicultural Citizenship*, ch. 7.

It should be noted, furthermore, that neither Kymlicka's reasons nor those I have offered above amount to justifying group representation on simple grounds of diversity, recognition, or the assertion of group identity.[32] As I argued in Chapter 3, the process of mobilizing the members of a group for their participation in representative institutions and their entrance into discussion of the society's issue agenda often rightly invokes self-images of group distinctiveness and pride. Groups do not deserve special representation in inclusive decision-making bodies, however, just so they can express their culture in public discussion or be recognized in their distinctiveness.[33]

Do these arguments for the representation of otherwise silenced social perspectives also imply that minority or disadvantaged interests or opinions should be specially represented? Before deciding that the same sort of reasoning applies to interests and opinions, we should recall their differences from perspectives. Social perspectives arise from broad social structures that position many people in similar ways whether they like it or not. This makes social perspectives basic in a way that many interests and opinions are not. Interests and opinions may be shared with a large number of others, or they may be quite idiosyncratic. Many are voluntarily formed and organized, and the potential number of interests and opinions in a given society is vast.

The primary relevant difference, however, between interests and opinions, on the one hand, and social perspectives, on the other, is that some asserted interests or opinions may be bad or illegitimate, whereas a social perspective is not in itself illegitimate. In a society of white privilege, for example, the social perspective of white people usually wrongly dominates the making of many public discussions, and it should be relativized and tempered by the social perspectives of those positioned differently in the racialized social structures. But the social perspective of white people is not itself wrong or illegitimate. White supremacist opinions, on the other hand, which would call for the forced segregation of all people of colour, are illegitimate, because they assert a refusal to recognize some members of society as equal participants in their society. A liberal society in which such opinions are held by a small minority might be obliged to let them express the opinions, but it is not obliged to give any special support to them just because they are at a disadvantage in getting a hearing.

---

[32] In Ch. 5 of his book *On Nationality* (Oxford: Oxford University Press, 1995), which I referred to in Ch. 3, David Miller suggests that this is a primary argument for group representation.

[33] See De Greiff, 'Deliberative Democracy and Group Representation'.

In general, liberal principles of free speech and association ought to govern the representation of interests and opinions. Everyone should have the freedom to express opinions and organize groups to publicize them. Everyone should be free to organize groups to promote particular interests. Both freedoms should be limited by rules that enable a similar freedom for others and which prohibit activities that wrongfully harm others. The content of this harm principle is notoriously contested, of course, and I will not enter that controversy here. The point is that, on the whole, maximizing liberty of speech and association should be the general principle guiding the representation of interests and opinions.

Some critics of interest group liberalism, however, observe that unbridled freedom of expression and association leads to gross unfairness in an economic system where some interests and opinions have much greater access to resources than others. In response to this concern, some of the reasoning used to argue for special measures to ensure that representation of perspectives might also support special measures to ensure the representation of interests or opinions in public debate. Political equality may require guaranteeing media access to interest groups with few resources, or limiting the ability of richer groups to dominate public influence. As Joshua Cohen and Joel Rogers suggest, moreover, a fair system of interest group representation ought to subsidize self-organization by those with legitimate interests but few resources.[34]

The argument that the perspective of differentiated social groups should all be represented in political decision-making does not specify *who* does the representing. Here two questions might be relevant. First, is it necessary that the person who represents a social group perspective in a particular political context be a member of that group? Secondly, does the proposal to represent group perspective rather than, say, group interest, go very far in addressing the problem of the one and the many? To close this section I will briefly consider each of these questions.

Can only persons with certain ascriptive attributes represent the perspective of a structural social group? If representation consists in a relationship between a constituency and representative in which the constituency contests within itself about the issues to be represented and calls the representative to account, then a social group constituency certainly can and should ask how well a person with the

[34] Joshua Cohen and Joel Rogers, 'Secondary Associations and Democratic Governance', in Eric Olin Wright (ed.), *Associations and Democracy* (London: Verso, 1996); compare Christiano, 248–57.

presumed descriptive attributes in fact represents a social perspective. It may be possible, furthermore, though I would argue not very common, for persons without the descriptive attributes to represent a perspective. To do so, however, the person should stand in social relations that provide him or her with similar experiences and social knowledge to those with the descriptive attributes. An Asian American man who grew up in a predominantly African American neighbourhood, who has many African American friends, and who now works for a community service in a neighbourhood with many African Americans, for example, might be able to represent an African American perspective in many discussions, but most Asian American men could not because they are rather differently positioned.

The second question asks whether we have really transcended the problem of the one representing the many by moving from representing group interest to representing group perspective. I argued earlier that the idea of perspective is more fluid and open than the idea of interest, because a perspective is a general orientation on the political issues without determining what one sees, and without dictating particular conclusions. Nevertheless, there are good grounds for questioning an assumption that a social perspective is unified to the extent that all those positioned by structures in a similar way will express issues conditioned by this situated perspective in the same way. For this reason a scheme of group representation would do best to *pluralize* group representation. Representation of the perspective of women in a commission or legislative body would be better done by means of a small committee of women rather than just one woman, for example. A committee can contain some of the perspectival differences that cross the group, as well as the differences in individual experience, skill, and judgement that can better enable the committee to analyse social situations from the gendered perspective of women and express this perspective to a wider public.[35]

## 6. *Application of the Argument for Group Representation*

I have argued that commitment to political equality entails that democratic institutions and practices take measures explicitly to include the representation of social groups whose perspectives would likely be excluded from expression in discussion without those measures. They

[35] See S. L. Weldon, 'The Political Representation of Women: The Impact of a Critical Mass', Paper presented to the American Political Science Association, San Francisco, Sept. 1996.

are either a relatively small minority, or they are socially or economically disadvantaged, or the prevailing political discourse is dominated by other perspectives. Social groups should be recognized and included in their specificity in communicative democratic processes.

The question now arises of how such specific group representation should be accomplished. Melissa Williams points out that many objections to the general principle of group representation actually object to particular forms of the implementation of group representation, such as reserved legislative seats.[36] There are many ways that democracies can apply the principle that discussion and decision-making should take special measures to include social groups whose perspectives would likely be excluded without those measures. Which are best depends on the political situation, on the nature of the structural cleavages of the polity, possible trade-offs with other political values, and the institutional context for representation. While many criticisms of group representation appear to have only national legislatures in mind, representing social perspectives may also occur in local legislatures, official political committees and commissions, organs of political parties, and in the wider world of corporate and civic associations. The goal of bringing more members of marginalized groups into such bodies can be achieved by many means, moreover, such as by designating places, electoral schemes, lotteries, designating functional constituencies, and so on.

Mindful that there is no general formula for applying a principle of inclusive representation, I can nevertheless review briefly some issues connected with several prominent implementation options. Although I think that many contexts additional to legislatures are at least as important for implementing these principles, this review will concentrate on proposals to increase group representation in legislatures. This is the context in which issues of group representation are most contested, both in public life and in academic literature.

One means of group representation is to reserve a specific number of seats or positions in a representative body for representatives of a particular group. Although in previous writing I have endorsed this opinion among others, some writers raise plausible and serious doubts about the method of reserved positions. Reserving seats for particular groups can tend to freeze both the identity of that group and its relations with other groups in the polity. Some more fluid procedure is desirable for adapting to changing social relations. At the same time, reserving seats can tend to freeze the specially represented group

---

[36] Williams, *Voice, Trust and Memory*, ch. 7.

members out of additional representational opportunities in other contested seats. Thus the specially represented group may be isolated and marginalized at the representational level. If groups know they have reserved seats, finally, they may not be very active in the process either of authorization or of accountability, the representatives can tend to be disconnected from the group constituents, and the seats liable to capture by parties or interests. If only the members of the group have a right to choose for the reserved seats, furthermore, this method generates difficult problems of determining who has the right to choose those representatives. One can argue, I think, that all of these problems beset the system of representation which reserved seats for Maori in New Zealand before the change to a system of proportional representation made it easier for a Maori party to elect Maori in general parliamentary elections.

These problems lead to the conclusion, it seems to me, that reserving seats in authoritative decision-making bodies should be a last resort and temporary option for representing otherwise excluded perspectives. Having group-designated seats in non-elected bodies such as commissions, however, seems less problematic, because these bodies usually are temporary and have a limited charge. These are representative bodies in a political sense, of course, only if there are some organized constituencies which claim the commission should be accountable to them.

Quotas for women in party lists, or rules about a certain proportion of racial or ethnic minority group members in party conventions, are often acceptable and desirable ways of promoting the inclusion of diverse perspectives and interests. This method does not ghettoize group members, but includes them in wider party deliberations. Depending on the number of parties and the voting procedures, voters from all groups continue to have several candidate options.

David Ryden argues that strengthening the formation and active deliberation of political parties is the best way to foster the representation of politically interested social groups with different perspectives. Special measures for social group representation in the formal state representative institutions, he argues, would tend to freeze group identity and fragment politics, and it is better to use party politics as the vehicle for contesting and constructing group representation.[37] I agree that political parties can be an important tool for applying principles of the inclusive representation of social perspectives. Without affirmative measures in party practices to attend to social group repres-

---

[37] Ryden, *Representation in Crisis*, 110–38.

entation in decision-making bodies, candidate lists, convention representation, and so on, however, especially large and established parties with some political power are likely to suffer the same biases towards representing the interests and perspectives of more privileged social segments that state institutions have. To promote the inclusion of all social perspectives in political communication and decision-making, then, political parties usually will require special attention to groups and compensatory measures for under-representation.

In the United States in recent years making claims on state officials and courts to create legislative districts with majorities of African Americans or Latinos has been one of the only methods tried to promote the representation of groups whose perspectives would otherwise be absent from public debate. The justice of drawing district boundaries specifically to ensure group representation is hotly contested, and I will not try to summarize the debates here. The weight of the debate brings me to the conclusion that geographical districting for the purposes of group representation is not the preferred option, but that it is not wrong or unjust to use this method. In a political system that relies on single-member, winner-take-all legislative districts, designing the districts so that structurally or culturally differentiated and socially disadvantaged minority groups are in the majority may be the only way that members of these groups will appear as representatives, and in most situations the social perspectives of the groups given voice in public discussion. Because political equality involves inclusion in this sense, such districting solutions are not wrong.[38]

Nevertheless, I agree with Lani Guinier's critique of majority–minority districts as the preferred solution to social group representation.[39] Districting presupposes that the marginalized groups are sufficiently spatially segregated to make a relatively homogeneous territory. Even in the United States, where this solution to the representation of racialized groups predominates, however, it is nearly impossible to construct a homogeneous district. When distinct lines have been drawn explicitly to promote the representation of a particular group's perspective, then the minority in the district less affiliated with that group may well feel justly that they are under-represented. Such feelings are less likely to obtain through a voting system that gives everyone more choices about what their vote means and with whom they ally in casting it.

[38] See Amy Gutmann, 'Responding to Racial Injustice', in Kwami Anthony Appiah and Amy Gutmann, *Color Conscious* (Princeton: Princeton University Press, 1996).
[39] Lani Guinier, 'Groups, Representation, and Race Conscious Districting', in *The Tyranny of the Majority* (New York: Free Press, 1995).

Guinier argues, I think cogently, that multi-member legislative jurisdictions with some form of cumulative voting and proportional representation best maximize such choices and encourage cross-group coalitions, at the same time that they provide organizational opportunities for marginalized or disadvantaged groups to be represented. In majority–minority districts, furthermore, results can be similar to reserved seats, in that they become 'safe'. The representatives from those districts are then liable to become separate from the constituents, and the citizens relatively passive in relation to the representatives. In a system with multi-member districts and proportional representation, citizens must be active to promote the representation of the interests and perspectives that most matter to them. Multi-member political units with proportional representation obviously provide a better solution for representing the perspectives of spatially dispersed groups.

Several recent discussions of political equality offer similar and well-developed arguments for voting schemes using one method or another of proportional representation based in multi-member districts. Proportional representation tends to increase party competition and enable more parties to obtain legislative seats than do winner-take-all systems. Systems of proportional representation, some argue, also allow voters more opportunity to join with others in 'communities of interest', such as a structural social group. I find these arguments persuasive as grounding the claim that proportional representation provides more opportunity for differentiated representation than does a system based on single-member, winner-take-all districts.[40]

Legislatures are not the only governmental bodies, however, in which arguments for group representation can and should be applied. Courts, public hearings, appointed committees and commissions, and consultative processes are among the other deliberative and decision-making bodies that should be candidates for inclusive representation, even when citizens do not directly vote on their composition. In recent decades more attention has been devoted to the representation of diverse groups in bodies and procedures such as these. A more democratic representative government would have various layers and sites of elected, appointed, and volunteer bodies that discuss policy options, make policy decisions, or review policy effectiveness. In such bodies it is possible and desirable to give specific representation to par-

[40] See Guinier, 'No Two Seats', and 'Groups, Representation, and Race Conscious Districting', in *The Tyranny of the Majority*; Christiano, *The Rule of the Many*, 224–42; Charles Beitz, *Political Equality* (Princeton; Princeton University Press, 1990), ch. 6.

ticular social group perspectives which might not otherwise be present. If more attention had been paid to special representation of oppressed or disadvantaged groups in the process of setting up the citizens' discussions that led to Oregon's health care rationing plan in 1990, for example, those discussion groups would probably not have been so dominated by white middle-class and college-educated perspectives.[41]

The processes of authorization and accountability that constitute the representative function, finally, should not be confined to official government bodies. I have already discussed how the free associative life of civil society contributes to the formation and expression of interests and opinions. Civil society is also an important site for the consolidation and expression of social perspectives. Organization and agitation in the public spheres of civil society, furthermore, are among the best methods of maintaining connections between representatives and constituents, and insisting that representatives be accountable. We deepen democracy when we encourage the flourishing of associations that people form according to whatever interests, opinions, and perspectives they find important. Strong, autonomous, and plural activities of civic associations offer individuals and social groups maximum opportunity in their own diversity to be represented in public life. Accordingly, the next chapter outlines a theory of how civil society contributes to inclusive communicative democracy.

[41] See Michael J. Garland and Romana Hasraen, 'Community Responsibility and the Development of Oregon's Health Care Priorities', *Business and Professional Ethics Journal*, 9/3 and 4 (Fall 1990), 183–200.

# CHAPTER 5

## Civil Society and its Limits

Recent interest by political theorists in the concept and practices of civil society has been spurred by the revolutionary events in eastern Europe, South Africa, and several Latin American countries, where apparently well-ensconced authoritarian regimes crumbled after being hollowed out by resistance movements of ordinary citizens in voluntary associations who withdrew their tacit support.

In several east European countries networks of underground publications, theatre groups, workers' organizations, and neighbourhood and village solidarity groups created opportunities and institutions outside the state in which to discuss issues and develop visions and material bases for organizing strikes, boycotts, and street demonstrations, as well as for protecting those in danger of arrest.[1] When the African National Congress called upon its supporters inside South Africa to withdraw their co-operation from the apartheid government, a host of civic organizations arose in the cities and townships to facilitate rent boycotts, organize community courts, provide some educational and social services, and organize strike support, street demonstrations, funeral attendance, and so on.[2] In both eastern Europe and South Africa this activity of creating and sustaining an oppositional civil society served as a school of democracy for citizens to activate democratic legal processes. While the success of civil soci-

---

[1] See H. Gordon Skilling, *Samizdat and an Independent Society in Central and Eastern Europe* (Oxford: Macmillan, 1989). See also Andra Bozoki and Milos Sukosd, 'Civil Society and Populism in the Eastern European Democratic Transition', *Praxis International*, 13/3 (Oct. 1993), 224–41. Jeffrey Isaac reflects on the meanings of this 'antipolitical politics' of civil society in his essay 'The Meanings of 1989', in *Democracy in Dark Times* (Ithaca, NY: Cornell University Press, 1998).

[2] For one account of the role of civic associations in the struggle to end apartheid, see Mzwanele Mayekiso, *Township Politics: Civic Struggles for a New South Africa* (New York: Monthly Review Press, 1996); see also Steven Friedman, 'An Unlikely Utopia: State and Civil Society in South Africa', *Politikon*, 19/1 (Dec. 1991), 5–19.

ety in eliminating authoritarianism and installing democratic legal processes in Latin American countries such as Argentina and Chile is less certain, nevertheless there too civic activity outside the state has been very important.[3]

Rediscovery of the concept of civil society, however, goes beyond these moments of opposition to authoritarian rule. Many claim for civil society a central role in promoting democracy and social welfare under liberal constitutionalist regimes as well. Civil society promotes trust, choice, and the virtues of democracy. Some theorists and political commentators even suggest that civil society is better equipped than the state to meet needs, deliver services, and further social solidarity. On this view, state institutions should be restricted in order to allow the flourishing of associational life to effect all these goods.

This chapter assesses these claims by asking about the function and limits of civic association in the context of societies guided by a rule of law that recognize basic liberties, and have democratic political practices, but where structural injustices exist. Associational activity provides important openings in the circle I described in Chapter 1, wherein formal democracy tends to reinforce social and economic inequality. The self-organization of marginalized people into affinity grouping enables people to develop a language in which to voice experiences and perception that cannot be spoken in prevailing terms of political discourse. At the same time civic activity autonomous from the state provides a base for social innovation, and the provision of goods and services less dominated by profit imperatives than conventional private enterprises. Civil society enables the emergence of public spheres in which differentiated social sectors express their experience and formulate their opinions. Perhaps even more importantly, the public sphere enables citizens to expose injustice in state and economic power and make the exercise of power more accountable. Through public discussion and agitation, moreover, citizens can and sometimes do influence the politics of state or corporate institutions or catalyse practical changes within civil society itself. Much of the activity and discussion of civil society is productively disorderly, filled with passion and play, and allowing space for enacting the values I will develop in Chapter 6 as those associated with differentiated solidarity. By encouraging plural associational activity, representative democracies can be participatory, and open diverse modes and axes of political representation.

[3] On Chile, see Joel M. Jutkowitz, 'Civil Society and Democratic Development in Chile', Paper presented to the American Political Science Association, Chicago, Sept. 1995.

This chapter aims to add conceptual clarity to contemporary theoretical discussions of civil society by reviewing the reasons for distinguishing it from the concepts of state and economy. Then it distinguishes three aspects of associational activity: private, civic, and public. I define some of the functions of associational life and the public spheres that sometimes emerge from it, and discuss the question of whether such public sphere activity is better thought of as singular or plural.

Despite the vital role of civil society in promoting inclusion, expression, and critique for deep democracy, I argue against those who suggest that civil society serves as a preferred alternative to the state today for promoting democracy and social justice. State institutions have unique capacities for co-ordination, regulation, and administration on a large scale that well-functioning democracy cannot do without. Though civil society stands in tension with state institutions, a strengthening of both is necessary to deepen democracy and undermine injustice, especially that deriving from private economic power. Each social aspect—state, economy, and civil society—can both limit and support the others. Thus social movements seeking greater justice and well-being should work on both these fronts, and aim to multiply the links between civil society and states.

My argument for the distinct virtues of state capacities over and above those of civil society assumes the two-part definition of social justice stated in Chapter 1. The concept of injustice covers both domination and oppression. Domination consists in institutional conditions which inhibit or prevent people from participation in decisions and processes that determine their actions and the conditions of their actions. The aspect of social justice that domination denies is self-determination. Oppression, the second aspect of injustice, consists in systematic institutional processes which prevent some people from learning and using satisfying or expansive skills in socially recognized settings, or which inhibit people's ability to play and communicate with others or to express their feelings and perspective on social life in contexts where others can listen. The aspect of social justice that oppression denies is self-development.

In this chapter I argue that the associational life of civil society can do much to promote self-determination. Precisely because of its plurality and relative lack of co-ordination, however, civil society can only minimally advance values of self-development. Because many of the structural injustices that produce oppression have their source in economic processes, state institutions are necessary to undermine such oppression and promote self-development.

State institutions and civil society thus stand in a certain tension with one another in their principles of organization. This tension can produce self-cancelling tendencies in democratic politics. Democratic politics that aim to promote justice need both forms of social activity, and they need to be connected with one another. In the final section I explore theories of associative democracy as one attempt to link state institutions and civil society in a way that reinforces each other's virtues without coming into conflict. While there are some useful ideas in these conceptions of associative democracy, I argue, they retain the tensions between state institutions and civic association. Thus democratic practice must live productively with these tensions.

## 1. The Idea of Civil Society

The words 'civil society', says Michael Walzer, 'name the space of uncoerced human association and also the set of relational networks—formed for the sake of family, faith, interest, and ideology—that fill their space'.[4] This is a good enough beginning to a definition, but, like most other definitions of civil society, it seems to include almost everything we know as social. Indeed, the idea of civil society does include a great deal, making attempts at a simple sentence definition inevitably vague. Theoretical elaboration of the idea of civil society requires not a sentence definition, but rather distinguishing and articulating terms describing social life. Accordingly, this section defines the social phenomena often referred to by the term 'civil society', in two steps. I argue that activities of voluntary associational life are usefully distinguished from those of both state and economy. State and economy are distinct from associational life because they co-ordinate action differently, and because institutions of state and economy exercise systematic power. I then distinguish three levels of associational life that are relatively autonomous from state and economy: private association, civic association, and political association.

In classical modern usages 'civil society' referred to the entirety of social life outside state institutions.[5] Civil society denoted the diverse and particular activities, institutions, and associations regulated and unified by the general legal and coercive apparatus of the state. Activities of private enterprise and market transaction, in this classical

---

[4] Michael Walzer, 'The Idea of Civil Society', in Walzer (ed.), *Toward a Global Civil Society* (Providence, RI: Berhahan Books, 1995), 7.

[5] See Nerra Chandhoke, *State and Civil Society* (Berkeley: Sage, 1992); and Keith Tester, *Civil Society* (London: Routledge, 1992).

usage, enjoyed a central place in civil society. The concept of civil society has evolved in the last century and a half, however, in response to significant changes in both states and the institutions and associations outside the state. While some theorists continue to include economic activity in the concept of civil society, many political theorists now distinguish the activities of voluntary associational life from both state and economy.[6] Distinguishing voluntary associational life from economy as well as state helps refine one of the guiding questions of this chapter, namely, what is the role of civil society in promoting social justice.

*State* refers to activities and institutions of legal regulation, enforcement backed by coercion, legislatively mandated co-ordination and public services, along with the managerial and technical apparatus necessary to carry out these functions effectively. In distinguishing *economy* from state I assume a capitalist economy, that is, an economy in which at least a large part of the society's goods and services are supplied by private enterprise operating through markets. Economic activity is profit- and market-oriented. *Civil society* refers to a third sector of private associations that are relatively autonomous from both state and economy. They are voluntary, in the sense that they are neither mandated nor run by state institutions, but spring from the everyday lives and activities of communities of interest. The associations of this third sector, moreover, operate not for profit. Most participate in economic activity only as consumers, fund-raisers, and sometimes employers. Even those activities of the third sector that involve providing goods and services for fees, however, are not organized towards the objectives of making profit and enlarging market shares.

It is useful to distinguish civil society from both state and economy in two respects. For the first I follow Jean Cohen and Andrew Arato in relying on Habermas's distinction between system and lifeworld.[7] State, economy, and civil society correspond to three distinct ways of co-ordinating action, the first through the medium of authorized power, the second through the medium of money, and the third through communicative interaction. State and economy are each *systemic* inasmuch as the actions of thousands or even millions of people are conditioned by respective system imperatives of bureaucratic

[6] Jean Cohen and Andrew Arato, *Civil Society and Political Theory* (Cambridge, Mass.: MIT Press, 1992); Jurgen Habermas, *Between Facts and Norms* (Cambridge, Mass.: MIT Press, 1996), ch. 7; Walzer, 'The Idea of Civil Society'; Kai Nielsen, 'Reconceptualizing Civil Society for Now: Some Somewhat Gramscian Turnings', in Michael Walzer (ed.), *Toward a Global Civil Society* (Providence, RI: Berhahan Books, 1995).

[7] Jurgen Habermas, *The Theory of Communicative Action*, ii (Boston: Beacon Press, 1984); Cohen and Arato, *Civil Society and Political Theory*.

routine or profit-making, and those co-ordinating people's actions need not directly communicate with one another. Both state and economy are systemic inasmuch as they bring together disparate people, places, and particular goals in action networks mediated by authorized power or money, where the particular actors are constrained by the imperatives of each to accomplish their particular goals within the system. They are systemic also inasmuch as each tends to extend its influence or effects, bureaucratizing or commodifying human needs and relationships ever more deeply.

Habermas designates as 'lifeworld' those activities and institutions which are structured primarily through communicative interaction rather than by systemic imperatives in relation to which actors reason instrumentally and strategically. Civil society corresponds to associative activities of the lifeworld. In the associations of civil society people co-ordinate their actions by discussing and working things out, rather than by checking prices or looking up the rules. Civil society includes a vast array of activities, institutions, and social networks outside state and economy, from informal clubs, to religious organizations, to non-profit service providers, to cultural producers, to political action groups.

The first reason to distinguish civil society from both state and economy, then, is to notice differing forms of the co-ordination of social action. The second reason is connected, but bears more directly on the issue of whether and how activities in this social sector can promote democracy and social justice. Recent political theory of civil society analyses how organizations and activities that are relatively autonomous from the state can limit state power, and make its exercise more accountable and democratic. If a purpose of theorizing the functions of civil society is to analyse the possibilities of free self-organization and their potential for limiting power and democratizing its exercise, however, then it is important to distinguish civil society from economy as well as state. Private firms, some of which are larger and more powerful than many states, dominate economic life in contemporary capitalist societies. Their internal organization is typically far less democratic than most governments, and persons whose lives are affected by the policies and actions of such economic institutions often lack the means to confront them. The structural consequences of market imperatives and profit-orientation as followed by these powerful economic actors, moreover, severely limit the options of individuals, groups, and sometimes states.

Theorists of civil society often use spatial or substantial language to define the concept, characterizing it as a realm, sphere, or space distinct from spheres of economy and state. Such spatial language suggests that society has three distinct parts that do not overlap. It also tempts us into placing each social institution into one and only one of these supposed spheres. The spatialized concept is not so useful for theorizing the possibility of democratization and social change, however, when thought of in such substantial terms with such specific borders. I suggest that a more process-oriented understanding of what civil society names helps clarify the theory. Rather than think of state, economy, and associative lifeworld as distinct spheres or clusters of institutions, we should think of them as *kinds of activities*. State designates activities of formal and legal regulation backed by legitimate coercive apparatus of enforcement. Economy designates market-oriented activity concerned with the production and distribution of resources, products, income, and wealth, which is constrained by considerations of profit and loss, cost-minimization, and so on. Civil society names activity of self-organization for particular purposes of enhancing intrinsic social values.

When we understand state, economy, and civil society as kinds of activity, we can see how many institutions include all three activities. Institutions where state or economic activities dominate may also contain or promote significant activities of voluntary association. People who work in state agencies or large corporations sometimes establish associations within them which raise issues of governance or policy in the organization and seek change in them. Much of the social movement work aimed at making professional workplaces more accepting of women and people of colour, for example, has involved such associational activity within private businesses.

Thus far I have refined Walzer's definition of civil society only to the extent of distinguishing uncoerced human associations and relational networks from systems of state and economy. This leaves a vast undifferentiated range of social life. To answer how activities of this associative lifeworld support democracy and promote social justice, it is helpful to distinguish levels of associative activity: private association, civic association, and political association.

*Private association* is self-regarding, in the sense that it is activity for the participants or members of the association. Families, social clubs, private parties and gatherings, many of the activities of religious organizations, are all examples of private association. More often than not, private association concerns enjoyment and suffering—light sociability, personal caretaking, consumption, entertainment, grieving, and spiritual renewal. Such activities are private in the Arendtian sense that they concern basic matters of life, death, need, and pleasure which in the extreme cannot be shared, and in the sense that the social relations carrying out these activities are usually more or less exclusive. Private associations tend to be inward-looking and particularist. I go to this club's functions because it is my club, where I know the other individuals and they know me; our meetings and events include only us and others whom we invite, and our purpose is to have a good time, or care for one another. Private society may also include inward-looking communities such as Amish, or certain ethnic or religious organizations which welcome strangers, but only strangers with whom the organization members claim a specific identity or affinity.

*Civic associations*, on the other hand, are primarily directed outward from those engaged in them to others. Activities with a civic purpose aim to serve not only members, but also the wider community. Civic associations claim to make some contribution to the collective life of the neighbourhood, city, country, or world. When civic associations claim to contribute to some community good, their participants assume that at least some of the beneficiaries are strangers, anonymous others who live in the community or who pass through, or others in faraway places. Thus a civic association that organizes volunteers to cut the vines that are choking the trees in a public park wishes to preserve the lushness of the park both for themselves and for others who might wander into it. The neighbourhood crime watch, the community arts centre, battered women's services, and journals of information and opinions about events and issues in the community, are all shaped and justified as knitting relations among strangers as well as acquaintances and friends. Unlike private association, civic association tends to be *inclusive* in this sense that it is open in principle to anyone.

A healthy civil society has a huge array of such civic activities and associations, not only small, *ad hoc*, and short-lived—such as some crime watch groups or neighbourhood clean-up crews—but also large, well-funded, and institutionalized over generations, such as the United Way. Most civic associations rely on volunteer work even when they employ paid staff, and all rely on donations of money and other resources to carry out their work. Some civic activities advance a partisan 'cause' and in this sense may be proto-political, such as associations working against the death penalty, promoting recycling, or wishing to save the spotted owl.

Robert Putnam famously argues that a rich associational life strengthens democratic institutions and culture.[8] His concept of

[8] Robert Putnam, *Making Democracy Work: Civic Traditions in Modern Italy* (Princeton: Princeton University Press, 1993).

associationalism, however, appears to include a great variety of groups and activities, from church groups to unions to reading the newspaper. He makes no distinctions between kinds of associations, nor does he try to account for just *how* some or all of them allegedly enhance democracy. It is important to distinguish between private and civic association, or between more inward-looking and outward-looking forms of association, because this distinction shows that some kinds of association may not enhance democracy very much or help change those structures that inhibit capabilities.[9] There is little reason to think that soccer clubs or bowling leagues, for example, do very much to enhance democracy or contribute to a solidarity of strangers. To be sure, members of such groups might develop skills in organizing schedules and leading meetings that non-joiners lack, and such skills may contribute to one's ability to be a citizen. Private clubs such as these, however, belong to that vast layer of association life where people do something they enjoy, in the company of friends and neighbours, for the sake of that enjoyment. Such private association is a wonderful thing, but it contributes little to the good of the wider society.

Private association, moreover, sometimes is depoliticizing or brazenly self-regarding. Some people and groups with a rich private associational life are indifferent to public life and restrict themselves to an enclosed group of family, friends, and career contacts. Whole communities or groups withdraw into associational privatism and even create defensive walls in the effort to keep the political and social concerns of the wider society at bay. There is nothing wrong with private association *per se* in a big and free society, as long as citizens and associations respect one another and are willing to do their part to contribute to the wider society. Too much private association relative to civil and political association, however, may weaken democracy and concern for social justice, because people and groups may care little for outsiders, and indeed may be hostile to others.[10]

*Political association* is distinct from both private and civic association, in that it self-consciously focuses on claims about what the social collective ought to do. Political activity consists in voicing issues for public debate about what ought to be done, what principles and priorities should guide social life, what policies should be adopted,

[9]  See Nancy Rosenblum, *Membership and Morals: The Personal Uses of Pluralism in America* (Princeton: Princeton University Press, 1998). Rosenblum argues that civil society poses dangers as well as opportunities to democracy, and illustrates some of these dangers by analysing a number of organizations and activities in the United States that come under this idea I am calling private society.

[10]  See Margaret Levi, 'Social and Unsocial Capital: A Review Essay of Robert Putnam's *Making Democracy Work*', *Politics and Society*, 24/1 (Mar. 1996), 45–55.

how the powerful should be held accountable, and what responsibilities citizenship carries. It allows conflict to surface, and proposes means of adjudicating conflict.

Many political associations aim to influence state policy formation or implementation, for example, parties, lobbying organizations, and special interest associations organizing to influence or protest state policy. Political association also refers to organized forms of public challenge directed at primarily economic institutions without using state policy. Thus a direct demand on the Gap to cease super-exploitation of teenagers in Central America is a political demand, even though it does not involve a claim on the state. Political activity is any activity whose aim is to *politicize* social or economic life, to raise questions about how society should be organized, and what actions should be taken to address problems or do justice. In ways I will discuss in the next section, political activity relies on a public sphere.

I refer to private, civic, and political association as *levels* of associational activity to indicate the ease of movement from one to another. Some voluntary associations are founded explicitly to move on all three levels. Others shift easily among levels even though they define their mission on one of them primarily. A gay bar, for example, usually serves as a site for private socializing. When it becomes a meeting-place and constituency for planning a rally in support of a city ordinance banning discrimination against gays and lesbians, however, it participates in political association. Civic associations often move to a political level when they find that their ability to achieve their civic goals is inhibited by the policies and practices of powerful agents in the state or economy, or when their activities come under public criticism or produce conflict. On the other hand, members of civic or political associations also often engage in private activity of enjoyment or mutual support.

To examine the uses and limits of associative activity for democratization and bringing about social justice, we need to move from this ontology of civil society to analysis of how civil society activities effect changes in state, economy, and civil society itself. Jean Cohen and Andrew Arato propose what they call a dualistic theory of civil society with 'defensive' and 'offensive' aspects. The first aspect refers to the way associations and social movements develop forms of communicative interaction that support identities, expand participatory possibilities, and create networks of solidarity. I call this aspect *self-organization*. In the second function associational activity aims to influence or reform state or corporate policies and practices. Along with theorists such as Cohen and Arato who work within a broadly

Habermasian framework, I refer to this aspect of civil society as the activity of the *public sphere*.[11]

Distinguishing the function of self-organization from those of public exposure and debate helps clarify how the activities of the associational lifeworld can contribute to supporting communicative democracy and social change. Among other things, self-organizing activities in civil society enable people who believe that their sorts of experiences, interests, and needs are socially and politically marginalized to find one another and develop their social voices. The aspect of civic activity producing public spheres, on the other hand, can and sometimes does deepen democracy by multiplying fora and aspects in which people are represented in public discussion, and by activities that make public officials and powerful private actors accountable.

This two-levelled interpretation of civil society maps onto the three-levelled interpretation I made in the previous section roughly as follows. The *self-organizing* level discussed here includes some activities of *private association*, but not all. Many of the activities of *civic association* belong to the self-organizing aspect, but some belong to or serve as conditions for public spheres. The second set of functions, *public spheres*, largely corresponds to *political association*, but includes some activities of civic association.

## 2. Self-Organizing Civil Society

In a free society people are liable to form all kinds of association with diverse identities and goals. Recent praise for civil society often neglects to acknowledge how many of such associations, even when voluntarily entered, are hierarchical or authoritarian in their rule. Associations founded with the intention of being democratic, moreover, are often even more susceptible to autocratic takeover than governments. The image of civic associations as free self-organization without the disciplinary regimes of coercion and bureaucracy is at best an exaggeration that feeds disenchantment with state institutions.[12] A

[11]   Cohen and Arato, *Civil Society and Political Theory*, 523–32. In a more recent paper Jean Cohen argues that mainstream American public discourse about civil society today leaves out the important concept and practices of the public sphere, and by doing so removes much of the critical force of the idea. See Cohen, *American Civil Society Talk*, Working Paper No. 6 (College Park: National Commission on Civic Renewal, University of Maryland, 1997). See also John J. Rodger, 'On the Degeneration of the Public Sphere', *Political Studies*, 32 (1985), 203–17.

[12]   From a Foucaultian point of view, which is helpful here, practices of 'governmentality' operate as much or more in some civic institutions as they do in state institutions. For

great number of voluntary associations, however, are directly democratic. People form and run them according to rules they collectively adopt. To this extent even private associations can be schools of self-government.

Beyond such general virtues of participation, the self-organizing activities of civil society contribute to self-determination, and, to a lesser degree, self-development, by supporting identity and voice, facilitating innovative or minority practices, and providing some goods and services.

*A voice for excluded.* In Chapter 1 I noted that in a formally democratic society where there are structural social and economic injustices, many of those who suffer such injustices are likely to be excluded, silenced, or marginalized in the formal democratic political process as well. This political inequality tends to create conditions in which the social and economic injustice or marginalization is not likely to be addressed as a problem by legislators and other public officials.

Civil society offers a way out of this circle, one of the only ways. However despised or disfranchised, in a liberal society (and even sometimes in illiberal societies) people who are disadvantaged or marginalized can find each other and form associations to improve their lives through mutual aid and articulation of group consciousness. Although they may lack the money, expertise, and social connections that others have, poorer or more marginalized people can exploit a resource which is more equally possessed by everyone: time.[13]

Activities of self-organization in civil society are the primary practical means for breaking through the silencing Lyotard calls the *differend*, which I discussed in Chapter 1. When a group's suffering or grievance cannot be expressed, or cannot fully be expressed, in hegemonic discourses, associational activity can support the development among those silenced new ways of seeing social relationships or labelling situations as wrong. In these self-organizing activities disadvantaged or marginalized sectors and groups sometimes articulate affirmative self-conceptions in response to denigrating or devaluing

one powerful analysis of governmentality outside, as well as inside, the state, see Barbara Cruikshank, *The Will to Empower: Technologies of Citizenship, Social Reform, and Democratic Government* (Ithaca, NY: Cornell University Press, 1999).

[13] In their massive study of the relationship between civic participation and social factors of privilege and disadvantage such as class, gender, and race, Sidney Vera, Kay Lehman Scholzman, and Henry E. Brady find that social and economic inequality correlates with relative lack of civic and political voice. They find less difference in the amount that structurally unequal groups contribute to civic and political activity in the way of time, however, than in money. See Vera, Scholzman, and Brady, *Voice and Equality: Civic Voluntarism in American Politics* (Cambridge, Mass.: Harvard University Press, 1995), esp. ch. 10.

positionings from the wider society. In Chapter 3 I suggested that this is one useful meaning for the label 'identity politics' to describe social movements reflecting on their socially differentiated positions. Through literature, theatre, song, visual art, social networking and exchange about civic projects, and critical analysis, relatively silenced social sectors envision and articulate new experiences and social perspectives. Associational life thus serves as a basis of social solidarity, cultural support, or resistance to domination and oppression.

*Social innovation.* In voluntary associations where people co-ordinate their action by discussion, people sometimes reach for new ideas and practices. Perhaps some people are dissatisfied with the prevailing conventions, or they are simply attracted to saying or doing something differently. Whether organic farming, herbal healing, evangelical religious worship, or car pooling, people often form associations in order to develop alternative practices. While some of these turn out to be crank or idiosyncratic, through their dissemination in the public sphere some come to be widely adopted, thereby facilitating social changes outside any legislative or legal mandates.

*Goods and services.* Associations of civil society provide many goods and services outside the framework of the state or profit-oriented economy. Non-profit social services such as tenants' advocates, health services, homeless or battered women's shelters, literacy centres, immigrant or exile settlement support services, after-school youth centres, and so on are often democratically organized, connected to their communities, and more empowering for clients than state-run services. While producer and consumer co-operatives rarely escape market forces and pressures, they often introduce elements of democratic decision-making or other substantive non-market values into the business process. Many experts and activists in less-developed countries regard civic organizations as important promoters of development: they improve the lives of some disadvantaged people by involving them directly in participatory projects such as small producer co-operatives, credit associations, and self-help housing construction. Civic associations worried about the revitalization of deteriorating inner cities in wealthier societies also aim to meet needs through non-profit non-governmental associational activity. In the United States non-profit associations such as Community Land Trusts or Habitat for Humanity have supplied units of decent affordable housing when both government and private developers apparently abandoned the task. Democracy and social justice would be enhanced in most societies if civic associations provided even more goods and services.

Not all of the identities, practices, or goods and services that flourish in civil society are necessarily good; nor do they coexist without conflict. By means of voluntary associations, however, people can take some control over the conditions under which they live and act, support affinities, develop practices, and provide goods and services in ways more under their direct control than activities of state and economy. In these ways civil society directly realizes the value of self-determination, and to a lesser extent self-development.

## 3. The Public Sphere

Many theorists of deliberative democracy implicitly or explicitly assume that state institutions such as legislatures and courts are the primary sites of deliberation. While Amy Gutmann and Dennis Thompson believe that deliberation in a strong democracy should occur in many fora, for example, most of their examples of the operation of deliberation involve public officials within state institutions.[14] Those writing in the tradition of discourse ethics, on the other hand, give more prominence to civil society as the site of deliberative politics.[15] A complete theory of communicative democracy identifies both state institutions and civic institutions as potential sites for democratic communication among citizens, and between citizens and public officials, where issues are discussed in an open and critical fashion.

Theorizing discursive democracy in the public sphere activities of civil society primarily forces two changes in typical understandings of deliberative democracy. First, as Habermas says in commenting on Joshua Cohen's formulation of a model of deliberative democracy, it is a mistake to think of the deliberatively democratic process as one that engages a unified people making decisions for society as a whole.[16] Instead, processes of deliberation in complex mass society must be understood as subjectless and decentred. Among other things, this implies abandoning traces of face-to-face interaction as the model of public discussion, and instead reinterpreting public debate as mediated among people dispersed in space and time.

Even those who understand processes of communicative democracy in this decentred and mediated way often ignore a second way

[14] Amy Gutmann and Dennis Thompson, *Democracy and Disagreement* (Cambridge, Mass.: Harvard University Press, 1996).
[15] See e.g. Simone Chambers, *Reasonable Democracy: Jurgen Habermas and the Politics of Discourse* (Ithaca, NY: Cornell University Press, 1997), esp. chs. 12 and 13.
[16] Habermas, *Between Facts and Norms*, 304–7.

that locating political discussion in civil society departs from a standard model of deliberative democracy. As Chapter 1 pointed out, implicit in the standard model of deliberative democracy are norms of orderly and dispassionate reason-giving. Expanding the idea of communicative democracy from formal sites of deliberation, such as parliaments, courtrooms, and chambers for hearing, to the streets, squares, church basements, and theatres of civil society requires us to include in democratic communication kinds of speech and interaction additional to making and criticizing arguments.

Public communication in civil society is often not unified and orderly, but messy, many-levelled, playful, emotional. Public communication covers not only making claims and giving reasons, though this is and ought to be a significant aspect. It also includes politicized art and culture—film, theatre, song, and story—intended to influence a wider public to understand the society or some of its members in particular and often different ways. If public communication aims at inclusion, debate, and promoting justice, furthermore, it must include multiple forms of protest action—rallies, marches, strikes, boycotts, commemorations and ceremonies, non-violent illegal blockades, and so on.[17] In what follows I first define the meaning of publicity and public spheres in civil society, and then I give an account of the specific functions the public sphere can serve for democratic process that aims to promote justice.

## What is the Public Sphere?

Chapter 1 discussed the role of publicity in democratic theory and practice. Here I shall elaborate that account more by focusing on three aspects of publicity. First, publicity refers to the constitution of a site for communicative engagement and contest. Secondly, it refers to a relationship among citizens within this site. Finally, publicity refers to the form that speech and other forms of expression take.

An event, building, outdoor space, or form of discussion is public just in so far as it is open to anyone. Print and electronic media are public, for example, in so far as anyone who understands their languages can easily access them. They are even more public where individuals and groups have easy access to them for expressing themselves.

---

[17] Theories of civil society inspired by new social movements emphasize this aspect of public communication; see Cohen and Arato, *Civil Society and Political Theory*; *Democracy in Capitalist Times* (Oxford: Oxford University Press, 1996). See also Andrew Szas, 'Progress through Mischief: The Social Movement Alternative to Secondary Association', in E. O. Wright (ed.), *Associations and Democracy* (London: Verso, 1995).

A park is public in so far as any person, whether resident of the neighbourhood or city, or not, can enter it and enjoy its environment and facilities. Thus the first sense of publicity refers to determinate spaces or fora to which anyone has access. For communicative democracy, it is important that public sites be available in both these ways. Citizens in a democracy should have formal access to both indoor and outdoor spaces for the staging of public events aimed at calling attention to issues, expressing opinions, and calling for action. They should be able to invite a general public to such events, and they should have access to public media in which to issue such invitations. To satisfy these latter conditions, as well as in order to expand public interaction beyond spatial proximity and simultaneity, citizens should have easy access to the public media, both print and electronic.

Publicity also refers to a particular kind of relationship among people reflexively created by such universally accessible sites and fora. As I discussed in Chapter 3, public sites or fora are populated by a plurality of actors with varying interests, priorities, values, and experiences. Events and expression that occur within these sites and fora are *exposed* to this plurality of points of view. They are witnessed by the mass of different people that constitute the public. Since a public forum is in principle accessible to anyone, appearing in public involves a kind of transcendence or indeterminacy which can be frightening. The public is plural, and none of us knows exactly *who* is in it, before whom, that is, public expression and actions are exposed. Many members of the public are strangers to one another at least in the sense that they know little about what has brought them to enter public sites, and do not know enough about their history and current projects to know the meaning that they will attribute to what they witness in public. Because the number of witnesses in principle is so large and because many of them are strangers in this sense, one whose words or deeds are public has little control over how the public will take up, interpret, and act in relation to what they see and hear.

The third aspect of publicity refers more specifically to the form of expression or action which is public. This is the aspect of publicity most emphasized by theorists of deliberative democracy. These theorists insist that the normatively reasonable and inclusive conditions of communicative democracy are not met unless people discussing public issues present their claims, arguments, appeals, stories, or demonstrations in ways that try to be accessible and accountable to anyone. There are often differences, then, between the way people can express things to their friends and associates, or to those who affirm a shared interest or group affinity, and the way politically responsible people ought to express themselves to a more general and indeterminate public. Contrary to some who theorize publicity, I do not conceive this difference as referring to a move from particular to more general content. Those who raise issues and make claims in public properly can and sometimes should be partial and particular in their concerns and perspectives. For their expressions to satisfy the publicity condition, however, they cannot assume the history, language, and shared perspective of a particular interest or group, but instead must recast the particularity of their concern in generally accessible images, concepts, and issues.

In this context, we can introduce some helpful distinctions into the debate about whether the public sphere should be conceived as singular or as many spheres. Despite the critical distance he has taken from his early formulation of the idea of a public sphere, for example, Jurgen Habermas continues to rely on the idea of a generalized public sphere as a process through which problems of the whole society are discussed, processed, and finally brought to influence the formation of authoritative law and public policy. In *Between Facts and Norms* Habermas defines the idea of public sphere thus: 'The public sphere can best be described as a network for communicating information and points of view (i.e., opinions expressing affirmative or negative attitudes); the streams of communication are, in the process, filtered and synthesized in such a way that they coalesce into bundles of topically specified *public* opinions.'[18] Along the lines I have just articulated, Habermas specifies that publicity refers neither to a function nor to the content of opinion or expression, but to the *social space* generated in communicative action. Associational life is the material from which public spheres emerge. 'In complex societies', he says,

the public sphere consists of an intermediary structure between the political system, on the one hand, and the private sectors of the lifeworld and functional systems, on the other. It represents a highly complex network that branches out into a multitude of overlapping international, national, regional, local, and subcultural areas. . . . Despite these manifold differentiations, however, all the partial problems constituted by ordinary language remain porous to one another.[19]

On this conception, it is important and necessary to describe the process of specifically public discussion as occurring in a single continuous arena of discourse and expression. In spite of the reservations I raised earlier about considering civil society a single sphere, referring to the public sphere with spatial metaphors is appropriate. The spatial

---

[18] Habermas, *Between Facts and Norms*, 360.      [19] Ibid. 373–4.

metaphor helps distinguish public discourse and expression not by content or import but as differently situated. The spatial metaphor also helps describe public discussion as a process which people enter and leave, but that it goes on even when some leave. The spatial metaphor, finally, enables the theory to say that a society has one continuous public sphere without reducing those who are 'in' it to common attributes or interests. Theorizing the public sphere as such a single continuous process or 'space' is necessary if the idea of public sphere is to be helpful in describing how a diverse, complex, mass society can address social problems through public action. The scope of activity, interaction, contradiction, and conflict requires an open flow of communication across neighbourhood, region, and associational networks.

Nancy Fraser, on the other hand, has questioned the claim that public discourse in democracy should be conceptualized as a single public sphere. While she directs her criticism at Habermas's early formulation of the role of the public sphere in democratic communication, it seems to me that the point applies as well to more recent accounts of the public sphere. In societies with social and economic inequalities, Fraser argues, when there is a public sphere it tends to be dominated, both in action and ideas, by more privileged groups. Even though formal access may be the same for all, the greater resources of wealth, power, influence, and information make access easier for some than others. The interests, opinions, and perspectives more associated with the privileged social actors, then, tend to monopolize discourse in the public sphere. Along lines I have discussed in Chapter 2, moreover, Fraser points to internal exclusions from the public sphere resulting from the group specificity of idiom, rhetoric, discursive style, and assertive confidence.

In societies with structural social and economic inequalities, Fraser concludes, 'arrangements that accommodate contestation among a plurality of competing publics better promote the ideal of participatory parity than does a single, comprehensive, overarching public sphere'.[20] Parallel to dominant publics, subordinated social groups such as workers, poor people, ethnic minorities, racialized groups, and women historically have sometimes organized their associational life in such a way that they created *subaltern counter-publics*. These have had and can have dual functions. On the one hand, the counter-publics can provide sites and fora for members of the subordinated group to

---

[20] Nancy Fraser, 'Rethinking the Public Sphere: A Contribution to the Critique of Actually Existing Democracy', in Bruce Robbins (ed.), *The Phantom Public Sphere* (Minneapolis: University of Minnesota Press, 1993), 14.

raise issues among themselves and discuss them, formulate analyses and positions, as well as develop aesthetic and discursive modes for expressing their social perspectives, autonomous from dominant discourses. Chapter 3 referred to the development and preservation of such group-specific counter-publics as one proper and positive meaning for a concept of 'identity politics'. Subaltern counter-publics also importantly function as places where members of subordinated groups develop ideas, arguments, campaigns, and protest actions directed at influencing a wider public debate, often with the goal of bringing about legal or institutional change.[21]

Is there or ought there to be a single public sphere in an inclusive communicative democracy, or are there or should there be many relatively autonomous public spheres distinguished by cultural style and/or structural social perspective? Democratic theory and practice, it seems to me, require both accepting Habermas's reasons for why democratic practice in broad mass society should encourage a single public sphere, and also accepting Fraser's arguments for nurturing subaltern counter-publics. Those committed to democratic process should reject political theories and practices which map the normative public–private distinction onto a distinction between issues or discourses that are general and those that are particular. Such theories distinguish issues, or kinds of discourses, that are properly public in the sense of being oriented on a single common good, on the one hand, from discourses and issues that are properly private because they are particularistic or divisive. Such theories and practices impose a unity on the public sphere that usually excludes or disadvantages some voices or perspectives. Democratic process ought to encourage and enable the organizing of multiple and contending discourses, forms of expression, and debates.

Unless multiple spheres are able to communicate with and influence one another, however, they are only parochial separatist enclaves with little role to play in a process of solving problems that cross groups, or problems that concern relations among the groups. Inclusiveness in democratic processes, then, suggests that there must be a single public sphere, a process of interaction and exchange through which diverse sub-publics argue, influence one another, and influence policies and actions of state and economic institutions. The public is open in the

---

[21] For accounts of the operations of subaltern publics of African Americans and women respectively, see Michael C. Dawson, 'A Black Counterpublic? Economic Earthquakes, Racial Agenda(s), and Black Politics', *Public Culture*, 7 (1994), 195–223; Maria Pia Lara, *Moral Textures: Feminist Narratives in the Public Sphere* (Cambridge: Polity Press, 1998).

sense that its diverse elements are porous to one another, as well as in the sense of its stage being exposed to the view of anyone.

## Functions of the Public Sphere

The conception of democracy I am developing in this book questions two disparate but common definitions of democracy. On the one hand, I question a thin conception of democracy which defines it as a political system in which élite decision-makers are elected and subject to the rule of law. To be sure, election of lawmakers and the rule of law are necessary conditions of democracy. This definition is incomplete, however, because it omits any connection between the ideas and interests of ordinary citizens and power élites. The classical definition of democracy as 'rule by the people', on the other hand, certainly emphasizes the ideas and interests of citizens. As I discussed in the previous chapter, however, it does so by naïvely collapsing the distance between powerful office-holders or private officials and those whose actions they condition.

If we admit distinctions of state, economy, and civil society, then we admit that there are important distinctions of power. The next section argues that the power of state institutions is not just a necessary evil, but rather that state institutions sometimes have uniquely positive capacities for limiting, though not eliminating, the potentially harmful effects of economic power. Under these circumstances of institutional complexity, I suggest, democracy is better thought of as a process that *connects* 'the people' and the powerful, and through which people are able significantly to influence their actions. Democracy is more or less strong and deep according to how strong are these connections and how predictable that influence.

The public sphere is the primary connector between people and power.[22] We should judge the health of a public sphere by how well it functions as a space of opposition and accountability, on the one hand, and policy influence, on the other. In the public sphere political actors raise issues, publish information, opinions, and aesthetic expression, criticize actions and policies, and propose new policies and practices. When widely discussed and disseminated, these issues, criticisms,

[22] Jean Cohen criticizes theories of civil society typical of American politics and academic discussion for failing to thematize the public sphere functions. Without thematizing the public sphere, the concept of civil society values only self-organized citizens and not their critical relation to powerful persons and institutions. See Cohen, *American Civil Society Talk*, Working Paper No. 6 (College Park: National Commission on Civic Renewal, University of Maryland, 1997).

images, and proposals sometimes provoke political and social change. I shall first discuss functions and examples of opposition and policy influence. Some social change does come about, however, because people act in civil society itself through the mediation of public criticism and discussion. Thus I will end my description of functions of the public sphere with some examples of society acting on society.

*Opposition and accountability.* Ian Shapiro takes recent political theory to task for concentrating on only one aspect of democracy, that of collective self-government. Once we thematize democratic politics as involving some separation between people and power, we must attend to another function of democracy, namely to oppose the arbitrary exercise of power.[23] This oppositional aspect of democracy exposes what the powerful do, often in order to bring moral pressure to shame powerful actors. Public exposure, protest, and shaming sometimes work effectively to prevent the powerful from exercising their private will, instead following a more publicly formed will. The public sphere is thus a main tool through which organized citizens can limit power and hold powerful actors accountable.

Although media attend to the persons of the powerful, and in particular to their rhetorical pronouncements, their handshakes, their school choices, their jogging and shopping trips, still, in modern states and corporations, power loves to hide. It lurks between the lines of quarterly reports, executive orders and memos, which circulate and get filed; it feeds on the dull routines of everyday professional life. The effects of power are clear: a Third World government cannot renegotiate the terms of its debt, and therefore is forced to devalue its currency, instantly lowering the standard of living of the masses of its people; 3,000 more workers are laid off as a corporate giant undergoes reorganization. But the forces of power, the responsible parties, cannot be located. Everyone's hands are tied, constrained by market and regulative imperatives. Spokespeople who represent institutions or governments read prepared statements articulating in tones of quiet reason what the rules are and how their actions are constrained. The operations of the system plod along, day by day, in the same grooves. Sometimes it becomes clear that these operations serve the interests of some people more than others. They empower or re-empower some and disempower others: but the power cannot be found.

Public communication and organizing help to limit arbitrary power by exposing it and demanding that persons with public and private

---

[23] Ian Shapiro, *Democratic Justice* (New Haven: Yale University Press, 1999), ch. 1; 'Elements in Democratic Justice', *Political Theory*, 24/4 (Nov. 1996), 579–619.

power give an account of themselves. Thus discussion and debate within diverse public networks contribute to realizing the processes of representation. Researchers, journalists, and activists publicize what is going on in the halls of government, and less often in the board rooms, and expose connections between decisions and consequences.[24] An affordable housing coalition demands to know why the city council has approved subsidized loans to developers of downtown office space instead of using the city's credit and power to promote affordable housing development. Events that people might have considered inevitable begin to appear as products of decisions that serve powerful interests.

Sometimes exposing power itself reduces the potential harm the powerful can do. In a society with a free public sphere that publicly scrutinizes powerful agents and institutions, it is difficult for these agents to act in obviously self-serving ways at the expense of others. Accountability fuelled by civic public spheres can help keep the actions of the powerful within the law and minimally honest. By exposing and criticizing the policies of state or corporate actors, public communication often reveals their power as arbitrary. When exposed, the powerful often appear selfish, bullying, or puny, and without legitimacy. Creative acts of civil disobedience often force power to become naked. Low-flying helicopters intimidate women encamped in protest of nuclear missiles in a New York field; marching nuns in the streets of Manila force soldiers to shoot or give up.

When civic movements expose power in public discussion and demand that the powerful give an account of themselves, they sometimes simply assert particular interests against others. Often, however, they make moral appeals about justice, rightness, or the collective good, rather than couching their criticism in solely self-interested terms. The freedom of civic activity arguably makes more possible such moral appeals than political action under the constraints of bureaucratic or profit-oriented imperative.[25] Sometimes the force of public moral appeals made by otherwise powerless people effects a change of policy because the powerful agents have been successfully *shamed*.

In June 1992 tens of thousands of environmental activists from all over the world created a critical civic public in the parks, streets, and hallways of Rio de Janeiro. Their purpose was both to discuss

[24] Alberto Melucci, *Nomads of the Present: Social Movements and Individual Need in Contemporary Society* (London: Radius, 1989).
[25] See Claus Offe, 'Bindings, Shackles, Brakes: On Self-Limitation Strategies', in *Modernity and the State* (Cambridge, Mass.: MIT Press, 1996).

environmental issues among themselves, and to pressure officials at the United Nations conference to adopt more far-reaching international resolutions to protect species, trees, and people from the damage of pollution and over-consumption. Among other things, they demanded that George Bush, then president of the United States, attend the conference. Rowdy demonstrations witnessed on televisions all over the world accused him of snubbing the world body and not caring about future generations. The protestors did not achieve all their objectives, of course, but their moral appeal did succeed in bringing the president to Rio, and many analysts credit the non-governmental public sphere in Rio with influencing some of the language of the treaties and resolutions adopted at the conference.

Public shame is sometimes the only weapon the weak have against private economic actors, but sometimes that weapon is powerful. Mexican employees of a US company subsidiary travel north to the site of a board of directors' meeting to protest their horrid working conditions, and the press is there. Not long after, the directors take actions aimed at improving conditions. Recent campaigns exposing the low wages and dismal working conditions of Asian or Latin American subcontractors employed by popular clothing manufacturers have been very successful at achieving wide public discussion and popular support that has led to policy changes in some of the targeted multinationals.

For relatively powerless people, the justice of their cause, combined with its effective public communication, is the only leverage they have; but in the politics of shame it sometimes works. Richard Mulgan argues that shame was the effective weapon of the Maori in their militant movement to change New Zealand's policies in the 1970s and 1980s.[26] Franke Wilmer similarly argues that stateless and powerless indigenous people all over the world have succeeded in putting their issues of self-determination, poverty, and culture rights on the international agenda and in shifting the policies of many states by means of a combination of moral rightness and effective organization and communication.[27]

Exposing powerful actors and institutions to public scrutiny and criticism, then, is an important means of breaking the circle by which social and economic inequality reinforces political inequality. Through public exposure and opposition relatively powerless people

---

[26] Richard Mulgan, *Maori, Pakeha, and Democracy* (Auckland: Oxford University Press, 1989).
[27] Franke Wilmer, *The Indigenous Voice in World Politics* (London: Sage, 1993).

sometimes gain a degree of political accountability that contributes social or economic change.

*Influence over policy.* The critical and oppositional functions of the public spheres of civil society perform irreplaceable functions for democracy. Nearly every society can benefit from enlargement of such critical public activity. Publicly criticizing state or corporate actions, however, is often easier than recommending positive action. Public spheres function to promote democracy and justice, however, also to the extent that they facilitate discussion and debate about what ought to be done by both the state, economic actors, and groups and individuals in civil society itself. In public spheres organized citizens often debate collective problems and what should be done about them, and organize to influence the policy-makers.

The next section criticizes arguments that law and public policy should not be used to regulate economic and social activity for the sake of promoting justice. For now I shall assume that state institutions should have many legitimate regulatory and programmatic functions. If citizens have no means of positively influencing state policy, then such policies cannot claim normative democratic legitimacy. Citizens exercise some measure of such influence, of course, by voting for legislative representatives. By itself, however, voting is a very thin form of influence. Civic organizing that raises issues and promotes policy objectives in the public sphere is an important supplement to the electoral process.

Habermas theorizes the public sphere as a sort of political thermostat. Its discussions and communication flows function to detect the emergence of social problems or wrongful harms. They transfer information about those problems and harms from the everyday activity in which they are experienced to the legislative and bureaucratic system that regulates the institutional background conditions, eventually producing a regulatory change meant to adjust the social environment to address the problems.

This image is of an ideal relationship between civil society, the public sphere, and state regulation, of course, one in which the regulatory results have democratic legitimacy. Law and policy are democratically legitimate to the extent that they address problems identified through broad public discussion with remedies that respond to reasonably reflective and undominated public opinion. The associational activity of civil society functions to identify problems, interests, and needs in the society; public spheres take up these problems, communicate them to others, give them urgency, and put pressures on state institutions to institute measures to address them. Crucial to such processes of democratic legitimacy, the arguments in the earlier chapters of this book suggest, are inclusive processes of communication. If some of the interests, opinions, and perspectives are suppressed, which would otherwise be formulated to persuade others of the importance of particular problems or solutions, or if some groups have difficulty getting heard for reasons of structural inequality, cultural misunderstanding, or social prejudice, then the agenda or the results of public policy are likely to be biased or unfair.

For these reasons, the public sphere will properly be a site of struggle—often contentious struggle. Precisely because norms of democratic legitimacy call for responding to policy agendas that emerge through broad public discussion, an effective way for more powerful or privileged actors to promote their political interests is to try to control the agenda of public discussion. It often takes considerable organizing, dramatic action, and rhetorical shrewdness for people whose concerns are excluded from that agenda to break through and gain access to public media that will fairly and widely disseminate their issues so that state institutions eventually deal with them.

Even in the vastly imperfect hierarchical democracies we live in, however, such legislative or policy shift sometimes happens. The process that led to the passage of the Americans with Disabilities Act of 1990 in the United States is one example of the success of citizens with serious social and policy concerns capturing a place in the public agenda and winning major legislative reform.[28] In the early 1990s AIDS activists in the United States engaged in disruptive protests of the regulatory policies of the Food and Drug Administration which prompted wide public discussion in diverse settings and eventually led to policy changes.

*Changing society through society.*  Sometimes public spheres aid social change projects without directly targeting the state or economy. Associational life enables people to experiment with ways of living and doing things, interacting or producing goods and distributing them, and with new norms of symbolic expression, or different ways of organizing associations. Sometimes people believe that these alternative norms and practices would be generally better for the society or some particular disadvantaged group if they were widely adopted. Public spheres then serve to spread the ideas and practices of this alternative.

---

[28] Joseph P. Shapiro, *No Pity: People with Disabilities Forging a New Civil Rights Movement* (New York: New York Times Books, 1993).

Many of the changes wrought by the contemporary feminist move-ment, for example, have had this character. Feminists effectively criti-cized the strong sexual division of labour in the family that makes men the public breadwinner and women the private domestic workers. While sexual equality in the family has by no means been achieved, decades of public discussion of the fairness of traditional arrangements have contributed to changes in attitudes and practices by masses of women and men. One might argue along similar lines that issues like pornography are best dealt with by means of intra-social transforma-tion rather than by means of legislation. Attempting to regulate or forbid the publication of books and movies degrading to women is fraught with problems of definition and application, thus endangering legitimate liberty. Feminists cannot take a 'live and let live' attitude towards such cultural products, however. Public discussion, demon-stration, and boycott are useful ways of calling directly on the public for people to examine their behaviour and desire.

The environmental movement offers another example of intra-society change outside state institutions. Environmentalists persuaded many consumers to reuse and recycle used consumer items, and de-veloped informal voluntary civic recycling systems, long before municipalities, private companies, and states entered the business of recycling. In this case, habits and attitudes first significantly changed in the lifeworld of civil society, where ideas and practices spread through public discussions. Only after significant social change had taken place did governments and private businesses extend the influ-ence of those changes by means of law, government, and corporate organization. This coupling of state or economic activity with a social change begun in civic activity is arguably one of the best ways to fos-ter social change.

Public organizing and engagement, then, can be thought of as processes by which the society communicates to itself about its needs, problems, and creative ideas for how to solve them. The democratic legitimacy of public policy, moreover, depends partly on the state institutions being sensitive to that communication process. The moral force of the processes of public communication and its relation to pol-icy, then, rests in part on a requirement that such communication be both inclusive and critically self-conscious.

To summarize, people collectively exercise positive power through civil society in a variety of ways. People acting in civil society to develop new ideas, disseminate alternative practices, or organize pub-lic criticism of state and economic power, form solidarities for both the privileged and the relatively disadvantaged. They invite members of the society to discuss problems either in order to change state or corporate policy, or to foster change in society directly. All these activities refer to the value of self-determination, the primary aspect of social justice that associative activity outside state and economy promotes. To the extent that associative activity enables public expression of particular ways of life or provides goods and services, it also contributes to promoting the value of self-development. Thus those who argue that diverse and broad civic associational life is a crucial basis for democracy have good grounds for their claims.

## 4. The Limits of Civil Society

The rediscovery of civil society, I have suggested thus far, is an important development in both contemporary political theory and practice. Especially when we understand civil society as a third sector outside of and anchoring both state and economy, the theory of civil society reveals powerful means of enhancing democracy and social solidarity. These functions have been relatively neglected by political theorists concentrating on state and economy. Renewed interest in civil society, however, coincides with new expressions of scepticism about state institutions. Anti-state sentiment in many parts of the world has helped to create conditions for dismantling state enterprises, regulatory and planning functions, and welfare services. Coincidentally, some political analysts regard civil society more highly than the state as a means for citizens to pursue social justice and well-being.

In this section I challenge this tendency to regard civil society as an alternative site for the performance of public-spirited, caring, and equalizing functions that have long been associated with governments. While civil society can promote democracy, social justice, and well-being in ways I have outlined, there are limits to what citizens can accomplish through institutions of civil society alone. Some argue that the fragmentation and plurality of civil society can undermine the trust and solidarity necessary for self-determining democracy,[29] and I think that there is merit to this argument. Here I will be more concerned with limits to the ability of civil society to address issues of justice as self-development. Especially because profit- and market-oriented economic activities inhibit the self-development of many people, citizens must rely on state institutions to take positive action to undermine oppression and promote justice. While state power must

---

[29] See Levi, 'Social and Unsocial Capital', and Rosenblum, *Membership and Morals*.

always be subject to vigilant scrutiny by citizens alert to dangers of corruption and domination, democratic state institutions nevertheless have unique and important virtues for promoting social justice.

I assume that no critics of state institutions today deny that states are important for policing, adjudicating conflict, and enforcing basic liberties. Nevertheless, many consider state institutions as necessary evils which ought to be kept to a minimum and are not to be trusted. We should not look to states, on this view, to take more expansive and substantial action to further the well-being of persons and groups. While it is always good to reduce suffering or injustice, solve social problems, and promote well-being, we should not depend on states to do it. Critics of the state have at least three kinds of argument for the claim that citizens should reject reliance on state institutions to solve social problems and promote justice as the equal opportunity for everyone to develop and exercise capacities: libertarian, communitarian, and post-Marxist. I will reconstruct each of these arguments, and then respond to them together.

The libertarian argument is familiar. Maximizing the liberty of individuals and organizations to pursue their own ends is the primary principle of justice. Coercive state institutions are justified only in order to enforce liberty, that is, to prevent some agents from interfering with others' legitimate exercise of their liberty. Although a society may contain many social and economic problems, many conflicts, injustices, and harmful inequalities, these are more properly addressed by voluntary co-operation in settings of private enterprise and civil society than by means of state regulation. It is wrong to use state institutions to try to produce substantive social outcomes in the way of resources use, income distribution, or the allocation of social positions. Aiming to do so, moreover, is likely to produce irrational or inefficient consequences. Minimizing the reach of state institutions is thus the social ideal.[30]

The communitarian argument differs from the libertarian in its positive concern for substantive values of caring, solidarity, and civic virtue. While communitarians endorse the value of liberty, protection of liberty is but one among several principles that ought to guide moral and political life, and may be overridden for the sake of promoting values of community. Communitarian morality, moreover, aims at

[30] I derive this argument primarily from Milton Friedman, *Capitalism and Freedom* (Chicago: University of Chicago Press, 1962). For the idea that it is wrong for state institutions to aim to produce distributive patterns, however, I am thinking of Robert Nozick's argument in *Anarchy, State and Utopia* (Cambridge, Mass.: Harvard University Press, 1974).

fostering and nurturing substantive ends of mutual aid and shared cultural symbols and practices. As grounds for preferring institutions of civil society to state institutions to realize the ends of mutual aid, caring, and social justice, some communitarians suggest the following. State bureaucratic institutions that provide social services, redistribute income, regulate economic activity, and so on, break down and distort local communities because they universalize and formalize these activities and curtail local autonomy. Government regulatory, redistributive, welfare, and social service bureaucracies, moreover, transform citizens into passive followers of orders and clients of services. State efforts to promote citizen well-being, furthermore, allow individuals and communities to shirk their personal and particular responsibilities to contribute to the well-being of community members. State actions break up the civic sources of mutual aid and solidarity. Government programmes to achieve substantive ends of equality or self-development generate an 'entitlement' mentality according to which citizens clamour for particular benefits to serve their interests without being willing to make social contributions, thus ultimately overloading and weakening the state. Good citizens are independent and autonomous, rather than dependent on others, at the same time that they manifest a commitment to promote the well-being of others and of the institutions and values of the community. Thus, rather than create and sustain bureaucratic state institutions to promote the well-being of citizens, public policy should devote itself to supporting civic education to instil in citizens a sense of obligation to others and the skills to organize civic institutions of solidarity and mutual aid.[31]

I call 'post-Marxist' those writers and activists in the socialist tradition who continue to be critical of capitalist economic processes and who argue for radical democracy, but who also criticize some aspects of historic Marxism. Post-Marxists express several reasons for turning to civil society as the arena for pursuing democracy and social justice, and for taking a distance from the state.

Most socialists traditionally understood their political project to consist in using state institutions to control the means of production and direct them to meeting needs and developing capacities. Some

[31] This argument is my own reconstruction, which I derive from contemporary public policy rhetoric in the United States and from the writings of Amitai Etzioni and William Galston. See Etzioni, *The Spirit of Community* (New York: Crown, 1993) and William Galston, *Liberal Purposes* (Cambridge: Cambridge University Press, 1991). Neither Etzioni nor Galston, however, would likely endorse the complete anti-state formulation I have attributed to the communitarian position here. Certain versions of African American community-based self-help discourse might also be said to fall within this general communitarian position.

post-Marxists question this state socialist project because it assumes that the state can be a single agent outside society directing its operations as a whole, when the state should be understood as part of society. Even if it holds democratic ideals, moreover, state socialism collapses the distinction between state and economy which helps the lifeworld of civil society to maintain its freedom and autonomy from coercive regulation.[32] The radical anti-capitalist pursuit of justice is better thought of as a project of democratizing both the state, corporate economy, and civil society than bringing all the production and distribution of goods under democratic state direction.

While most post-Marxists support existing social insurance and welfare programmes, they also raise critical questions about capitalist welfare states. Interventionist and redistributive policies in the context of capitalism can be sustained under conditions of rapid growth and relative insulation from foreign competition. Without these conditions, the fiscal and managerial tensions of supporting large welfare states become manifest, and states retreat from economic regulation and welfare provision.[33] Activities to meet needs and provide social services that come under the bureaucratic rationality of the state, moreover, disorganize the democratic communicative potential of family and community, replacing them with normalizing, dominating, and pacifying regulatory regimes to which clients must submit or do without help.[34]

Like traditional Marxists, finally, some post-Marxists argue that in capitalist societies states do not neutrally represent all social sectors, but rather respond most to the imperatives of capital accumulation. States that try to control investment and service provision in ways that conflict with the interests of big economic actors are faced with capital flight and disinvestment. When states are thus dominated by economic power, social change movements of environmentalists or economic egalitarians are bound to be co-opted if they try to work within the state. Movements for social justice should thus limit their activity to pressuring state and economy from outside in civil society, and to enlarging the activity of democratic associations and economic co-operatives in the independent sector.[35]

[32] See Cohen and Arato, *Civil Society and Political Theory*, 418, 466, 481.

[33] Ibid. 462–8; see also Claus Offe, *Contradictions of the Welfare State* (Cambridge, Mass.: MIT Press, 1984); and Iris Marion Young, *Justice and the Politics of Difference* (Princeton: Princeton University Press, 1990), ch. 2.

[34] This process is part of what Habermas refers to as the 'colonization of the lifeworld'. See *The Theory of Communicative Action*, ii; see also Nancy Fraser, 'Struggle over Needs', in *Unruly Practices* (Minneapolis: University of Minnesota Press, 1989).

[35] John Dryzek, 'Political Inclusion and the Dynamics of Democratization', *American Political Science Review*, 90/1 (Summer 1996), 475–87; *Democracy in Capitalist Times*.

Each of these arguments gives primary value to self-determination. The libertarian position above all values individual self-determination defined as the negative liberty of persons and enterprises. Both communitarians and neo-Marxists hold that libertarians do not recognize how the power of large organizations often seriously inhibits an individual's self-determination, and how the interdependence of modern social life transforms the meaning of self-determination. Because individual well-being depends on communicative and associative relations with others, and because social and economic processes generate collective problems, individuals can determine the conditions of their action primarily as participants in democratic decisions about community affairs. In my view, all three of these arguments tend to forget that social justice involves not only self-determination but also self-development.

As I discussed the idea in Chapter 1, self-development means being able actively to engage in the world and grow. Just social institutions provide conditions for all persons to learn and use satisfying and expansive skills in socially recognized settings, and enable them to play and communicate with others or express their feelings and perspective on social life in contexts where others can listen. Self-development in this sense certainly entails meeting people's basic needs for food, shelter, health care, and so on. It also entails the use of resources for education and training. Self-development does not depend simply on a certain distribution of materials goods. Using satisfying skills and having one's particular cultural modes of expression and ways of life recognized also depend on the organization of the division of labour and the structures of communication and co-operation. While self-development is thus not reducible to the distribution of resources, market- and profit-oriented economic processes particularly impinge on the ability of many to develop and exercise capacities. Because this is so, pursuit of justice as self-development cannot rely on the communicative and organizational activities of civil society alone, but requires positive state intervention to regulate and direct economic activity.

Before making that argument, I should make clear that I agree with the post-Marxist critique of state socialism for its totalizing tendencies. State power threatens freedom and self-determination, and should be limited by markets and independent economic enterprise, on the one hand, and strong independent networks of civic and political associations, on the other. Confining state institutions to enforcing agreements, adjudicating disputes, and protecting private liberties, however, cedes too much scope for economically based oppression.

Social justice requires the mutual limitation of state, economy, and civil society.

Profit- and market-oriented economic processes impede the ability of many people in most societies to develope and exercise capacities, due to at least the following factors. Business cycles, along with technological and organizational changes aimed at reducing labour costs, regularly throw people out of work. Commodity markets increasingly favour big producers over the small farmer or craftsperson. Vast numbers of people are thereby economically marginalized, without meaningful work and means of subsistence. Many unemployed people are so worried about survival that they have little time and energy for volunteer contributions to their communities, and many employed people also lack the time. Many currently employed people live at the edge of economic insecurity. This would not count as remediable injustice if their society lacked resources for remediation. Both locally and globally, however, there are such vast inequalities of wealth, comfort, and privilege that structural change could enable more people to develop and exercise capacities. Rationalization of production or service delivery to minimize costs per unit by mechanization often subdivides the work process so thoroughly that performing it does not require learning and using satisfying skills even when the work requires significant concentration. Market-driven investment and pricing decisions encourage the proliferation of gadgets and cheap entertainment at the same time that they fail to provide housing, health care, and quality education and training affordable to everyone. Markets produce numbers of harmful or socially costly consequences as 'externalities' difficult to charge to particular responsible parties, such as pollution, congestion, needs to travel greater distances, despoliation of city and countryside, and other damages to the collective quality of life.

If promoting social justice means that societies should, as much as possible, aim to make conditions for self-development available for everyone, then these endemic consequences of profit- and market-oriented economic processes ought to be corrected. The most direct and rational response entails, on the one hand, socially directed investment decisions to meet needs, provide education and training, and create and maintain quality infrastructure, parks, pleasant and well-lighted streets, and other such public spaces; and, on the other hand, the organization of the necessary, useful, and creative work of the society so that everyone able to make social contributions has the opportunity to do so.

The associations of civil society certainly can respond to the failures of firms and markets to enable the development exercise of capacities.

Civil society alone, however, cannot do the major work of directing investment towards meeting needs and developing skills and usefully employing its members. Ensuring investment in needs, infrastructure, and education and training enough to support self-development for everyone and the organization of the work of society so that everyone who is able does meaningful work requires much society-wide decision-making and co-ordinated action. Precisely the virtues of civil society, however—voluntary association, decentralization, freedom to start new and unusual things—mitigate against such co-ordination. Indeed, the activities of civil society may exacerbate problems of inequality, marginalization, and inhibition of the development of capabilities. For persons and groups with greater material and organizational resources are liable to maintain and even enlarge their social advantages through their associational activity. Especially to the extent that their associational life is private as distinct from civicly oriented, their associational activities often reinforce unequal opportunities for developing capabilities. Associations of civil society, moreover, cannot mobilize the amount of resources necessary to support conditions for the self-development of everyone.

State institutions in principle are the most important means of regulating and directing economic life for the sake of the self-development of everyone. Only state institutions have the kind of power that can limit the power of large private enterprises and facilitate the use of that private power for the collective well-being. Well-organized states accomplish large-scale collective goals by facilitating social co-ordination among individuals and groups. To manage such co-ordination states must be centralized and regulative: they must gather useful information, monitor implementation and compliance, and rely on coercion in case of non-compliance. Only state institutions can facilitate the co-ordination required for a society to ensure investment in needs, skills development, infrastructure, and quality environment for everyone, and to organize many useful occupations so that those not self-employed or working for private enterprise have options for meaningful work. Democratically legitimized states are not necessary evils; potentially and sometimes actually, they exhibit uniquely important virtues to support social justice in ways no other social processes do.[36]

The claim that citizens ought to promote justice as self-development as well as self-determination, and that state institutions

---

[36]   Robert Goodin, 'The State as a Moral Agent', in *Utilitarianism as a Public Philosophy* (Cambridge: Cambridge University Press, 1995).

are the most important means of doing so, raises many questions about how this should be done. Reasonable people disagree about what values and priorities come under the umbrella of social justice. They disagree as well about what policies are most efficient and effective for promoting the well-being of citizens, and require the fewest trade-offs with other values. Addressing all these debates would require much more than I can accomplish here. The point of this argument is not to advocate particular policy solutions to problems of poverty, segregation, or economic domination. It is rather only to argue that democratic citizens should look to law and public policy to address these and related problems, and should consider state institutions and their actions major sites of democratic struggle, not merely for the sake of resisting corruption and the abuse of power, but also for taking action to foster social changes to promote greater justice.

Libertarians, of course, object that the use of the state to promote particular social outcomes wrongly interferes with the liberty of individuals, organizations, and firms. I have assumed that social justice requires that everyone has an equal opportunity to develop and exercise capacities. I have argued that such opportunities are by no means guaranteed by the workings of private enterprise and civil society, and further that profit- and market-oriented economic activity contributes to the inhibition of the capacities of many. As Robert Goodin argues, the libertarian claim that each should be allowed to attend to his or her own business without interference does not apply where discharging a moral obligation is the business of nobody in particular.[37] Under such circumstances, the state is the means by which the collective discharges its obligations, and it is permissible for the democratic state to compel everyone to contribute to those moral priorities.

From both communitarians and post-Marxists might come the dependency-domination objection. If states co-ordinate investment and the division of labour in ways to ensure that everyone can develop and exercise capacities, they do so at the cost of making citizens dependent on state action and submitting them to bureaucratic rules. Society-wide co-ordination of action through the state does generate formal regulation and bureaucracy which can have pacifying and dominating effects. The proper response to such dangers is not to reject state action to achieve objectives best achieved by governments, but rather to couple that action with the flexibility and critical accountability of civil society. In the next section I will explore some proposals for such linkage.

---

[37] Ibid.

One of the post-Marxist arguments for restricting the pursuit of social justice to activities in civil society may work most directly against the image of the virtuous state I have offered. Don't I assume that the state is a neutral instrument citizens can use to co-ordinate their collective lives towards particular ends? Isn't it rather the case that the very economic powers I argue ought to be regulated for the sake of ensuring self-development and well-being themselves manipulate states for the sake of their own interests? There is considerable truth in this claim, especially in these days of globalization, when economic powers larger and more powerful than states hamper the ability of most states to fashion policies that will promote the self-development of their citizens. Multinational corporations, trade agreements, financial institutions such as the International Monetary Fund exercise significant power to influence the policies of many states in ways that often make ordinary working and poor people worse off. To the extent that this is a global reality it should be recognized, but not accepted as either necessary or good.

At this point, however, we return to the role of civil society, as the lived world where social and systemic problems are felt, and the world of communicative organizing that by protest and persuasion shifts public opinion and the forces that influence state policies. Both social movement activists such as Zapatistas and scholars of international relations appeal to expanded activities of an international civil society as a means for citizens to respond to the economic powers that transcend states. People organized across borders can expose the power of transnational economic actors and work to develop and strengthen democratic international regulation and co-operation. Both within and across societies, strengthening the associative life of civil society for the sake of promoting self-determination and self-development for everyone remains a crucial project. This chapter has discussed how civil society performs unique functions of social solidarity, identity support, and criticism of state and economic actors. To perform these functions associations must remain independent enough of state institutions both to provide alternative spaces for public action and to criticize state action. Chapter 7 will focus on issues of democracy in the context of transnational power and interaction.

## 5. Associative Democracy

This chapter has supported the claim that a free, active and diverse civil society is crucial for democracy. Associational activity promotes communicative interaction both in small groups and across large publics. It fosters democratic inclusion by enabling excluded or marginalized groups to find each other, develop counter-publics, and express their opinions and perspectives to a wider public. The public sphere arising from civic organizing and communication both serves a crucial oppositional function and develops knowledge and ideas for political action. Civic organizing and public discussion enable individuals collectively to authorize modes and sites in which aspects of their lives are represented in political discussion. At the same time, such organizing and discussion provides one of the most effective ways of holding representatives accountable. Civil society limits the ability of both state and economy to colonize the lifeworld, and fosters individual and collective self-determination.

Particular attributes of civil society make possible its self-determining, oppositional, communicative, and creative aspects. The value of civil society lies precisely in the fact that its activities are voluntary, diverse, plural, often locally based, and relatively uncoordinated among one another. Civic associations deepen democracy and promote self-development because they are relatively autonomous from both state and economy and from each other, potentially and often actually subject to participatory democratic governance by their members.

I have also argued, however, that civic activity cannot substitute for critical functions that state institutions have often fulfilled at least to some degree in twentieth-century democracies. State institutions ought not merely to provide a framework of rights and their enforcement to support civic and economic activity. Promoting social justice requires attending to issues of self-development as well as self-determination. Left to themselves, both the organization and consequences of capitalist market activity impede the self-development of many people. Authoritative state regulation can limit the harmful effects of economic power. Economic and infrastructure planning, redistributive policies, and the direct provision of goods and services by the state can minimize material deprivation and foster the well-being of all members of society.

State institutions can be a tool limiting economic power and promoting general well-being, however, only because and to the extent that they can co-ordinate action across a broad and complex social field by means of authoritative rules backed by coercion. The virtues of state institutions, that is, are quite the contrary of the virtues of civic activity. They are centralized, have formal rules and procedures, layers of bureaucracy, and systems of review. When strong they have

significant power to motivate actions, either by threatening or offering, so that their collective effects will achieve authoritatively decided
results.

A democratic society and politics that would promote justice needs
economic activities of production, distribution, service provision,
resource development, and financing. To promote justice these economic goals need to be balanced with activities of civil society and
state institutions. In theory civil society and state institutions perform
complementary functions, both limiting the potentially harmful
effects of unfettered and merely self-regarding economic activity, and
each correcting the potential excesses of the other. In practice, however, it could be argued that these two aspects of social and political life
tend to pull against each other. The authoritative power of state institutions can and sometimes does repress the creativity of civic activity
and the ideas expressed in public spheres. The centralized and formally
regulated nature of state-co-ordinated programmes sometimes enacts
service or distributive biases, renders citizens passive and dependent,
frustrates attempts at innovation, wastes resources, or fails to take
account of individual, group, and local differences. The anarchistic and
particularistic impulses of civil society, on the other hand, sometimes
mean that plural organizations pursue their own ends either ignorant
of or in direct competition with others. Far from promoting broad
social trust, plural and diverse civic activity can produce both inequality, exclusion, and generally unco-ordinated activity. Too much civic
voluntarism and oppositional organizing can undermine the possibility of co-ordinated positive state action. That may be just what
democracy requires when the state is tyrannical, but when the state is
formally democratic and liberal, such fragmentation and incapacity
robs less advantaged citizens of tools they and their allies can use to
improve their lives.

Democratic institutions thus face a certain dilemma. On the one
hand, state and civil society are both necessary elements in a democratic process that aims to do justice. On the other hand, their attributes
and actions seem to undermine one another. Some theorists and
activists recently have proposed a way out of this dilemma by linking
state and civic institutions more closely. I will now briefly examine
these proposals for what some call *associative democracy.* The general
idea of associative democracy has many potential virtues, I will argue,
and democratic processes might well benefit from having more institutions along the lines of associative democracy. Despite its promise,
however, I conclude that associative democracy cannot resolve the
tensions between state and civic institutions.

I rely on two theories of associative democracy, one proposed by Paul Hirst and another proposed by Joshua Cohen and Joel Rogers. While the two theories are similar in many respects, they are different enough to warrant separate analyses. Together the two theories exhibit, more than resolve, the tensions between state institutions and civil society that I have uncovered. While each theory has the tension implicit within it, this tension appears more salient when seeing them together. Each theory aims to overcome the ways civic and state institutions can undermine one another by balancing and linking the two forms of institutions. In fact, however, each theory tends to resolve the tension by allowing one side to dominate the other. Hirst's theory of associative democracy gives greater weight to the decentralized, voluntary, and local virtues of civic associations, while Cohen and Rogers put greater weight on the centralizing, co-ordinating, and enforcing functions more characteristic of state institutions.

Paul Hirst thinks of associative democracy as an institutionally different way of organizing economic production, distribution, and service provision. While state and market economy remain alongside this alternative set of institutions, he envisions that many of the functions and activities performed now by either state institutions or private for-profit enterprises are increasingly taken over by voluntary associations governed by and accountable to the persons whom they serve or represent. As I understand Hirst's vision, services such as health care, garbage collection, or postal service are to be administered through such voluntary associations. He also proposes a larger role for relatively small, democratically run associative enterprises to produce and distribute goods.

In Hirst's theory, the primary value served by associative democracy is self-governance. The ideal is to expand the range of social activity over which affected persons have collective control by means of membership in democratic associations. For the most part, these are local and functionally differentiated. Citizens relate to them voluntarily. They themselves decide which associations they want to provide needed or wanted services for them, from which associations they will buy goods, and which associations will represent them in regional, national, or global political discussions.

As much as possible, for Hirst, the authoritative functions of state regulatory and welfare bureaucracies should be devolved onto such associations, which serve local populations to which they are also accountable and in relation to which they can be flexible in policy implementation. Hirst questions institutions of state sovereignty in the form of encompassing and central authority over multiple functions in a large contiguous territory. He argues that authority should be functionally differentiated and devolved as locally as feasible while accomplishing their objectives. Without articulating details, he suggests that principles of federalism should put both associations, functions, and locales in co-ordinated relations to one another. Chapters 6 and 7 will say more about issues of local governance and federalism.

Despite its devolution of many authoritative functions, on Hirst's account there remain many important functions for state institutions. A centralized, co-ordinating, and authoritatively coercive state is the most important mechanism for funding associations. Hirst follows Philippe Schmitter's proposal that associations should be funded through a voucher system paid for by taxes. Under such a system, citizens would each have the right to designate a certain proportion of tax dollars to the associations of their choice; perhaps the state would limit the number of associations each citizen can name, and specify standards associations must meet to get on the list. Both Schmitter and Hirst offer such a system of voluntary funding as a way of increasing citizen influence over associational life as well as ensuring that relatively disadvantaged or minority groups receive funding.

On Hirst's model, other important functions for state institutions include setting standards for products and services, ensuring peace among associations, enforcing rights, formulating and enforcing a common regulatory framework for associative activity, reviewing the associations' spending practices, and monitoring compliance. Thus Hirst envisions state institutions as enabling associative activity and setting a regulatory and legal framework for the relation between individuals and associations, and the relation between associations. Ideally most services and many goods are supplied, however, by democratically run membership associations. Hirst thus emphasizes the civic principles of localism and voluntary membership. On this account, the state is a kind of handmaid to associations.[38]

For Cohen and Rogers, on the other hand, the primary purposes of associative democracy seem to be to promote equality and efficiency. As I understand their proposals, the institutions of associative democracy are a means by which state institutions can compensate for the unfair political advantages of the wealthy and implement welfare and regulatory policies most efficiently.

Cohen and Rogers envision associative democracy as a means of implementing special representation for oppressed and disadvantaged

[38] Paul Hirst, *Associative Democracy* (Amherst: University of Massachusetts Press, 1993).

groups, the principle that I argued for in Chapter 4. The rules and regulations of associative democratic institutions can locate or help create
organizations of various under-represented groups: poor people,
minorities, or groups whose interests and social perspectives offer
legitimate contributions to public discussion but which in the free play
of competition among groups tend to lose influence and lack
resources. In the Cohen and Rogers model, funding of associations
seems crucially different from Hirst's. For them, it appears that the
state directly subsidizes the formation or maintenance of associations
for the purposes of compensating for unequal influence on public
policy.

It seems that Cohen and Rogers envision a narrower role for associations linked to state institutions than Hirst. Their primary purpose
is to set basic economic, regulatory, and welfare policy and especially
to follow through on the implementation of policies. Cohen and
Rogers worry about the factional and divisive quality of market and
civic life; they propose to remedy such unworkable anarchy by
encouraging associations that are encompassing in the groups they
represent, that co-ordinate action through centralized institutions,
and which are able effectively to discipline their members. The associations that Cohen and Rogers envision working together with each
other and the state to deliberate about and implement economic plans
and regulations, that is, take on state-like function in many of their
important activities.[39]

These models of associative democracy clearly raise many questions. Exactly which sort of functions and decisions are appropriate
for voluntary associations, and which are not. Should we think of
associative democracy as a form of the organization of all of society, or
as one among many policy tools? If states decide to organize and
subsidize associations, by what process and criteria should this be
undertaken? How does associative democracy deal with the many
conflicts and disagreements that would surely to arise about each of
these questions?

Despite the gaps in these accounts of associative democracy, it
would be a mistake to dismiss them. As I have argued, contemporary
disaffection with state institutions as tools for promoting justice and
well-being is misplaced. Vigorous state institutions have unique regulatory and co-ordinative capacities necessary for enacting society-
wide plans, limiting the dominative power of private institutions,

[39] Joshua Cohen and Joel Rogers, 'Secondary Associations and Democratic
Governance', in Eric Olin Wright (ed.), *Associations and Democracy* (London: Verso,
1995).

providing universally available services, as well as defining and enforcing rights. The power state institutions require to accomplish these things, and states' tendency to grow in bureaucratic complexity, however, means that state institutions are prone to abuse their power and become unresponsive to the concerns of the citizens they are supposed to serve. Prudence calls for a mistrust of state institutions, even when we affirm their importance.

Thus the general idea of linking civic institutions more directly to state institutions in formal processes of decision-making, representation, and review may help us to conceptualize how strong states can be better used for promoting ends of democracy, justice, and well-being. Various experiments of this sort have been performed around the world in recent years. For example, government officials have found it increasingly difficult to impose decisions on localities about the siting of risky facilities, and for this reason increasingly have instituted processes of deliberation and consultation that formally involve civic organizations.[40] Movements have been growing in the United States and elsewhere for citizen panels with authority to review the actions and policies of state institutions such as police departments. While many find the forms of corporatism typical of some European countries too élitist and exclusionary to be called democratic and representative, some polities have experimented with new forms of diverse representation of social segments in state-level decision-making bodies. A nation-wide body of representatives of business, labour, and civic non-profit and community organizations in South Africa, for example, has a formal role in setting the legislative agenda, preparing studies to support that agenda, and publicly discussing policy issues. The April 1998 peace agreement for Northern Ireland, to take another example, called for the creation of a Civic Forum composed of representatives from diverse civic organizations to influence policy discussion alongside the legislative assembly. Citizens wishing to deepen democratic communication across social difference and to promote social justice thus have a number of models available for linking official state authority to the creativity, diversity, and fluidity of civil society.

Creating such institutions, however, is not likely to reduce the tension between these two aspects of social organization. Whenever civic associations are more strongly tied to authoritative state procedures, their independence from state imperatives, and therefore their ability

---

[40] Christian Hunold and Iris Marion Young, 'Justice, Democracy and Hazardous Siting', *Political Studies*, 46/1 (1998), 82–95.

to hold state institutions accountable to citizens, is threatened. Whenever procedures are created to link state and civil society for purposes of policy-making, implementation, or evaluation, these procedures risk becoming another layer of bureaucracy disciplining citizens or insulating them from influencing the process. On the other hand, when deliberation and decision-making authority are dispersed among diverse locales, associational interests, and perspectives, they are liable to lose a generalized vision of the co-ordinated action of the whole society. Citizens in a deep democracy must be aware of these ever present tensions and liabilities, be vigilant in monitoring the actions and effects of both state, economy, and civil society, and actively promote the limitation and balance of each by the others.

# CHAPTER 6

## Residential Segregation and Regional Democracy

Earlier chapters used metaphors of social location to describe aspects of relations among people, and to ground a claim that structural locations give rise to different social perspectives. Spatial metaphors of structure, position, location, field, and perspective aim to evoke the multidimensionality and differentiated privileges of these relationships. Social relationships defined by location that have consequences for democracy and justice are not only metaphorical, however. Space itself matters. Few theories of democracy, however, have thematized the normative implications of spatialized social relations. Both this chapter and the next take up this task. This chapter focuses on the local and regional spaces of metropolitan areas, whereas the next chapter considers more global social and spatial relations.

Processes that produce and reproduce residential segregation are obvious forms of social, economic, and political exclusion. Defining segregation as a process of exclusion, this chapter reviews the harms it causes or exacerbates. Residential segregation enacts or enlarges many material privileges of economic opportunity, quality of life, power to influence actions and events, and convenience. At the same time it obscures the fact of such privileges from many of their beneficiaries. Most salient for issues of democracy, segregation impedes communication among the segregated groups.

My discussion of segregation focuses first on residential racial segregation in the United States. The harms of segregation are not confined to racial segregation, however, nor are they experienced only in the United States. Thus I discuss issues of class-based segregation as well as race-based segregation. I refer, moreover, to processes of both race and class segregation outside the United States, particularly in Europe.

Having detailed both economic and political harms of segregation, I explore normative ideals that should guide practices and policies to respond to these harms. Most critical reactions to existing residential patterns are guided by certain ideals of integration that promote the mixing of segregated groups, and specifically the entrance of racial minorities or lower-income people into the more privileged sites and enclaves. While equal opportunity and freedom of movement are, in my view, basic values, and highlight the need to remove remaining discriminatory barriers in contemporary urbanized democracies, I argue in this chapter against this model of integration as the best ideal to guide inclusively democratic practice. Group-differentiated residential and associational clustering is not necessarily bad in itself, inasmuch as it may arise from legitimate desires to form and maintain affinity grouping. Spatial group differentiation, however, should be voluntary, fluid, without clear borders, and with many overlapping, unmarked, and hybrid places. To the extent that a model of integration as mixing and dispersal ignores the primary issues of the spatial distribution of benefits, I argue that this ideal focuses on the wrong set of issues.

I offer an alternative ideal of social and political inclusion that I call *differentiated solidarity*. This ideal shares with an ideal of integration a commitment to combat exclusion and foster individual freedom. But, unlike at least some formulations of an ideal of integration, differentiated solidarity also affirms the freedom of association that may entail residential clustering and civic differentiation. At the same time, the ideal of differentiated solidarity notices and affirms that locally and culturally differentiated groups dwell together in a wider region whose structural and environmental conditions affect them all, and where actions and interactions often have distributive consequences that tend to benefit some over others. Thus the ideal of differentiated solidarity affirms that groups nevertheless dwell together, whether they like it or not, within a set of problems and relationships of structural interdependence that bring with them obligations of justice.

Chapter 1 introduced the question of what is the morally appropriate scope of an inclusively democratic polity, but postponed further discussion of that issue. This chapter thematizes this question of the proper scope of the polity at local and regional levels of interaction, and the next chapter addresses the question of scope in the context of global interaction. The scope of the polity, I argue, ought to include all those who dwell together within structural relations generated by processes of interaction, exchange, and movement that create unavoidable conditions of action for all of them. The harms of residential segregation are enacted in many places, most notably in the United States, by the construction or maintenance of small political jurisdictions within metropolitan areas of dense interaction. Against such metropolitan fragmentation, I argue for political jurisdictions that include broad metropolitan regions and discourage the form of jurisdictional separation that currently allows many small municipalities to ignore obligations of justice towards differentiated others in neighbouring towns. Under contemporary conditions of urbanized interdependence, capital investment and market exchange, communications, and environmental experience, the region is the necessary substratum of political community.

Proponents of deeper and more participatory democracy are often suspicious of institutional changes that would subordinate local community or town process to wider regional political institutions. Any gains in efficiency and equity obtained through regionalization, they suggest, come at the expense of democracy. While these fears are often well founded, I argue that regional governance institutions can, and should, be designed so as to preserve or create neighbourhood and town voice and participation. The norms of differentiated solidarity can be applied by means of institutions of regional federalism that grant a prima-facie value to local autonomy but require intergovernmental negotiation, mediation, joint planning, and regulation.

## 1. Residential Racial Segregation

While there are many sites of racial and class segregation, here I focus on residential segregation for two reasons. First, especially where segregation is not legally mandated and enforced, *de facto* residential segregation is a major cause of other segregations, such as of children in schools or in employment. Secondly, because of its spatial and jurisdictional aspects, residential segregation has far-reaching consequences for democratic practice.

### Segregation in the United States

In *American Apartheid* Douglas Massey and Nancy Denton document the great extent of racial residential segregation in American cities through most of the twentieth century. Despite the passage of the Fair Housing Act in 1968, and even though, according to polls, many more whites now than thirty years ago say that Blacks should be able to live where they wish, degrees of residential racial concentration have declined very little. Chicago remains the nation's most segregated city. According to the standard measure of degree of segregation, 91 per cent of Blacks in Chicago would have to move in order to achieve a racial mix in the city in proportion to the total numbers of Blacks and whites. In Cleveland, Newark, St Louis, Philadelphia, Los Angeles, and New York, at least 80 per cent of Blacks would have to move to achieve a desegregated residential pattern; and all but two of the eighteen largest northern American cities have indexes in excess of 70 per cent.[1] Levels of Black–white segregation in suburban areas are somewhat lower, but still high. Latinos also tend to be spatially concentrated, especially in some parts of the country, but, according to Massey and Denton, less so than Blacks.[2] Some might assume that this segregation is a legacy of enforced segregation in the South. The patterns of racial concentration that Massey and Denton find, however, are generally more pronounced today in northern cities which did not have explicit policies of racial exclusion than in the southern cities that did.

Massey and Denton refute two common-sense explanations for the persistence of racially concentrated neighbourhoods. One might think that the patterns of residence can be sufficiently explained by the fact that Blacks have lower than average income; Massey and Denton show, however, that many higher-income Blacks also live in racially concentrated communities. As I will discuss later, class structure intersects with residential racial segregation, but it seems clear that income cannot entirely account for patterns of racial concentration.

[1] Douglas Massey and Nancy Denton, *American Apartheid* (Cambridge, Mass.: Harvard University Press, 1993), 61–7. I have heard some people object to the phrasing of the measure of segregation that Massey and Denton use: 80% of Blacks would have to move in New York to achieve a desegregated living pattern there. This phrasing, which can sound so neutral and merely statistical to some ears, to others carries objectionable white integrationist assumptions. Why construct an index of segregation that pictures the Blacks as moving while the whites stay where they are? Really to achieve lower racial concentration, don't both groups have to move? The definition of the index also suggests that the desirable goal is a proportionate mixing of whites and people of colour through all residential areas. Later in this chapter I will question this picture of desirable residential living patterns. It is important, I believe, to have ways of measuring degrees of racial concentration. In some cities or regions it would make little sense to phrase such a measure in terms of whites having to move, because whites are the majority of people in the United States, and they are widely dispersed. As a measure, describing racial concentration by saying that 90% of Blacks would have to move to achieve proportionate racial mix is acceptable, even appropriate. It is important, however, to raise questions about the images, however benign, of whose lives must change and what goals are desirable underlie statements of the problem, and to be aware of such assumptions.

[2] Ibid. Especially for discussion of segregation of Latinos in certain parts of the United States, see also Paul A. Jargowsky, *Poverty and Place: Ghettos, Barrios, Slums and the American City* (New York: Russell Sage, 1996).

Others might say that these patterns of residence can be explained by African American preference to live primarily near other African Americans. If this were the explanation, then there might be nothing wrong with the patterns. I will argue shortly that affinity grouping in social life and neighbourhood is not wrong and may be a positive good for some. Massey and Denton cite survey data, however, showing that most Blacks prefer a mixed neighbourhood. The vast majority say they do not want to live in an all-Black neighbourhood, and most say they would prefer roughly half-Black. The high concentrations of many Black neighbourhoods, then, cannot be explained by the preferences of African Americans.[3]

In fact there is a large body of evidence that residential segregation in the United States has been produced and is maintained by legal and illegal discrimination by landlords, home owners, real estate agents, banks, and other individuals and institutions. Until 1968 in the United States it was not illegal for a property owner to discriminate in the sale or rental of housing, and in many other countries it is not illegal today. Whether technically legal or not, a great many property owners believe they are entirely within their rights to decide who will or will not live in their property, according to whatever criteria they choose. Real estate agents often lie, falsely or selectively advertise, and 'steer' white clients to some neighbourhoods and people of colour to others.[4] People of colour are denied mortgage loans far more frequently than whites of comparable income. Banks, developers, and insurance companies often avoid investing in neighbourhoods with significant concentrations of people of colour, thus contributing to their decline.[5]

Thus in the United States residential racial segregation is the product largely of the discriminatory actions of private market actors, who self-consciously discriminate by race, or who manipulate a racist market for the sake of making profits. Government policy is by no means exempt from causal responsibility for racial residential patterns in the United States, however. As detailed by Massey and Denton, from the

---

[3] Massey and Denton, *American Apartheid*, 88–96. These data do reveal a *clustering* preference among African Americans, which I will discuss later. Most Blacks also say they do not wish to live in a mostly white neighbourhood. Combined with a marked preference by whites for neighbourhoods at least 75% white, the clustering preferences of Blacks and whites together do help explain the actual residential patterns. The point is that African Americans' preferences do not correspond to the nearly all-Black neighbourhoods to which many are confined.

[4] Ibid. 96–109.

[5] See George C. Galster and Edward W. Hill, 'Place, Power, and Polarization,' in Galster and Hill (ed.), *The Metropolis in Black and White* (New Brunswick, NJ: Center for Urban Policy Research, 1992) for another account of the self-perpetuating cycle of privilege that maintains segregation.

early twentieth century to the present there have been a series of both federal, state, and local policies and programmes that have contributed directly to producing and reproducing segregation. These include zoning practices, public housing policies from the 1930s to the present, post-Second World War mortgage subsidy programmes, urban renewal, and urban redevelopment grants.[6]

## Residential Racial Segregation in European Cities

While many would like to claim that *de facto* racial segregation is a specifically American problem, my reading of the literature leads me to think that this is not so. Among majority white liberal democracies the United States is perhaps extreme in the size and homogeneity of its Black neighbourhoods, but other countries show patterns of racial residential concentrations. While not nearly in such a pronounced way as in the United States, for example, New Zealand cities such as Auckland and Wellington tend to crowd poor and working-class Maori and Pacific Islanders into a few neighbourhoods.[7] No doubt many other examples could be obtained from around the world. I focus here on racial residential concentrations in European cities, primarily in order to show that racialist social structures of privilege and disadvantage do not seem to be restricted to North America, and apparently can appear in advanced social welfare democracies as well as in undemocratic or less developed societies.[8]

---

[6] Massey and Denton, *American Apartheid*, pp. 51–57.

[7] According to a government report, in Wellington 50% of the Pacific Island population and 28% of the Maori population would need to change the area in which they live to achieve the same residential distribution as Pakeha, or New Zealanders of European descent. Research on Maori and Pacific Islanders' access to accommodation discovered that 83.9% of Auckland land agents acted to the detriment of Maori and Pacific Island applicants. See J. MacDonald, *Racism and Rental Accommodation* (Auckland: Social Research and Development Trust, 1986). See also Edward M. K. Douglas, *Fading Expectations: The Crisis in Maori Housing*, Report for the Board of Maori Affairs, (Wellington, June 1986); Elizabeth Mleay, 'Housing Policy', in Jonathan Boston and Paul Dalziel (eds.), *The Decent Society? Essays in Response to the Nation's Economic and Social Policies* (Auckland: Oxford University Press, 1992).

[8] Some students of comparative residential segregation find significant segregation in some European cities, but argue that European cities are not now and are not likely to become the 'hypersegregated' racial enclaves that characterize some neighbourhoods and communities in the United States. See e.g. Barbara Schmitter Heisler, 'Housing Policy and the Underclass: The United Kingdom, Germany, and the Netherlands', *Journal of Urban Affairs*, 16/3 (1994), 203–20. I am not quarrelling here with this assessment; it may be that the United States has a higher degree of segregation and a more intractable problem of undermining it. The point of these examples is only to suggest that the harms of segregation and the problems it generates for democracy go beyond the United States.

Several British cities show concentrations of South Asians and Afro-Caribbeans in neighbourhoods of less desirable public housing and rental property.[9] Several German cities with relatively large migrant populations from Africa, Asia, and the Middle East, such as Hamburg, Frankfurt, and Berlin, show tendencies of residential concentration of these people.[10] Amsterdam and Brussels have some of the highest segregation indexes of Europe,[11] and there are noticeable concentrations of non-European migrants in the outer suburbs of cities such as Paris[12] and Stockholm.[13] Scholars debate about whether the European societies that show such residential concentrations are becoming racialized ghettos which Europeans leave and avoid and in which economic disadvantage and social problems will increase.[14]

Since most of those who are concentrated in racially or ethnically marked neighbourhoods are immigrants with cultural affinities, it is

[9] Susan Smith, *The Politics of 'Race' and Residence* (Oxford: Blackwell, 1988); 'Residential Segregation and the Politics of Ritualization', in Malcolm Cross and Michael Smith (eds.), *Racism, the City and the State* (London: Routledge, 1993); David McIvoy, 'Greater London in Britain's First Ethnic Census', in Curtis C. Roseman, Hans Dieter Laus, and Gunther Threme (eds.), *EthniCity: Geographic Perspectives on Ethnic Change in Modern Cities* (Lanham, Md.: Rowman & Littlefield, 1996).

[10] See e.g. Klaus Ronneberger, 'Zitadellenökonomie und soziale Transformation der Stadt', in Noller, Prigger, and Klaus Ronneberger (eds.), *Stadt-Welt* (Frankfurt, 1994); Jurgen Friedricks (ed.), *Spatial Disparities and Social Behavior* (Hamburg: Hans Christian Verlag, 1992); several articles in this collection discuss processes of discrimination and residential concentration of immigrants in several German cities, including Hamburg and Berlin.

[11] Matthijs Breebaart, Sako Musterd, and Wim Ostendorf, 'Patterns and Perception of Ethnic Segregation in Western Europe', in H. Häussermann and Ingrid Orwald (eds.), *Stadtentwicklung und Zuwanderung* (Opladen: Sonderheft Leviathan, 1997). See also Hartmust Häussermann and Rainer Marz, 'Migration und Minderheiten in den zentraleuropäischen Metropolen. Berlin, Brüssel, Budapest und Wien', in *Migranten Berlin. Zuwanderung* (Berlin: Gesellschaftliche Problem politische Ansatz, Fakultät Institut Sozialwissenschaften, Humbolt University, 1995).

[12] Scholars apparently disagree on whether these concentrations should be thought of as racial segregation. Loci J. D. Wacquant, for example, argues that in France social exclusion is more of a lower-class youth problem than a racial issue; see '"Race", Class and Space in Chicago and Paris', in Katherine McFate, Roger Lawson, and William Julius Wilson (eds.), *Poverty, Inequality and the Future of Social Policy* (New York: Russell Sage, 1995); Sophi Body-Gendrot, on the other hand, conceptualizes processes of social and spatial exclusion in France more in terms of the racialization and essentialization of experienced cultural difference; see Body-Gendrot, 'Immigration and Marginality in France', in McFate, Lawson, and Wilson (eds.), *Poverty, Inequality and the Future of Social Policy*; see also Body-Gendrot, 'Migration and the Racialization of the Postmodern City in France', in Malcolm Cross and Michael Keith (eds.), *Racism, the City and the State* (London: Routledge, 1993).

[13] Joachim Vogel, 'Urban Segregation in Sweden: Housing Policy, Housing Markets, and the Spatial Distribution of Households in Metropolitan Areas', *Social Indicators Research*, 27 (1992), 139–55.

[14] Margaret Weir, 'The Politics of Racial Isolation in Europe and America', in Paul E. Peterson (ed.), *Classifying by Race* (Princeton: Princeton University Press, 1995).

reasonable to assume that these residential patterns result at least partly from a preference members of these groups have for living near those with whom they feel affinity. In the terms that Peter Marcuse uses, these neighbourhoods may simply be ethnic enclaves rather than ghettos resulting from exclusion by the white majority.[15] If residential concentrations simply reflect a preference for living near certain kinds of people, then their existence should not present a problem. But how do we tell the difference between residential segregation and residential clustering in these multicultural cities? This is not the place to analyse which are and which are not segregated, but I propose the following criteria for observing the difference; these criteria are probably not exhaustive. If studies show that migrants or others marked as racially or ethnically different experience housing discrimination in majority neighbourhoods, then this means that many members of these groups are confined in their housing options to racially concentrated neighbourhoods. If residents of the city 'know' where racial and ethnic minorities are said to be living, and if these neighbourhoods carry associations of danger or boundedness to city residents, then those living in them are likely to suffer stigma that affects other opportunities. If members of the majority cultural group are moving out of neighbourhoods associated with racialized groups, there is probably a segregating process. In addition, if both public and private resource and property owners fail to invest in the racially concentrated neighbourhoods, and the latter decline in quality, we probably have a segregation process. If the neighbourhoods in which racialized groups cluster have notable disadvantages compared to others, such as having poor transportation access, poor-quality housing for the price, location near unpleasant industrial facilities, and so on, then the cluster is partly a matter of privilege. To the extent that discriminatory attitudes and behaviour force or induce members of racial or ethnic minorities to live in certain neighbourhoods when they might otherwise seek housing elsewhere, they live in segregated conditions. Even more importantly,

---

[15] Peter Marcuse, 'The Enclave, the Citadel, and the Ghetto: What has Changed in the Post-Fordist U.S. City', *Urban Affairs Review*, 33/2 (Nov. 1997), 228–64. Marcuse develops conceptual distinctions among these three types of residential patterns. An enclave is a clustering of persons according to affinity groups, whereas a ghetto is the exclusion and confinement of a subordinate group by a dominant group. A citadel is an exclusive community of class and race privilege, from which others are restricted access. An enclave is a positive and empowering social structure, according to Marcuse, whereas a ghetto perpetuates disadvantage. Many spaces of racial or ethnic concentration share characteristics of each. While the distinctions Marcuse makes are useful, he offers no criteria for determining whether an observed residential concentration is an enclave or a ghetto or a citadel, or is in transition from one to another.

if their housing conditions, neighbourhood location, and general quality of residential life are inferior, then their segregation contributes to conditions of structural inequality. The literature I have cited above gives strong indication that many of the racially and ethnically concentrated neighbourhoods in European cities meet several of these criteria.

Such circumstances can have varying causes. The processes of housing discrimination against people of colour in Britain, for example, according to Susan Smith, have operated more through public policy and the decisions of policy administrators, though private markets play a complementary role. After the Second World War, the most desirable rental housing in metropolitan areas tended to be the public council housing. Government bureaucracy plays a larger role than markets in the allocation of units of council housing. For many years public housing rules stated that a person had to reside in Britain for five years before becoming eligible for council housing. Even after this rule was lifted, other rules tended to restrict the opportunities of immigrants or people of colour, such as marriage rules, family size, income, or creditworthiness. In some districts during some periods of the last forty years, moreover, administrators allocating public housing units acted on their ideas about which sort of people belonged in which sort of units, and sometimes would claim that the existing resident did not want to live near Blacks when they allocated units to Blacks in other, often inferior, units.

The restriction of choice in public rental housing forced South Asians and Afro-Caribbeans into the private rental housing market in the inner cities. This housing was generally the oldest, poorest quality, and located in the neighbourhoods with fewest amenities.[16] The privatization of a significant proportion of public housing in Britain beginning under the Thatcher government may have changed these segregation dynamics somewhat, but racially marked residential patterns were well established by then.

## 2. The Wrongs of Segregation

The term 'segregation' usually carries a negative normative connotation. But just what is wrong with it? Some people seem to attribute the wrong of racial segregation to group clustering itself. Such a view would suggest that group differentiation itself is problematic, because it creates potential for disrespect, conflict, and lack of communication.

[16] Smith, *The Politics of 'Race' and Residence*, chs. 3 and 4.

I believe it is a mistake, however, to focus on the patterned fact of group clustering as the moral problem with segregation; focusing on patterned group differentiation deflects from the more important problems, which concern processes of exclusion from privileges and benefits. These processes of exclusion do indeed have grave consequences for the possibility of democratic peace and co-operation, but this is due more to the structural inequalities they generate than the group identities they magnify.

Here I discuss specifically four wrongs of residential racial segregation. First, segregation violates a principle of equal opportunity and thus wrongly limits freedom of housing choice. Secondly, and most importantly, processes of segregation produce and reinforce serious structures of privilege and disadvantage. The very processes that produce segregation, thirdly, also obscure the fact of their privilege from those who have it. As a result, finally, the social and spatial differentiation segregation produces seriously impedes political communication among segregated groups, thus making it difficult to address the wrongs of segregation through democratic political action.

*Wrongly limits choice.* Processes of segregation are wrong because they inhibit the freedom of people to live where they wish, or at least to have the opportunity to compete for housing in the communities of their choice. Some restriction on housing choice occurs, of course, because housing in some neighbourhoods costs more than in others. Insufficient income limits housing choice. Other restrictions, however, involve racial discrimination. To the extent that neighbours, landlords, real estate brokers, banks, and governments discriminate in their treatment of persons marked as belonging to racially or ethnically othered groups, they violate a principle of equal opportunity and wrongly restrict housing choice. Either intentionally or unconsciously, they exclude people of colour from communities which the latter might otherwise find desirable, and leave them little alternative but to reside in less desirable neighbourhoods often already populated predominantly by members of racially marked groups.

*Reproduces structures of privilege and disadvantage.* People who live in neighbourhoods or communities with a high concentration of people of colour often have a worse quality of life than do those who live in all-white or nearly all-white neighbourhoods. People in segregated neighbourhoods often must pay more for poorer-quality housing than those in white neighbourhoods.[17] Class intersects with race in

---

[17] See Phillip L. Clay, 'The (Un)housed City: Racial Patterns of Segregation, Housing Quality and Affordability', in George Galster and Edward Hill (eds.), *Metropolis in Black*

many predominantly Black neighbourhoods; because the racially marked groups have lower average incomes, their concentration in space magnifies the market effects of lower incomes.[18] Business establishments are less able to sustain themselves, especially if there is an economic downturn, and property owners are sometimes less able to maintain their property. Businesses thus exit and new ones are reluctant to enter, because the neighbourhood is perceived as deteriorating and property values are falling. Remaining commercial and residential property owners have little incentive to invest in the improvement or even maintenance of their property, and the spiral continues. As a result, people living in these neighbourhoods often have fewer stores, restaurants, offices, private services, movie theatres, and the like than those who live in even modest white neighbourhoods.

As a consequence of many factors of market, transportation, prejudice, and preference, in the United States both large and small employers are locating further and further from minority-identified neighbourhoods and towns. Those who live in these neighbourhoods find themselves isolated from access to information about jobs and the social networks that both disseminate this information and refer acquaintances to employers. Even if they manage to learn of openings and are considered for them, moreover, segregated residents find that poor access to transportation can be a major impediment to taking or keeping jobs. Thus segregation helps reproduce the looser relation to labour markets of many members of segregated groups.[19] Those who live in segregated neighbourhoods, finally, often have access to fewer and lower-quality public and private services than those in integrated or white neighbourhoods. Transportation systems often serve them poorly, and their streets are the last to be ploughed of snow. Their residential clustering often gives them less clout in city hall than others in the city, and for this reason they may be relatively under-served in fire and police protection.[20] Their schools are often of poor quality, both physically and academically, and they often have poor access to medical services.

Processes of segregation, then, exacerbate class differences of income, education, and skill to produce racially structured differences

*and White: Place, Power, and Polarization* (New Brunswick, NJ: Center for Urban Policy Research, 1992).

[18] Massey and Denton, *American Apartheid*, esp. ch. 5.

[19] See William Julius Wilson, *When Work Disappears* (New York: Knopf, 1997); Galster and Hill, 'Place, Power and Polarization'. Discussions of the consequences of racial and class segregation in Europe also point to such consequences for employment opportunity; see e.g. Waquant, '"Race", Class and Space in Chicago and Paris'.

[20] Massey and Denton, *American Apartheid*, 153–60.

in privilege and opportunity. These structures in turn reinforce racial discrimination by creating less desirable places associated with the subordinate groups. These places themselves are racially marked by the dominant society as unworthy, and those who live there are held responsible for the physical neglect of their environment. The aversive racial marking of segregated neighbourhoods thus boomerangs onto their inhabitants, rationalizing further discrimination against them because of where they they live.

Many who live or have lived in neighbourhoods inhabited predominantly by African Americans or Latinos in the United States, or by South Asians or those of Caribbean descent in England, for example, are made uncomfortable by a discourse that focuses exclusively on the disadvantages such segregation usually brings. They often experience life in these neighbourhoods as personally supportive, lively, and neighbourly, with culturally distinct institutions and strong civic networks. I agree that discussions of racial residential concentration are too often one-sided. Later I shall argue that affinity group clustering, as distinct from segregation, is not wrong in itself; I will also argue that certain interpretations and attempts to implement an ideal of integration fail to recognize the positive contribution such clustering makes to some people's lives.

Most scholars of residential racial segregation also focus on such facts of relative disadvantage and absolute deprivation. They often fail to highlight the correlative privilege of those in predominantly white neighbourhoods and communities that attends these same facts. Even though housing demand in white neighbourhoods might be higher if the market were truly open to all bidders, segregation helps keep housing prices high by constructing in them a desirable amenity over and above location and quality of structures: the whiteness of their neighbourhoods. High property values in these neighbourhoods encourage investment in the neighbourhood, thus maintaining or raising the property values. Their neighbourhoods more often have better shopping and entertainment, transportation access, public and private services, gardens and green spaces. It is fair to say, moreover, that at least to a certain extent, the predominantly white neighbourhoods and communities often *have* such amenities *because* the segregated neighbourhoods do not. If city or regional economies often can support only a certain number of grocery stores, theatres, coffee-houses, and so on, then the choice of their location has critical distributive effects. Presumably a city government has limited funds for garbage pick-up or fire protection. Thus if some neighbourhoods have the privilege of excellent service, it is likely at the expense of other neighbourhoods where service is poor.

*Obscures the privilege it creates.* Segregation, I have argued, reserves certain privileges for some whites, and excludes many people of colour from those privileges and benefits. The very same process that produces these relations of privilege, moreover, obscures that privilege from those who have it. In order to see themselves as privileged, the white people who live in more pleasant neighbourhoods must be able to compare their environment with others. But this comparison is rarely forced upon them because those excluded from access to the resources and benefits they themselves have are spatially separated and out of sight. Another place defines their lives. Whites often avoid experiencing those other places, but usually we do not even need to think about such avoidance, because our daily lives and social spaces are so constructed that we have no reason to go where the others live.

As a consequence, those who have privileged lives compared to the disadvantages in the quality of life produced by segregation can think of their lives as normal, average. Life does not feel privileged for the white family with two working adults paying a hefty mortgage and dealing with the hassles of child care, freeways, and too many demands at work. Being able to stop off at a gourmet grocery on the way home, to count on police protection and snow removal, and to walk or drive a short distance to see a first-run movie seem like the most minimal rewards for an arduous week of work. Segregation thus makes privilege doubly invisible to the privileged: by conveniently keeping the situation of the relatively disadvantaged out of sight, it thereby renders the situation of the privileged average.

Making privilege invisible to the privileged has the effect of inoculating against what sense of injustice they might have. Those who lead relatively privileged lives in a segregated society see no injustice in their situation. Indeed, they often become indignant at the suggestion that they benefit from injustice, because they experience their lives as so average, normal, and full enough of troubles. Many of these people who think of themselves as average, good, and decent could be made uncomfortable by frequent everyday human encounters with those excluded from these benefits, within their daily living environment. Their sense of justice might be pricked; some of them might even think that something should be done to change the situation. But the everyday separation of the lives of the more and less privileged that is part of the process of residential racial segregation makes it unnecessary for the privileged to think about social injustice except in the most abstract terms.

*Impedes political communication.* In Chapter 1 I traced the circle that often goes from structural social inequality to political inequality, so that a formally democratic process often operates to reinforce structural inequality. Formally democratic processes do seem often to reinforce rather than undermine the harms of segregation, partly because the processes exclude and marginalize members of segregated groups from political influence.[21] To the extent that privileged groups often dominate the public policy process, these policies often fail to notice and address the harms of segregation; as we have seen above, often public policies sometimes even magnify the harms of segregation.

In earlier chapters I have argued that inclusive communicative democracy is one of the only ways to break this circle by which formally democratic politics reinforces structural social inequality. The theory of communicative democracy says that policy change to undermine structural inequality is more likely to occur if subordinated groups are politically mobilized and included as equals in a process of discussing issues and problems that lead to decisions. If some people suffer injustices, the first step in redressing them is being able to make claims upon others in a shared public forum that together they should take action to address these problems. If those with such claims can participate equally with members of dominant groups in political discussion and decision-making, they may be able to change the way others see the social relations in which they stand together, the problems they generate, and the priorities they should have for action.

The very processes of segregation that produce structural privileges for many white people, however, also impede the establishment of such inclusive political fora. The conditions of segregation impede the emergence of both civic and state-sponsored sites where differentiated groups come together to debate whether there are injustices and, if so, what should be done about them. The economic and social privilege that many whites have relative to many African Americans and Latinos in the United States tends to translate into a political privilege where a white perspective dominates political bodies like city councils or state legislatures. Blacks have a strong if not dominant voice in some municipalities in the United States, of course, precisely because of processes of segregation which have isolated them in inner cities and inner, often economically depressed suburbs. Where African Americans or other segregated groups are able to dominate local politics, in the United States they usually preside over vast problems and

---

[21] Michael Dawson and Cathy Cohen analyse the relationship between political marginality and segregation in distressed African American neighbourhoods. See 'Neighborhood Poverty and African American Politics', in *American Political Science Review*, 87/2 (June 1993), 286–302.

a narrow tax base with which to address them. More privileged neighbours live in other towns to which they have little political relationship; the political separation of municipalities in such cases means that there are few sites and fora for political communication between groups. I will return to the problem of jurisdictional separation shortly.

Suppose inclusive fora of democratic communication do bring together groups structurally differentiated by processes of segregation. The effects of segregation impede communication within them in other ways. Because structures of segregation have given groups rather different everyday experiences, because they may also be culturally distinct and segregation impedes significant awareness of these cultural differences, because they often have different assumptions about what is important, they are very likely to misunderstand and misrepresent one another. Segregation, that is, exacerbates prejudicial attitudes that group members may have towards others, thus making it difficult to engage in productive debate and discussion. Especially the more privileged are liable to make assumptions about social realities and experience that do not hold for the others. Since the privileged allow themselves to construct their lives as average, when they learn of the difference between their lives and those less privileged, this encounter may as likely feed stereotypes and deprecating judgements as much as it may produce sympathetic understanding. Under such circumstances there is even greater need for discourses of greeting and recognition of others, and for listening to narratives of experience and perspective.

## 3. Residential Class Segregation

Discriminatory acts and policies are major causes of residential racial segregation. Many of the privileges and disadvantages associated with racial segregation, however, are also intimately tied to structures of class privilege and disadvantage, including processes of residential class segregation. For the purposes of this discussion, I mean by residential class segregation practices and processes that tend to homogenize the income and wealth level, occupational status, and lifestyle consumer tastes of communities. Residential class segregation is by no means an inevitable consequence of class differences themselves. Indeed, historically many societies have enacted and reinforced hierarchies of privilege, wealth, and leisure through the proximity and interaction of members of upper and lower classes. It was not until industrial urbanism was well developed in the nineteenth century that well-to-do people separated themselves from others and that practices of city planning encouraged segregation of the poor.[22] Many of the urban centres of the twentieth century still had many spaces where well-to-do homes were mixed with more modest apartment houses, and people of various strata often mingled in city streets and parks.

In the United States the two decades after the Second World War saw a decrease in residential class segregation, as the middle class expanded and people of all income levels sought suburban housing. In the following two decades, however, there was a marked increase in residential segregation, and all the signs point to more spatial differentiation of the well-to-do, the working class, and the poor.[23] Residential class segregation is certainly not unique to the United States, moreover, but is common all over the world, and appears also to be increasing in many parts of the world.[24]

Most broadly, class segregation refers to an entire way of life in which relatively well-off people can conduct nearly all of their everyday activities insulated from encounters with those less well-off, their faces, their dwellings, their working conditions, and so on. Segregation is thorough when well-off people are spatially enclosed and protected from encounter with those less well-off not only in their residential neighbourhoods, but in their working day, their shopping trips and nights out, their vacations, and in travelling from their residences to any of these places. Not only do many desire this sort of privilege and insulated life, but many can fulfil their desire.

Class segregation must be produced and maintained by active and policed exclusion. Whether by erecting walls or carving out separate municipal jurisdictions, class segregation most often works by constructing and policing strict boundaries. To be sure, market forces contribute mightily to patterns of class residential concentration. Many

[22] See Douglas S. Massey, 'The Age of Extremes: Concentrated Affluence and Poverty in the Twenty-First Century', *Demography*, 33/4 (Nov. 1996), 395–412.

[23] See Christopher J. Mayer, 'Does Location Matter?', *New England Economic Review*, (May/June 1996), 26–40; Massey, 'The Age of Extremes'; Stephen Hegley, *Privilege, Power and Place: The Geography of the American Upper Class* (Totowa, NJ: Rowman & Littlefield, 1995).

[24] On class segregation in European cities, see Jordi Borja and Manuel Castells, *Local and Global: Management of Cities in the Information Age* (London: Earthscan, 1997), 37, 146. On the segregation of wealth and poverty in Britain, see Anne E. Green, *The Geography of Poverty and Wealth* (Warwick: Institute for Employment Research, 1991). Massey reports class segregation trends for several developed and developing countries; 'The Age of Extremes'. For a comparison of residential class segregation in São Paulo and Los Angeles, see Teresa P. R. Caldeira, 'Fortified Enclaves: The New Urban Segregation', *Public Culture*, 8 (1996), 303–28.

people cannot buy or rent homes or apartments because these command too high a price that others are eager to pay. Unregulated real estate markets can also work in unpredictable ways, however, producing mixed use and mixing income and occupation in close proximity.[25] The demand for housing associated with neighbourhood privilege reaches far down the income pyramid, and often enough there are investors willing and able to cater to this market if they are allowed to. Zoning laws that restrict the form of building and use of property in better-off neighbourhoods ensure they are not allowed to.[26]

Where neighbourhoods and towns have an income mix, those less well-off benefit from the 'neighbourhood effects' of dwelling together with those with more resources. Neighbourhoods and towns with a mix of affluent and less affluent people can support better parks, public buildings, and streets than can towns populated with mostly lower-income people. If they have public schools, they are likely to have better facilities. Their dollars attract more shops, restaurants, and entertainment venues. Even when the homes and grounds of the wealthy are gated and inaccessible, lower-income people who live near them benefit from their green spaces. It is certainly arguable that affluent people sacrifice little or nothing by sharing city spaces with less affluent people in this way, and that they gain benefits of interacting with differently situated people.

Walled and gated citadels are the extreme opposed to such potential sharing of environments. They exist precisely to prevent openness towards neighbours. Many gated communities enclose gardens, shops, and services for the use only of those who live within the walls. Some walled enclaves encourage community among their residents; thus they are not entirely private spaces. But their purpose is to insulate residents from the surrounding city, its people, and its problems.

The form of active exclusion characteristic of affluent suburbs is different. Building regulations and lot size usually ensure that the communities are reserved for affluent residents. Road access to the communities is limited, and rarely do roads connect with public transportation service. Thus unwelcome lower-class visitors rarely wander in; if and when they do, police or neighbourhood watch groups are liable to challenge their right to be there.

---

[25]   Robert H. Nelson argues that freer markets would produce more income diversity in property ownership than exists in many suburbs. See Nelson, *Zoning and Property Rights: An Analysis of the American System of Land-Use Regulation* (Cambridge, Mass.: MIT Press, 1977).

[26]   See Hegley, *Privilege, Power and Place*, esp. ch. 3.

Does class segregation magnify privilege at the same time that it obscures privilege, as I have argued happens with racial segregation? Just by virtue of their wealth the affluent have significant privilege in land, dwellings, and amenities. Segregation magnifies this privilege by offering residents a collective space of comfort, finery, and enclosed security. Class segregation insulates the well-off from the normal annoyances and problems of urban life—noise, dirt, and litter, industrial and warehouse sites, pollution, crowded streets and public transport, disorderly and diverse mixed architecture and activities, crime and the threat of crime.

Living in such segregated communities also obscures class privilege; the well-off can avoid situations in which they experience the circumstances of those less well-off. Capitalist democratic societies have less incentive to obscure class privilege than to obscure race privilege, however, because the dominant values do not question class privilege as they do race domination. Consequently, like all conspicuous consumption, one of the reasons to create walled communities and homogeneously affluent towns is to create a setting of privilege that residents are aware of each time they enter.

Class segregation endangers democracy in at least three ways. First, it discourages public spaces and public encounters. Like residential racial segregation, secondly, class segregation impedes communication between groups. Most importantly, by segregating themselves in enclosed enclaves or separate political communities, those more well-off can abandon a sense that wealthier citizens share problems with their less well-off neighbours and should co-operate with them to produce public goods.

Chapter 5 discussed publicity as a necessary aspect of democratic participation and as a basis for communication among citizens for the sake of exposing the actions of political and economic élites, holding them accountable, and positively influencing their actions. A public sphere may be enacted partly through print and electronic media, and to that extent does not require open physical spaces. To the extent that physical public space shrinks, however, or to the extent that many citizens withdraw from embodied public space, open communicative democracy is in danger.

A public space, recall, is one to which anyone has access, a space of openness and exposure. The physical open spaces of public streets, squares, plazas, and parks are what I have mind with the term *embodied* public space. These are large spaces where many people can be present together, seeing, being seen, exposed to one another. In them one may encounter anyone who lives in the city or region as well as outsiders passing through. They importantly contribute to democratic inclusion because they bring differently positioned strangers into one another's presence; they make concrete the fact that people of differing tastes, interests, needs, and life circumstances dwell together in a city or region.[27] Used by various constituencies for festivals or rallies, they announce to a wide public the interests and enjoyments of the constituencies, which others may share or be persuaded to support. Thus they are also crucial to democracy as unique sites of political expression and demonstration, where public opinion can show its strength.

Both walled enclaves and tucked-away suburbs devalue and discourage embodied public space. They may have indoor and outdoor gathering-spaces for residents and their invited guests. Since they are not accessible to anyone and they are not situated so that localized neighbourhoods open onto them, however, these spaces are not public.

Class segregation minimizes encounters between members of well-off and less well-off groups. When they do interact, it is most often on terms specified by the well-off and for their benefit, such as the interactions between enclave dwellers and the people who clean or repair their homes. While city, state, or national policy making discussions may imagine the groups as together politically in a formal and abstract way, such abstract togetherness has little basis in experience for any of them. Segregation reduces the living communication differently situated economic groups have, however, and thus the opportunity to understand the problems and perspectives of the others. Because these problems and perspectives are perceived to affect them, however, the segregated groups may talk among themselves about the others, often formulating one-dimensional and deprecating stereotypes. If members of the segregated groups then should find themselves in fora where they discuss public issues, false impressions and assumptions are liable to fuel further misunderstanding and frustrate communication.

Class segregation, finally, enables those who are wealthier and with more economic power to ignore the problems and interests of those less privileged and simply attend to furthering their own well-being and perceived interests. Enclosed in comfortable enclaves, they can be indifferent to the needs and interests of others and withdraw from the

---

[27] Gerald Frug discusses the importance of such diversified encounter in public space. See *City Making: Building Communities without Building Walls* (Princeton: Princeton University Press, 1999), ch. 6. See also Teresa Caldeira's discussion of the importance of public space; 'Fortified Enclaves: The New Urban Segregation'.

problems of interdependent urban life. Social and political indiffer-
ence is especially easy when privileged classes live in separate political
jurisdictions, when borders allow residents of affluent suburbs to keep
resources for themselves and insulate themselves from the needs and
problems of the less advantaged. In the United States most metropolitan areas have scores of distinct municipalities, some of which are
wealthy and most of which are not. Jurisdictional boundaries allow
people to express local political concern for only the situations and
policies of their town, and to ignore people in nearby towns and cities.
Some scholars argue that this self-regarding privilege results in
reduced civic and political involvement among residents of affluent
communities, as compared with people of the same income level who
live in more diverse settings. Relatively satisfied with their schools and
services, and without others to challenge their privilege and produce
conflict, many suburban dwellers have little motivation to volunteer
to improve the well-being of their communities or to get involved in
political debates.[28]

Some readers may be impatient with this criticism of class *segregation* as an impediment to democracy, because they think that class difference itself is the major impediment to political equality. As I noted
in Chapter 1, I sympathize with the view that structural class inequality creates a political inequality that in turn enables the privileged class
to reinforce its privilege using formally democratic processes. On this
view, structural class inequality itself should be reduced or eliminated.

Many people in the imperfect democracies we live in, however, do
not agree with this analysis, or the value of economic equality it
assumes. If they express a commitment to democratic values, however,
then they must believe that all members of a polity ought in principle to
have the opportunities to participate with others in political decision-
making, to make claims of justice upon them, and attempt to persuade
them of the rightness of these claims. The problem with class *segregation*, as distinct from class structure itself, is that it conflicts with this
commitment to democratic participation. Even those who find nothing wrong with unequal accumulation of wealth and economic power
should find the consequences of the residential and political segregation of classes problematic for democratic values. Undermining that
segregation, then, can open more possibilities for those who believe
that economic inequality itself ultimately conflicts with democracy to

[28] J. Eric Oliver, 'Civic Involvement in Suburbia: The Effects of Metropolitan Economic
Segregation on Participation in Local Civic Affairs', Paper presented to the American
Political Science Association, Washington, Sept. 1997.

try to persuade others to enact egalitarian policies in a democratic process.


## 4. Critique of an Ideal of Integration

Residential racial segregation, along with class segregation, produces the harms I have reviewed. What norms and ideals ought to guide policies and actions aiming to reverse these harms? Many critics of racial segregation are guided by a notion of integration in which spatial group differentiation itself is the problem and residential mixing is the solution. In an ideally integrated city, no neighbourhood would be dominated by a minority group, nor would any neighbourhood be inhabited exclusively by a majority group. Instead, each neighbourhood would contain people of different groups in rough proportion to their incidence in the general population. In this section I question such an ideal as an appropriate guide for action to eliminate the harms of residential racial segregation. This ideal tends wrongly to focus on patterns of group clustering while ignoring more central issues of privilege and disadvantage. I have four objections to this way of conceiving the goals of desegregation and inclusion.

First, attempts to bring about integration tend to leave the dominant group relatively undisturbed while requiring significant changes from members of the excluded groups. Pro-integration housing policies, for example, usually involve the movement of members of the segregated groups to white neighbourhoods, rather than the reverse. More generally, practical efforts at integration too often mean that the socially dominant groups set the terms of integration to which the formerly segregated groups must conform. Members of the excluded groups are expected to 'fit' into the society and expectations of the dominant groups.

Secondly, an ideal of integration rejects the validity of people's desire to live and associate with others for whom they feel particular affinity. People often want to cluster in affinity groups defined by ethnicity, religion, language, sexual orientation, or lifestyle, and modern urban processes usually enable them to do so. People often settle in a new city near family or friends, or near those with whose particular tastes, language, religious practices, and so on they believe they will be most comfortable. They seek to enter friendly networks for locating housing or jobs, and these are often particularized by affinity groupings.

Such residential and civic clustering is not in itself wrong. Especially when members of a cultural group experience discrimination, deprecating stereotypes, exclusion, and comparative disadvantage, the neighbourhood clustering of the group can serve as an important source of self-organization, self-esteem, relaxation, and resistance. Similar resources derive from any clustering. Such relative separation of a group is not wrong when its purpose is mutual aid and culture-building among those who have affinity with one another, as long as this process of clustering does not exclude some people from access to benefits and opportunities.

Such a clustering desire based on lifestyle or comfort is not wrong even when acted on by privileged or formerly privileged groups, fur-thermore, if it can be distinguished from the involuntary exclusion of others and the preservation of privilege. To take a particularly con-tentious but important example, the desire of white Afrikaners in the new South Africa to preserve their language and retain a sense of con-tinuity with how they interpret their history is a legitimate desire, and may require some residential and civic group clustering to be fulfilled. As long as members of this group also participate on an equal basis in the process of forging inclusive democratic institutions, and support measures to bring equal opportunity and economic development to historically oppressed people, and so on, a desire on the part of some of them to retain a sense of group affinity is not morally objectionable in itself.

The third problem with the ideal of integration usually implicit in discussions of race and residence, therefore, is that it is likely to meet with resistance and failure, and when it fails, the fault seems to lie with the segregated group. The project of integration may fail because seri-ous commitment and resources have not been devoted to it, or because well-intentioned whites persist in exclusionary acts that they rational-ize in bad faith. To the extent that integration requires members of the segregated group to change their lives and conform to the expectations of the dominant group, it puts the onus for success on the relatively more disadvantaged groups. Resistance of the formerly segregated group to dispersing its affinity groups, or failure to measure up to the dominant norms and expectations, seem to be more noticeable obs-tacles to successful integrations. Members of the dominant group committed to the project of integration then throw up their hands and blame the subordinate group members who cannot or will not integ-rate on these terms.

Finally, and most importantly, the ideal of integration tends to focus on the wrong issue. According to this ideal, the problem of segrega-tion is that groups are spatially and institutionally distinguishable, and the remedy is spatial and institutional mixing in proper proportions.

I have argued above that the primary wrong of segregation is not that groups are distinguished, however, but that through its processes certain groups establish or retain material privilege. Actions or policies that aim to mix members of segregated groups in spaces and institutions of dominant groups usually operate very slowly, a few individuals at a time, and leave untouched the material disadvantages created by exclusionary spatial processes.

In the United States calls for policies of housing integration often sound to African Americans or Latinos like a condemnation of the neighbourhoods they have often loved and tried to improve, where they have experienced strong churches and civic institutions, and good times socializing. For some of these people the policies promoting integration amount to removing individuals from their sources of solidarity and isolating them, further disempowering them. While nearly everyone who lives in segregated neighbourhoods wants better housing, transportation access, public parks, and so on, many resist the implication that they must give up their culturally specific institutions and social networks to mix with strangers who are likely to be distant if not disrespectful.[29]

Some public housing policies in the United States can illustrate the sometimes perverse implications of taking clustering itself as the problem and mixing as the solution. The US Housing and Urban Development agency at one time had guidelines for low-income housing that encouraged reserving some spaces for whites in order to promote integration in projects. These often resulted in empty units reserved for white applicants who did not appear, at the same time that waiting lists for African Americans and Latinos were years long. Court action eventually brought such integration-promoting methods into question, and the practice has been more or less abandoned.[30]

---

[29] See Alex J. Johnson, 'Bid Whist, Tonk and *United States* vs. *Fordice*: Why Integrationism Fails African Americans Again', *California Law Review*, 81/6 (Dec. 1993), 1401–70. Johnson argues here for the virtues of separate African American educational institutions, but his points apply to valuing distinctly African American neighbourhoods and institutions within them. The ideal of integration, Johnson argues, can only be achieved by respecting the unique culture of groups through the maintenance and operation of separate institutions that allow African Americans to join together in collective associations that have educational and social dimensions. Integration is a long-term process that requires affirming group-differentiated separation on the way. In analysing the *Fordice* decision, Johnson argues that attempting to change racial patterns by coercion is wrong, at least partly because it limits African American choices to cluster.

[30] See Richard Thompson Ford's discussion of *United States* v. *Starrett City Associates*, 1988, in his articles 'Boundaries of Race: Political Geography in Legal Analysis', *Harvard Law Review*, 107/8 (June 1994), 1896–7.

In Europe the issue of integration is discussed today most often in terms of the situation of members of groups who have migrated to European countries from Asia, Africa, the Middle East, and the Caribbean. Although many of these people were born in these countries, often dominant society treats them all as foreigners. They are often relatively segregated in European cities, partly as a result of voluntary clustering and partly because of processes of exclusion. Many maintain a distinct language, religious practices, social networks, and other cultural affinities. Often they have meagre opportunities for employment and economic improvement. Many European cities and states aim to promote integration of members of these groups.

In his influential book *Multicultural Citizenship* Will Kymlicka argues that integration is the proper normative ideal for the relationship between immigrants and the nations into which they immigrate. Whereas national minorities have rights to self-organization and cultural separation because they have historically occupied a territory, immigrants have joined another society voluntarily in order to better their lives. While they need protections from discrimination, and special resources to enable them to learn the dominant language and develop skills necessary to compete on the labour market, the goal of their movement and these policies ought to be their integration into the dominant national culture.[31] Kymlicka here fails to distinguish the goals of economic opportunity and political inclusion from incorporation into a dominant national culture. Most migrants do in fact wish to be integrated into labour markets and political institutions of the societies they have joined; many, however, resist the suggestion that they should acquire the dominant national culture and privatize their native culture as a condition of these economic and political opportunities. This distinction has generated some conflict in some European cities.

Yasmin Nohaglu Soysal distinguishes two kinds of policies that European states follow towards the inclusion of immigrants and their children. Some policies provide opportunities for language-learning, training, etc., at the same time that they discourage groups from forming group-specific organizations. Others allow or even encourage the self-organization of migrant groups to provide services and represent the interests and perspectives of these groups in politics and policy.[32] The former sort, I suggest, tend to guided by an ideal of integration, while the latter align more with the ideal of differentiated solidarity I

[31] Kymlicka, *Multicultural Citizenship*, ch. 5.
[32] Yasmin Nohaglu Soysal, *Limits of Citizenship: Migrants and Postnational Membership in Europe* (Chicago: University of Chicago Press, 1994).

will argue for below. The arguments I have offered above against an ideal of integration that discourages group clustering in civic life apply as much to the situation of cultural minorities in Europe, I suggest, as to the context of the United States.

Some scholars of European cities argue that an implicit or explicit ideal of integration allows the dominant national majority to set the terms of acceptance and inclusion for those judged racially and/or culturally different. The stance of tolerant integration requires that the migrants be perceived as affirming the values and sociocultural accomplishments of the majority society. They often fail their perception test, however, either because they retain group-specific organizations and practices or because the majority constructs their difference in ways that preclude sharing in the national culture and pride.[33]

With respect to housing allocation in particular, some European policies that focus on mixing whites and people of colour in residential settings have had some of the same coercive implications as US policies and, like them, have failed to address the issues of housing and social disadvantage. The British 'dispersal' public housing allocation policies of the 1970s and early 1980s, for example, forced Blacks out of clustered living situations into neighbourhoods not of their choosing, but for the most part without improving the quality of their housing.[34] Quotas for different groups was at the centre of Dutch pro-integration housing policy in the 1980s. The policy was eventually abandoned, however, because many protested the way it limited choices for the migrant minorities it was supposed to help.[35]

The clustering of people who feel particular affinity with one another because they share religion or other cultural practices, and/or because they share similar difficulties and stigmas which they can resist together, is no more wrong in the European context than in the American. Residential clustering can and often does offer benefits of civic organization and networking among group members. It also often allows opportunities for the spatial and social support of the *public* expression of cultural specificity that some argue is necessary if

[33] See Jan Blommaert and Jef Verschieren, 'European Concepts of Nation-Building', in Edwin N. Wilmsen and Patrick McAllister (eds.), *The Politics of Difference* (Chicago: University of Chicago Press, 1996).

[34] Smith, *The Politics of 'Race' and Residence*.

[35] See Ger Mik, 'Housing Segregation and Policy in the Dutch Metropolitan Environment', in Elizabeth D. Huttman (ed.), Wim Blauw and Juliet Satman (co-eds.), *Urban Housing Segregation of Minorities in Western Europe and the United States* (Durham, NC: Duke University Press, 1991).

people are to use cultural resources to support personal identity and civic sociability.[36]


## 5. An Alternative Ideal: Differentiated Solidarity

Assuming that the criticisms I have made of a common form of an ideal of integration are valid, then we need to formulate a different ideal of social and political inclusion. I propose to call this alternative ideal *differentiated solidarity*. Like the ideal of integration, norms of differentiated solidarity oppose actions and structures that exclude and segregate groups or categories of persons. Differentiated solidarity assumes respect and mutual obligation.

Unlike an ideal of integration, however, differentiated solidarity allows for a certain degree of separation among people who seek each other out because of social or cultural affinities they have with one another that they do not share with others. Differentiated solidarity does not presume mutual identification and affinity as an explicit or implicit condition for attitudes of respect and inclusion.[37] Affinity group differentiation can be affirmed if it is structured in a context of co-operation that discourages group-based selfishness, prejudice, or hatred. Differentiated solidarity, then, aims to balance values of generalized inclusion and respect with more particularist and local self-affirmation and expression.[38] I will elaborate its principles of both

[36] Yael Tamir discusses the need for public culture in this sense; see Tamir, *Liberal Nationalism* (Princeton: Princeton University Press, 1993).

[37] The ideals and principles I offer under the concept of differentiated solidarity are similar to the ideals expressed by Roy Brooks under the label of 'limited separation in alliance with racial integration'; Brooks, *Integration or Separation: A Strategy for Political Equality* (Cambridge, Mass.: Harvard University Press, 1996), esp. pt. III. Limited separation, Brooks says, is 'cultural and economic integration within African American society' (p. 184). 'Limited separation is voluntary racial isolation that serves to support and nurture individuals within the group without unnecessarily trammeling the interest of other individuals or groups. Racial isolation that results from a conscious choice or strategy of self-support by African-Americans and that does not unnecessarily subordinate whites individually or collectively is what I mean by limited separation' (p. 190). I find this definition somewhat too strong in stating an approval of 'isolation'. Racial 'isolation' is neither desirable nor possible; 'limited separation' is a more descriptive term.

[38] The articulation of an idea of differentiated solidarity draws on some ideas of previous work. Partly inspired by the struggles of Maori in New Zealand and the policy changes in that society towards greater cultural and political autonomy for Maori in the context of dwelling together with others in a wider New Zealand polity, I developed an earlier form of this idea in an essay, 'Together in Difference: Transforming the Logic of Group Political Conflict', in Will Kymlicka (ed.), *The Rights of Minority Cultures* (Oxford: Oxford University Press, 1995). Despite important institutional changes in New Zealand in the last twenty years problems of segregation and exclusion remain serious. Other aspects of these

solidarity and differentiation, and then indicate how this ideal can guide desegregating actions and policies.[39]

*Solidarity.* With this term I intend to invoke a sense of commitment and justice owed to people, but precisely not on the basis of a fellow feeling or mutual identification. Most uses of this term 'solidarity' presume such unifying fellow feeling, as do synonyms such as 'community'. Ideals of inclusion in our complex, plural, and populous societies, however, must rely on a concept of mutual respect and caring that presumes distance: that norms of solidarity hold among strangers and those who in many ways remain strange to one another.[40] If not fellow feeling, what is the moral basis for such attentiveness across social distance?

It is that people live together. They are together in a locale or region, whether they like it or not. Because they are together, they are all affected by and relate to the geographical and atmospheric environment, and the structural consequences of the fact that they all move in and around this region in distinct and relatively unco-ordinated paths and local interactions. They are all potentially affected by an earth-

---

ideas of differentiated solidarity recall earlier discussions of what I have called a 'heterogeneous public'. See 'Impartiality and the Civic Public: A Critique of the Ideal of University Citizenship', in *Throwing Like a Girl and Other Essays in Feminist Philosophy and Social Theory* (Bloomington: Indiana University Press, 1990); see also *Justice and the Politics of Difference* (Princeton: Princeton University Press, 1990), ch. 5. These ideas are also based on the ideal of openness to unassimilated others which I articulated in earlier formulations of an ideal of city life; see 'The Ideal of Community and the Politics of Difference', in Linda Nicholson (ed.), *Feminism/Postmodernism* (New York: Routledge, 1990).

[39] The ideals of differentiated solidarity I articulate here also owe something to recent formulations of norms of political community and inclusion that Jurgen Habermas has made. Habermas rejects notions of political community that reject an assumed pre-political 'nation' or other group affinity as the basis for mutual respect and commitment to co-operation working political institutions require. He offers instead a concept of 'constitutional patriotism' to unify members of a political community, which can allow for cultural distinctions within it. See 'Citizenship and National Identity: Some Reflections on the Future of Europe', *Praxis International*, 12/1 (Apr. 1992), 1–19; and 'The European Nation-State: On the Past and Future of Sovereignty and Citizenship', in *The Inclusion of the Other: Studies in Political Theory* (Cambridge, Mass.: MIT Press, 1998). The concept of differentiated solidarity shares with Habermas's notion of constitutional patriotism the desire to dissociate the bases of political solidarity from mutual identification. Habermas's ideal assumes, however, an already existing jurisdiction covered by a single set of procedures and laws. His concept does not so usefully explain normative groups for creating or changing jurisdictions covered by constitutional procedures. As I will discuss further at the end of this chapter and in Ch. 7, jurisdictional boundaries are often drawn in ways that intentionally or unintentionally exclude some people affected by actions and policies from having to be considered. Normative theory and political practice wishing to correct this mismatch cannot rely on a concept of solidarity based on the prior assumption of shared jurisdiction or constitution.

[40] Jodi Dean, *Solidarity of Strangers* (Berkeley: University of California Press, 1994).

quake, reduction in electrical service, or complex rush hour traffic jams, the latter two of which they often help cause. Distant strangers often need to care about and co-operate with one another enough to respond to local circumstances and problems that potentially affect most of them, which often originate from the confluence of their individualized actions.

Strangers in modern societies also live together in a stronger sense. Their daily activities assume dense networks of institutional relations which causally relate them in the sense that the actions of some here pursuing these ends potentially affect many others whom they do not know and may not have thought about. Economic activities and their institutions most deeply connect the dwellers of a region. Institutions and relations of mass communication, relations of law, contract, and service delivery, whether public or private, also bring strangers together in communicative and causal relations that link their actions and the conditions of their action.

Few theorists of justice ask what is the scope of persons or other creatures over whom obligations of justice ought to extend. They usually assume the polity to which principles of justice ought to apply as already given, and that principles of justice apply to all who take themselves to be in the same polity. As I pointed out in Chapter 1 and will again discuss at the end of this chapter and in Chapter 7, however, many polities are arbitrarily defined or defined on purpose to exclude some persons. Thus it is appropriate to ask whether the boundaries of a given polity correspond to the definition the polity ought to have in order properly to respond to moral requirements of justice. How, then, do we learn what the scope of obligations of justice is, if not by looking at the scope of existing polities?

Onora O'Neill offers a useful answer to this question. She argues that people (and perhaps some other creatures) who dwell together in the ways I have discussed stand in relations where principles of justice ought to apply. An agent stands in relations of justice with all those others whose actions that agent assumes in the background of his or her own action. In going about our own business we assume that many others will or will not do things whose institutional and causal consequences can affect our lives and actions, and we likewise implicitly assume our actions as institutionally and causally connected to the lives and actions of others. On O'Neill's account, people have obligations of justice to others in so far as and on account of this fact that they assume the specific agency of others as premises for their own action.[41]

---

[41] Onora O'Neill, *Toward Justice and Virtue* (Cambridge: Cambridge University Press, 1996), ch. 3.

I tune in to the traffic report at 8.30 a.m., and learn that several of my usual commuting routes are slower than normal; I decide to wait an hour before leaving for work. This simple act presupposes many other actors: those who prepare the traffic report, the radio station operators, all those other unknown commuters leaving for work. I grab a cup of coffee at the service station where I fuel my car. With these simple actions I presuppose the actions of possibly millions of others who are instrumental in making hot-brewed coffee and gasoline cheaply available to me. Obligations of justice arise among persons set in such institutional relations and causal chains of effect and influence. Because of these institutional and causal relationships, my actions here flow together with many others' to have far-reaching effects on distant others.

O'Neill argues that this conceptualization implies that the scope of obligations of justice is global. I agree with her, and in the next chapter I will explore that argument and discuss its normative implications for political institutions and democratic practice. The point for now, however, is to specify the claim that strangers with diverse loyalties, local affinities, and goals dwell together in complex causal relationships in metropolitan regions. Because they dwell together in this way, they have obligations of justice to one another. Obviously this does not mean that each of the thousands or millions of people who dwell together in a city or region has specified and individualized obligations to pay attention to the situation of every other individual in relation to all the others, and personally to rectify the situation of each person he or she finds suffering injustice. It means instead that every person dwelling in this institutional and causal nexus is obliged to do what he or she can to constitute and support institutions of collective actions organized to bring about relations of justice among persons, that is to say, political organizations. The ideal of differentiated solidarity specifically recognizes such obligations of collective action to undermine injustice and promote justice among the strangers who dwell together in a region.

*Differentiation.* The social and political ideal of differentiated solidarity holds that segregation is wrong, but that social group distinction is not wrong. The ideal affirms a freedom to cluster, both in urban space and in religious, cultural, and other affinity group associations. This freedom should be balanced with a commitment to non-discrimination; spatial and social clustering, that is, cannot be based on acts of exclusion, but rather on affinity attraction.

The freedom to cluster should also be paired with an openness to unassimilated otherness. Persons differentiated into social and cultural

affinity groups recognize their togetherness with other affinity groupings and affirm their being together with them in relations of justice.
Openness to unassimilated others involves affirming relationship with
them at the same time as one affirms a respectful distance. Such a
stance of recognition or acknowledgement of the others can be
described neither as tolerance nor as communal identification. To be
tolerant usually implies a willingness to let them alone but not to
affirm a relationship with them. Tolerance is too weak a norm for promoting inclusion. As I have already discussed and will again in the next
chapter, however, inclusive political institutions do not require that all
the members of the polity mutually identify. Differentiated solidarity
requires only that these who mutually identify over here in this respect
affirm their openness to and engagement with those with different situations and affinities. As I discussed in Chapter 2, recognition in this
sense is more a condition for political discussion and decision-making
than one of its goals. It affirms the need for group-based organization
and voice at the same time that it expresses openness to listening to
others and engaging with them in shared public spaces.

The normative ideal of differentiated solidarity also challenges
boundaries, both conceptual boundaries that differentiate groups and
spatial boundaries that contain and exclude. If there are different
groups, they do not have clear borders but shade into one another and
overlap. To be open to unassimilated otherness means not only
acknowledging clear differences, but also affirming that persons have
multiple memberships, and that some persons, either by choice or by
accident, do not fit any characterization.

As manifest spatially, differentiated solidarity normatively privileges spatial shadings and hybrids along with clustering. Urban spaces
instantiating differentiated solidarity might look something like this.
The region has some neighbourhoods and communities generally
recognized as group-differentiated—as characteristically Jewish, or
African American, or gay, or Maori, or straight white European neighbourhoods. None of them is homogeneous, however; while some may
have a dominant differentiated character, statistically speaking the
neighbourhoods are hybrid. This urban space also has many neighbourhoods and districts with little group clustering. A traveller in this
urban region of spatial separations without exclusions finds no clear
borders between neighbourhoods; they flow into one another without
the abrupt border between fancy façades and boarded windows
that now appear in many American cities.[42] In this ideal of city life

---

[42] See Richard Thompson Ford, 'Geography and Sovereignty: Jurisdictional Formation
and Racial Segregation', *Stanford Law Review*, 49/6 (July 1997), 1365–1446. Ford quotes

everyone has their homeplace, the place of their immediate residence and local community participation. No one feels that another part of the city or region is closed to him or her, however, because of the behaviour and attitude of its residents. People relate to other districts, moreover, as their places of work, or for shopping, entertainment, and visiting friends. Urban space instantiating differentiated solidarity, finally, contains many outdoor and indoor public spaces where any of those who dwell together in the region might be found at concerts, festivals, rallies, and public discussions.

*Application.* These two ideals, integration and differentiated solidarity, share some values and diverge on others. As much as the ideal of integration, differentiated solidarity affirms principles of non-discrimination. Policy guided by an ideal of differentiated solidarity would prohibit all group-based discrimination. It would also forbid acts and policies aimed at class exclusion in offering economic, social, and political opportunities, such as municipal zoning or requiring certain lot sizes or against multi-unit dwellings.

Perhaps even more than an ideal of integration, moreover, differentiated solidarity promotes the liberty of housing consumers. Social policies aimed at desegregation and at promoting norms of differentiated solidarity should open opportunities for individuals and allow them liberty to pursue their own chosen goals for their personal lives, especially their place of residence. People should not be forced to move, for example, to achieve desegregation objectives, any more than they should be removed for the sake of segregation. Allocation of housing should rely primarily on price-regulated or subsidized markets; where housing is assigned it should be as much as possible according to the preferences of residents rather than according to some integrated patterned outcome decided by allocators.

While the preferences of housing consumers should be respected as much as possible, the same is not true for the institutions and owners whose actions contribute to housing opportunities or the conditions of neighbourhoods. Most existing patterns and processes of residential racial segregation cannot be reversed in ways that will increase options for individual choice, without monitoring and regulating the activities of landlords, financial institutions, developers, and other private agents whose actions most affect the social meaning of urban space.

Kenneth Jackson's description of the meeting of the racially concentrated poor and dilapidated East Side of Detroit with the suburb of Grosse Pointe, whose wide lawns and clipped hedges are visible from some front stoops of the East Side. Ford points out that law and social policy seem not to be worried about the social and jurisdictional boundaries that allow such stark separation of conditions of privilege and disadvantage, at the same time that the law is very worried about boundaries of majority Black electoral districts.

Policy-makers cannot rely on even honest commitments to group blindness and non-discrimination, because these often accompany actions that reinforce segregated privilege and disadvantage. Processes of segregation are reproduced in liberal society not primarily by design but more by the confluence of many apparently innocuous or self-deceiving acts. It is thus necessary to intervene actively in those processes. It is legitimate to limit the liberty of property owners and housing-related institutions for the sake of promoting the freedom of individuals to live in decent housing in decent neighbourhoods where some choose group-specific clusters.

With respect to resource allocation and political process, policy guided by ideals of differentiated solidarity diverge from those guided by integration. The latter usually aim to open predominantly white neighbourhoods to others. Often they provide opportunities for members of racialized groups to move from poorer-quality, racially concentrated neighbourhoods to places with better housing and quality of life. Some policies encourage whites to settle or stay in racially mixed neighbourhoods. Policies such as these concentrate on the situation and action of individual home-owners or renters. Many of them are useful in combating discrimination or promoting choice. Because they are relatively small in comparison to the problem, however, and focus on the movement of individuals, they make hardly a ripple in the processes that reproduce the privileges of segregation.

Policy guided by an image of the city as group-differentiated in some spaces, but in a context where citizens understand that they are together across that difference and have a sense of justice towards one another, focuses more on the movements of resources than that of people. Disadvantaged neighbourhoods of high racial concentration need massive public and private investment in housing renovation and development, commercial spaces and businesses, public spaces like community centres, parks, and playgrounds, and job-creating enterprises. Programmes mandated by the US Community Reinvestment Act or even 'enterprise zones' act on these sort of principles, but their scale is so small and their activities usually so relatively isolated that they often have little effect on neighbourhood quality.

Policy that aims to move resources to people addresses directly the inequalities of material privilege and disadvantage processes of segregation produce. Such policies do not force some to face the choice of leaving the familiarity of home or be excluded from benefits and opportunities open to others. Moving resources in ways that have noticeable and lasting effect in the improvement of the quality of life in neighbourhoods, moreover, is likely to affect the movement of people; some outsiders may be attracted to living in the neighbour-hoods. Policies aiming to invest resources in racially concentrated, relatively under-served neighbourhoods need not, and should not, replace open housing and non-discrimination policies, of course.

## 5. Local Participation and Regional Governance

More than thirty years ago Robert Dahl highlighted a dilemma for democracy in a world of increasing population density, ease of com-munication, and economic interdependence. On the one hand, values of participation, communicative interaction, and citizen influence over public decisions lead democrats to favour small political units. Given the density of interdependence across regions and countries, however, decentralized units have little power to influence far-reaching relations and actions that fundamentally affect their local conditions. The wider the scope of political jurisdiction, the more possible it is to regulate such far-reaching conditions. Dahl summarizes the dilemma thus:

At the extremes, citizens may participate in a vast range of complex and cru-cial decisions by the single act of casting a ballot; or else they have almost unlimited opportunities to participate in decisions over matters of no import-ance. At one extreme, then, the people vote but do not rule; at the other they rule—but they have nothing to rule over.[43]

The small unit of democratic governance has unique virtues and functions. The smaller the number of people in a political unit, the more influence potentially each member has over decision in it. In a small unit members have more opportunities to know and directly interact with other members in associations and communication net-works, to create dense, rich, and many-sided relations. In small units of governance citizens have easier access to meetings, hearings, and the offices that implement decisions. Thus they are able most easily to monitor the implementation and hold public officials accountable. Local governance units can best encourage and enable the active par-ticipation of citizens in raising issues, shaping the political agenda, making decisions, and implementing them.

Small political jurisdiction, however, in today's world often func-tions to separate people administratively whose actions nevertheless profoundly affect one another, and who dwell together in environ-

---

[43] Robert Dahl, 'The City in the Future of Democracy', *American Political Science Review*, 61/41 (Dec. 1967), 953–70. Compare Robert Goodin's discussion of participation and centralization in *Green Political Theory* (Oxford: Polity Press, 1992), ch. 4.

ments and structural processes that institutionally and causally relate them. Processes of racial and class residential segregation that I discussed above are often facilitated by creation or maintenance of municipal jurisdictions that contain disadvantage and preserve privilege. Autonomous local jurisdictions exclude some people and activities through their use of zoning regulation; with their tax powers wealthy communities run high-quality schools and first-rate services while a neighbouring poorer municipality has a much lower tax base and need for more costly and complex service provision. The planning and development decisions of one jurisdictionally autonomous unit affect the investment patterns and atmosphere of many neighbouring communities who have no say in these decisions.

The scope of a polity, I argued above, ought to coincide with the scope of the obligations of justice which people have in relation to one another because their lives are intertwined in social, economic, and communicative relations that tie their fates. Because of such social linkage, people assume actions of many unknown and differently situated strangers as premises of their own actions. Decisions not to run a bus line to certain neighbourhoods and shopping districts, and to erect walls around affluent communities, assume that some less well-off people would try to enter those spaces if access were easier. According to O'Neill's theory of the scope of obligations of justice that I have summarized, these people stand in relations of justice. I have suggested that dense relations of causal influence and background action obtain across metropolitan regions. When the political organization of such regions institutionalizes political discussion and decision-making only within separate small jurisdictions, and people in them feel they need to concern themselves only with the others in their jurisdictional community, then such political separation is illegitimate because it does not correspond to the scope of relations of justice.

In the United States such jurisdictional separation is often one source of continuing social exclusion and inequality.[44] Some scholars argue that in the United States the economic well-being of suburbs is tied to the economic well-being of their city cores; yet jurisdictional separation allows suburbs to benefit from that economic interdependence without sharing with central cities their administrative service provision and economic development costs.[45] The United States is

[44] See Ford, 'Geography and Sovereignty: Jurisdictional Formation and Racial Segregation'.
[45] See David Rusk, *Cities without Suburbs* (Washington: Woodrow Wilson Center Press, 1993); Hank V. Savitch and Ronald K. Vogel, 'Ties that Bind: Central Cities, Suburbs and the New Metropolitan Region', *Economic Development Quarterly*, 7/4 (Nov. 1993), 341–58.

perhaps unique in the degree of jurisdictional fragmentation of such regional economies, but not in the degree of economic interdependence across regions.[46] For these reasons a wide scope of political regulation, extending across a region, is desirable from a normative point of view, as well as from the point of view of efficiency or efficacy.

We appear to have a normative dilemma. On the one hand, self-determination, cultural specificity, participation, and accountability seem best realized in relatively small political units. On the other hand, values of taking into account the needs and interests of differently situated others with whom local affinity groups dwell are best realized in political units wide in scope, comprising at least broad metropolitan regions. Is there any way out of this dilemma that can balance local self-determination with a region-wide acknowledgement of the legitimate interests of others?

Gerald Frug offers a model of urban politics designed to respond to this dilemma. The theoretical key to the model, he suggests, is to conceive of decentralized political units as 'decentered'.[47] Decentred decentralization rejects the understanding and institutionalization of local autonomy most common in local government law. On this inadequate interpretation, a municipality has autonomous authority just in so far as it is a bounded jurisdiction separate from others in the sense that each abides by a principle of non-interference. What goes on within the jurisdiction is our business, and others outside may not interfere, and we in this jurisdiction likewise need not and should not concern ourselves with the problems and decisions of neighbouring jurisdictions. This bounded, or as Frug calls it 'centered', understanding of local autonomy gives to citizens and governments in one municipality licence to pursue only the interests of residents in their locality without regard for the consequences of their actions and policies on those outside, and without having to attend to region-wide interactions.

If local autonomy were absolute in this sense, modern societies might be unworkable; but they are not. State and provincial governments limit the autonomy of municipalities precisely in order to facilitate regulation of wider social processes and issues of justice. State power in this way also operates under the centred model of sovereignty. State, provincial, and national governments centralize regulative control in institutions removed from local participation; they

[46] Michael Storper, *The Regional World: Territorial Development in a Global Economy* (London: Guilford Press, 1997); Borja and Castells, *Local and Global*.

[47] Frug, 'Decentering Decentralization', *University of Chicago Law Review*, 60/2 (Spring 1993), 253–338; Frug's model is most well developed in his book *City Making*.

stand as overrides to local government, with primarily jurisdictional power over many issues, leaving local governments with residual powers. Frug argues that a better way to institutionalize political relations of co-ordination and concern across a broad region would rely on an altered concept of local autonomy. Following some feminist theorists of autonomy, I shall refer to this revised concept as relational autonomy.[48]

Under a relational concept, autonomy means that agents can choose their ends and have capacities and support to pursue those ends. The social constitutions of agents and their acting in relations of interdependence means that the ability to separate and be independent of others is rare if it appears at all. Thus, on this interpretation, an adequate concept of autonomy should promote the capacity of persons to pursue their own ends in the context of relationships in which others may do the same. While this concept of autonomy entails a presumption of non-interference, it does not imply a social scheme in which atomized agents simply mind their own business and leave each other alone. Instead, it entails recognizing that agents are related in many ways they have not chosen, by virtue of kinship, history, proximity, or the unintended consequences of action. In these relationships agents are able to thwart one another or support one another. Relational autonomy consists partly, then, in the structuring of relationships so that they support the maximal pursuit of all individual ends.

Frug adapts this concept of relational autonomy to urban politics. He calls for institutions of regional government with which locales have a relational autonomy.[49] First, local autonomy means a presumption of agency and non-interference. Local units should be small enough to allow for meaningful citizen participation in discussion and decisions, and local governments should have non-trivial decisions to make about how the environment, public life, and opportunities of its citizens are shaped. In his revision of local governance concepts, then, Frug proposes to retain local municipal jurisdictions and even to create neighbourhood councils in larger jurisdictions. Secondly, in so far

[48] See Jennifer Nedelsky, 'Relational Autonomy', *Yale Women's Law Journal*, 1/1 (1989), 7–36; 'Law, Boundaries, and the Bounded Self', in Robert Post (ed.), *Law and the Order of Culture* (Berkeley: University of California Press, 1991). See also Anna Yeatman, 'Beyond Natural Right: The Conditions for Universal Citizenship', in *Postmodern Revisions of the Political* (New York: Routledge, 1994); 'Feminism and Citizenship', in Nick Stevenson (ed.), *Cultural Citizenship* (London: Sage, 1998). These feminist theories are about how the autonomy of individuals should be conceived by law and political governance.

[49] Frug, *City Making*. Compare the proposals of Ford, '*The United States* vs. *Starrett City Associates 1988*'; 'Geography and Sovereignty: Jurisdictional Formation and Racial Segregation'.

as the activities and decisions of a locale may adversely affect others, or generate conflict, or implicate their interdependent relationships, other locales have a legitimate right to make claims on autonomous locales, negotiate the terms of their relationships, and mutually adjust their effects. Thus Frug proposes to institutionalize mechanisms that require locales to take one another's interests and needs into account and which create regional bodies for negotiation of jurisdiction and decision-making about region-wide concerns. The relationship between local governments and metropolitan or regional governance institutions is based largely on intergovernmental negotiation, then, rather than a legal hierarchy in which the regional government subordinates the local.[50]

It would take another book to work out in detail the institutional design of local and regional government based on a concepts of differentiated solidarity and relational autonomy. Such a project would need to consider many alternatives about many matters of local government, take positions on them and defend them, and compare its normative conclusions with existing institutions of regional government in various parts of the world. My purpose here in introducing arguments about local control and regional scope is to fill out a concept of differentiated solidarity as a response to the harms of racial and class segregation. With that limited purpose in mind, I will sketch some elements of this model of local governance as I understand them.

First, what is a region, in this model? I have in mind primarily the metropolitan centres in which nearly all the world's population is projected to dwell within the next few decades. These are centres of high-density economic processes and movement across them, where the density of interaction fades at the edges. A region is also a geographical centre, defined by specific climatic conditions, vegetation, topography, and waterways. A region is the radius of local labour and consumer markets; it spans the radius of broadcast for a strong radio signal. Many people dwell not only in their neighbourhoods and local communities, but also in the whole region. They travel across the region frequently to work, play, shop, and visit family and friends.

As I understand it, these are some of the elements of this model of the autonomy of local governments in institutionalized relation to others in a region. We begin with locally autonomous units of participation and decision-making. Jordi Borja and Manuel Castells characterize such decentred units as follows:

[50]   Compare Borja and Castells, *Local and Global*, ch. 8.

Decentralization should be based on units or territorial zones (districts) which possess historical geographical and/or socio-cultural characteristics, i.e., of a kind making the existence or construction of a collective identity possible. They should also have as clear a physical image a possible (it is better if major arteries define districts, uniting rather than separating them), and it is desirable that they be or can become multi-purpose in social and functional terms. Districts need to be big enough by inhabitants and are to make the exercise or management of functions and services possible.[51]

Where people desire to cluster according to affinities of religion, culture, or way of life, this model of local government would design institutions of political participation and decision-making to correspond to such groupings, but would also discourage exclusion and encourage many diverse and hybrid locales. Much of the association life that implementation of ideas of associative democracy might draw on occurs within these local districts. The model calls for participatory decision-making institutions at this local level which are deeper than those that now exist in many cities and towns.

The model constitutes these local governments as autonomous in the sense that their citizens through their political institutions have the right to decide the form and policies of social services including schools, within the limits of equal respect and non-discrimination for all served by them. A concept of relational autonomy says, however, that such local autonomy cannot be only inward-looking and self-regarding. This model of regional governance requires that local governments take the interests of others in the region into account, especially where outsiders make a claim on them that they are affected by the actions and policies of that locale. A set of regional governance institutions enforces this requirement. These include procedures for negotiations and co-operation between local governments. As I envision it, if one locale claims that activities or policies of another do or may adversely affect their locale and its residents, the local governments must enter a process of deliberation about their conflicts of interests in which third parties have a mediating role. Regional governance also entails a regional legislature to set the framework for these mandated negotiating procedures, as well as serving several other regulatory functions, such as those to do with tax policy and revenue-sharing, transportation and construction planning, and environmental protection. Regional government creates intergovernmental institutions of local government co-operation to render service provision high quality and efficient across a region,

[51] Ibid. 190.

and access to services offered in one locale should not be restricted to residents of that locale.[52]

How does this model of local self-determination in the context of regional government instantiate an ideal of differentiated solidarity? It aims to strike a balance between attention to the needs and interests of diverse and distant strangers that commitment to justice requires, on the one hand, and desires for differentiated affiliation in more closely identifying communities of interest. Groups differentiated by culture or lifestyle can have a certain measure of autonomy, on this model, and can be represented in wider regional institutions. An important function of regional institutions ought to be to create fora where such particularist groups meet for public discusison about region-wide concern. In order to avoid local parochialism that representation only by locale fosters, Frug proposes that a regional legislature and other institutions of regional governance rely on forms of cross-local representation of structural or functional groups, as well as on the representation of locales. Institutions might specially represent otherwise under-represented structural positions, for example, such as those of women or young people, which cross the region. They might have institutions for representing specific interests, such a those of consumers or parents.

This model of regional government differs in important ways from many existing structures of local governments in relation to state, provincial, or national governments. First, the scope of a region in this model is narrower than the scope of many states. Secondly, as already mentioned, regional government in this model does not simply limit and override the powers of local government, as occurs in most relations between local and state governments. Nor does it function simply as a higher level of authority more removed from the local participation of citizens. Instead, regional government sets a framework for inter-local negotiation, conflict resolution, and co-operation whose issues are on the local, as well as regional, public agenda.

Many forces have been collaborating recently to pressure local governments in the United States to institute stronger metropolitan governance structures with wider powers than in the past.[53] Federal and state government policy recently has passed more administrative responsibilities such as welfare to the local level, at the same time that

---

[52]   See Frug, *City Making*, ch. 8; in '*The United states* vs. *Starrett City Associates 1988*', and 'Geography and Sovereignty: Jurisdictional Formation and Racial Segrgation', Richard Ford also emphasizes access to city services.

[53]   See Hank V. Savitch and Ronald K. Vogel (eds.), *Regional Politics: America in a Post-City Age* (Thousand Oaks, Calif.: Sage, 1996).

local governments worry more about revenues and the costs of their programmes and services. Some local governments respond by looking for ways to co-operate on a regional level. Increasing transnational investment activity also motivates local governments to organize regionally to compete with other regions for economic development opportunities. Similar pressures have prompted metropolitan regions all over the world to take steps to create or restructure regional government.[54]

I have presented a sketch of a model of regional government whose purpose is to enhance the sense of justice across a region, as well as institutional capacity to implement equity-promoting decisions, while sacrificing little of the values of local participation. Many existing regional governments do not have these intentions. Wider regional governance institutions do not necessarily preserve or enhance participation, reduce exclusion and segregation, and cultivate an ethic of regard for the legitimate interests of others across the region. Given the realities of power, metropolitan governments are even more likely to reduce democratic participation and accountability and increase the power of more privileged and affluent districts at the expense of the less privileged. Everything depends on the institutional design and the political pressures of organized citizens to use regional institutions for undermining exclusion and promoting more equality in neighbourhood quality and access to services. Experiments in redistribution by means of regional government like those in Minneapolis–St Paul or Johannesburg convince me that regional institutions of differentiated solidarity are possible.

[54] See Borja and Castells, *Local and Global*; Storper, *The Regional World*.

# CHAPTER 7

# Self-Determination and Global Democracy

The nation-state system enacts exclusions that are sometimes grave in their consequences yet widely accepted as legitimate. States claim the right to exclude non-citizens who wish to live within their borders. They also claim a right against interference from other states or international bodies concerning the actions and policies they take within their jurisdictions. States and their citizens claim that they have no obligation to devote any of their intellectual and material resources to enhance the well-being of anyone outside their borders. Some political theorists argue against the legitimacy of these exclusions, and promote a more cosmopolitan conception of moral obligation and political action. Others contest this cosmopolitanism, arguing for the moral value and legitimacy of nationalism in a form compatible with liberal democratic principles and institutions.

This chapter considers issues of exclusion, inclusion, and relationships in a global context. It extends the question concerning the proper scope of the polity to issues of justice between peoples across the world. With cosmopolitans I argue against the widespread belief that obligations of justice extend only to co-nationals or only members of the same nation-state. Especially under contemporary conditions of global interdependence, obligations of justice extend globally. If the scope of democratic political institutions should correspond to the scope of obligations of justice, then there ought to be more global institutional capacity to govern relations and interactions among the world's peoples.

Many people rightly distrust projects of cosmopolitan governance, however, on grounds of cultural homogenization or dangers of domination of some people by others. This chapter takes such suspicions seriously. With those who theorize the value of national loyalty, I suggest that commitments to justice among peoples across the world entail recognizing the importance of the distinctness of peoples for the well-being of many individuals. I review arguments that the moral value of political recognition provides an important source of the self. Nationalist interpretations of the distinctness of peoples, however, tend to be inappropriately essentialist and exclusionary. Instead, peoples should be understood as relationally constituted, and the political recognition of the distinctness of peoples would be able to accommodate the millions of people who think of their identities as hybrids of national membership, or who construct a cosmopolitan identity.

Those who theorize the importance of recognizing distinct peoples in politics are right to emphasize a principle of self-determination. Today we still tend to interpret this principle, however, as the claim for a right to an independent sovereign state. This interpretation of self-determination as non-interference is not consistent with requirements of global justice. Nor can it support a claim that all peoples should be able to exercise the right of self-determination. Building on the concept of relational autonomy developed in Chapter 6, I argue that the normative idea of self-determination should be reconceived in relational terms that cohere with openness and interdependence. Self-determination should be conceived as about non-domination, rather than non-interference. Coupled with arguments for global governance, this conception of the self-determination of peoples produces a vision of local and cultural autonomy in the context of global regulatory regimes. Thus this chapter aims to invoke the ideal of differentiated solidarity on the global level.

To lend concreteness to this vision, I suggest that a social movement for global democracy might build on some existing institutions of global regulation and international law, particularly some of the institutions in the United Nations system. It is important that any vision of global governance be democratic, however, and on this count the existing institutions of the United Nations require serious reform. The chapter discusses some of the requirements of global democratic interaction, recalling the norms of communicative democracy and public spheres developed earlier.

## 1. The Nation-State and Obligations of Justice

Many people think that if they have obligations of justice, they are only to those who live in the same political society as they, governed by the same constitution. They do not stand in relations of justice to inhabitants of other nation-states. As Margaret Canovan points out, liberal political theorists typically make this assumption without even noticing that they do so.[1] Rarely have political theorists explicitly addressed the question I raised in the previous chapter and which now returns: what is the proper scope of obligations of justice to which political institutions ought to correspond?[2]

The received answer, usually implied, is that the scope of issues and claims of justice is the nation-state. Persons within a given society defined by sovereign state jurisdiction have obligations of justice to one another. They are obliged to listen to the claims urged by their fellow citizens, for example, that laws or institutions treat them unfairly, and they are obliged to contribute to support policies and programmes that aim to rectify injustice and promote justice. State institutions are obliged to listen impartially to the justice claims of citizens and to enforce judgements of justice among them. Neither the state nor the people living within its jurisdiction, however, have obligations of justice to those outside the society. On the contrary, the state's obligation is to maximize its own interests and those of its citizens without equal consideration for how this pursuit may affect the interests of outsiders, so long as in doing so the state does not directly interfere with the internal affairs of other states. Outsiders have no moral right to make claims upon a state other than their own or upon its citizens except under the laws of that state. From a moral point of view, the people of each society are and ought to be entirely independent of one another.

How is this position justified? As already mentioned, many merely assume it without justification. I reconstruct three types of justification, which I call positivist, nationalist, and associationalist. My analysis and critique will dwell on the nationalist justification because it seems most plausible and has received significant recent rehabilitation in theory and practice.

[1] Margaret Canovan, 'The Skeleton in the Cupboard: Nationhood, Patriotism, and Limited Loyalties', in S. Caney, D. George, and P. Jones (ed.), *National Rights, National Obligations* (Boulder, Colo.: Westview Press, 1997); see also Canovan, *Nationhood and Political Theory* (Cambridge: Cambridge University Press, 1996).

[2] In *A Theory of Justice* (Cambridge, Mass.: Harvard University, 1971) Rawls does make explicit the assumption that the subject of justice is the basic institutions of a particular society understood as independent and closed from others, but he does not justify this assumption. In more recent work he acknowledges the need for a 'law of peoples', but he continues to assert that his two principles of justice apply only within a given state. See Susan Hurley, 'Democracy, Rationality and Leady Boundaries', in Ian Shapiro and Casiano Hacker-Cordon (eds.), *Democracy's Edges* (Cambridge: Cambridge University Press, 1999). See Kok-Chor Ten, 'Kantian Ethics and Global Justice', *Social Theory and Practice*, 23 (Spring 1997), 53–62.

*Positivist justification.* Confronted with the question of why we think
we think we have obligations of justice only to those who live in our
nation-state, some might be inclined to reply that it is simply the fact
that we are governed by the same political constitution that accounts
for our obligations to them and only them. With a version of ought
implies can, this justification might add that claims of justice are mean-
ingless unless there are institutions to adjudicate and discharge them.
The state supplies these, but only with respect to the people under its
jurisdiction. Therefore, we have such obligations only to each other
and none to outsiders.

I call this a positivist account because it makes moral obligations of
justice contingent on the existence of particular political jurisdictions.
Like all positivism, however, such a position robs principles and practices of justice of any *moral* force. They become as arbitrary as borders
that happen to be drawn, and can change as borders change. It cannot
be right, however, that the scope of justice is determined by the scope
of political institutions which recognize some as insiders who can
make justice claims and some as outsiders who must go to another tri-
bunal. If obligations of justice are contingent on political jurisdictions
in this way, then people can remove their obligations simply by
redrawing borders.

On this account, there was no injustice in the 'bantustan' policy of
apartheid South Africa. That policy created 'homelands' for several
Black African peoples in South Africa, on some of the worst land in
the region, which the South African state declared to be independent
states. It forced many Blacks to move to these 'homelands' and forced
them to carry passports to enter the borders they called South Africa.
They set up Black-run governments and told their leaders to take care
of their own and not to come to white South Africa with claims of
injustice. Most of the world judged this policy, premised on the claim
that political jurisdiction justifies excluding those outside the jurisdiction from claims of justice, as one of the supreme evils of the apartheid
regime.

When put so starkly, few would endorse the positivist account, precisely because it is so arbitrary. Political actors often wish to define
political jurisdictions that include some and exclude others; when they
have the power to implement their will, they claim that those who
have been made jurisdictional outsiders have no claims of justice on
the insider state or its subjects. Since the definition of jurisdictions is
so often a result of victor's spoils or expedient resolution of conflict, it
cannot be a basis for the moral justification of the scope of obligations
of justice.

*Nationalism.* Claimed ties of national membership and identification serve more commonly and plausibly as grounds for the claim that obligations of justice extend only within a society and that states should further the interests of their own citizens alone with little regard for the interests of outsiders. David Miller gives two forms of an argument that national identification is the moral basis for obligations of justice. Nations are communities of obligation, and to affirm one's national membership is to affirm the particular obligations to one's co-nationals, and only to one's co-nationals, that national identification entails. These include obligations to help preserve and nurture the national culture and institutions, to defend the nation and its members from attack by outsiders, and to resist any efforts to dominate or repress the nation's culture and people. These obligations also include obligations of justice. The constitution of national community means that members of the nation have obligations to co-nationals to assume that their needs are provided for and to share with them their national resources and their product.

The distributive and redistributive policies of many states have their basis in these obligations. 'It is because we have prior obligations of nationality that include obligations to provide for the needs of members that the practice of citizenship properly includes redistributive elements of the kind that we commonly find in contemporary states.'[3] The relationship of nationality to obligations of justice accounts for why from a moral point of view each nation should have its own state, namely as a means by which its members can discharge their obligations of justice to one another. Members of a nation have some moral obligations to outsiders—obligations of hospitality, to keep agreements made, or to respect the autonomy of other nations. However miserable and needy outsiders may be, though, and however much insiders have for themselves, they have no obligations of redistributive justice to those outsiders. Other nations have a moral obligation to take care of their own. If the members of other nations fail in their obligation to take care of their own, then we have no obligation to make up for that failure, and outsiders have no claim of justice upon us; we may owe them obligations of charity only if it is strictly impossible for the members of the other nations to take care of their own.[4]

Miller also offers a motivational argument for the connection between obligations of justice and national community. State policies responding to obligations and demands of justice often require some

---

[3] David Miller, *On Nationality* (Oxford: Oxford University Press, 1995) 72.
[4] Ibid. 76–9.

people to contribute or do what they might otherwise not be willing to do or contribute. Without national identification people will not be willing to make such sacrifices.

If we believe in social justice and are concerned about winning democratic support for socially just policies, then we must pay attention to the conditions under which different groups will trust one another, so that I can support your just demand on this occasion knowing that you will support my just demand at some future moment. Trust requires solidarity not merely within groups but across them, and this in turn depends upon a common identification of the kind that nationality alone can provide.[5]

It is certainly plausible that people who identify with one another as members of groups distinguished from others by culture and history have special obligations to those with whom they specially identify in this way that they do not have to any others. Such obligations concern the fostering of this cultural and historical identity.[6] The claim that members of national groups have obligations of justice *only* to fellow nationals, however, appears to be based on contingent psychological and historical circumstances rather than moral principle. That claim runs into the difficult problem of multicultural societies, moreover, where a single common national identity is weak or where national and cultural minorities are suppressed in order to promote the unified national identities. Later I will question the very idea of nation itself on these grounds that it arbitrarily elevates some cultural groups over others.

Miller's argument, and that of others[7] who endorse the application of principles of justice only to co-nationals, makes obligation

---

[5] Ibid. 140. Compare Yael Tamir: 'The "others" whose welfare we ought to consider are those we care about, those who are relevant to our associative identity. Communal solidarity creates a feeling, or an illusion, of closeness or shared fate, which is a precondition of distributive justice. It endows particularistic relations with moral power, supporting the claim that "charity begins at home". Moreover, the morality of community can serve as grounds for justifying the allocation of resources to the well-being of future generations, and to the study and preservation of the communal past. Consequently, the community-like nature of the nation-state is particularly well suited, and perhaps even necessary, to the notion of the liberal welfare state'; *Liberal Nationalism* (Princeton: Princeton University Press, 1993), 121.

[6] Arthur Ripstein argues along these lines in his essay 'Context, Continuity, Fairness', in Robert McKim and Jeff McMahon (eds.), *The Morality of Nationalism* (Oxford: Oxford University Press, 1997).

[7] Margaret Canovan argues that nationalism provides the political 'engine' that makes the state strong enough to mobilize political resources to enact welfare policies and to enforce them. The achievement of the modern state is universalist in the sense that nationalist movements and commitments motivate individuals to expand their sense of obligation beyond the members of their family, clan, or village to strangers with whom they identify as belonging to the same cultural and historical community. See *Nationhood and Political Theory*.

contingent on sentiment. Arguments that people have obligations of justice to others cannot depend on their having feelings of identification with those others. At best, feelings of identification can sometimes explain why some people sometimes recognize the obligations they have (or believe they have obligations they do not have). In fact we most often need to make arguments that some people have obligations of justice to others when those with the obligations fail to recognize them; and people often deny their obligations because they feel little affinity for those others or positively dislike them. Moral arguments for obligations of justice must rest on more objective and normative grounds than feelings of familiarity or cultural affinity.

In Chapter 6 I summarized Onora O'Neill's more objective criteria for deciding what are the scope of obligations of justice. Her account is similar to that offered by writers such as Charles Beitz and Thomas Pogge who focus on the question of whether and to what degree there are transnational or global obligations of justice. Wherever people act within a set of institutions that connect them to one another by commerce, communication, or the consequences of policies, such that systemic interdependencies generate benefits and burdens that would not exist without those institutional relationships, then the people within that set of interdependent institutions stand in relations of justice.[8] As I shall discuss more in the next section, global social and economic relations today do not support the claim that such interdependencies are confined with the borders of nation-states.

Persons who are asked to contribute to collective institutions designed to promote the well-being of all certainly must be motivated to do so, especially if some people ought to contribute more than others. One way to cultivate such motivation is to rely on feelings of local identification or cultural affinity. Nevertheless, while there may be reason to say that commitments to justice *begin* in such local and particularist relationships, that does not imply that they should end there. According to political theorists such as Miller and Canovan, the nation-building era helped create sentiments of solidarity among millions of distant strangers that made the modern welfare state possible. While I believe there may be reasons to doubt such an account of the origins of the welfare state, even if we accept it for the sake of argument, it shows that feelings of solidarity are not timeless and natural, but can be constructed. Why not, then, say that transnational sentiments of solidarity ought to be constructed to correspond to

[8] Charles Beitz, *Political Theory and International Relations* (Princeton: Princeton University Press, 1979); Thomas Pogge, 'Cosmopolitanism and Sovereignty', *Ethics*, 103 (Oct. 1992), 48–75.

transnational obligations, rather than fall back on the supposed facts of nationalist motivation?[9]

The claim that persons have obligations of justice only to fellow nationals is particularly problematic in multinational and multicultural contexts, and today such contexts are more the rule than the exception. All over the world groups who understand themselves as historically or culturally distinct dwell alongside and interspersed with one another. In some cases a nationalist project had brought together several groups under the domination of one and now these national minorities assert their specificity. In others immigrants and refugees have significantly changed the relative homogeneity of the societies in which they and their children have made their home.

The position that obligations of justice are limited to co-nationals is often taken to legitimize rejection of redistributive policies perceived to benefit groups with whom many citizens do not identify. White Anglo-Americans appear increasingly reluctant to support redistributive policies, partly because many of them erroneously believe that these policies primarily benefit African Americans and Latinos, with whom they feel few ties of common culture and shared history. The feelings of redistributive solidarity for which many Europeans have long been admired are coming under significant strain today in those societies with significant numbers of non-European immigrants, such as those of Turkish, North African, or South Asian origin. Some supporters of social democratic welfare policies now argue for stricter immigration restrictions on the grounds that they are necessary to renew popular support for redistributive welfare policies.[10] Of course, such arguments can fuel more xenophobia towards those perceived different from the dominant national culture despite the fact that they are members of the society.

[9] Jurgen Habermas argues that nationalism historically has served the function of promoting motivations of solidarity among strangers in a broad territory. Under contemporary conditions, he argues, however, appeals to a nation have wrongful exclusionary and discriminatory consequences. He argues that in this period commitments of solidarity can be fostered by experiences of democracy and the rule of law. See 'The European Nation-State: On the Past and Future of Sovereignty and Citizenship', and 'On the Relation between the Nation, the Rule of Law, and Democracy', both in *The Inclusion of the Other* (Cambridge, Mass.: MIT Press, 1998). Such an evolutionary story of the initially progressive and then regressive function of the idea of the nation ignores the ways that from the beginning nationalism has fuelled imperialist domination of some peoples by others. Still, Habermas's analysis is useful for reminding us of the historically constructed nature of both nationalism and solidarity, and thus the possibility of reconstruction of that latter without the former.

[10] See Alan Wolfe and Jyette Lausen, 'Identity Politics and the Welfare State', *Social Philosophy and Policy*, 14/2 (Summer 1997), 231–55.

Miller wishes to distance his argument from the implication that dominant nationals do not have the same obligations of redistribution to members of ethnic or immigrant minorities as to the dominant national group. Within the jurisdiction of a given nation-state, he believes, all members of the society, whatever their national or ethnic origin, should be entitled to the same rights and benefits. Multicultural societies, however, he suggests, are inherently unstable. If the society wishes to avoid trimming the role of the state down to the most minimal keeper of the peace and enforcer of liberty, only two options are available. Either partition the state so that each national group has a state of its own, by means of which it can promote the welfare of its own, or assimilate national and ethnic minorities into the dominant nation so that everyone in the society will identify with one another sufficiently to support general welfare policies. Neither alternative is viable.

Later I will support the view that a certain degree of separation and self-governance among peoples who consider themselves distinct is morally appropriate in certain respects. Such self-determination cannot entail, however, that peoples have no obligations of justice to one another. A 'partition' response to cultural difference, moreover, is not viable for many situations involving peoples with long histories of interaction and interspersal. The current political configuration and tension in Northern Ireland, for example, is itself the result of an effort to resolve a conflict by partition, and almost no one thinks that further partition would be desirable or possible. The differently identifying groups of Northern Ireland share many experiences and problems because they dwell together; though often in conflict they are in the same society. Because of their togetherness and dense interaction they have obligations of justice to one another. The fact that many do not identify with one another and that some in one group positively hate members of the other group may well mean that they refuse to recognize and act on such obligations of justice; but that is no basis for denying that these obligations exist.

The assimilationist answer to the alleged instability of multicultural societies is at least as problematic as the partitionist. On this view, Maori who make claims upon the New Zealand state for increased health services, better housing, funds to subsidize Maori development projects, and so on should not also insist on the right to administer such funds in their own institutions, nor should they continue publicly to celebrate Maori cultures. On this assimilationist account, it is legitimate for majority cultural or national groups to require minorities to change their sense of identity as a condition of receiving the full benefits of a welfare state. Surely such a position endorses illegitimate domination, however, as much of the recent literature on minority rights demonstrates.

*The associationalist position.* There remains one account of why obligations of justice obtain only among those within the jurisdiction of a single sovereign state, which I call the associationalist account. Unlike the previous account, this one is not based on group identification. Those who dwell together in a nation-state have exclusive obligations to one another, on this account, because their living together under a common constitution enables and fosters their social and economic interactions. The state provides a framework of social co-operation which allows members of the society to pursue their ends in association with others in the society. Associating with one another within this framework, they can pursue their individual and collective well-being. Their obligations to care about the well-being of other members of the society, and to rectify unfairness resulting from particular actions, the organization of their institutions, or chance, derives from the fact that they dwell together in this framework of association in which they all to some extent rise or fall together.[11]

This associationalist argument may indeed show that there are *some* obligations that people dwelling within a state jurisdiction have towards one another that they do not have to outsiders. Because they dwell together and acknowledge one another as members of the same political community, they have obligations to support one another in sustaining the framework of their association in so far as it enables all members to flourish. The rules and policies of the public and private institutions within which they dwell, in so far as these are not unjust or promote justice, may generate particular obligations towards others in the society. To the extent that they are unjust, they generate obligations to correct them. The fact that the political framework of association within a given state jurisdiction may generate special obligations not owed to outsiders, however, does not show that those within a state jurisdiction have no relations with outsiders sufficient to generate obligations of justice. State institutions are not the only forms of association that bind people with special obligations; some of these may cross states. Other connections that ground obligations of justice,

---

[11] Compare Samuel Scheffler, 'Liberalism, Nationalism and Egalitarianism', in Robert McKim and Jeff McMahon (eds.), *The Morality of Nationalism* (Oxford: Oxford University Press, 1997), 191–208. Scheffler argues against national identification as constituting a moral basis for applications of principles of justice. He suggests that states and societies are instead united by a political culture their institutions foster where members of the society see themselves as mutually willing to share risks for one another over the long term.

moreover, arise from the unintended effects of the confluence of many actions.

None of these three arguments for a uniquely state-specific understanding of justice work, then. In the next section I will review an argument for the claim that obligations of justice extend globally in today's world. I detail some of the regulatory problems and issues of justice that many people think cross state borders today, and I conclude that adequately to respond to such problems and issues requires stronger institutions of global governance.

## 2. Trans-border Justice and Global Governance

I referred above to the arguments that some political theorists make that today the scope of issues of justice is global as well as local and regional. Wherever people act within a set of institutions that connect them to one another by commerce, communication, or the consequences of policies, such that systematic interdependencies generate benefits and burdens that would not exist without those institutional relationships, then the people within that set of interdependent institutions stand in relations of justice. Beitz, Pogge, and O'Neill, among others, argue that the scope and complexity of economic, communication, and many other institutional systems constitute a sufficiently tight web of constraint and interdependence that today we must speak of a global *society*. Recent empirical and social theoretical scholarship about globalization has raised a number of issues about globalized processes of interaction and effect in various aspects of social life, including economic interaction. Similarly, there has been no dearth of challenges to the new theses of increasing globalization. A review and analysis of these issues would occupy another book. Details of the manner and extent of globalization need not be settled, however, before we can cite some general conditions of global society that raise issues of justice.

The first concerns the fact of the global distribution of natural resources in the context of a world economic system where some kinds of resources are more valuable than others. Resources such as fertile land, economically valuable minerals, and so on are by no means evenly distributed around the globe. Some states preside over a wealth of such resources, whereas others have relatively little. Charles Beitz questions the moral right of states to keep for themselves all the benefits derived from the natural resources that happen to lie within their borders. Because the placement of resources is morally arbitrary, no state is entitled to treat them as private property to be used only for its own benefit. Beitz argues that because some resources are necessary for the productive capacity of all societies, they must be considered a global commons. Their use and the benefits of their use should be globally regulated under a co-operative framework of global justice.[12] Just how such a global framework might justly regulate access to and use of resources is another complex question.

Many issues of environmental damage and sustainability are widely recognized as global in their implications. As passengers on spaceship earth, all the world's peoples are inextricably together. If the ozone layer thins, it potentially affects all of us; we are all affected by trends of global warming. Pollutants that enter the air or water may not affect all the world's peoples, but they do not respect state borders. The decade of the 1990s saw several significant conferences and treaties premissed on the assumption of a need for global environmental regulation. In each issues of justice have been high on the agenda: What is a fair distribution of the burdens and benefits of global environmental regulation, given the fact that people in the relatively rich developed world have had the chance to use those resources and pollute the environment for centuries, while those in less developed countries now face potential environmental impediments to their industrialization? Are not the peoples of the developed world obliged for this reason to take more of the burden for saving the earth and to compensate the peoples of less developed countries for their contributions to global environmental preservation? Again, raising such issues of global justice does not say how they should be addressed. The point here is that such issues of justice cannot be dismissed by saying that the scope of obligations of justice extend only as far as the borders of state jurisdictions.

The manner and degree to which there is one global economic system that affects all the world's people is a matter of dispute. Few question that there are deep economic interdependencies among people in the world, however, that cross state boundaries. These make it impossible to support the image of global society as a system of sovereign independent states each of whose policies affects only its own people except in so far as states or their people contract agreements. A change in the value of currency or interest rates within one country often has ripple effects on the financial markets of the whole world. Commodity prices on the world market are determined by the interaction of many

---

[12] Beitz, *Political Theory and International Relations*, pt. III, ch. 2. Interestingly, David Miller accepts this argument; he says that every nation-state has a right to the resources that will give each equal opportunity for economic well-being; *On Nationality*, ch. 2.

agents across borders; a change in the price of some key commodities on that market can profoundly affect the lives and well-being of people within a state, but often that state is relatively powerless to control or influence either the prices or their effects.

That interdependencies of this sort raise issues of justice between people in different parts of the world is perhaps less controversial than other claims that some people make, to the effect that historical and current relations of exploitation among the world's peoples raise profound issues of justice between them. Some scholars argue that the current wealth of Europe and North America compared to societies of Africa, Latin America, and South Asia is due in part to the persistence of colonial relations between North and South.[13] The economies of the South depend on capital investment controlled from the North and most of whose profits return to Northern-held corporations. Their workers are often too poorly paid by multinationals or their local contractors to feed their families, and farmers and miners of the South obtain unfavourable prices on a global resource market.

Such deprivation has forced many economies and governments of the southern hemisphere into severe debt to Northern banks and international finance agencies. This indebtedness restricts the effective sovereignty of many Southern states, because powerful financial institutions outside them exercise effective control over their internal economic policies. The standard of living and well-being of many people within their jurisdictions declines because of structural adjustment policies outsiders press them to adopt for the sake of foreign investor confidence or international financial stability.[14] Centrally the rich and powerful within these countries should not be excused from responsibility for the condition of their less well-off compatriots. However the empirical details play out at particular times and places, there can be little doubt that conditions like these raise profound issues of economic justice among the world's peoples. The operations of trade, finance, investment, and production are global in their implications, and within those processes some people benefit more than others. In

[13] The work of Samir Amin is classic here; see *Class and Nation* (New York: Monthly Review Press, 1980). For a different and more recent formulation of an analysis coming to a similar conclusion, see Fernando Henrique Cardoso, 'North–South Relations in the Present Context: A New Dependency', in M. Carnoy, M. Castells, S. Cohen, and F. Cardoso (eds.), *The New Global Economy in the Information Age* (University Park: Pennsylvania State University Press, 1993).

[14] See Stephen Haggard, 'Markets, Poverty Alleviation, and Income Distribution: An Assessment of Neoliberal Claims', *Ethics and International Affairs*, 5 (1991), 175–96; Barry Wilkins, 'Debt and Underdevelopment: The Case for Cancelling Third World Debts', in Robin Attfield and Barry Wilkins (eds.), *International Justice and the Third World* (London: Routledge, 1992).

this sense there exists a global society spanned by issues and obligations of justice.

In such a world as this the borders of state jurisdictions sometimes function to allow some people wrongly to ignore the interests of others whose lives their actions affect, simply because they lie outside those borders. The citizens of some states have some of their options constrained as a result of the policy decisions of other states or actors within those states, but those citizens have no institutional vehicle for influencing those decisions. Perhaps even more challenging to principles of democracy and the rule of law, the activities of some international actors, such as transnational corporations, sometimes escape the regulatory net of any state because they can shift jurisdictions.[15] In these ways, as well as others, states today find their ability to regulate the institutional conditions within which their citizens live and work severely curtailed.

Economic and environmental relations raise the most obvious trans-border issues of justice. Other relationships suggest additional issues, however. Developments in the kinds and costs of communication media and transportation, for example, help to produce denser social interactions among the world's people. Among other things, the increased ease of communication raises issues of justice to do with cultural difference and control over communicative form and content. Peace and security issues have been candidates for international regulation for centuries, but contemporary conditions now raise additional issues of justice consequent on war. For example, when war forces hundreds of thousands of people to flee their homes, how should the responsibility for their protection and care be assigned, what are they entitled to, and from whom? Economic, environmental, and media interactions motivate millions of people to migrate from one state to another, creating serious conflicts about rights and responsibilities of both migrants and others in the societies they leave and enter.[16]

From all these considerations I conclude that the scope of relationships across which principles of justice apply is often global. Let me be clear, however, about what this conclusion does *not* imply. The claim that there are global obligations of justice does not imply that everyone in the world has just the same obligations regarding everyone else in the world. Two sorts of consideration enter in considering the weight of obligations, and to whom they are owed. Since institutional

---

[15] See Ulrich Beck's discussion of the 'virtual taxpayer', in *Was ist Globalisierung?* (Frankfurt: Suhrkamp Verlag, 1997), ch. 1.

[16] See Rainer Bauböck, *Transnational Citizenship: Membership and Rights in International Migration* (Aldershot: Edward Elgar, 1993).

and causal connections are the basis for standing in relations over which principles of justice apply, the greater the connections, the more principles of justice apply. Thus people who live within the state political jurisdiction and/or who are closer rather than further away from one another are likely to have stronger claims of justice on one another than those more distant. The reason to presume stronger claims of justice among those in the same region or country, however, is neither national identification, common constitution, nor geography *per se*, but rather the scope and density of social and economic ties. Responsibility for promoting global justice, moreover, just like responsibility for promoting justice within a particular institution or city, falls more heavily on those whose actions more profoundly affect the condition of the actions of others.

To say that obligations of justice extend globally, moreover, does not mean that moral action requires that every actor consider all other individuals in the world in her or his deliberations. Obligations of social justice are not primarily owed by individuals to individuals. Instead, they concern primarily the organization of institutions.[17] Individuals usually cannot act alone to promote justice; they must act collectively to adjust the terms of their relationships and rectify the unjust consequences of past and present social structures, whether intended or not. They need authoritative institutions through which to act collectively. The primary obligations of individuals regarding global justice, as well as local and regional justice, is to do what they can to promote institutions and policies that aim for fair relations among people across the globe.

Other things being equal, I have argued in the previous chapter, the scope of political institutions ought to correspond to the scope of obligations of justice. Thus if the scope of some obligations of justice in the world today is global, there ought to be stronger and more democratic organizations of global governance with which to discharge those obligations. Before I elaborate on that claim, however, we

---

[17] Thomas Pogge distinguishes two approaches to social justice, an institutional and an interactional approach. Whereas the international approach focuses only on the actions of particular individuals as they affect identifiable persons, the institutional approach theorizes moral responsibility for the fate of others in so far as agents participate in institutions and practices that may do harm to them. As distinct from an interactional approach, an institutional approach makes issues of international justice and moral responsibility with respect to distant strangers more visible. I make a similar distinction between a distributive approach to justice and an approach that focuses on the way institutions produce goods and their distributions; see Iris Marion Young, *Justice and the Politics of Difference* (Princeton: Princeton University Press, 1990). Focusing on how structures and institutional relations produce distributive patterns makes more visible a connected international society and the relations of moral responsibilities of distant peoples within it.

need to ask how this argument for global governance responds to continued strong political claims for local autonomy and the right of distinct peoples for self-determination.

## 3. Recognition of Distinct Peoples without Nationalism

So far in this chapter the argument aligns itself with cosmopolitan criticisms of the moral particularism often associated with nationalism.[18] In this cosmopolitan position we are all simply individuals with human rights and their correlative obligations. This cosmopolitanism responds to the historical condition of dense trans-border interaction and influence that has produced more limited powers for nation-states. These arguments do not respond, however, to what might be thought of as an opposing historical trend, namely the challenge of ethnic and cultural minorities to the legitimacy of existing nation-states to rule over them. All over the world groups that seemed to be well absorbed into a larger nation-state project have been asserting claims that the sovereignty of those states over them is illegitimate and that they have rights to self-determination. Such claims have several origins and motives, both noble and base. Sometimes they are promulgated by would-be élites wishing to gain greater power. In other circumstances they express the aspiration of members of a group to resist economic and social marginality and exploitation by privileged others in a nation-state or cross-national framework. Many such claims express a desire for greater associational and cultural freedom. Since claims to self-determination more often than not have diverse motives, they are often complex and ambiguous in their implications. Usually they generate conflict, too often intractable and bloody. Many seem to regard that fact as a reason to reject any such claims, and to declare the very notion of distinct peoples and their claims for self-determination intrinsically pernicious. Such a stance remains rhetorically and practically impotent in response to such claims, however. Indeed, some would argue that a refusal on the part of some public

[18] For recent examples of a cosmopolitan position, see Martha Nussbaum, 'Patriotism and Cosmopolitanism', in Joshua Cohen (ed.), *For Love of Country* (Boston: Beacon Press, 1996); Veit Bader, 'Citizenship and Exclusion: Radical Democracy, Community and Justice, or What is Wrong with Communitarianism?', *Political Theory*, 23/2 (May 1995), 211–46. In more recent work, however, Bader is less unambiguously cosmopolitan, giving more attention to ethnic-cultural commitments; see 'The Cultural Conditions of Transnational Citizenship', *Political Theory*, 25/6 (Dec. 1997), 771–813; Jeremy Waldron, 'Minority Cultures and the Cosmopolitan Alternative', in Will Kymlicka (ed.), *The Rights of Minority Cultures* (Oxford: Oxford University Press, 1995).

actors to take such claims seriously itself sometimes contributes to the conflict they generate. Since so many people in the world have strong feelings about local affinity and either potential or actual domination of some people by others across such affinities, a vision of global democracy must take such claims seriously and conceptualize principled responses to them.

Can a normative and social-theoretical account be formulated which preserves a place for the positive valence of the distinctness of peoples without endorsing the exclusions typical of nationalism? Is there a place for the self-determination of peoples in an argument for democratic practices global in their scope? Only a theory and practice that aims to balance global solidarities with the specificities of local and cultural affinity does justice to the social complexities of our world, and would have any hope of inspiring people to act. In this section I move towards such an account by rejecting the idea of nation while affirming that of a distinct people. A concept of distinct peoples relies on a relational social ontology, rather than the substantial logic typical of nationalism.

Nationalist ideologies tend to define their groups in either/or terms. They conceptualize the nation as strictly bounded between insiders and outsiders, and seek to define attributes of national identity or character that all members share. As I argued in Chapter 3, claiming such an essence for the nation sometimes oppresses individuals within who do not conform to these national norms, and sometimes oppresses outsiders against whom national members set themselves in opposition.

Yael Tamir argues against such essentialist understandings of the nation, and suggests instead that members of a distinct cultural group have a 'family resemblance' to one another.[19] Several attributes may distinguish one cultural group from another, including language, lineage, historical narrative and perspective, artistic tradition, and religion. Individual members of a group all of whom affirm their relation to the group often nevertheless differ in the degree to which they share the same attributes or the manner in which they interpret and act on their relationship to them. Essentialist nationalism attempts to repress these differences within and forge a bounded unity of national membership.

In Chapter 3 I argued for a relational rather than substantial ontology of social groups. A social group exists and is defined as a specific

---

[19] Tamir, *Liberal Nationalism*. Compare James Tully's use of family resemblance to conceptualize cultural difference and membership, in *Strange Multiplicity* (Cambridge: Cambridge University Press, 1995), 120–2.

group in interactive relations with others. Social group identities emerge from the encounter and interaction among people who experience some differences in their ways of life and forms of association. On this view, social difference may be stronger or weaker, and it may be more or less salient, depending on the point of view of comparison. A group is internally constituted to the extent that people interact with one another to affirm their similarity and belonging together. It is also externally constituted to the extent that its members distinguish themselves from others and others affirm a distinctness from them. These relations of similarity and distinctness can and often do change, however, and in the flux of interaction they are rarely all or nothing. Those I affirm as like me in one respect are different in others, and I may perceive similarities with those whom I affirm as distinct. Conceiving group differentiations as a function of relationships, comparison, and interaction, then, allows for overlap and hybridity among groups. Individual modulation, multiple memberships, and degrees of identification with a cultural group are important to recognize and conceptualize for national or culture groups in this fluid and mobile world.[20]

If we abandon the either/or conception of nation, then the distinctness of peoples emerges as a matter of degree.[21] Social and cultural difference may be stronger or weaker, and it may be more or less salient, depending on the point of view of comparison. People experience themselves as sharing affinity with some and as distinct from others in many possible respects: language, historical connection with a territory, self-understanding as having a shared history, religious practice, artistic styles and meanings, a dialogic consciousness of dwelling together distinctly, being segregated and stereotyped by another group, and so on. Some groups are distinct from one another in only some of these ways, while others are distinct from each other in all these respects. The Scots are distinct from the English in respect to historical religious affiliation, history, and territory. Where language once was a major distinction between the peoples, this distinction has diminished, though it is still present to a degree. When they think of themselves in relation to Russians or Chinese, however, we might

---

[20] Compare Kwami Anthony Appiah, 'Cosmopolitan Patriots', in *Cosmopolis: Thinking and Feeling beyond the Nation* (Minneapolis: University of Minnesota Press, 1998). For a theoretical examination of the forms of identification and motivation consistent with a post-nationalist relational conception of group affinity, see Martin J. Matustick, *Postnational Identity: Critical Theory and Existential Philosophy in Habermas, Kierkegaard, and Havel* (New York: Guilford Press, 1993).

[21] I have proposed to replace the dichotomy Kymlicka makes between nation and ethnic group with a continuum of more or less distinct people; see Young, 'A Multicultural Continuum: A Critique of Will Kymlicka', *Constellations*, 4/1 (Apr. 1997), 48–53.

suppose that most Scots think of themselves as more like the English than not.

Perhaps more important than nationalism's tendency to define membership in essentialist terms is its aspiration to have an independent and separate political community coincide with one and only one distinct people or nation. In principle, nationalist sentiments call for an independent state for every nation and one nation for every state. On this interpretation, self-determination entails rights of non-intervention and exclusion that I challenged earlier. Nationalists demand that their members together have sovereign and exclusive control over a contiguous and bounded territory. They often assert the right to exclude non-members and that non-members have no claim upon their internal activities. Citizens of this nation-state have obligations of loyalty and mutual aid to one another that they do not have to others. Their political organization as a state is designed to advance their national goals, without consideration for the interests of others except to respect their rights to separate sovereign statehood.

There are thousands of groups in the world today who consider themselves distinct peoples—whose members share cultural characteristics and histories by which they consider themselves distinguished from others, and who recognize one another as in the same distinct group in some respect or to some degree. Some of those who consider themselves distinct peoples in the world today are called nations; others are not, but would like to be so called, and in too many cases those called nations dominate those not so designated either culturally, politically, or economically. Since the concept of nation is implicitly linked to statehood, and since the international system resists the recognition of new states, many who legitimately consider themselves distinct peoples do not receive the regional and/or international recognition they deserve. When we conceive the distinctness of peoples relationally and as a matter of degree, then cultural or historical groups that differentiate themselves from one another are also usually tied together to a significant degree. Many Catalonians who assert their distinctness in the context of the contemporary Spanish state recognize that they define themselves in relation to others in the peninsula, and that their histories are intertwined and mutually influencing. They claim to be distinct from others in specific respects, but also to have shared problems and projects with others.

In response to the suggestion that we should be suspicious and critical of the idea of a nation, and instead endorse the looser, more relational and continuous idea of a people, many wish to know just what does and does not count as a people. Such an impulse to draw legalistic distinctions among types of peoples, saying that one type deserves recognition as distinct while other types do not, however, is a major cause of conflict and domination. Political principle must be content with a more vague and ambiguous set of intuitions about when a group of people have sufficient affinities and cultural projects to warrant distinction, and that their claim to be so provides prima-facie grounds. The conception of self-determination I wish to defend detaches the concept of a people from nationalism, that is, from the claim that being a people entails rights to a distinct, contiguous, and bounded territory over which the group has exclusive jurisdiction and with which others may not interfere. Such detachment from bordered territory lessens the urgency to have clear borders within the idea of a people.


## 4. Rethinking Self-Determination

Many peoples suffer at the hands of nation-building efforts to suppress or assimilate culturally distinct peoples. Many have been deprived of lands and livelihoods by colonial and post-colonial systems of appropriation and exploitation, and have been driven into poverty in the process. Others have had their freedom of religion, association, or linguistic and cultural practice suppressed. Many of these peoples claim a right of self-determination as a means to throw off the yoke of cultural imperialism and gain some control over resources as a base for the life and development of their people.

The claims of indigenous peoples in particular resonate in this regard, in that they have generated a global social movement that challenges the global system of state sovereignty.[22] Most of the world's indigenous peoples claim rights of self-determination against the states that assert sovereign authority over them. States organized according to currently accepted principles of sovereignty, however, find it difficult or impossible to accommodate these claims. Because they claim rights to use land and resources, and to develop governance practices continuous with pre-colonial indigenous practices, indigenous peoples' demands do not easily cohere with the more formal and bureaucratic governance systems of modern European law. Despite unjust conquest and continued oppression, however, few indigenous peoples seek to establish an independent, internationally recognized state with ultimate authority over matters within a determinately bounded

[22] See Franke Wilmer, *The Indigenous Voice in World Politics* (Newbury Park, Calif.: Sage, 1993).

territory. For the most part indigenous peoples seek greater and more secure autonomy within the framework of a wider polity.[23]

I dwell on the situation and claims of indigenous peoples because they challenge the states system in a fundamental way. Nevertheless, there are other peoples who claim to be oppressed or lack sufficient recognition by the states which the international system recognizes as having jurisdiction over them. Distinct peoples have prima-facie claims to self-determination, that is, to participate with others of the group in institutions of self-government. There are two kinds of argument for this claim, one more concerned with culture and identity and one more concerned with power and domination. Several recent moral theories of the significance of cultural difference argue that cultural membership, or membership in historical peoples, is an important 'source of the self'. The language or languages one grows up hearing and speaking are a deep reservoir for personal identity formation, as are the stories told and songs sung in those languages. Many people gain a particular joy and sense of stability from symbols, practices, monuments, sites, and texts associated with distinct cultural or historical groups. While most people evolve their own personal identities partly in relation to such cultural affinities, as I discussed in Chapter 3, this does not mean that those positioned as members of the group all have the same attitude towards that membership. To the extent that the well-being of individuals partly depends on the flourishing of the meanings and practices that serve as sources of their selves, however, then those people should have the means collectively to decide how to maintain and promote their flourishing as a people.[24]

The second circumstance that calls for self-determination is often tied to the first, but carries additional implications. Structures of power, exploitation, and domination build easily on experienced social and cultural differentiation. By relying on perceived difference, some people exclude others from material benefits or are able to exploit their labour for their own benefit. A more benign form of domination can occur when the language or practices of a large majority simply overwhelm those of smaller minorities. In such situations, institutions of self-government can serve as a means to resist exclusion, discrimination, exploitation, or minority status. Doubtless group membership is

---

[23] See Hector Diaz Palanco, *Indigenous Peoples in Latin America; The Quest for Self-Determination*, trans. Lucia Rayas (Boulder, Colo.: Westview Press, 1997), esp. ch. 2.

[24] See Will Kymlicka, *Liberalism, Community and Culture* (Oxford: Oxford University Press, 1989), esp. chs. 4, 5, and 8; Charles Taylor, 'Multiculturalism and the Politics of Recognition', in Amy Gutmann (ed.), *Multiculturalism* (Princeton: Princeton University Press, 1992); Tamir, *Liberal Nationalism*, chs. 1 and 2.

sometimes plural, ambiguous, and overlapping. For this reason it is sometimes difficult to say decisively whether a particular collection of individuals counts as a distinct people. In many cases such ambiguities can only be resolved by argument and negotiation in which values and consequences beyond those of self-determination should also be taken into account. These difficulties do not negate the fact, however, that historical and cultural groups have often been and continue to be dominated and exploited by other groups often using state power to do so. Nor do ambiguities about membership negate the fact that self-government and autonomy are important to many who consider themselves members of distinct peoples because they find such collective autonomy important for their own freedom and well-being.

Many peoples who claim a right of self-determination today seek a sovereign state of their own with a single continuous territory enclosed by unambiguous borders. This ambition to form territory-contiguous and bounded states that claim independence from outsiders threatens to oppress new minorities and generate bloody conflict over territories to which several groups lay claim. Proliferation of independent sovereign states, moreover, probably works against the need for greater capacity for global regulation and co-operation which I argued for above. So we have a dilemma. On the one hand, claims of the self-determination of peoples have prima-facie validity. On the other hand, recognizing those claims by awarding each people an independent territorially bounded jurisdiction constantly threatens peace and freedom. A way can be found out of this dilemma by conceiving self-determination in relational terms as non-domination rather than non-interference.

On a non-interference model of self-determination, a people or government has the authority to exercise ultimate control over what goes on inside its jurisdiction, and no outside agent has the right to make claims upon or interfere with what the self-determining agent does. Reciprocally, the self-determining people have no claim on what others do with respect to issues within other jurisdictions, and no right to interfere in the business of the others. Just as it denies rights of interference by outsiders in a jurisdiction, this concept entails that each self-determining entity has no inherent obligations with respect to outsiders.

Freedom interpreted as non-interference assumes that agents, whether individual or collective, are independent of one another except in so far as they choose to exchange and contract. The arguments that I made above about the scope of justice and global interdependence of peoples, however, challenges such an assumption of the independence of nations or states. A theory of self-determination for peoples should recognize that peoples are interdependent and, for this reason, that non-interference is inadequate as an interpretation of self-determination.

In Chapter 6 I referred to feminist critiques of this idea of independence as inappropriate for a moral theory of autonomy and their alternative concept of relational autonomy. Relational autonomy entails a presumption of non-interference, but does not imply a social scheme in which atomized agents simply mind their own business and leave each other alone. Instead, it entails recognizing that agents are related in many ways they have not chosen, by virtue of economic interaction, history, proximity, or the unintended consequences of action. In these relationships agents are able either to thwart one another or to support one another. Relational autonomy consists partly, then, in the structuring of relationships so that they support the maximal pursuit of agent ends. In Chapter 6 I applied the concept of relational autonomy to a normative model of local government. In that context, relational autonomy presumes local control over local issues and practices, but in the context of federated intergovernmental relations and a regional regulatory framework. This concept of relational autonomy, I suggest, can also be applied to shift a principle of self-determination away from independence towards autonomy in the context of interdependent relations among peoples.[25] To complement the feminist notion of relational autonomy, I draw on Philip Pettit's critique of freedom interpreted as non-interference and his alternative notion of freedom as non-domination.[26]

Interference, according to Pettit, means that one agent blocks or redirects the action of another in a way that worsens that agent's choice situation by changing the range of options. On Pettit's account, non-interference, while related to freedom, is not equivalent to it. Instead, freedom should be understood as non-domination. An agent dominates another when the agent has power over that other and is thus able to interfere with the other *arbitrarily*. Interference is arbitrary when it is chosen or rejected without consideration of the interests or opinions of those affected. An agent may dominate another, however, without ever interfering with that agent. Domination con-

[25] In the context of conceptualizing the meaning of indigenous people's claims for self-determination, Craig Scott proposes a more relational understanding of the claim. See Scott, 'Indigenous Self-Determination and Decolonization of the International Imagination: A Plea', *Human Rights Quarterly*, 18 (1996), 814–20.

[26] Philip Pettit, *Republicanism* (Oxford: Oxford University Press, 1997).

sists in standing in a set of relations which makes an agent *able* to interfere arbitrarily with the actions of others.

Real freedom means the absence of such relations of domination. Pettit argues that institutions should promote and preserve non-domination for everyone. To do so there must be regulations that sometimes interfere with actions in order to restrict dominative power and promote co-operation. Interference is not arbitrary if its purpose is to minimize domination, and if it is done in a way that takes the interests and voices of affected parties into account. Like the concept of relational autonomy, then, the concept of freedom as non-domination refers to a set of social relations. 'Non-domination is the position that someone enjoys when they live in the presence of other people and when, by virtue of social design, none of those others dominates them.'[27]

I propose that a principle of self-determination for peoples should be interpreted along lines of relational autonomy or non-domination, rather than simply as independence or non-interference. On such an interpretation, self-determination for peoples means that they have a right to their own governance institutions through which they decide on their goals and interpret their way of life. Other people ought not to constrain, dominate, or interfere with those decisions and interpretations for the sake of their own ends, or according to their judgement of what way of life is best, or in order to subordinate a people to a larger 'national' unit. Peoples, that is, ought to be free from domination. Because a people stands in interdependent relations with others, however, a people cannot ignore the claims and interests of those others when the former's actions potentially affect the latter. In so far as outsiders are affected by the activities of self-determining people, those others have a legitimate claim to have their interests and needs taken into account even though they are outside the government jurisdiction. Conversely, outsiders should recognize that when they themselves affect a people, the latter can legitimately claim that they should have their interests taken into account in so far as they may be adversely affected. In so far as their activities affect one another, peoples are in relationship and ought to negotiate the terms and effects of the relationship. When self-determining peoples understand themselves as constituted in relation to one another, they recognize that there are many respects in which they live and act together with others. For example, they inhabit territories with others and need some of the same local resources; or, they are similarly affected by natural, social, or economic disasters.

[27] Ibid. 67.

Self-determining peoples morally cannot do whatever they want without interference from others. Their territorial, economic, or communicative relationships with others generate conflicts and collective problems that oblige them to acknowledge the legitimate interests of others as well as promote their own. Pettit argues that states can legitimately interfere with the actions of individuals in order to foster institutions that minimize domination. A similar argument applies to actions and relations of collectivities. In a densely interdependent world, peoples require political institutions that lay down procedures for co-ordinating the actions of all of them, resolving conflicts and negotiating relationships.

This argument for a concept of self-determination understood as relational autonomy in the context of non-domination applies as much to large nation-states as to small indigenous or 'ethnic' groups. Those entities that today are considered self-determining independent states in principle ought to have no more right of non-interference than should smaller groups. Self-determination for those entities now called sovereign states should mean non-domination. While in this principle we should include a presumption of non-interference, the principle stipulates that outsiders may have a claim on a people's activities, in order to prevent dominative harm or enlist co-operation necessary for collective action. Thus the interpretation of self-determination as non-domination ultimately implies limiting the rights of existing nation-states and setting these into different, more co-operatively regulated relationships. Just as promoting freedom for individuals involves regulating relations in order to prevent domination, so promoting self-determination for peoples involves regulating international relations to prevent the domination of peoples. Such international regulation must be inclusively democratic, however, which means that all those whose actions are regulated must participate together in the process of formulating regulatory institutions and procedures.

I do not introduce this discussion of an alternative meaning of self-determination as the starting-point for institutional design. My primary interest is to state and justify the normative principles of governance that I believe best correspond to a global understanding of differentiated solidarity. Some discussion of what it might mean to apply this interpretation of a principle of self-determination, however, helps to make the interpretation more plausible.

First, application of this principle does not mean that each people has a right to sole governance of a single, bounded, contiguous territory inhabited only by members of their own group. Unfortunately, this is the vision of many groups who claim self-determination today; it is this aspiration to a single, homogeneously occupied, contiguously bounded territory, rather than the aspiration to self-determination as such, that has instigated too much death and ethnic cleansing in this century. Understood as non-domination, self-determination must be detached from territory.[28] Given that a plurality of peoples inhabits most territories, and given the hybridity of peoples and places that characterizes many territories, institutions of governance ought not be defined as exclusive control over territory and what takes place within it. On the contrary, jurisdictions can be spatially overlapping or shared, or even lack spatial reference entirely.

On the other hand, governance cannot be divorced from land, its resources, and a sense of place. People dwell *somewhere*, and they are neighbours to *these* people. Many of the self-determination claims of oppressed minorities, such as those of most indigenous peoples, concern access to land and resources in order to enhance their economic well-being. The cultural and historical distinctness of many groups, moreover, is often tied to particular natural or built sites, and some of the worst cases of nationalist conflict focus on group-contested sites.

No formula can be laid down in advance for how to do it, but in principle the implementation of self-governance institutions often should recognize the importance of land, resources, and place without assuming that self-determination requires exclusive control over a large and contiguous bounded territory. In many cases this should mean that locales are heterogeneous and multicultural, perhaps enacting procedures of group representation along lines I argued in Chapter 4. In other cases particular groups may have specific rights to land and resources without having exclusive control over a territory. Negotiations between indigenous and non-indigenous peoples in some parts of the world concern this sort of accommodation.[29] In a third way for recognizing locales and resources, some forms of group autonomy may be territorially based, but attached to interlocking federal arrangements that also help assure the freedom and flourishing of internal minorities.

---

[28] See John Gerard Ruggie, 'Territoriality and Beyond: Problematizing Modernity in International Relations', *International Organization*, 47/1 (Winter 1993), 139–74.

[29] See Roger Maaka and Augie Flera, 'From Entitlement to Re-engagement as Indigenous Affairs Agenda: *Tino Rangatiratanga* and the Politics of Indigeneity in Aotearoa/New Zealand', in Paul Patton and Duncan Ivason (ed.), *Political Theory and Indigenous Peoples* (Cambridge: Cambridge University Press, 2000). Recent negotiations between some First Nations and Canadian provinces also have in view working out a just accommodation to plural claims to land and resource use.

Claims to self-determination emerge precisely because collectives of individuals who perceive themselves differentiated to some degree or in some respects nevertheless also stand in relation to one another and sometimes come into conflict. In practice recognizing a right of self-determination in ways that minimize dominative implications must take different forms, depending on the degree of hybridity and multi-culturalism among the contestants, the ways other individuals and groups may be affected, the manner and degree to which the contest-ants differentiate themselves, and the history of a region. Self-determination as non-domination should allow many multicultural or cosmopolitan jurisdictions. Where governance institutions are group-based, they may be so to different degrees and only in certain respects, in accord with the above mentioned position that the degree to which peoples themselves are distinct may vary.

Some group-based jurisdictions should be associated with place in order to serve as anchor for identities that have hybrid, inter-regional character. For example, many Jews of the world consider themselves American, or Australian, or South African, etc., as well as Jewish. For many of them, however, the existence of place that is associated with the Jewish people, Israel, is an important vehicle for the retention of their hybrid identities. On my argument, however, the right to a place to exercise self-determination does not entail exclusive rule of the bounded territories Israel now claims. Because Palestinians also have legitimate claims to self-determination, certain vital resources, such as water, must be fairly shared, and certain spaces, such as the city of Jerusalem, must also be shared jurisdictions.

Because interpretation of self-determination as non-interference retains theoretical and practical hegemony in the world, we can find few instances of governance arrangements that try to apply a more relational understanding. The 1998 negotiated peace agreement for Northern Ireland is one of the most interesting examples of a pro-posed set of governance institutions which both aims to recognize the distinctness of peoples, but also aims to define their governance rela-tionally in the context of wider interlocking institutions, at the same time that it aims to protect the rights of individuals and groups with little or no affiliation with the two major groups.

As of this writing, implementation of the agreement has been obstructed by a dispute over arms decommissioning, and the parties seem to be returning to intractable polarization. So far as I can tell, however, this dispute does not arise from the terms of the agreement itself. The institutional design of the 1998 agreement offers a good example of relational autonomy. The agreement recognizes all the inhabitants of the territory known as Northern Ireland as a self-determining people with their own government. It also recognizes that there are two main groups with historic relations to that territory and whose fates have been intertwined for centuries, and gives each of them special rights in the governance structure, on terms that aim to recognize a 'parity of esteem' between them. The agreement calls for additional governance institutions linking Northern Ireland *both* to the United Kingdom and to the Republic of Ireland. Not only do these commissions recognize both English and Irish, both Protestant and Catholic, claims, but they serve as a way that members of either group in Northern Ireland can feel protected and supported. The agreement also contains strong language about human rights and non-discrimination, however, aimed particularly at protecting the many inhabitants of Northern Ireland who do not strongly identify with either group. The major flaw in the agreement, at least from the point of view of some, is that it does not remove the state sovereignty of the United Kingdom from ultimate authority over the territory; it does, however, empower the citizens of Northern Ireland to do so in a referendum.[30] This flaw highlights the limitations of trying to apply a principle of self-determination as non-domination in a world where state sovereignty remains and where its hegemonic interpretation remains non-interference.

But what is the 'self' of a supposedly self-determining people, some might want to know. The very idea that there is a people with sufficient unity to be self-determining may be questionable.[31] Any tribe, city, nation, or other designated group is a collection of individuals with diverse interests and affinities, prone to disagreements and internal conflicts. One rarely finds a set of interests agreed upon by all members of a group for guiding their autonomous government. Too often, moreover, some members of the group stand in relations of structural inequality or domination towards other members of the group. Under these circumstances, promoting self-determination of the group may further the domination of some of its members. Sometimes it is ambiguous, moreover, who belongs to a particular group, and many individuals have a reasonable claim to have affinity with more than one. Might it not be that such difficulties vitiate the idea of self-determination?

[30] See Shane O'Neill, 'Mutual Recognition and the Accommodation of National Diversity: Constitutional Justice in Northern Ireland', in Alain G. Gagnon and James Tully (eds.), *Struggles for Recognition in Multicultural Societies* (Cambridge: Cambridge University Press, 2000).

[31] See Russell Hardin, *One for All* (Chicago: University of Chicago Press, 1995) for a critique of the notion of collective common interests in the context of nationalist politics; also see Hardin's response to my discussion of self-determination as non-domination in Ian Shapiro and Stephen Macedo (eds.), *Designing Democratic Institutions*, NOMOS 31 (New York: New York University Press, 2000).

I think not. Any collection of people that constitute themselves as a political community must worry about how to respond to conflict and dissent within the community, and about whether the decisions and actions carried out in the name of the group can be said to *belong* to the group. In so far as a collective has a set of institutions through which that people make decisions and implement them, the group sometimes expresses unity in the sense of agency. Whatever conflicts and disagreements may have led up to that point, once decisions have been made and action taken through collective institutions, the group itself can be said to act. Such a discourse of group agency and representation of agency to wider publics need not falsely personify the group or suppress differences among its members. Most governments claim to act for 'the people', and their claims are more or less legitimate to the extent that the people in the society accept the government and its actions as theirs, and even more legitimate if they have had real influence in this decision-making process. Self-determining peoples ideally, then, should govern themselves democratically. They cannot be said to be self-determining, however, if democracy, or particular interpretations of democracy, is imposed on them. Others can only try to encourage a regional or global institutional context in which democracy is easier for peoples to establish and maintain, but they cannot require it.

Outsiders can morally require, however, that self-governing peoples respect equally the basic human rights of all individuals who come within their jurisdiction. This is an important implication of the non-domination interpretation of self-determination. No people or jurisdiction can claim that they have a right not to be interfered with by outsiders if some of their members claim that they suffer systematic abuses of their rights. Such claims ought to trigger a hearing before some third-party entities, preferably broadly multilateral entities. Some states today claim to protect the human rights of individuals under the jurisdiction of other states, but in fact are also dominating those states and their people. Although NATO's stated motive for its 1999 war against Yugoslavia involved serious human rights abuses in Kosovo, for example, both the fact that NATO acted without international sanction and its manner of carrying out that war make it a case of wrongful domination that also failed miserably to protect human rights. With such examples in mind, some critics revert to an international principle of non-interference. This is not the proper response to such dominative moralism, however; the cure is rather to establish strong global regulatory institutions concerning human rights the formulation of whose policies should involve all the world's peoples.

Protection of human rights is also the best answer to the problem of disputed membership. Peoples should have the prima-facie right to define the meaning and terms of membership in its self-determining institutions. When some individuals claim membership that is disputed by those institutions, they should first have special protection of their persons, and then have fora in which their claims may be heard and adjudicated.

Understood as non-domination, then, the self-determination of peoples has the following elements. First, self-determination means a presumption of non-interference. A people has the prima-facie right to set its own governance procedures and make its own decisions about its activities within its jurisdiction, without interference from others. In so far as these activities may adversely affect others, however, or generate conflict for other reasons, self-determination entails the right of those others to make claims on the group, negotiate the terms of their relations, and mutually adjust their effects. Thus self-determining peoples require recognized and settled institutions and procedures through which they negotiate, adjudicate conflicts, and enforce agreements. Self-determination does not imply independence, but rather that peoples dwell together within political institutions which minimize domination among them. Finally, the self-determination of peoples requires that the peoples have the right to participate in designing and implementing intergovernmental institutions aimed at minimizing domination. In these ways a non-domination interpretation of a principle of self-determination enacts ideals of differentiated solidarity, in principle on a global scale.

## 5. Global Democracy

I have argued that the scope of obligations of justice extends globally today on many issues. Many actions and policies in one place presuppose institutions that link distant actors across borders, and their consequences, both intended and unintended, often have far-reaching effects. Ideally, the scope of political community and government regulation should extend as widely as the scope of obligations of justice. Global actors would be better able to address many issues of justice today, then, with more global capacity for co-ordination and regulation. In contrast to most current international regulatory institutions, global governance should be organized democratically.

At the same time I have argued that many peoples over whom nation-states presently claim jurisdiction have rights of self-determination. Rather than interpreting self-determination as a right of non-interference, however, this principle should be understood as requiring that a group be able to set its own ends in a context of relations that minimize domination. In Chapter 6 I also argued for local and regional relational autonomy as important for democratic participation.

These goals appear to conflict: greater capacity for global regulation and more local and regional autonomy. Some recent theorizing of possibilities for global democracy, however, calls for just such a combination of global regulatory frameworks and local self-determination. Far from standing in tension, stronger and more democratic global regulatory capacities can support a desire for the autonomy of distinct people and multicultural metropolitan regions.

In calling for global regulatory capacity, many contemporary theorists reject the vision of a single, centralized, global state whose power and authority would be structured on the model of existing large nation-states. Not only does such a vision seem very difficult to act on, but many find such a goal undesirable. State power is best held in check and accountable if it is pluralized.

Several theorists thus propose a vision of global democracy that combines both devolution of power from the level of existing nation-states to more local and regional units with a strengthening of regulatory authority and capacity with jurisdiction wider than nation-states, and ultimately including all peoples. In this vision arguments for global regulatory capacity and a greater sub-state self-determination do not conflict; instead these writers conceive each side as the complement of the other. Thus Jordi Borja and Manuel Castells, for example, argue that stronger global regulatory frameworks are necessary to manage processes of finance, investment, and communications, among other processes, that now partly escape the regulatory power of nation-states, often to the detriment of particular peoples and regions. At the same time they call for enabling greater local autonomy, both for the sake of cultural preservation and because the management and governance of metropolitan regions brings regulation closer to the lives of people. Thus, for example, legal changes should be enacted to make it easier for cities and regions currently under the jurisdiction of different nation-states to partner one another on issues of economic development, and political or cultural exchange.[32]

David Held presents a relatively well-developed model of global democracy which articulates global regulatory institutions with

---

[32] See Jordi Borja and Manuel Castells, *Local and Global: Management of Cities in the Information Age* (London: Earthscan, 1997).

devolved local autonomy. Along lines I have argued above, Held finds that promoting values of peace and justice requires expanding global regulatory institutions to address such issues as security, environmental sustainability, investment, and the global distribution of wealth. Such global regulatory institutions should be democratic, which means that systems of representation and accountability should be developed for them. For the sake of democratic participation and bureaucratic simplicity, however, Held argues that governance should normally be local. A principle of subsidiarity ought to guide the relationships of local, regional, state, and global governance. Problems or conflicts felt only locally should be resolved locally according to localized designed procedures. A higher level of governance should enter to address them only when they involve conflicts between locales or when the problems affect several local units together. Held envisions the creation of transnational legislatures and referendum procedures in order to make processes democratic.[33]

These approaches provide good points of departure for thinking about global political community coupled with local self-determination. As part of such a vision I propose a global system of regulatory regimes to which locales and regions relate in a federated system. These regimes lay down rules regarding that small but vital set of issues around which peace and justice all for global co-operation. I envision seven such regulatory regimes, though of course the number could be larger or smaller, and the jurisdictions defined differently: (1) peace and security, (2) environment, (3) trade and finance, (4) direct investment and capital utilization, (5) communications and transportation, (6) human rights, including labour standards and welfare rights, (7) citizenship and migration. I imagine that each regulatory regime has a distinct functional jurisdiction, with some need for overlapping responsibility and co-ordination. Each provides a thin set of general rules that specify ways that individuals, organizations, and governments are obliged to take account of the interests and circumstances of one another. By distinguishing regimes functionally, such as global governance systems, deterritorializes some aspects of sovereignty.

Each of these issue areas today has an evolving regime of international law and organization on which to build in order to create a global regime with greater enforcement strength and resources for carrying out its purpose. For the most part, however, only the activities

---

[33] See David Held, *Democracy and the Global Order* (Cambridge, Mass.: Polity Press, 1995), pt. IV; 'Democracy and Globalization', in Daniele Archibugi, David Held, and Martin Kohler (eds.), *Re-imagining Political Community: Studies in Cosmopolitan Democracy* (Cambridge, Mass.: Polity Press, 1998).

of states are currently subject to regulation under those treaty regimes. An important aspect of decentring governance through global regulatory regimes would consist in bringing at least some of the activities of non-state organizations, such as municipalities, private for-profit and non-profit corporations, and individuals directly under global regulation, with regional and local governments as tools of implementation.

Within the context of global regulatory regimes, everyday governance ought to be primarily local. Locales consist in first-level autonomous units of governance. What defines a locale may vary according to the way people affiliate—their history, priorities, and relationship with others. Some might be defined as self-determining peoples. While rooted in place, these might not be associated with a single contiguous territory. The Ojibwa people could count as a self-determining local unity, for example, even if some of their members are dispersed territorially. As I have already discussed, however, many locales ought to be heterogeneous and multicultural. Thus metropolitan regions are primary candidates for self-determining units. Such autonomous governance units should be institutionalized as *open*, in both a territorial and a jurisdictional sense. Autonomous peoples or communities may overlap in territories, and their governance needs to recognize the conditions and problems they share with others, as well as how their actions may affect the conditions of action of other units and their members. Local units, in this vision, are autonomous in the sense that their members construct their own institutions of governance as they choose, within limits of global regulation. The global level of governance is properly 'thin', in the sense that it only lays down rather general principles regarding the sorts of issues I listed above. Local jurisdictions 'thicken' them into administrable programmes and rules by interpreting and applying them according to their own procedures, priorities, and cultural understandings.[34]

A major purpose of global regulatory regimes, in the model I imagine, is to protect local units and their members from domination. Self-determination understood as non-domination, recall, means a presumption of non-interference for autonomous units that are embedded in institutionalized relationships that protect them from dominative threats. Some local units are more vulnerable than others to such threats. Global regulatory regimes should aim to minimize domination both of individuals and of self-determining locales. To the

---

[34] A federated relationship between self-determining entities might be interpreted as a way of implementing the relationship between 'thin' and 'thick' principles that Michael Walzer advocates; see *Thick and Thin: Moral Argument at Home and Abroad* (Notre Dame, Ind.: Notre Dame University Press, 1994), 63–84.

extent that peoples and locales have often experienced domination by neighbouring peoples or nation-states that have claimed jurisdiction over them, one purpose of global regulation is to protect such vulnerable peoples and locales. Just as importantly, regulatory institutions should protect both individuals and groups from the domination that powerful private economic actors today are sometimes able to exercise, especially over small and poor peoples. In these ways local self-determination and cultural autonomy can be understood not as conflicting with, but rather as requiring, strong global regulation.

A vision of global governance with local self-determination ought to make the inclusion of democratic values and institutions paramount. Those regimes and institutions existing today that co-ordinate and regulate global interaction beyond the jurisdiction of states, however, are not very democratic. The growing global power of multinational corporations is explicitly undemocratic, for example. Existing tribunals of international law have few channels of democratic accountability. Especially because of the power and structure of the Security Council, the United Nations is not a democratic institution. Scholars and journalists bemoan the 'democratic deficit' they observe in the operations of today's most complex and thoroughly developed transnational governance body, the European Union.[35]

Of course there are large questions of institutional design for democratizing processes and institutions of global governance, and in the next section I will explore such issues briefly by reference to the United Nations system. At the level of vision, here are some of the issues of democratization.[36] First, one of the reasons to advocate localism, the devolution of authority onto more local units from the level of existing nation-states, is to promote democracy. Participation and citizenship are best enacted at a local level. Democratic federated regimes of global regulations, however, do require institutions of representation and policy deliberation at levels far removed from the local. A global environmental regulatory decision-making body, for example, would not need to be any *more* removed from ordinary citizens than many national regulatory bodies currently are. Once we move beyond a local level, any polity is an 'imagined community' whose interests and problems must be discursively constructed as

[35] See Thomas Pogge, 'Creating Supra-national Institutions Democratically: Reflections on the European Union's "Democratic Deficit"', *Journal of Political Philosophy*, 5/2 (June 1997), 163–82.

[36] Susan Hurley gives some very suggestive ideas about how democratic relations need to be conceptualized 'laterally' rather than hierarchically in envisioning global democratic institutions. See 'Democracy, Rationality, and Leaky Boundaries'.

affecting everyone, because people do not experience most of the others in the polity. I believe that this problem is no bigger for transnational and global regulation than it is for large nation-states.

Activities of global governance ought to be public. Simple as this sounds, the deliberations of some of the most powerful global actors today, such as the International Monetary Fund or the World Trade Organization, are not public, and their leaders are not accountable to those their decisions affect. In Chapter 5 I discussed the important functions of civil society in fostering independent public spheres through which individuals and groups expose the activities of powerful state and economic actors, express their opposition to or criticism of some of those activities, and hold powerful actors accountable. Global democratic processes could not be very strong without such public spheres that in principle included all the world's peoples.[37] Already the possibilities of transportation and communication in the world today see the formation of incipient public spheres composed of active citizens in global civil society.[38] In the last two decades exciting transnational civic associations have involved millions of people in cross-border organizing, practical aid, arts exchange, and networks of civic associations have worked together to pressure powerful global actors to change their policies. A remarkable example of the effect of such a global public sphere was the 1998 exposure of the World Trade Organization's proposal for a multilateral agreement on investment that would have enabled transnational corporations to circumvent many existing regulations of nation-states, not for the sake of coordinated global regulation, but for the sake of increasing their own freedom. Protestors demanding more transparency and democratic accountability of the WTO in Seattle in 1999 suggest that this global public sphere may be widening.

Institutions through which distinct peoples and locales can participate in formulating policies of global regulatory regimes would help render such global regulation compatible with a principle of self-determination. Self-determination does not mean an ultimate right of exclusion and non-interference, I have argued. It does entail, however, that to the extent that self-governing entities are obliged to follow

[37]  See Jurgen Habermas's discussion of the need and potential for a global public sphere in his essay 'Kant's Idea of Perpetual Peace: At Two Hundred Years' Historical Remove', in Ciaran Cronin and Pablo De Greiff (eds.), *The Inclusion of the Other: Studies in Political Theory* (Cambridge, Mass.: MIT Press, 1998).

[38]  Richard Falk, 'The Global Promise of Social Movements', in *Explorations at the Edge of Time: Prospects for World Order* (United Nations University, 1992); Ronnie D. Lipschutz, 'Reconstructing World Politics: The Emergence of Global Civil Society', *Millennium*, 21/3 (Winter 1992), 389–420.

more encompassing regulations, they have had a real opportunity to participate with others in formulating those regulations.

I have suggested above, for example, that there ought to be a stronger global regime to formulate global standards of individual human rights, and monitor and enforce compliance with those standards. Having such a human rights regime would not impinge on local self-determination, I am arguing, as long as two conditions were met: (1) the peoples and communities obliged to observe these standards have had the opportunity to participate as a collective in their formulation; (2) they have significant discretion in how they apply these standards for their local context, and the means they use locally to implement them. As I understand their protests, those nations and groups in the world today who question the application of existing human rights covenants to their context do not reject general principles of human rights. They argue that the particular formulations of those rights applied today were developed largely by Western powers, and that in these changed times these formulations should be subject to review in a process that includes them.[39]

Ideally, global democratic institutions would be designed to encourage inclusive communication in ways that I have theorized in earlier chapters. Representative institutions should be designed, for example, so that the fissures of structural inequality receive expression, so that structurally differentiated global perspectives have explicit voice. Poor people of the world, for example, deserve a specific voice on the global stage. Despite their vast differences in ideological commitments, religion, family structure, and so on, women everywhere have specific issues of subordination and vulnerability that any global forum ought regularly to hear. Attention to structural differences such as these on a global, as well as local and regional, level can mitigate the dangers some might fear in the self-organization of culturally or historically distinct peoples.

## 6. In the Short Term: United Nations Reform

Improved global regulatory institutions will only come about by means of determined social movements working together from many parts of the world. In this and previous chapters I have already mentioned some examples of global social movements that have affected

[39] See Nikhil Aziz, 'The Human Rights Debate in an Era of Globalization', in Peter van Ness (ed.), *Debating Human Rights: Critical Essays from the United States and Asia* (New York: Routledge, 1999).

policies of international institutions. Movements critical of structural adjustment policies and indebtedness that hurt many people in less developed countries, for example, have affected both the discourse and the policies of international financial institutions. Assuming that a global social movement for stronger global regulatory institutions tied to principles of global and local democracy can be mobilized, what might its focus be in the near term? In concluding this chapter I suggest that reform of the United Nations System is one reasonable goal for such a movement.

Why focus on the United Nations? Although the General Assembly imperfectly represents the diverse peoples of the world, it is the only institution that in principle represents nearly all the world's people. Although many individuals and states complain that UN institutions are inefficient and ineffective, even powerful states such as the United States and China regularly seek legitimacy for some of their international actions using UN processes. While institutions of the United Nations have often been manipulated by states eager to promote their own interests, the United Nations has also sometimes served as an instrument for principled co-operation among states to confront domination or promote well-being.

Not only do states often work through UN institutions, or at least work to appear to be co-operative and interested in justice, but especially in the last two decades some of the most significant organization of international civil society has related to UN-sponsored conferences and covenants on issues as diverse as the environment, human rights, and women's issues. Though resource-poor and flawed in their design and operation, many institutions of the United Nations are the best existing starting-points for building global democratic institutions. From their experiences working within and with some UN institutions, the failures as well as the modest successes, many people have learned about what effective peace enforcement or development assistance seem to entail. This is not the place to review and evaluate the many criticisms of the existing UN system and the various proposals for reform.[40] I shall only outline a few of the ideas for system change that appear to derive from a vision of global democracy consistent with the one I have stated.

[40] For useful sources, see Erskine Childers and Brian Urquhart, *Renewing the United Nations System* (Uppsala: Dag Hammarskjöld Foundation, 1993); see also Erskine Childers, 'The United Nations and Global Institutions: Discourse and Reality', *Global Governance*, 3 (1997), 269–76; Chadwick F. Alger (ed.), *The Future of the United Nations System: Potential for the Twenty-First Century* (New York: United Nations University, 1998); Daniele Archibugi, 'The Reform of the UN and Cosmopolitan Democracy: A Critical Review', *Journal of Peace Research*, 30/3 (1993), 301–15.

Movements for democratic global governance must start with some existing institutions, but the United Nations system nevertheless requires major overhaul to become more democratic, just, and effective. First, the Security Council must be radically transformed. Presently that body allows the states which are its permanent members to use UN institutions to promote their own objectives while the rest of the world remains powerless to object. A Security Council should be more representative of the world's peoples, and no state should have veto power. The General Assembly is a relatively democratic institution; in principle each member state has equal standing. Since it mirrors the existing states system, however, the General Assembly's activities encourage neither more global regulation nor more local self-determination. The last two decades of the twentieth century saw an increasingly formal role in the United Nations for participation of non-governmental organizations, and this is a trend on which social movements can build. Indigenous peoples have used such NGO status to their advantage, for example, in gaining recognition for many distinct peoples and having access to forums and programmes of UN agencies. In addition to these possibilities for expanding participation in UN institutions, some UN reformers call for the establishment of a People's Assembly to which individuals all over the world would elect representatives directly.[41] Among other things, a People's Assembly could help create a global citizenship status for all persons, so that they would not have to depend on a state for acknowledgement of their basic rights.

UN institutions do not serve well two of the most crucial functions envisioned at its founding: promoting peace and equitable economic interaction. The states of the world, especially the most powerful, refuse to allow the development of strong peace-keeping institutions under UN auspices. The idea of impartial multilateral humanitarian intervention and peace enforcement will remain a cynical joke as long as actions with that name are organized and led by the United States primarily with hardware and personnel under its national command. The United Nations needs its own military force under its own military command available for peace enforcement.[42]

The most powerful global economic regulatory institutions, the International Monetary Fund, the World Bank, and the World Trade

[41] In response to the objection that organizing world-wide parliamentary elections would be impossible, Erskine Childers says it would be like organizing eight Indian parliamentary elections.

[42] Raimo Vayrynen, 'Enforcement and Humanitarian Intervention: Two Faces of Collective Action by the UN', in Alger (ed.), *The Future of the United Nations System.*

Organization, are also effectively under the national control of the world's richest nations, and the world's most powerful private corporations have significant influence over their policies. Since voting power within the IMF and the World Bank depends on economic contribution to them, they do not even pretend to be inclusive and democratic. The World Trade Organization gives equal votes to all member nations, but its proceedings and activities lack transparency. These institutions have evolved independently of the public spheres and global inclusion more characteristic of some other UN institutions. The world's economic powers often seek to bypass UN economic institutions altogether, moreover, relying on economic groups such as the G7 and the Organization for Economic Co-operation and Development for international economic regulation. Other UN institutions have always been available for strengthening global economic co-operation in inclusive and equitable ways. The UN Conference on Trade and Development was originally conceived as serving this function, and could be used again, and the resources of the UN Development Programme could be enhanced. Some writers suggest that the General Assembly should create a global Council of Ministers for Economic and Social Affairs which would also oversee regional economic commissions.[43]

None of this could be useful and effective without enhanced and better-organized resources for the UN organizations. According to Erskine Childers, the entire staff of all the allegedly bloated UN bureaucracies numbers about that of the state of Wyoming. The budgets these organizations work with are tiny compared to the budgets of major corporations and most of the world's states. Any social movement for strengthening global democracy and inclusion must work to shame states such as the United States, which refuses to pay the dues it owes to the United Nations at the same time that it exercises its Security Council power. More broadly, however, institutions of global governance certainly require equitable financing that draws not only on the resources of states, but also on private economic powers.

Social movements for global democracy and justice should try not only to build on and create global legal and regulatory institutions, but also to expand possibilities for transnational association and public spheres. Currently some of the most creative social movement activities in the world involve people seeking equitable development of their local economies in demanding transnational attention to matters

---

[43] Ho-Waon Jeong, 'The Struggle in the UN System for Wider Participation in Forming Global Economic Policies', in Alger (ed.), *The Future of the United Nations System*.

of democracy and distributive justice. Issues of debt forgiveness for the most indebted poor countries, for example, have received serious discussion in recent years, at least partly because of a persistent global social movement.

This chapter has argued that principles of inclusive democracy should be extended to a global level, because the scope of many social and economic interactions today extends globally. At the same time I have argued that global governance institutions ought to be coupled with recognition of the self-determination of peoples, who should be represented as peoples in such governance institutions. Whether at the level of metropolitan government, discussed in Chapter 6, or at wider regional and global levels, democratic participation should maximize the local autonomy of collectives, at the same time that it recognizes the relationships in which locales stand to one another, and regulates these relationships in settled federated processes of negotiation and co-operation.

# REFERENCES

ABRAMS, KATHRYN, 'Hearing the Call of Stories', *California Law Review*, 79/4 (July 1991), 971–1052

ALCOFF, LINDA MARTIN, 'The Problem of Speaking for Others', *Cultural Critique*, 20 (Winter 1991), 5–32.

—— *Real Knowing: New Versions of Coherence Theory* (Ithaca, NY: Cornell University Press, 1996).

ALGER, CHADWICK F. (ed.), *The Future of the United Nations System: Potential for the Twenty-First Century* (New York: United Nations University, 1998).

ALLEN, DANIELLE, 'Good Will and Equitable Persuasion: Reading Aristotle's *Rhetoric* for a Theory of Democratic Judgement', Paper presented to the American Political Science Association, Boston, Sept. 1998.

AMIN, SAMIR, *Class and Nation* (New York: Monthly Review Press, 1980).

ANZALDUA, GLORIA (ed.), *Making Face, Making Soul/Haciendo Caras* (San Francisco: Aunt Lute Foundation, 1990).

APPIAH, KWAMI ANTHONY, 'Identity, Authenticity, Survival: Multicultural Societies and Social Reproduction', in Amy Gutman (ed.), *Multiculturalism* (Princeton University Press, 1994).

—— 'Cosmopolitan Patriots', in *Cosmopolis: Thinking and Feeling beyond the Nation* (Minneapolis: University of Minnesota Press, 1998).

ARCHIBUGI, DANIELE, 'The Reform of the UN and Cosmopolitan Democracy: A Critical Review', *Journal of Peace Research*, 30/3 (1993), 301–15.

ARENDT, HANNAH, *The Human Condition* (Chicago: University of Chicago Press, 1998).

ARONOWITZ, STANLEY, 'Is a Democracy Possible? The Decline of the Public in the American Debate', in Bruce Robbins (ed.), *The Phantom Public Sphere* (Minneapolis: University of Minnesota Press, 1993).

AZIZ, NIKHIL, 'The Human Rights Debate in an Era of Globalization', in Peter van Ness (ed.), *Debating Human Rights: Critical Essays from the United States and Asia* (New York: Routledge, 1999).

BADER, VEIT, 'Citizenship and Exclusion: Radical Democracy, Community and Justice, or What is Wrong with Communitarianism?' *Political Theory*, 23/2 (May 1995), 211–46.

—— 'The Cultural Conditions of Transnational Citizenship', *Political Theory*, 25/6 (Dec. 1997), 771–813.

BARBER, BENJAMIN, *Strong Democracy* (Berkeley: University of California Press, 1984).

BARWELL, ISMAY, 'Towards a Defense of Objectivity', in Kathleen Lennon and Margaret Whitford, eds. *Knowing the Difference: Feminist Perspectives in Epistemology* (London: Routledge, 1994).

BAUBÖECK, RAINER, *Transnational Citizenship: Membership and Rights in International Migration* (Aldershot: Edward Elgar, 1994).

BAYNES, KENNETH, *The Normative Grounds of Social Criticism* (Albany: State University of New York Press, 1992).

BECK, ULRICH, *Was ist Globalisierung?* (Frankfurt: Suhrkamp Verlag, 1997).

BEITZ, CHARLES, *Political Theory and International Relations* (Princeton: Princeton University Press, 1979).

—— *Political Equality* (Princeton: Princeton University Press, 1990).

BENHABIB, SEYLA, 'Sexual Difference and Collective Identities: The New Global Constellation', *Signs: A Journal of Women in Culture and Society*, 24/2 (Winter 1999), 335–62.

—— 'Toward a Deliberative Model of Democratic Legitimacy', in Benhabib (ed.), *Democracy and Difference* (Princeton: Princeton University Press), 67–94.

BEVERLEY, JOHN, 'The Margin at the Center: On *Testimonio* (Testimonial Narrative)', *Modern Fiction Studies*, 35/1, 11–28.

—— '"Through All Things Modern": Second Thoughts on *Testimonio*', *boundary 2*, 18/2, 1–21.

BICKFORD, SUSAN, *The Dissonance of Democracy* (Ithaca, NY: Cornell University Press, 1996).

—— 'Beyond Reason: Political Perception and the Political Economy of Emotion Talk', Paper presented to the American Political Science Association, Boston, Sept. 1998.

—— 'Reconfiguring Pluralism: Identity and Institutions in the Inequalitarian Polity', *American Journal of Political Science*, 43/1 (Jan. 1999), 86–108.

BLAU, PETER, *Inequality and Heterogeneity* (New York: Free Press, 1977).

BLOMMAERT, JAN, and JEF VERSCHIEREN, 'European Concepts of Nation-Building', in Edwin N. Wilmsen and Patrick McAllister (eds.), *The Politics of Difference* (Chicago: University of Chicago Press, 1996).

BODY-GENDROT, SOPHI, 'Immigration and Marginality in France', in Katherine McFate, Roger Lawson, and William Julius Wilson (eds.), *Poverty, Inequality and the Future of Social Policy* (New York: Russell Sage).

—— 'Migration and the Racialization of the Postmodern City in France', in Malcolm Cross and Michael Keith (eds.), *Racism, the City and the State* (London: Routledge, 1993).

BOHMAN, JAMES, 'Emancipation and Rhetoric: The Perlocutions and Illocutions of the Social Critic', *Philosophy and Rhetoric*, 21/3 (1988), 185–203.

—— *Public Deliberation* (Cambridge, Mass.: MIT Press, 1996).

—— 'The Coming of Age of Deliberative Democracy', *The Journal of Political Philosophy* Vol. 6, No. 4, December 1998, pp. 400–425.

—— and WILLIAM REHG (eds.), *Deliberative Democracy* (Cambridge, Mass.: MIT Press, 1996).

BONDI, LIZ, 'Locating Identity Politics', in Michael Keith and Steve Pile (eds.), *Place and the Politics of Identity* (London: Routledge, 1993).

BORJA, JORDI, and MANUEL CASTELLS, *Local and Global: Management of Cities in the Information Age* (London: Earthscan, 1997).

BOZOKI, ANDRA, and MILOS SUKOSD, 'Civil Society and Populism in the Eastern European Democratic Transition', *Praxis International*, 13/3 (Oct. 1993), 244–1.

BREEBAART, MATTHIJS, SAKO MUSTERD, and WIM OSTENDORF, 'Patterns and Perception of Ethnic Segregation in Western Europe', in H. Haussermann and Ingrid Orwald (eds.), *Stadtentwicklung und Zuwanderung* (Opbaden: Sonderheft Leviathan, 1997).

BROOKS, ROY, *Integration or Separation: A Strategy for Political Equality* (Cambridge, Mass.: Harvard University Press, 1996).

BROWN, WENDY, *States of Injury* (Princeton: Princeton University Press, 1995).

CALDEIRA, TERESA P. R., 'Fortified Enclaves: The New Urban Segregation', *Public Culture*, 8 (1996), 303–28.

CANOVAN, MARGARET, *Nationhood and Political Theory* (Cambridge: Cambridge University Press, 1996).

—— 'The Skeleton in the Cupboard: Nationhood, Patriotism, and Limited Loyalties', in S. Caney, D. George, and P. Jones (eds.), *National Rights, National Obligations* (Boulder, Colo.: Westview Press, 1997).

CARDOSO, FERNANDO HENRIQUE, 'North–South Relations in the Present Context: A New Dependency' in M. Carnoy, M. Castells, S. Cohen, and F. Cardoso (eds.), *The New Global Economy in the Information Age* (University Park: Pennsylvania State University Press, 1993).

CARENS, JOSEPH, and MELISSA WILLIAMS, 'Muslim Minorities in Liberal Democracies: Justice and the Limits of Toleration', in Carens (ed.), *Culture, Citizenship, and Community: A Contextual Exploration of Justice as Evenhandedness* (Oxford: Oxford University Press, 2000).

CHAMBERS, SIMONE, *Reasonable Democracy: Jurgen Habermas and the Politics of Discourse* (Ithaca, NY: Cornell University Press, 1996).

CHANDHOKE, NERRA, *State and Civil Society* (Berkeley: Sage, 1992).

CHILDERS, ERSKINE, 'The United Nations and Global Institutions: Discourse and Reality', *Global Governance*, 3 (1997), 269–76.

—— and BRIAN URQUHART, *Renewing the United Nations System* (Uppsala: Dag Hammarskjöld Foundation, 1993).

CHRISTIANO, THOMAS, *The Rule of the Many* (Boulder, Colo.: Westview Press, 1996).

CLAY, PHILLIP L., 'The (Un)Housed City: Racial Patterns of Segregation, Housing Quality and Affordability', in George Galster and Edward Hill (eds.), *Metropolis in Black and White: Place, Power, and Polarization* (New Brunswick, NJ: Center for Urban Policy Research, 1992).

COHEN, CATHY J., 'Straight Gay Politics: The Limits of an Ethnic Model of Inclusion', in Ian Shapiro and Will Kymlicka (eds.), *Ethnicity and Group Rights*, NOMOS 29 (New York: New York University Press, 1997).

COHEN, JEAN, *American Civil Society Talk*, Working Paper No. 6 (College Park: National Commission on Civic Renewal, University of Maryland, 1997).

COHEN, JEAN, and ANDREW ARATO, *Civil Society and Political Theory* (Cambridge, Mass.: MIT Press, 1992).

COHEN, JOSHUA, 'An Epistemic Conception of Democracy', *Ethics*, 97 (Oct. 1986), 26–38.

—— 'Deliberation and Democratic Legitimacy', in Alan Hamlin and Philip Pettit (eds), *The Good Polity* (London: Blackwell, 1989).

—— 'The Economic Basis of Deliberative Democracy', *Social Philosophy and Policy*, 6/2 (Spring 1989), 25–50.

—— and JOEL ROGERS, 'Secondary Associations and Democratic Governance', in Eric Olin Wright (ed.), *Associations and Democracy* (London: Verso, 1996).

COLLINS, PATRICIA HILL, *Black Feminist Thought* (New York: Routledge, 1991).

CONNOLLY, WILLIAM, *Identity/Difference* (Ithaca, NY: Cornell University Press, 1993).

CORTESE, ANTHONY, *Ethnic Ethics* (Albany: State University of New York Press, 1990).

COWARD, ROSALIND and JOHN ELLIS, *Language and Materialism* (London: Routledge & Kegan Paul, 1977).

CROCKER, DAVID, 'Functioning and Capability: The Foundations of Sen's and Nussbaum's Development Ethic', in Martha Nussbaum and Jonathan Glover (eds.), *Women, Culture and Development: A Study in Human Capabilities* (Oxford: Oxford University Press, 1995).

CROSS, MALCOLM, and MICHAEL SMITH, *Racism, the City and the State* (London: Routledge, 1993).

CRUIKSHANK, BARBARA, *The Will to Empower: Technologies of Citizenship, Social Reform, and Democratic Government* (Ithaca, NY: Cornell University Press, 1999).

CULLER, JONATHAN, 'Communicative Competence and Normative Force', *New German Critique*, 35 (Spring–Summer 1985), 133–44.

CUNNINGHAM, FRANK, *Democratic Theory and Socialism* (Cambridge: Cambridge University Press, 1987).

—— *The Real World of Democracy Revisited* (Atlantic Highlands, NJ: Humanities Press, 1994).

DAHL, ROBERT, 'The City in the Future of Democracy', *American Political Science Review*, 61/41 (Dec. 1967), 953–70.

—— *Democracy and its Critics* (New Haven: Yale University Press, 1989).

DAWSON, MICHAEL, 'A Black Counterpublic? Economic Earthquakes, Racial Agenda(s), and Black Politics', *Public Culture*, 7 (1994), 195–223.

—— and CATHY COHEN, 'Neighborhood Poverty and African American Politics', *American Political Science Review*, 87/2 (June 1993), 286–302.

DEAN, JODI, *Solidarity of Strangers* (Berkeley: University of California Press, 1994).

DE GREIFF, PABLO, 'Deliberative Democracy and Group Representation', in Jorge Gracia and Pablo De Greiff (eds.), *Hispanics/Latinos in the US* (New York: Routledge, 2000).

DERRIDA, JACQUES, *On Grammatology* (Baltimore: Johns Hopkins University Press, 1973).

—— *Speech and Phenomena and Other Essays: Husserl's Theory of Signs* (Evanston, Ill.: Northwestern University Press, 1973).

—— 'Sending: On Representation', trans. Peter Dews and Mary Dews, *Social Research*, 49 (Summer 1982), 294–326.

—— 'Force of Law: The "Mystical Foundation of Authority"', in Drucilla Cornell, Michel Rosenfeld, and David Gray Carlson (eds.), *Deconstruction and the Possibility of Justice* (New York: Routledge, 1992).

DEWEY, JOHN, *The Public and its Problems* (Chicago: Swallow Press, 1927).

DHANDA, MEENA, 'Justifications for Gender Quotas in Legislative Bodies: A Consideration of Identity and Representation', *Women's Philosophy Review*, 20 (Winter 1998–9), 44–62.

DISCH, LISA, 'More Truth than Fact: Storytelling as Critical Understanding in the Writings of Hannah Arendt', *Political Theory*, 21/4 (Nov. 1993), 665–94.

—— *Hannah Arendt and the Limits of Philosophy* (Ithaca, NY: Cornell University Press, 1994).

DOUGLAS, EDWARD M. K., *Fading Expectations: The Crisis in Maori Housing*, Report for the Board of Maori Affairs (Wellington, June 1986).

DRYZEK, JOHN, *Discursive Democracy* (Cambridge: Cambridge University Press, 1990).

—— *Democracy in Capitalist Times* (Oxford: Oxford University Press, 1996).

—— 'Political Inclusion and the Dynamics of Democratization', *American Political Science Review*, 90/1 (Summer 1996), 475–87.

DYSON, MICHAEL, 'Essentialism and the Complexities of Racial Identity', in David Theo Goldberg (ed.), *Multiculturalism* (Cambridge, Mass.: Blackwell, 1994).

ELSHTAIN, BETHE JEAN, *Democracy on Trial* (New York: Basic Books, 1995).

ESTLAND, DAVID, 'Making Truth Safe for Democracy', in D. Copp, J. Hampton, and J. Roemer (eds.), *The Ideal of Democracy* (Cambridge: Cambridge University Press, 1993).

—— 'Beyond Fairness and Deliberation: The Epistemic Dimension of Democratic Authority', in James Bohman and William Rehg (eds.), *Deliberation and Democracy* (Cambridge, Mass.: MIT Press, 1998).

ETZIONI, AMITAI, *The Spirit of Community* (New York: Crown, 1993).

FAJER, MARC A., 'Can Two Real Men Eat Quiche Together? Storytelling, Gender-Role Stereotypes, and Legal Protection for Lesbians and Gay Men', *University of Miami Law Review*, 46 (Jan. 1992), 524–8.

FALK, RICHARD, 'The Global Promise of Social Movements', *in Explorations at the Edge of Time: Prospects for World Order* (New York: United Nations University, 1992).

FARRELL, THOMAS B., *Norms of Rhetorical Culture* (New Haven: Yale University Press, 1993).

FISHKIN, JAMES, *The Voice of the People* (New Haven: Yale University Press, 1995).

FORD, RICHARD THOMPSON, '*The United States* vs. *Starrett City Associates 1988*, Boundaries of Race: Political Geography in Legal Analysis', *Harvard Law Review*, 107/8 (June 1994), 1896–7.

—— 'Geography and Sovereignty: Jurisdictional Formation and Racial Segregation', *Stanford Law Review*, 49/6 (July 1997), 1365–446.

FRASER, NANCY, 'Struggle over Needs', in *Unruly Practices* (Minneapolis: University of Minnesota Press, 1989).

—— 'Rethinking the Public Sphere: A Contribution to the Critique of Actually Existing Democracy', in Bruce Robbins (ed.), *The Phantom Public Sphere* (Minneapolis: University of Minnesota Press, 1993).

—— 'From Redistribution to Recognition: Dilemmas of Justice in a "Post Socialist" Age', *New Left Review*, 212 (July–Aug. 1995), 68–99.

FRIEDMAN, MILTON, *Capitalism and Freedom* (Chicago: University of Chicago Press, 1962).

FRIEDMAN, STEVEN, 'An Unlikely Utopia: State and Civil Society in South Africa', *Politikon*, 19/1 (Dec. 1991), 5–19.

FRIEDRICKS, JURGEN (ed.), *Spatial Disparities and Social Behavior* (Hamburg: Hans Christian Verlag, 1992).

FRUG, GERALD, 'Decentering Decentralization', *University of Chicago Law Review*, 60/2 (Spring 1993), 253–338.

—— *City Making: Building Communities without Building Walls* (Princeton: Princeton University Press, 1999).

FRYE, MARILYN, 'Oppression', in *The Politics of Reality* (Trumansburg, NY: Crossing Press, 1983).

FUSS, DIANA, *Essentially Speaking: Feminism, Nature and Difference* (New York: Routledge, 1989).

GALSTER, GEORGE C., and EDWARD W. HILL, 'Place, Power, and Polarization', in Galster and Hill (eds.), *The Metropolis in Black and White* (New Brunswick, NJ: Center for Urban Policy Research, 1992).

GALSTON, WILLIAM, *Liberal Purposes* (Cambridge: Cambridge University Press, 1991).

GARLAND, MICHAEL J., and ROMANA HASRAEN, 'Community Responsibility and the Development of Oregon's Health Care Priorities, *Business and Professional Ethics Journal*, 9/3 and 4 (Fall 1990), 183–200.

GIDDENS, ANTHONY, *The Constitution of Society* (Berkeley: University of California Press, 1984).

GITLIN, TODD, *Twilight of Common Dreams* (New York: Metropolitan Books, 1995).

GOODIN, ROBERT E., 'Inclusion and Exclusion', *Archives of European Sociology*, 37/2 (1966), 343–71.

—— *Green Political Theory* (Oxford: Polity Press, 1992).

—— 'The State as a Moral Agent', in *Utilitarianism as a Public Philosophy* (Cambridge: Cambridge University Press, 1995).

GOULD, CAROL, *Rethinking Democracy: Freedom and Social Cooperation in*

*Politics, Economy and Society* (Cambridge: Cambridge University Press, 1988).

GREEN, ANNE E., *The Geography of Poverty and Wealth* (Warwick: Institute for Employment Research, 1991).

GREEN, PHILIP, *Retrieving Democracy* (Totowa, NJ: Rowman & Allenheld, 1985).

GUINIER, LANI, *The Tyranny of the Majority* (New York: Free Press, 1995).

GUTMANN, AMY, 'Responding to Racial Injustice', in Kwami Anthony Appiah and Amy Gutmann (eds.), *Color Conscious* (Princeton: Princeton University Press, 1996).

—— and DENNIS THOMPSON, *Democracy and Disagreement* (Cambridge, Mass.: Harvard University Press, 1996).

HABERMAS, JURGEN, *The Theory of Communicative Action*, i and ii (Boston: Beacon Press, 1984).

—— *Moral Consciousness and Communicative Ethics* (Cambridge, Mass.: MIT Press, 1990).

—— 'Citizenship and National Identity: Some Reflections on the Future of Europe', *Praxis International*, 12/1 (Apr. 1992), 1–19.

—— *Between Facts and Norms* (Cambridge, Mass.: MIT Press, 1996).

—— *The Inclusion of the Other: Studies in Political Theory* (Cambridge, Mass.: MIT Press, 1998).

—— 'Kant's Idea of Perpetual Peace: At Two Hundred Years' Historical Remove', in Ciaran Cronin and Pablo de Greiff (eds.), *The Inclusion of the Other: Studies in Political Theory* (Cambridge, Mass.: MIT Press, 1998).

HÄUSSERMANN, HARTMUST, and MARZ RAINER, 'Migration und Minderheiten in den zentraleuropäischen Metropolen. Berlin, Brüssel, Budapest und Wien', *Migranten Berlin. Zuwanderung* (Berlin: Gesellschaftliche Problem politische Ansatz, Fakultat Institut Sozialwissenschaften, Humbolt University, 1995).

HAGGARD, STEPHEN, 'Markets, Poverty Alleviation, and Income Distribution: An Assessment of Neoliberal Claims', *Ethics and International Affairs*, 5 (1991), 175–96.

HAMPTON, JEAN, *Political Philosophy* (Boulder, Colo.: Westview Press, 1997).

HARAWAY, DONNA, 'Situated Knowledges: The Science Question in Feminism and the Privilege of Partial Perspective', in *Simians, Cyborgs, and Women* (New York: Routledge, 1991).

HARDIN, RUSSELL, *One for All* (Chicago: University of Chicago Press, 1995).

HARDING, SANDRA, *Whose Science? Which Knowledge? Thinking from Women's Lives* (Ithaca, NY: Cornell University Press, 1991).

HARVEY, DAVID, *Justice, Nature and the Geography of Difference* (Oxford: Blackwell, 1996).

HEGLEY, STEPHEN, *Privilege, Power, and Place: The Geography of the American Upper Class* (Totowa, NJ: Rowman & Littlefield, 1995).

HEISLER, BARBARA SCHMITTER, 'Housing Policy and the Underclass: The United Kingdom, Germany, and the Netherlands', *Journal of Urban Affairs*, 16/3 (1994), 203–20.

HELD, DAVID, *Democracy and the Global Order* (Cambridge, Mass.: Polity Press, 1995).

—— 'Democracy and Globalization', in Daniele Archibugi, David Held, and Martin Kohler (eds.), *Re-imagining Political Community: Studies in Cosmopolitan Democracy* (Cambridge, Mass.: Polity Press, 1998).

HENRY, CHARLES, *Culture and African American Politics* (Bloomington: Indiana University Press, 1990).

HIRST, PAUL, *Representative Democracy and its Limits* (Oxford: Polity Press, 1990).

—— *Associative Democracy* (Amherst: University of Massachusetts Press, 1993).

HOCHSCHILD, JENNIFER, *Facing up to the American Dream: Race, Class, and the Soul of the Nation* (Princeton: Princeton University Press, 1995).

—— 'Where you Stand Depends on What you See: Connections among Values, Perceptions of Fact, and Prescriptions', in James Kuklinski (ed.), *Citizens and Politics: Perspectives from Political Psychology* (Cambridge: Cambridge University Press, 2000).

HONIG, BONNIE, *Political Theory and the Displacement of Politics* (Ithaca, NY: Cornell University Press, 1993).

HONNETH, AXEL, *The Struggle for Recognition* (Cambridge, Mass.: MIT Press, 1995).

—— 'Democracy as Reflexive Cooperation: John Dewey and the Theory of Democracy Today', *Political Theory*, 26/6 (Dec. 1998), 763–83.

HUNOLD, CHRISTIAN, and IRIS MARION YOUNG, 'Justice, Democracy, and Hazardous Siting', *Political Studies*, 46/1 (1998), 87–95.

HURLEY, SUSAN, 'Democracy, Rationality, and Leaky Boundaries', in Ian Shapiro and Casiano Hacker-Cordon (eds.), *Democracy's Edges* (Cambridge: Cambridge University Press, 1999).

INGRAM, DAVID, *Reason, History, and Politics* (Albany: State University of New York Press, 1995).

ISAAC, JEFFREY, *Democracy in Dark Times* (Ithaca, NY: Cornell University Press, 1998).

JARGOWSKY, PAUL A., *Poverty and Place: Ghettos, Barrios, Slums and the American City* (New York: Russell Sage, 1996).

JEONG, HO-WAON, 'The Struggle in the UN System for Wider Participation in Forming Global Economics Policies', in Chadwick F. Alger (ed.), *The Future of the United Nations System: Potential for the Twenty-First Century* (New York: United Nations University, 1998).

JOHNSON, ALEX J., 'Bid Whist, Tonk and *United States* vs. *Fordice*: Why Integrationism Fails African Americans Again', *California Law Review*, 81/6 (Dec. 1993), 1401–70.

JUTKOWITZ, JOEL M., 'Civil Society and Democratic Development in Chile',

Paper presented to the American Political Science Association, Chicago, Sept. 1995.

KNIGHT, JACK, and JAMES JOHNSON, 'Aggregation and Deliberation: On the Possibility of Democratic Legitimacy', *Political Theory*, 22/2 (May 1994), 277–98.

KYMLICKA, WILL, *Liberalism, Community, and Culture* (Oxford: Oxford University Press, 1989).

—— *Multicultural Citizenship* (New York: Oxford University Press, 1996).

—— (ed.), 'Together in Difference: Transforming the Logic of Group Political Conflict', in *The Rights of Minority Cultures* (Oxford: Oxford University Press, 1995).

LARA, MARIA PIA, *Moral Textures: Feminist Narratives in the Public Sphere* (Cambridge: Polity Press, 1998).

LARMORE, CHARLES, *Patterns of Moral Complexity* (Cambridge: Cambridge University Press, 1987).

LEFORT, CLAUDE, *The Political Forms of Modern Society* (Cambridge, Mass.: MIT Press, 1986).

LEVI, MARGARET, 'Social and Unsocial Capital: A Review Essay of Robert Putnam's *Making Democracy Work*', *Politics and Society*, 24/1 (Mar. 1996), 45–55.

LEVINAS, EMMANUEL, *Otherwise than Being, or Beyond Essence*, trans. Alphonso Lingis (The Hague: Nijhoff, 1981).

LIPSCHUTZ, RONNIE D., 'Reconstructing World Politics: The Emergence of Global Civil Society', *Millennium*, 21/3 (Winter 1992), 389–420.

LUGONES, MARIA, 'Purity, Impurity and Separation', *Signs: A Journal of Women in Cultural and Society*, 19/2 (Winter 1994), 458–79.

LYOTARD, JEAN-FRANÇOIS, *The Differend: Phrases in Dispute* (Minneapolis: University of Minnesota Press, 1988).

MAAKA, ROGER, and AUGIE FLERA, 'From Entitlement to Re-engagement as Indigenous Affairs Agenda: *Tino Rangatiratanga* and the Politics of Indigeneity in Aotearoa/New Zealand', in Paul Patton and Duncan Ivason (eds.), *Political Theory and the Rights of Indigenous Peoples* (Cambridge: Cambridge University Press, 2000).

MCCARTHY, THOMAS, 'Practical Discourse: On the Relation of Morality to Politics', in Craig Calhoun (ed.), *Habermas and the Public Sphere* (Cambridge, Mass.: MIT Press, 1992).

MACDONALD, J., *Racism and Rental Accommodation* (Auckland: Social Research and Development Trust, 1986).

MCIVOY, DAVID, 'Greater London in Britain's First Ethnic Census', in Curtis C. Roseman, Hans Dieter Laus, and Gunther Threme (eds.), *EthniCity: Geographic Perspectives on Ethnic Change in Modern Cities* (Lanham, Md.: Rowman & Littlefield, 1996).

MACPHERSON, C. B., *The Life and Times of Liberal Democracy* (Oxford: Oxford University Press, 1977).

MANDELBAUM, SEYMOUR, 'Telling Stories', *Journal of Planning Research*, 10/3 (1991), 109–214.

MANSBRIDGE, JANE, *Beyond Adversary Democracy* (New York: Basic Books, 1980).

—— 'Feminism and Democratic Community', in John W. Chapman and Ian Shapiro (eds.), *Democratic Community*, NOMOS 35 (New York: New York University Press, 1991).

—— 'A Deliberative Perspective of Interest Representation', in Mark P. Patracca (ed.), *The Politics of Interest: Interest Groups Transformed* (Boulder, Colo.: Westview Press, 1992).

—— 'Self-Interest and Political Transformation', in George E. Marcus and Russell L. Hanson (eds.), *Reconsidering the Democratic Public* (University Park: Pennsylvania State University Press, 1993).

—— 'Activism Writ Small, Deliberation Writ Large', Paper presented to the American Political Science Association, Washington, Sept, 1997.

MARCUSE, HERBERT, *One Dimensional Man* (Boston: Beacon Press, 1964).

MARCUSE, PETER, 'The Enclave, the Citadel, and the Ghetto: What has Changed in the Post-Fordist U.S. City', *Urban Affairs Review*, 33/2 (Nov. 1997), 228–64.

MARTIN, BILL, *Matrix and Line* (Albany: State University of New York Press, 1993).

MASSEY, DOUGLAS S., 'The Age of Extremes: Concentrated Affluence and Poverty in the Twenty-First Century', *Demography*, 33/4 (Nov. 1996), 395–412.

—— and NANCY DENTON, *American Apartheid* (Cambridge, Mass.: Harvard University Press, 1993).

MATUŠTÍK, MARTIN J., *Postnational Identity: Critical Theory and Existential Philosophy in Habermas, Kierkegaard, and Havel* (New York: The Guildford Press, 1993).

—— 'Back to the Future: Marcuse and New Critical Theory', foreword to William Wilkerson and Jeffrey Paris (eds.), *New Critical Theory: Essays on Liberation* (Lanham, Md.: Rowman & Littlefield, 2000).

MAY, LARRY, *The Morality of Groups* (Chicago: University of Chicago Press, 1988).

—— *Sharing Responsibility* (Chicago: University of Chicago Press, 1993).

MAYEKISO, MZWANELE, *Township Politics: Civic Struggles for a New South Africa* (New York: Monthly Review Press, 1996).

MAYER, CHRISTOPHER J., 'Does Location Matter?', *New England Economic Review* (May–June 1996), 26–40.

MELUCCI, ALBERTO, *Nomads of the Present: Social Movements and Individual Need in Contemporary Society* (London: Radius, 1989).

METGE, JOAN, *The Maoris of New Zealand: Tauhai* (London: Routledge & Kegan Paul, 1976).

MEYERS, DIANA TIETZEJS, *Subjection and Subjectivity* (New York: Routledge, 1994).

MICHELMAN, FRANK, 'Traces of Self-Government', *Harvard Law Review*, 100 (1986), 4–77.

MIK, GER, 'Housing Segregation and Policy in the Dutch Metropolitan Environment', in Elizabeth D. Huttman (ed.), and Wim Blauw and Juliet Satman (co-eds.), *Urban Housing Segregation of Minorities in Western Europe and the United States* (Durham, NC: Duke University Press, 1991).

MILL, JOHN STUART, *On Liberty* (New York: MacMillan, 1999).

MILLER, DAVID, *On Nationality* (Oxford: Oxford University Press, 1995).

—— 'Deliberative Democracy and Social Choice', in David Held (ed.), *Prospects for Democracy* (Oxford: Polity Press, 1993).

MINOW, MARTHA, *Making All the Difference* (Ithaca, NY: Cornell University Press, 1990).

MLEAY, ELIZABETH, 'Housing Policy', in Jonathan Boston and Paul Dalziel (eds.), *The Decent Society? Essays in Response to the Nation's Economic and Social Policies* (Auckland: Oxford University Press, 1992).

MOHANTY, SATYA, 'The Epistemic Status of Cultural Identity', *Cultural Critique*, 24 (Spring 1993), 41–80.

MONROE, KRISTIN RENWICK and LINA HADDA KREIDI, 'The Perspective of Islamic Fundamentalists and the Limits of Rational Choice Theory', *Political Psychology*, 18/1 (1997), 19–43.

MOUFFE, CHANTAL, *The Return of the Political* (London: Verso, 1993).

—— 'Democracy, Power, and the "Political"', in Seyla Benhabib (ed.), *Democracy and Difference* (Princeton: Princeton University Press, 1996).

MOYA, PAULA, 'Postmodernism, "Realism" and the Politics of Identity: Cherrie Moraga and Chicana Feminism', in Chandra Talpade Mohant and M. Jacquie Alexander (eds.), *Feminist Genealogies, Colonial Legacies, Democratic Futures* (New York: Routledge, 1997).

MULGAN, RICHARD, *Maori, Pakeha, and Democracy* (Auckland: Oxford University Press, 1989).

NEDELSKY, JENNIFER, 'Relational Autonomy', *Yale Women's Law Journal*, 1/1 (1989), 7–36.

—— 'Law, Boundaries, and the Bounded Self', in Robert Post (ed.), *Law and the Order of Culture* (Berkeley: University of California Press, 1991).

NELSON, HILDE, 'Resistance and Insubordination', *Hypatia: A Journal of Feminist Philosophy*, 10/2 (Spring 1995), 23–40.

NELSON, ROBERT H., *Zoning and Property Rights: An Analysis of the American System of Land–Use Regulation* (Cambridge, Mass.: MIT Press, 1977).

NICHOLSON, LINDA (ed.), *Feminism/Postmodernism* (New York: Routledge, 1990).

NIELSEN, KAI, 'Reconceptualizing Civil Society for Now: Some Somewhat Gramscian Turnings', in Michael Walter (ed.), *Toward a Global Civil Society* (Providence, RI: Berhahan Books, 1995).

NOZICK, ROBERT, *Anarchy, State and Utopia* (Cambridge, Mass.: Harvard University Press, 1974).

NUSSBAUM, MARTHA, 'Patriotism and Cosmospolitanism', in Joshua Cohen (ed.), *For Love of Country* (Boston: Beacon Press, 1996).

OFFE, CLAUS, *Contradictions of the Welfare State* (Cambridge, Mass.: MIT Press, 1984).

—— 'Bindings, Shackles, Brakes: On Self-Limitation Strategies', in *Modernity and the State* (Cambridge, Mass.: MIT Press, 1996).

OKIN, SUSAN, *Justice, Gender and the Family* (New York: Basic Books, 1989).

OLIVER, J. ERIC, 'Civic Involvement in Suburbia: The Effects of Metropolitan Economic Segregation on Participation in Local Civic Affairs', Paper presented to the American Political Science Association, Washington, Sept. 1997.

O'NEILL, ONORA, *Toward Justice and Virtue* (Cambridge: Cambridge University Press, 1996).

O'NEILL, SHANE, 'Mutual Recognition and the Accommodation of National Diversity: Constitutional Justice in Northern Ireland.', in Alain G. Gagnon and James Tully (eds.), *Struggles for Recognition in Multicultural Societies* (Cambridge: Cambridge University Press, 2000).

PALANCO, HECTOR DIAZ, *Indigenous Peoples in Latin America: The Quest for Self-Determination*, trans. Lucia Rayas (Boulder, Colo.: Westview Press, 1997).

PETTIT, PHILIP, *Republicanism* (Oxford: Oxford University Press, 1997).

PHILLIPS, ANNE, *Democracy and Difference* (University Park: Pennsylvania State University Press, 1993).

—— *The Politics of Presence* (Oxford: Oxford University Press, 1995).

PITKIN, HANNA, *The Concept of Representation* (Berkeley: University of California Press, 1971).

PLOTKE, DAVID, 'Representation is Democracy', *Constellations*, 4/1 (Apr. 1997), 19–34.

POGGE, THOMAS, 'Cosmopolitanism and Sovereignty', *Ethics*, 103 (Oct. 1992), 48–75.

—— 'Creating Supra-national Institutions Democratically: Reflections on the European Union's "Democratic Deficit"', *Journal of Political Philosophy*, 5/2 (June 1997), 163–82.

PUTNAM, HILARY, 'A Reconsideration of Deweyan Democracy', *Southern California Law Review*, 63/6 (Sept. 1990), 1671–97.

—— 'Pragmatism and Moral Objectivity', in Martha Nussbaum and Jonathan Glover (eds.), *Women, Culture and Development* (Oxford: Oxford University Press, 1995).

PUTNAM, ROBERT, *Making Democracy Work: Civic Traditions in Modern Italy* (Princeton: Princeton University Press, 1993).

PZEWORSKI, ADAM, and IMMANUEL WALLTERSTEIN, 'Structural Dependence of the State on Capital', *American Political Science Review*, (1989), 11–29.

RAWLS, JOHN, *A Theory of Justice* (Cambridge, Mass.: Harvard University Press, 1971).

—— *Political Liberalism* (New York: Columbia University Press, 1993).

REHG, BILL, 'Reason and Rhetoric in Habermas's Theory of Augumentation', in Walter Jost and Michael Hyde (eds.), *Rhetoric and Hermeneutics in our Time* (New Haven: Yale University Press, 1997).

REMER, GARY, 'Political Oratory and Conversation: Cicero versus Deliberative Democracy', *Political Theory*, 27/1 (Feb. 1999), 39–64.

RIPSTEIN, ARTHUR, 'Context, Continuity, Fairness', in Robert McKim and Jeff McMahon (eds.), *The Morality of Nationalism* (Oxford: Oxford University Press, 1997).

ROBBINS, BRUCE (ed.), *The Phantom Public Sphere* (Minneapolis: University of Minnesota Press, 1993).

RODGER, JOHN J., 'On the Degeneration of the Public Sphere', *Political Studies*, 32 (1985), 203–17.

RONNEBERGE, KLAUS, 'Zitadellenökonomie und soziale Transformation der Stadt', in X. Noller, X. Prigger, and Klaus Ronneberger (ed.), *Stadt-Welt* (Frankfurt, 1994).

ROSENBLUM, NANCY, *Membership and Morals: The Personal Uses of Pluralism in America* (Princeton: Princeton University Press, 1998).

ROSS, THOMAS, 'Despair and Redemption in the Feminist Nomos', *Indiana Law Review*, 69/1 (Winter 1993), 101–36.

RUGGIE, JOHN GERARD, 'Territoriality and Beyond: Problematizing Modernity in International Relations', *International Organization*, 47/1 (Winter 1993), 139–74.

RUSK, DAVID, *Cities without Suburbs* (Washington: Woodrow Wilson Center Press, 1993).

RYDEN, DAVID, *Representation in Crisis: The Constitution, Interest Groups, and Political Parties* (Albany: State University of New York Press, 1996).

SANDERS, LYNN, 'Against Deliberation', *Political Theory*, 25/3 (June 1997), 347–76.

—— and DONALD KINDER, *Divided by Color: Racial Politics and Democratic Ideals* (Chicago: University of Chicago Press, 1996).

SARTRE, JEAN-PAUL, *Critique of Dialectical Reason*, trans. Alan Sheridan-Smith (London: New Left Books, 1976).

SAVITCH, HANK V., and RONALD K. VOGEL, 'Ties that Bind: Central Cities, Suburbs and the New Metropolitan Region', *Economic Development Quarterly*, 7/4 (Nov. 1993), 341.

—— —— *Regional Politics: America in a Post-City Age* (Thousand Oaks, Calif.: Sage, 1996).

SCHEFFLER, SAMUEL, 'Liberalism, Nationalism, and Egalitarianism', in Robert McKim and Jeff McMahon (eds.), *The Morality of Nationalism* (Oxford: Oxford University Press, 1997).

SCHWARTZ, NANCY, *The Blue Guitar: Political Representation and Community* (Chicago: University of Chicago Press, 1988).

SCOTT, CRAIG, 'Indigenous Self-Determination and Decolonization of the International Imagination: A Plea', *Human Rights Quarterly*, 18 (1996), 814–20.

SEIDMAN, STEVEN, 'Identity and Politics in a "Postmodern" Gay Culture', in *Difference Troubles: Queering Social Theory and Sexual Politics* (Cambridge: Cambridge University Press, 1997).

SEN, AMARTYA, *Inequality Reexamined* (Cambridge, Mass.: Harvard University Press, 1992).

—— 'Justice: Means versus Freedoms', *Philosophy and Public Affairs*, 19 (Spring 1990), 111–21.

SHAPIRO, IAN, 'Elements of Democratic Justice', *Political Theory*, 24/4 (Nov. 1996), 579–619.

—— *Democratic Justice* (New Haven: Yale University Press, 1999).

SHAPIRO, JOSEPH P., *No Pity: People with Disabilities Forging a New Civil Rights Movement* (New York: New York Times Books, 1993).

SILVERS, ANITA, 'Formal Justice', in Anita Silvers, David Wasserman, and Mary B. Mahowald (eds.), *Disability, Difference, Discrimination: Perspectives on Justice in Bioethics and Public Policy* (Lanham, Md.: Rowman & Littlefield, 1998).

SKILLING, H. GORDON, *Samizdat and an Independent Society in Central and Eastern Europe* (Oxford: Macmillan, 1989).

SMITH, KIMBERLY K., 'Storytelling, Sympathy, and Moral Judgement in American Abolitionism', *Journal of Political Philosophy*, 6/4 (1998), 356–77.

SMITH, SUSAN, *The Politics of 'Race' and Residence* (Oxford: Blackwell, 1988).

—— 'Residential Segregation and the Politics of Ritualization', in Malcolm Cross and Michael Smith (eds.), *Racism, the City and the State* (London: Routledge, 1993).

SOMMER, DORIS, 'Not Just a Personal Story: Women's *Testimonios* and the Plural Self', in Bella Brodzski and Celeste Schenk (eds.), *Lifelines: Theorizing Women's Autobiography* (Ithaca, NY Cornell University Press, 1988).

SOYSAL, YASMIN NOHAGLU, *Limits of Citizenship: Migrants and Postnational Membership in Europe* (Chicago: University of Chicago Press, 1994).

SPARKS, HOLLOWAY, 'Dissident Citizenship: Democratic Theory, Political Change, and Activist Women', *Hypatia: Journal of Feminist Philosophy*, 12/4 (Fall 1997), 74–109.

SPELMAN, ELIZABETH V., *Inessential Woman* (Boston: Beacon Press, 1988).

SPRAGENS, THOMAS, *Reason and Democracy* (Durham, NC: Duke University Press, 1990).

STEVENSON, NICK (ed.), *Cultural Citizenship* (London: Sage, 1998).

STORPER, MICHAEL, *The Regional World: Territorial Development in a Global Economy* (London: Guilford Press, 1997).

SUNSTEIN, CASS R., 'Preferences and Politics', *Philosophy and Public Affairs*, 20 (Winter 1991), 3–34.

—— *The Partial Constitution* (Cambridge, Mass.: Harvard University Press, 1993).

SZAZ, ANDREW, 'Progress through Mischief: The Social Movement Alternative to Secondary Associations', in E. O. Wright (ed.), *Associations and Democracy* (London: Verso, 1995).

TAMIR, YAEL, *Liberal Nationalism* (Princeton: Princeton University Press, 1993).

TAN KOK-CHOR, 'Kantian Ethics and Global Justice', *Social Theory and Practice*, 23 (Spring 1997), 53–62.

TAYLOR, CHARLES, 'Multiculturalism and the Politics of Recognition', in Amy Gutmann (ed.), *Multiculturalism* (Princeton: Princeton University Press, 1992).

TESTER, KEITH, *Civil Society* (London: Routledge, 1998).

TULLY, JAMES, *Strange Multiplicity* (Cambridge: Cambridge University Press, 1995).

VAN PARIJS, PHILIPPE, 'Justice and Democracy: Are they Incompatible?', *Journal of Political Philosophy*, 4/2 (June 1996), 101–17.

VAYRYNEN, RAIMO, 'Enforcement and Humanitarian Intervention: Two Faces of Collective Action by the UN', in Chadwick F. Alger (ed.), *The Future of the United Nations System: Potential for the Twenty-First Century* (New York: United Nations University, 1998).

VERBA, SIDNEY, KAY LEHMAN SCHOLZMAN, and HENRY E. BRADY, *Voice and Equality: Civic Voluntarism in American Politics* (Cambridge, Mass.: Harvard University Press, 1995).

VOGEL, JOACHIM, 'Urban Segregation in Sweden: Housing Policy, Housing Markets, and the Spatial Distribution of Households in Metropolitan Areas', *Social Indicators Research*, 27 (1992), 139–55.

WACQUANT, LOIC J. D., '"Race", Class and Space in Chicago and Paris', in Katherine McFate, Roger Lawson, and William Julius Wilson (eds.), *Poverty, Inequality and the Future of Social Policy* (New York: Russell Sage, 1995).

WALDRON, JEREMY, 'Minority Cultures and the Cosmopolitan Alternative', in Will Kymlicka (ed.), *The Rights of Minority Cultures* (Oxford: Oxford University Press, 1995).

WALKER, MARGARET, *Moral Understandings: Feminist Studies in Ethics* (New York: Routledge, 1997).

WALTON, DOUGLAS, *The Place of Emotion in Argument* (University Park: Pennsylvania State University Press, 1992).

WALZER, MICHAEL, *The Company of Critics: Social Criticism and Political Commitment in the Twentieth Century* (New York: Basic Books, 1990).

—— *Thick and Thin: Moral Argument at Home and Abroad* (Notre Dame, Ind.: Notre Dame University Press, 1994).

—— 'The Idea of Civil Society', in Walzer (ed.), *Toward a Global Civil Society* (Providence, RI: Berhahan Books, 1995).

WARREN, MARK, 'What should we Expect from More Democracy? Radically Democratic Responses to Politics', *Political Theory*, 24/2 (May 1996), 241–70.

WEIR, MARGARET, 'The Politics of Racial Isolation in Europe and America', in Paul E. Peterson (ed.), *Classifying by Race* (Princeton: Princeton University Press, 1995).

WELDON, S. L., 'The Political Representation of Women: The Impact of a Critical Mass', Paper presented to the American Political Science Association, San Francisco, Sept. 1996.

WENDELL, SUSAN, *The Rejected Body* (New York: Routledge Press, 1996).

WHITE, STEPHEN, *Political Theory and Postmodernism* (Cambridge: Cambridge University Press, 1991).

WILKINS, BARRY, 'Debt and Underdevelopment: The Case for Cancelling Third World Debts', in Robin Attfield and Barry Wilkins (eds.), *International Justice and the Third World* (London: Routledge, 1992).

WILLIAMS, MELISSA, *Voice, Trust and Memory: Marginalized Groups and the Failure of Liberal Representation* (Princeton: Princeton University Press, 1998).

WILMER, FRANKE, *The Indigenous Voice in World Politics* (London: Sage, 1993).

WILSON, WILLIAM JULIUS, *When Work Disappears* (New York: Knopf, 1997).

WOLFE, ALAN, and JYETTE LAUSEN, 'Identity Politics and the Welfare State', *Social Philosophy and Policy*, 14/2 (Summer 1997), 231–55.

WRIGHT, ERIC OLIN, *Class Counts* (Cambridge: Cambridge University Press, 1997).

YEATMAN, ANNA, 'Beyond Natural Right: The Conditions for Universal Citizenship', in *Postmodern Revisions of the Political* (New York: Routledge, 1994).

—— 'Minorities and the Politics of Difference', in *Postmodern Revisions of the Political* (New York: Routledge, 1994).

—— 'Feminism and Citizenship', in Nick Stevenson (ed.), *Cultural Citizenship* (London: Sage, 1998).

—— and MARGARET WILSON (eds.), *Justice and Identity: Antipodean Practices* (Wellington: Bridget Williams Books, 1995).

YOUNG, IRIS MARION, 'The Ideal of Community and the Politics of Difference', in Linda Nicholson (ed.), *Feminism/Postmodernism* (New York: Routledge, 1990).

—— 'Impartiality and the Civic Public: A Critique of the Ideal of University Citizenship', in *Throwing Like a Girl and Other Essays in the Feminist Philosophy and Social Theory* (Bloomington: Indiana University Press, 1990).

—— *Justice and the Politics of Difference* (Princeton: Princeton University Press, 1990).

—— 'Rawls's *Political Liberalism*', *Journal of Political Philosophy*, 3/2 (June 1995), 181–90.

—— 'Together in Difference: Transforming the Logic of Group Political Conflict', in Will Kymlicka (ed.), *The Rights of Minority Cultures* (Oxford: Oxford University Press, 1995).

—— 'Communication and the Other: Beyond Deliberative Democracy', in Seyla Benhabib (ed.), *Democracy and Difference* (Princeton: Princeton University Press, 1996).

—— 'A Multicultural Continuum: A Critique of Will Kymlicka', *Constellations*, 4/1 (April 1997), 48–53.

—— 'Asymmetrical Reciprocity: On Moral Respect, Wonder, and Enlarged

Thought', in *Intersecting Voices: Dilemmas of Gender, Political Philosophy and Policy* (Princeton: Princeton University Press, 1997).

—— 'Gender as Seriality: Thinking about Women as a Social Collective', in *Intersecting Voices: Dilemmas of Gender, Political Philosophy and Policy* (Princeton: Princeton University Press, 1997).

—— 'Unruly Cateogries: A Critique of Nancy Fraser's Dual Systems Theory', *New Left Review*, 222 (Mar.–Apr. 1997), 147–60.

—— 'Justice, Inclusion and Deliberative Democracy', in Stephen Macedo (ed.), *Deliberative Politics: Essays on Democracy and Disagreement* (Oxford: Oxford University Press, 1999).

# INDEX